Out to Eat
Sydney 2001

Lonely Planet Publications
Melbourne • London • Paris • Oakland

Lonely Planet *Out to Eat – Sydney*

2nd edition – October 2000

Published by Lonely Planet Publications

Lonely Planet Offices
Australia PO Box 617, Hawthorn, VIC 3122
From Jan 2001 Locked Bag 1, Footscray, VIC 3011
USA 150 Linden St, Oakland, CA 94607
UK 10a Spring Place, London NW5 3BH
France 1 rue du Dahomey, 75011 Paris

Photographs Simon Bracken

Series publishing manager: Adrienne Costanzo
Acting publishing manager: Katie Cody
Series design: Wendy Wright
Layout: Vicki Beale
Mapping: Alison Lyall
Cover design: Simon Bracken
Coordinating author: Kath Kenny
Coordinating editor: Katharine Day

ISBN 1 86450 141 3

text & maps © Lonely Planet 2000
photos © Lonely Planet Images 2000

Printed by McPherson's Printing Group Pty Ltd
Printed in Australia

All rights reserved. No part of this publication may be reproduced, stored in a retrieval system or transmitted in any form by any means, electronic, mechanical, photocopying, recording or otherwise, except brief extracts for the purpose of review, without the written permission of the publisher and copyright owner.

LONELY PLANET and the Lonely Planet logo are trade marks of Lonely Planet Publications Pty Ltd.

Lonely Planet books provide independent advice. Lonely Planet does not accept advertising in its books, nor do we accept payment in exchange for listing or endorsing any restaurant. Lonely Planet reviewers do not accept discounts or free meals in exchange for positive coverage of any sort.

> If you wanted a change of food from the Puddin', all you had to do was to whistle twice and turn the basin round.
>
> **Norman Lindsay,** *The Magic Pudding*

OUT TO EAT – PEOPLE

Specialist Lonely Planet Authors

After spending years in Japan eating sushi and

This book is the result of more than a year's planning, thousands of meetings, and the creative efforts of a hungry team that includes experienced food writers, food-mad editors,

soba, Simon Richmond wrote On Your Plate Japanese and reviewed many Japanese restaurants. Alison Cowan wrote On Your Plate Thai having travelled extensively in Asia and conquered the hottest Thai curry.

Self-confessed Italian food snob Sally Webb wrote On Your Plate Italian. After living in Italy for 5 years she is now resident in Sydney. On Your Plate Chinese was written by Margaret Burke who has had years of eating the real thing in China.

designers, cartographers, guidebook authors, a chef or two and a sprinkling of publishers. Fuelled by equal parts Alka Seltzer and passion for good food, the core **team of writers** comprised: Margaret Burke, Sam Chapman, Alison Cowan, Marise Donnelley, Susan Gray, Nikki Hall, Kath Kenny, Simon Richmond, Will Swan Jacqui Taffel and Sally Webb. For **additional assessments**, thanks to Liz Ginis. Coordinating author Kath would like to thank all the dining partners for their excellent taste and fine company, especially her constant dinner date Andrew.

Chapter introductions and **features** by Courtney Centner, Katharine Day, Marise Donnelley, Carolyn Holbrook, Kath Kenny, Will Swan, Jacqui Taffel and Donna Wheeler.

Coordinating Author

Kath Kenny has authored reviews and opinion pieces covering stories

From the Publisher

This book was coordinated by Katharine Day, edited and proofed by Courtney Centner, Katharine Day, Susannah Farfor, Jocelyn Harewood, Carolyn Holbrook, and Donna Wheeler. Vicki Beale and Wendy Wright were responsible for layout and design. Alison Lyall designed the maps and coordinated the mapping, with assistance from Paul Clifton and Katie Butterworth. Thanks to Dan Levin for technical know-how and support and to Allyson de Fraga for research and editorial assistance.

ranging from Australian aid programs in Cambodia to new apartment developments in East Sydney. She co-authored the book *DIY Feminism*, was coordinating author on *Out to Eat - Sydney 2000* and reviewed restaurants for the first *Out to Eat - London*. During her research for this edition, Kath tried the best pizza of her life in Haberfield and learnt to love lentil ice cream in Rozelle.

OUT TO EAT – THE BOOK	**9**
A GUIDE TO THE GUIDE	**10**
OUT TO EAT READERS	**12**
SYMBOLS	**14**
Central Sydney	**15**
Introduction & Best List	*22*
Circular Quay, Circular Quay East, City, Cockle Bay, Darling Harbour, Haymarket, Pyrmont, The Rocks, Walsh Bay	
Back for More	*52*
Inner East	**53**
Introduction & Best List	*57*
Darlinghurst, East Sydney, Elizabeth Bay, Kings Cross, Potts Point, Redfern, Surry Hills, Woolloomooloo	
Back for More	*86*
Inner West	**87**
Introduction & Best List	*94*
Annandale, Ashfield, Balmain, Camperdown, Chippendale, Drummoyne, Dulwich Hill, Enmore, Erskineville, Glebe, Haberfield, Leichhardt, Marrickville, Newtown, Petersham, Rozelle	
Back for More	*126*
Eastern Suburbs	**127**
Introduction & Best List	*132*
Bellevue Hill, Bondi, Bondi Junction, Bronte, Double Bay, Moore Park, Paddington, Rose Bay, Vaucluse, Woollahra	
Back for More	*158*
South Eastern Suburbs	**159**
Introduction & Best List	*163*
Brighton-Le-Sands, Coogee, Cronulla, Eastlakes, Kensington, Kingsford, Maroubra, Randwick	
Back for More	*176*
North Shore	**177**
Introduction & Best List	*181*
Balmoral, Berowra Waters, Brooklyn, Castlecrag, Chatswood, Clontarf, Cremorne, Crows Nest, Hornsby, Kirribilli, McMahons Point, Mosman – The Spit, Neutral Bay, North Sydney, Terrey Hills, Thornleigh, Wahroonga, Westleigh, Willoughby	
Back for More	*206*

Northern Beaches	**207**
Introduction & Best List	210
Avalon, Clareville, Collaroy, Cottage Point, Dee Why, Harbord, Manly, Narrabeen, North Curl Curl, Palm Beach, Whale Beach	
Back for More	226
Outer West	**227**
Introduction & Best List	231
Auburn, Bankstown, Beverly Hills, Cabramatta, Campsie, Lakemba, North Strathfield, Parramatta, St Marys	
Back for More	242
Blue Mountains	**243**
Introduction & Best List	246
Blackheath, Katoomba, Leura	
Back for More	250
FEATURES	
Circular Quay East	25
I Want To Be Alone	28
Cafe Crawl – City	35
On Your Plate – Chinese	43
Cafe Crawl – Inner East	62
Bar Brawl	70
Crown Street, Surry Hills	78
The Joy of Food	82
Pizza and Pide To Go	98
Enmore Rd, Enmore	103
On Your Plate – Italian	112
Cafe Crawl – Inner West	118
Campbell Pde, Bondi	135
Lick It Up	141
Reel to Reel Meals	148
Grand Parade, Brighton Le Sands	165
Cafe Crawl – East/South-East	168
Lowdown on Loos	183
On Your Plate – Thai	188
On Your Plate – Japanese	200
Manly	214
Cafe Crawl – North	219
Frying Kangaroo	224
Manic Organic	235
Church St, Parramatta	239
On the Grapevine	251
Best Australian Wine	252
GLOSSARY	**254**
INDEXES	**258**

Map Contents

Chapter 1 Central Sydney
Map 1	Rocks & Quay	16
Map 2	Darling Harbour (Inset: Pyrmont)	18
Map 3	Central Sydney (Inset: The Domain)	20
Map 4	Chinatown	21

Chapter 2 Inner East
Map 5	Kings Cross & Potts Point	54
Map 6	East Sydney & Darlinghurst	55
Map 7	Inner East & South	56

Chapter 3 Inner West
Map 8	Inner West	88
Map 9	Newtown & Enmore	90
Map 10	Glebe	91
Map 11	Balmain & Rozelle	92
Map 12	Leichhardt	93

Chapter 4 Eastern Suburbs
Map 13	Paddington & Woollahra (Inset: Vaucluse)	128
Map 14	Bondi	130

Chapter 5 South Eastern Suburbs
Map 15	South-East (Inset: Airport)	160
Map 16	Brighton Le Sands (Inset: Cronulla)	162

Chapter 6 North Shore
Map 17	North Sydney	178
Map 18	Middle Harbour	179
Map 19	Hornsby (Inset: Westleigh)	180
Map 20	Outer North (Inset: Terrey Hills)	180

Chapter 7 Northern Beaches
Map 21	Manly (Inset: Narrabeen)	208
Map 22	Avalon & Palm Beach (Inset: Cottage Point)	209

Chapter 8 Outer West
Map 23	Outer West (Inset: Auburn, Bankstown, Cabramatta, Campsie, Fairfield, Lakemba, North Strathfield)	228
Map 24	Parramatta (Inset: St Marys)	230

Chapter 9 Blue Mountains
Map 25	Blue Mountains (Inset: Leura, Wentworth Falls)	244
Map 26	Katoomba	245
Map 27	Blackheath	245

Locator Maps
Map 28	Regional Sydney	281
Map 29	Greater Sydney	282
Map 30	Central Sydney	284

Public Transport
Map 31	Trains	286
Map 32	Ferries	287
Legend		288

Out to Eat – The Book

Lonely Planet

For more than 25 years travellers have looked to Lonely Planet for independent advice, not only on where to go and what to see, but on where and what to eat. Every Lonely Planet guidebook is, in part, devoted to food and the best places to eat it. So we thought, why stop there? It's time to go the whole hog – and so here's our restaurant guide created for Sydney locals and visiting food lovers alike.

The Second Edition

Trying to sum up the Sydney dining scene is tricky. As soon as you say 'figs are big' the jackfruit is back. As soon as you say fusion food is in again, the traditional Italian trattoria is winning new fans. What we can say is that in Sydney today you can order the world's cuisines without crossing more than a couple of suburbs. And with restaurants increasingly keeping later hours, you can now place an order at almost any time of the day or night.

Out to Eat is for everyone seeking Sydney's very best places to eat – not the easiest of tasks in a city with so many choices. Out to Eat helps you narrow down the myriad options and make the best decision. The complete spectrum of budgets is covered in Out to Eat – from down-to-earth eateries offering great food at low prices to to-die-for options where money is no object.

The book draws on the vast resources of local knowledge of its Sydney writers. The Out to Eat team brings in-depth cuisine knowledge, restaurant industry experience and intimacy with Sydney to each review. Insights are added by Lonely Planet guidebook authors, seasoned travellers who bring their in situ knowledge of culinary culture culled from spending years on the road.

For the second year running our reviewers have been out there sipping, slurping and sampling to select Sydney's best for you. And you won't find any hype. While we love staying in touch with all the gossip that's generated by Sydney's thriving scene, our reviews focus primarily on the food, not on who's who. Not being part of that industry (except, of course, as diners) means that we are not afraid to tell it like it is.

We've rounded up the best bars, choicest cafes and the pick of pizzas. We know where you can simultaneously grab a feast and catch a flick, where the sauciest dishes and sexiest chefs are - we'll even show you the loos with the best views.

Improvements to this edition owe much to those readers who took time out from eating to give us feedback on the first edition. You've congratulated us on our attention to vegetarian eating and highlighting options for smoke-free and noise-free dining. We've moved our locator maps from the front of the book to the back for easier reference, and we've made some improvements to our icons.

Finally, and importantly, this guidebook is free from advertising. This means a clean read for you, and uncompromised opinion from us. With more than 400 independently appraised places to choose from, we hope you'll discover a corner of Sydney that's new to you and worth going out for.

A Guide to the Guide

Organisation *Out to Eat – Sydney* is organised according to locality. The names of the chapters represent convenient groupings of neighbourhoods (ie East, Inner West, North Shore, etc) and do not refer to actual districts. Within the chapters the listings are organised alphabetically and according to suburb. Feature asides are sprinkled throughout the book.

Best Because Out to Eat includes such a diversity of listings, there are no 'stars', or points scored out of 20. But there are places that are outstanding in their field – look for them in the 'Best' lists at the beginning of each chapter. Old favourites are not forgotten in the Back for More listings at the end of each chapter. Readers also have their say on pages 12 and 13.

The Listings Each review offers a snapshot of one reviewer's experience of one or more visits to the restaurant, bar, pub, shop or cafe. We emphasise that the opinion outlined in each listing should be taken as a guide only, and not as hard evidence of what you may expect. Dishes are seasonal, prices change, staff and owners move on. The reviews attempt to encapsulate the spirit of a place and provide solid opinion on whether the place delivers what it promises. Every listing is a recommendation. The bottom line for inclusion is that the food must be good or better than good. A handful of places where the food was just OK have been included because they had something unique to offer (such as location, historical interest or atmosphere).

Lesser-known cuisine terms which have an asterisk* next to them are explained in the glossary, on page 254.

Opening Hours Many restaurants open for longer hours during daylight-saving time (normally late Oct to late March). Many restaurants say they are open until 'late', but this generally means that business closes for the night at the restaurateur's discretion and not that the business is open until a late hour (ie, until midnight or later). If the listing includes a 'kitchen closes' time, it means that cooked meals are no longer available after that time but that you may still buy a drink, and perhaps snacks, until closing.

Reservations Details whether the business accepts reservations and, if so, when they are necessary.

Licensing A restaurant with a BYO (Bring Your Own) licence allows you to bring alcohol that you have purchased elsewhere to be served with your meal. Almost all restaurants with a BYO licence allow only bottled wine or beer to be brought in and served. 'Unlicensed' means that it is illegal to consume alcohol on the premises. At a 'licensed' restaurant (or bar, cafe etc) you can purchase alcohol to consume with your meal. Licensed restaurants that allow BYO usually charge a corkage fee.

Smoking A Bill before the NSW State Parliament bans smoking in all restaurants and cafes. In pubs and bars, smoking is banned in the dining area, or where the predominant activity is the consumption of food. If the bill is passed this could be in effect by Spring 2000.

Map Reference Each listing is cross-referenced to a numbered map.

Price Fields Price fields show the complete range of prices on each restaurant's menu, for example 'starter: $5-$11', where $5 is the price of the least expensive starter on the menu and $11 is the most expensive. Prices were correct at the time of research.

Set Menu/Banquet Prices Indicates that set menus and banquets are available, usually without prior arrangement.

Credit Cards & Eftpos Abbreviations show credit and debit facilities offered by the restaurant. AE: American Express, BC: BankCard, DC: Diners Club,

JCB: Japanese Credit Bureau card; MC: MasterCard; V: Visa Card; Eftpos: Electronic Funds Transfer at Point Of Sale.

GST As we all know by now, restaurant, takeaway and prepared food is subject to a federal GST. Please note that while some prices in this book reflect the addition of the tax, most do not.

Tipping A service charge is generally not added to restaurant meals in Australia. Tipping is seen as a discretionary token of goodwill and thanks to both the service and kitchen staff. That said, it is an accepted practice to leave roughly ten per cent of the total bill. More will demonstrate that you were especially appreciative of the level of service you received. So long as the tip is voluntary, no GST applies.

Wheelchair Access Restaurants equipped with a toilet that has been purpose-built or adapted for wheelchair access are the only listings carrying the words 'wheelchair access'. 'Access' suggests wheelchairs will also easily get into the restaurant and have ease of movement once inside. We can't guarantee this, so please telephone ahead to confirm facilities.

Dress Code Very few Sydney restaurants claim to have an official dress code. The relevant listings include the details.

Entertainment Gives details of in-house entertainment (dance, live music, performances).

Glossary (and Glossary of Special Orders) A glossary of the lesser-known cuisine terms which have been mentioned in the listings, and a glossary of special dietary needs.

Indexes Restaurants are grouped in three indexes – index by cuisine, index by suburb, and an alphabetical index. The alphabetical index also provides a quick reference for finding restaurants that have wheelchair access, are suitable for business, have outdoor seating, serve breakfast, are easy on the pocket (restaurants where you can get mains for $15 or under) and are child friendly (given to restaurants with either highchairs or children's serves (or both)).

Write to us

Things change – prices go up, opening hours change, good places go bad and bad places go bankrupt – nothing stays the same. So, if you find things better or worse, recently opened or recently closed, please tell us and help make the next edition even more accurate and useful.

Every morsel of information you send will be read and acknowledged by the appropriate author, editor or publisher. The best contributions will be rewarded with a free Lonely Planet book and excerpts may appear in future editions of *Out to Eat – Sydney*, so please let us know if you don't want your letter published or your name acknowledged.

Write to us:
Lonely Planet Out to Eat
PO Box 617, Hawthorn VIC 3122
☎ 03 9819 1877 fax 03 9819 6459
email: out2eat@lonelyplanet.com.au

from Jan 2001:
Locked Bag 1, Footscray VIC 3011
☎ 03 9689 4666 fax 03 9689 6833
email: out2eat@lonelyplanet.com.au

Out to Eat Readers

There are a lot of reasons why we go back to a place time and time again, and they change according to the occasion – for some having a reliable 'local' is paramount, while others will travel to the other side of town to satisfy a craving, and some hungry souls only go out to celebrate anniversaries and birthdays. One thing we can say is that Out to Eat readers have eclectic tastes – recommendations roam through the city, suburbs and beyond, and reflect Sydney's diversity of cuisines. Most of our readers' favourites are reviewed within the book, but the few that aren't will be considered for the next edition. We don't have the space to list every recommendation, but here are some of the best comments received:

Yulla, Bondi & Onde, Darlinghurst
A new Middle Eastern/Mediterranean place in Bondi called Yulla is cheap and stylish (owned by the people from DOV). But my favourite is still Onde in Darlinghurst, for incredibly good value bistro food. (Daniel N, Tamarama)

The Malabar, Crows Nest
We love this Southern Indian restaurant. It's speciality is dosa – really good. They also do a great thali and are always crowded. (Debbie W, Lane Cove)

Rockpool, The Rocks
Even though it's incredibly expensive and the design is très '80s, the food, service and attention to detail are consistently excellent. (Meena S, Coogee)

Burgerman, Bondi
Handy to drop in to when sandy on the way home from the beach for great tasting burgers that please kids (plain hamburger with sauce) and adults (grilled chicken or fish, rocket, chilli etc) alike. (Lola T, St Kilda)

Billy Kwong, Surry Hills
Swish but affordable. Try taste treats like the jellyfish salad, priced for friends to share. Love the warm cool interiors and graphics by Sydney's rising stars. (Glenn W, Surry Hills)

The Blue Water Cafe, Manly
Great atmosphere with big chunky wooden tables and cushioned stools. Great post-surf breakfasts – from porridge to a full fry-up and good coffee. (Peter M, Lane Cove)

Prasit's Northside Takeaway, Surry Hills
Worth queuing to eat the best Thai in Sydney – from delicious fish cakes, squid salad and heavenly beef to richly flavoured curries, including the fabulous red duck curry. (Chris C, Bronte)

Fish Face, Darlinghurst
Just the best fish and seafood. Always absolutely delish. Service fab – they come get you from the pub when your table is ready. BYO too (seems to be less around than a year or two ago). (Eugenie S, Mosman)

Sean's Panaroma, North Bondi
Great ambience, tucked away location and beautiful farm-style cooking. (Karen R, Tamarama)

The Orange Peel Cafe, Balmain
Good vegetarian foccacias, great cakes and muffins. In a quaint sandstone building, small and cosy, and you can sit outside. (Miranda W, email)

Fifi's Lebanese Restaurant, Enmore
Quite unlike any other Sydney Lebanese restaurant (no belly dancers, no cushions, no grot). Fabulous food (including the world's best baba ganoush and felafels), cheap prices, friendly service, simple but classy decor. (Kim N, email)

Bathers' Pavilion, Balmoral Beach
Bathers' Pav is a great theatrical experience (low key but nonetheless theatrical) - with a view at night of the shark net lit up and its chorus line of red-shoed seagulls. Food is great – forces you to try unusual things – last time I had sea urchin! (Rebecca B, Mosman)

Touch of Thai, Woolloomooloo & Savion, North Bondi
Touch of Thai is a tiny place that serves the best value Thai in Sydney. If it's really full they will bring your meal to the Irish pub next door. Also the Middle Eastern kosher cafe called Savion – they have the most hygienic chip fryer in Sydney. (Nadine F, Elwood)

Uchi Lounge, Surry Hills
Fab, elegant, hip Japanese. (Madeleine S, email)

Kyushu, Neutral Bay & Cloudstreet, Kirribilli
Kyushu's always busy. Fresh, light and very tasty Japanese food. The best part is the price – it's a struggle to spend $30. Also Cloudstreet – don't let the restaurant's appearance from the street fool you – excellent service and modern Australian cuisine at its absolute creative best awaits inside. You can BYO wine, too. (Leon W, email)

Barzura, Coogee
Excellent food at reasonable Sydney prices. Right on the beach, casual and pretty rowdy. Great for breakfast, lunch and dinner. (Peter C, email)

Sailors Thai, The Rocks
Sailors Thai serves wonderful, considered food in a stark but sensual space. Bravo the calm, knowledgeable staff who welcomed and fussed over our toddler (who also loved the food). (Joseph G, Palm Beach)

Una's, Darlinghurst
I noticed one of my faves, Una's in Victoria St, wasn't in Out to Eat 2000. It serves good ol' fashioned schnitzels and all sorts of hearty German food. (Paul C, email)

The Maltese Cafe, Surry Hills
I do miss the very-Valletta old shop, but no complaints about the best (and cheapest) little pastries around. Stick with the traditional pea or ricotta, and take some frozen ones home for later on. Date biscuits are also yum. (Rumer G, Fitzroy)

Bar Baba, Leichardt
We go there for the buzz, Italian-style food and varied menu. One of the few places in Sydney that does risotto well – the fresh crab risotto is sensational. (Hélène T, Bronte)

Milsons, Kirribilli
A strong aesthetic appeal in everything they do – from the stunning decor to the way the superb Asian influenced food appears on the plate. The service is friendly and professional without being ingratiating. (Margaret C, Glebe)

Corinthian, Marrickville
Greek with no frills. Lamb skulls in the bain-marie, platters filled with huge chunks of meat on the bone. (Mike & Rina, Balmain)

Symbols

 Totally smoke free.

 Smoking Text accompanying this symbol explains whether there are smoking restrictions, separate smokefree dining or smoking throughout. (Note: Upcoming legislation banning smoking in enclosed public spaces including cafes and restaurants will override these restrictions – see p 10 for further details.)

Vegetarian Options
Each restaurant has been rated for the quality and range of vegetarian dishes (those that contain no meat, including fish and seafood) on offer on the regular menu. 'Carrot' icons indicate the rating.

 Various and/or interesting vegetarian options.

 All-vegetarian menu or excellent vegetarian options.

 Quiet Noticeably quiet, even when busy.

 Medium noise Not noticeably quiet, and you can generally hear conversation at your own table without straining.

 Noisy Can be very noisy when busy (either due to music or the acoustics of the space). You may have to raise your voice considerably to be heard in conversation.

 Romantic Make a date. Something about this place makes romance seem very likely.

 Open fireplace Open fireplace for chilly days or nights.

 Outdoors Outdoor dining options for fine days or nights.

 Parking Free private parking on premises, valet parking, or discounted validated parking at a nearby commercial carpark.

 Business Exercise the expense account. This place is suitable for business occasions. Expect professional table service, compatible clientele, adequate table spacing and comfortable noise levels.

CENTRAL SYDNEY

 Circular Quay

Circular Quay East

City

Cockle Bay

Darling Harbour

Haymarket

Pyrmont

The Rocks

Walsh Bay

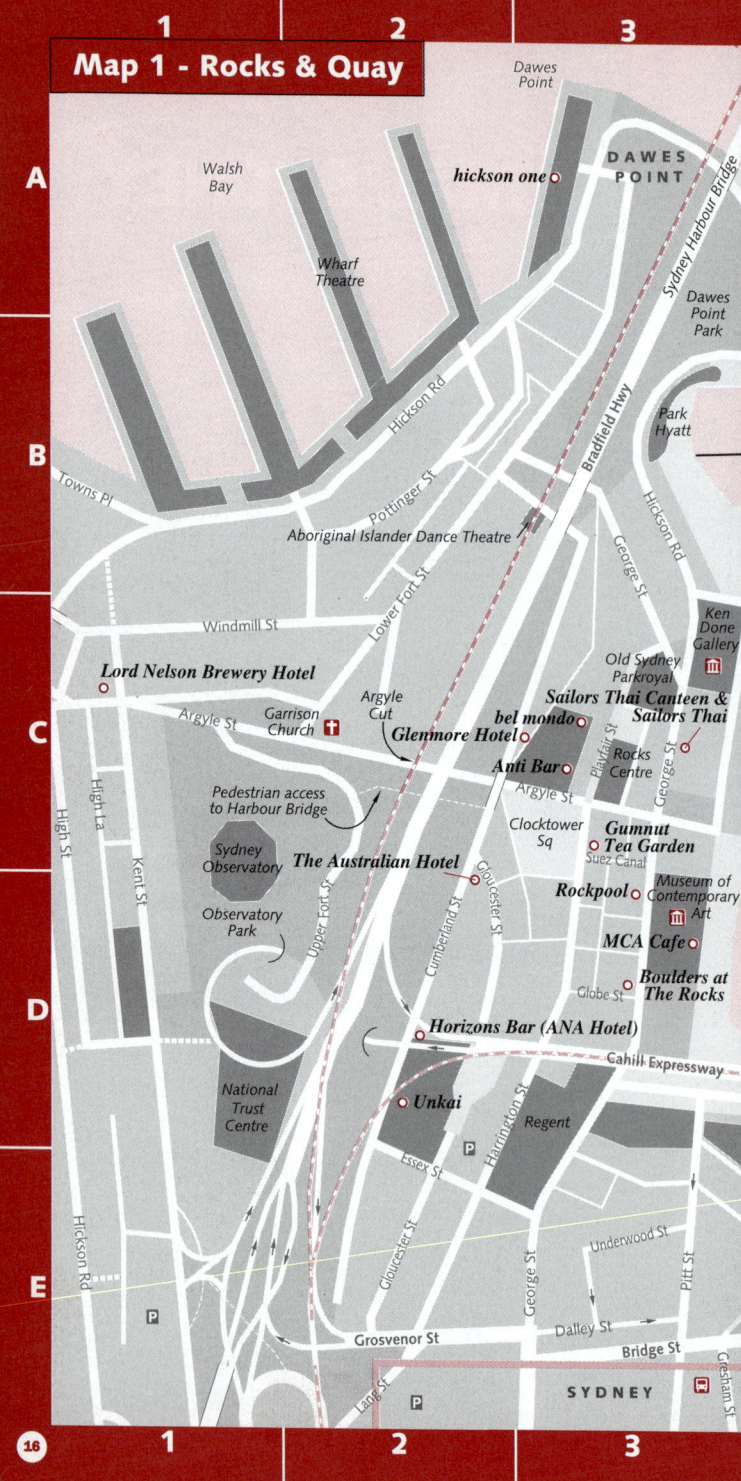

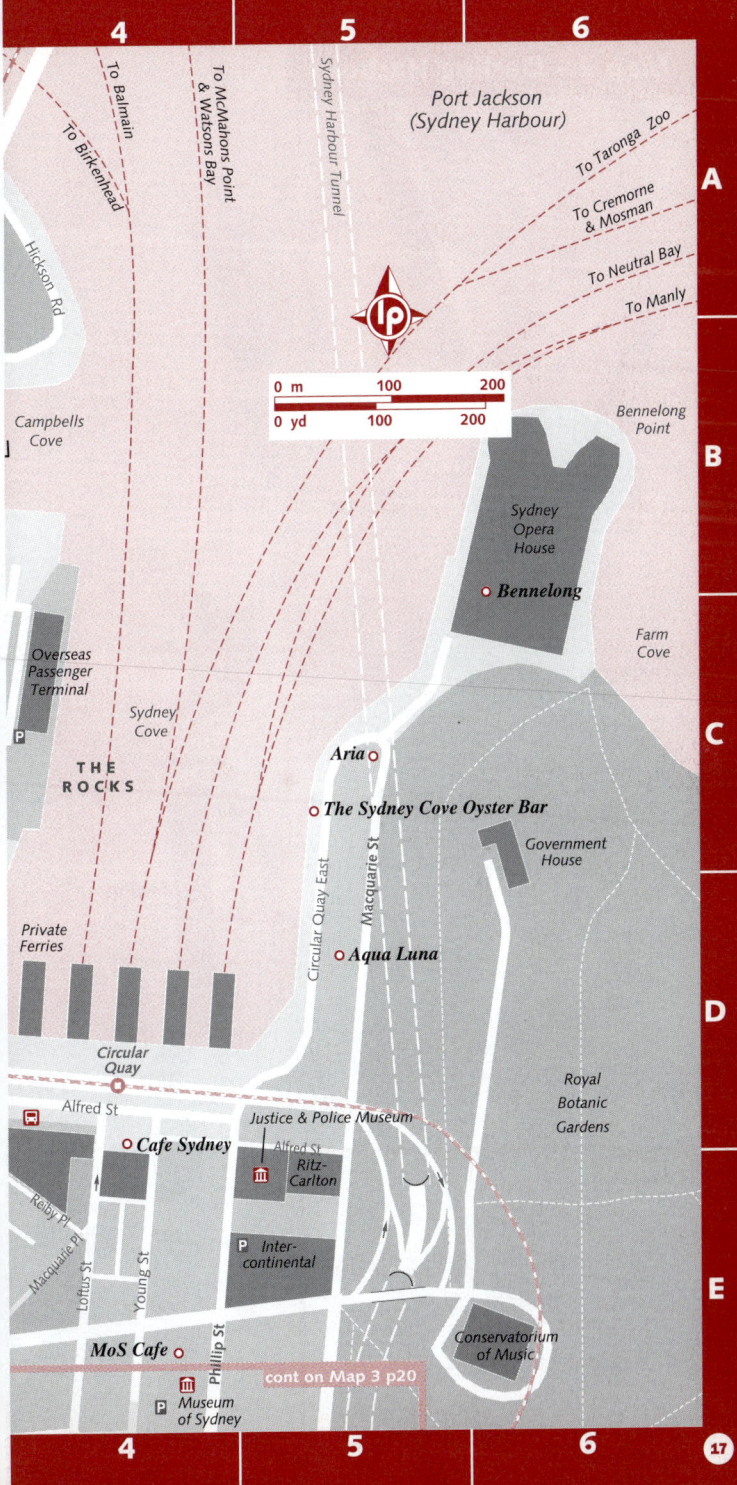

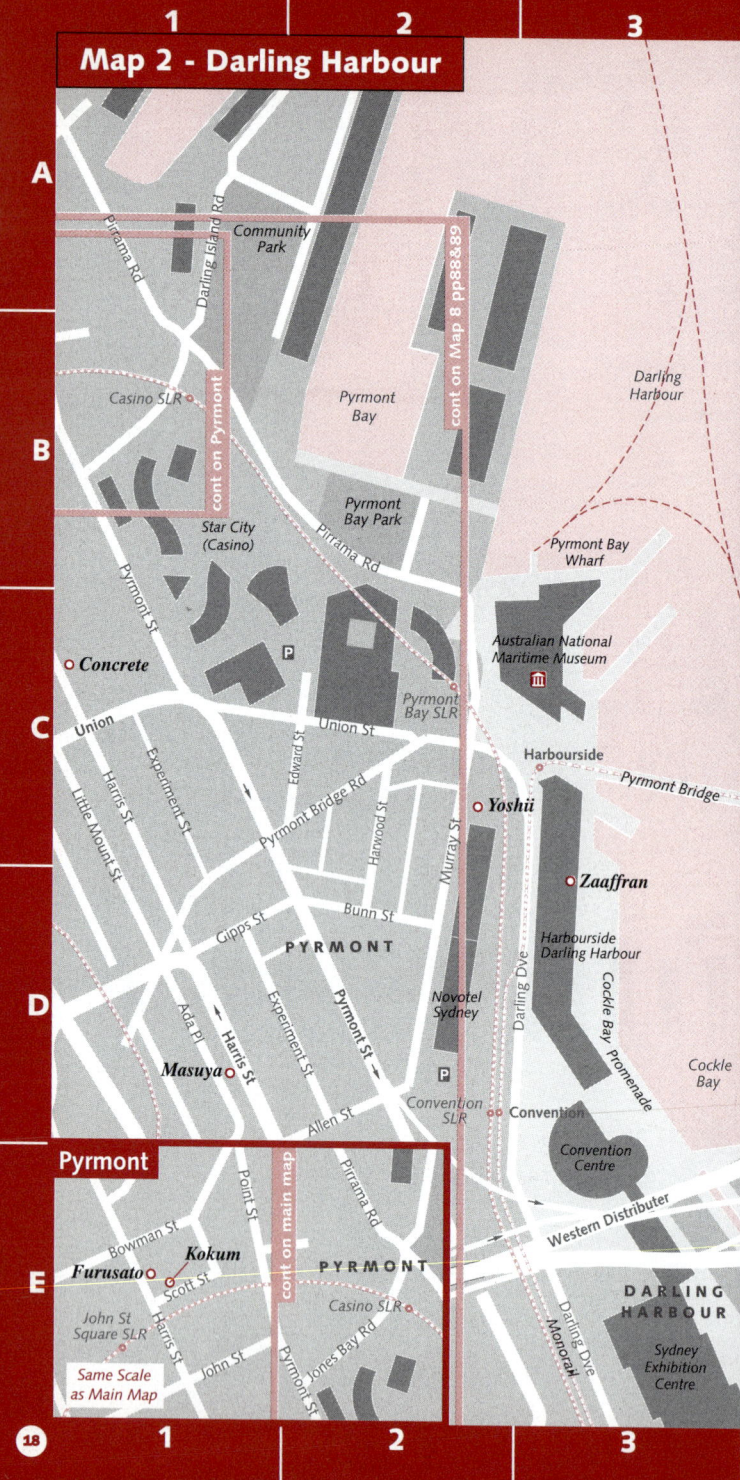

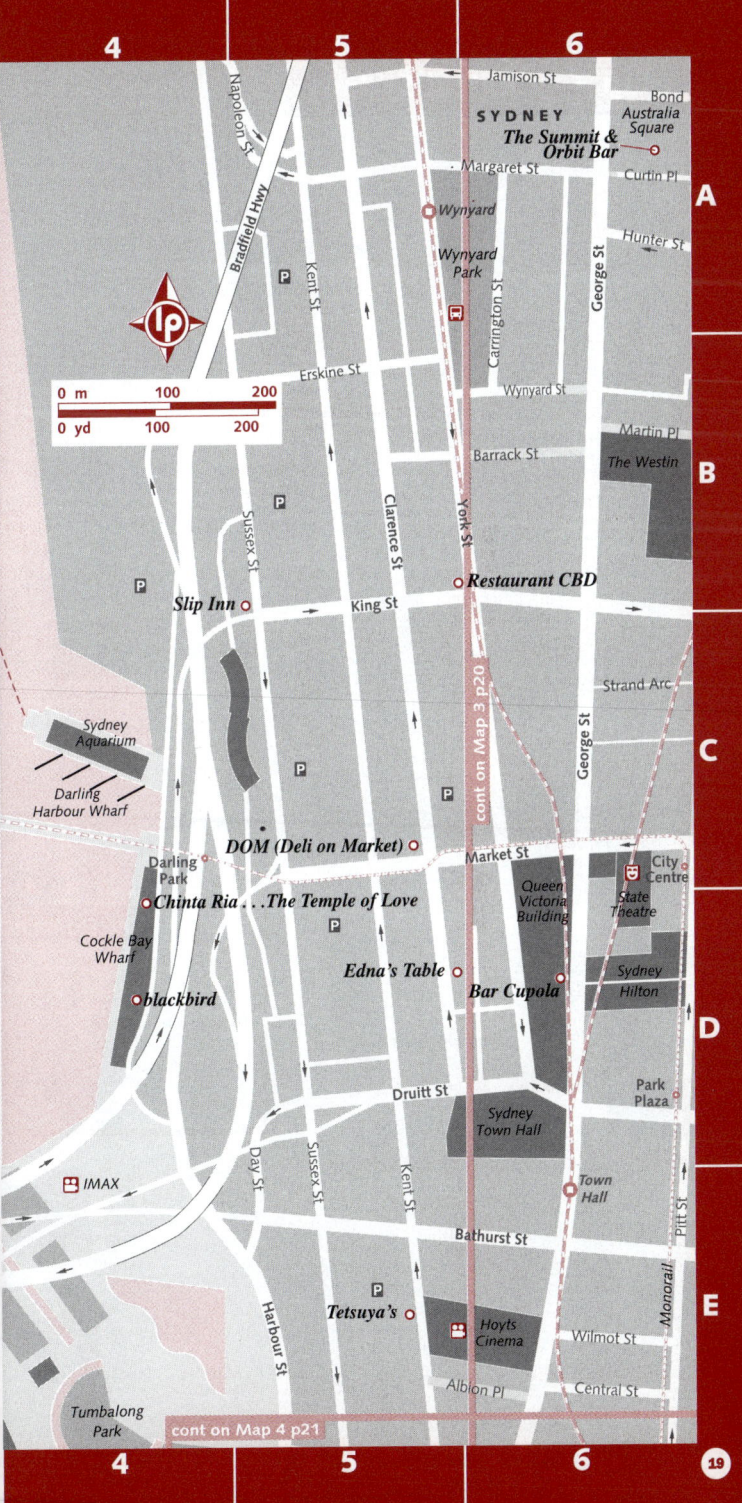

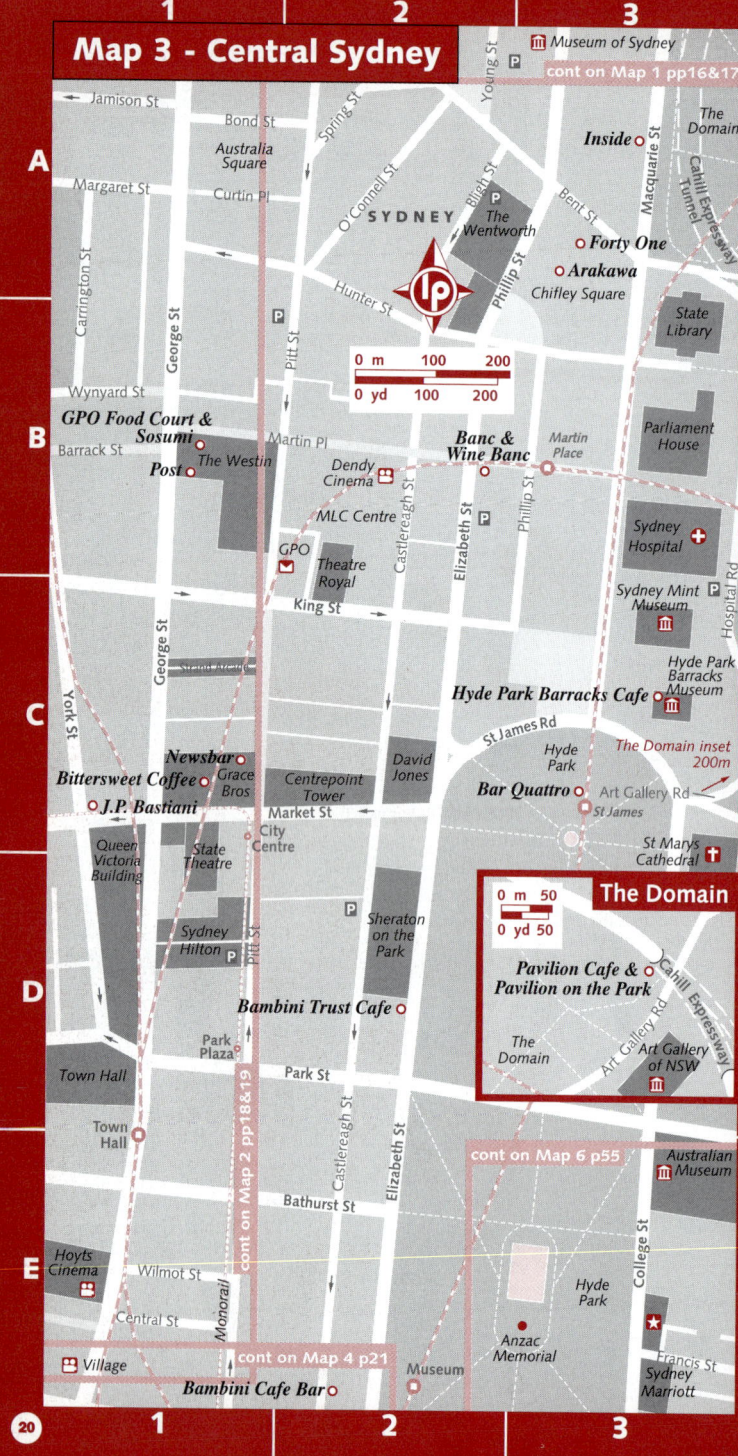

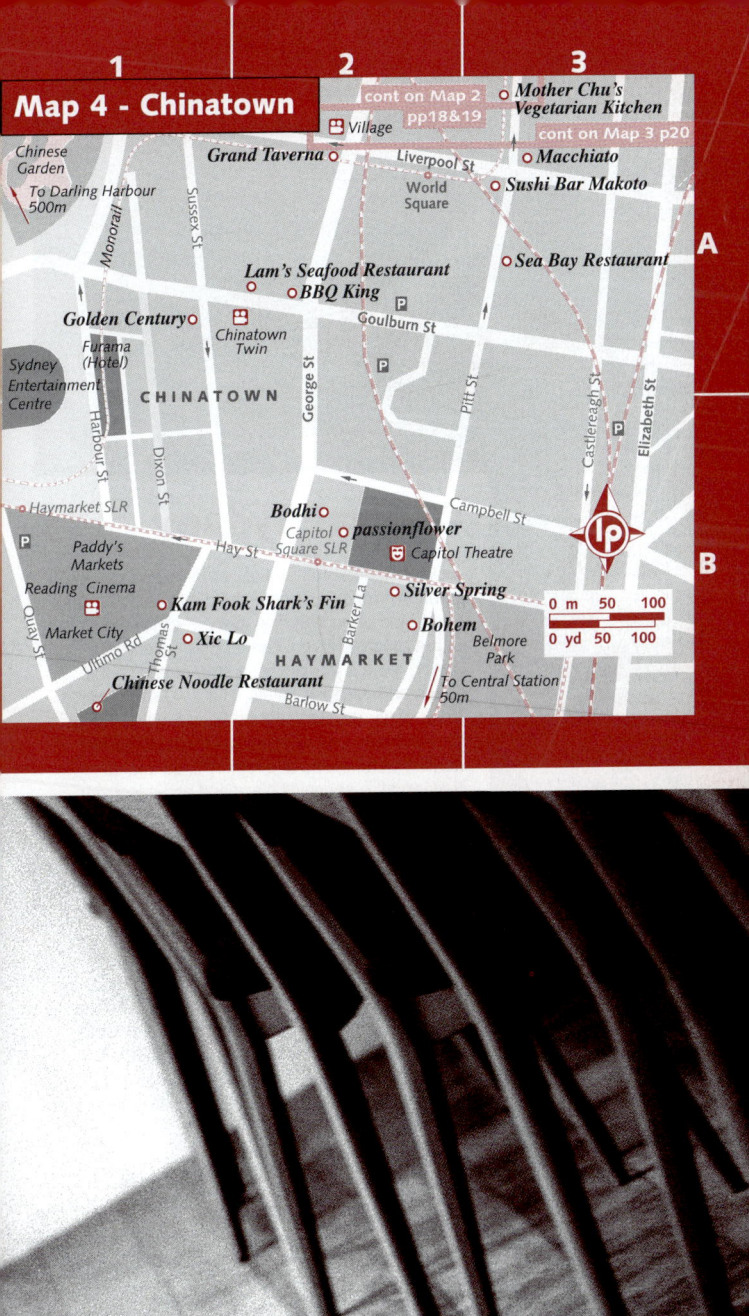

BEST

■ **Aria**
Symphony of flavours and harbour views

■ **Banc**
French fine dining with elegance

■ **Post**
The old GPO delivering great food

■ **Rockpool**
Supermodel of mod Oz cuisine

■ **Sailors Thai Canteen**
Excellent Thai at mess prices

■ **Tetsuya's**
Japanese/French fusion master now in the city

■ **Xic Lo**
Value Vietnamese in slick surrounds

Central Sydney

Just outside Central Station, at Belmore Park, a group of Sydney's Chinese residents go about their own brand of body buffing every weekday morning with a tai chi session. Farther north, along Pitt Street, there's Chinatown, a strip of adult bookshops and decaying hotels, and a 40-storey office tower under development at World Square. Westwards is Darling Habour – a wasteland of derelict warehouses and railway lines until a Segaworld, a shopping plaza and an underwater aquarium transformed it into Australia's most-frequently visited tacky tourist hub (though you'll find some surprisingly top class restaurants here). The city centre is roughly marked by Centrepoint Tower, Sydney's 'mood ring' (it turned pink for the Mardi Gras). Farther northwards, along Martin Place, you'll find snazzy new bars and the General Post Office, recently revamped into a swish hotel and food hall. Keep going northwards for Circular Quay and the Opera House, where you can take in some of the world's finest food with some of the world's finest views. With all this, and almost all of the world's great cuisines within a few square miles, Sydney is indeed a truly international city.

CIRCULAR QUAY

Bennelong
Modern Australian

☎ **9250 7548**
Sydney Opera House, Bennelong Point

This is one venue where the food can only try to keep up with the stunning surrounds, under the ribbed vaults of Utzon's shells. Whether lounging in a Swan chair at the cocktail bar, or dining on the lower level amid the mesmerizing artichoke lamps, it's an exciting place. Such architectural pressure may explain why the food is so painstakingly described. Wood mushroom ragoût with an oven confit of lamb (from Gippsland, $38), roasted saddle of Mirrawa squab (with foie gras and truffle jus, $38). Our seared trout (from the ocean) had a lovely salt and cracked pepper crust and came with a mustard and lemon sauce and sprightly asparagus spears. Another Aussie icon, the 'Bennelong Pav' ($16) is almost as well constructed as Utzon's pad – a cascade of fruit appearing like a miniature Carmen Miranda hat. A yoghurt topping (with double cream) drags it into the new millenium.

Mon-Sat 5.30pm-11.30pm; reservations necessary; licensed, no BYO

Map 1 B6

Opera House Car Park ($20 after 5.30pm)

Smoking at bar only

starter: $18-$32
main: $26-$38
dessert: $16
Pre-theatre set menu $50 or $60 (6pm-7.30pm)

AE BC DC MC V

Cafe Sydney
International

☎ **9251 8683**
Level 5, Customs House, 31 Alfred St

Cafe Sydney is all dark wood, booths and low wattage – like an old-fashioned steakhouse that went to finishing school in Manhattan. The ringside balcony overlooking Circular Quay makes it a gotta-go once sort of place. Perhaps the universal appeal of its position has dictated the universal appeal of the menu? You could start with a mixed plate of plain and sweet naan ($2) then move on to a rocket and pancetta salad ($9.50), a Thai vegetable curry ($15) or beef with creamed celery ($27.50). But don't bother with the vegetarian risotto ($18). There's an array of seafood dishes, and a char-grilled steak of swordfish ($25.50), deliberately raw on the inside, is very good. For dessert, a 'chocolate and macadamia cake with Malibu cream' ($11.50) sounds like it's just flown in from the Gold Coast (we recommend instead the lime tart with a sublime mango sorbet, $10.50).

Open: daily noon-3pm, Mon-Sat 6pm-11pm, light snacks daily 3pm-6pm (to 4pm Sunday); reservations essential; licensed, no BYO

Map 1 D4

Valet parking from 6pm, $15

Wheelchair access

Smoking at bar and terrace only

Terrace tables

starter: $9.50-$18.50
main: $18-$29.50
dessert: $9.50-$13.50

AE BC DC MC V

CIRCULAR QUAY EAST

Map 1 D5
Opera House car park
Wheelchair access
Smoking at bar only
Promenade tables in bar

Aqua Luna
Italian

☎ 9251 0311
5–7 Macquarie St

Now that the controversial East Circular Quay developments are as done as burnt toast, Sydneysiders have become as blithely nonchalant about their hulking silver forms as Aqua Luna diners are when high profile politicians and well-known actors wander in. There's a continual low roar as a full house heartily tucks into their meals and their conversations. Everything tastes as if the flavour volume has been turned up to maximum, starting with the extra virgin olive oil for bread dipping and a salmon entrée ($18) that's like a dip in the sea. A veal and thyme lasagne ($19) is one of the best versions ever, while succulent grilled lamb is served with a crescent of roasted pumpkin and an overly salty tapenade ($30). If you try the River Cafe's cocoa-saturated 'chocolate nemesis' cake, order your partner an espresso gelati – it's a match made in dessert heaven ($15.50 & $10).

starter: $11-$25
main: $27.50-$32
dessert: $8-$15
AE BC DC MC V; Eftpos

Open: Mon-Fri noon-3pm, Mon-Sat 6pm-11pm; reservations essential; licensed, no BYO

Map 1 C5
Wheelchair access
Smoking at the bar only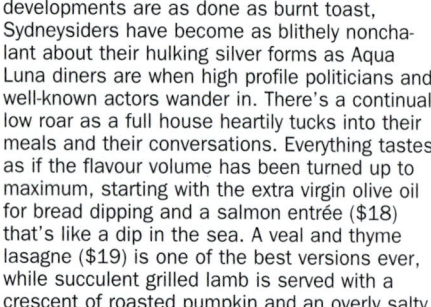

Aria
Modern Australian

☎ 9252 2555
1 Macquarie St

Like a snatch of opera, the booming tenor voice of chef Mathew Moran sings out from the kitchen, 'Service Now! Yabbies away, table 15! Go, go, go.' His libretto is a dramatic introduction to Aria, the newest star in Sydney's fine-dining firmament. Moran is a chef striving for perfection, so while the histrionics may be overcooked, the food is close to faultless. His mind-blowing mod Oz masterpieces would taste great eaten in the dark; they're even better when accompanied by elegantly attired waiters, double damask tablecloths, decanted wine and eye-boggling views of the Opera House and Harbour Bridge. A blue swimmer crab consommé ($24) afloat with sea bass tortellini and slivers of shiitake is full of clean, delicate flavours. And, served sashimi-style, a char-grilled tuna fillet with baby olives and garlicky mash ($40) is a paean to ultra-fresh ingredients and confident cooking. Desserts fall into the die-for category, particularly an assiette of art-directed Valrhona chocolate treats ($18).

starter: $22-$32
main: $36-$40
dessert: $16-$18
AE BC DC MC V

Open: Mon-Fri noon-2.30pm, Mon-Sat 5.30pm-11.30pm (pre-theatre menu 5.30pm-7pm), Sun 6.30pm-10pm; reservations essential; licensed, no BYO

Circular Quay East

The sun came up through the Heads and stole its way into the Quay, far over the bay. Each of the tiny waves turned to flame, and as the sun rose higher it left pearly tracks across the water. A month would not be long enough to imbibe such beauty...

Miles Franklin, *My Career Goes Bung* (1946)

Franklin's words appear on a brass plaque on the 'Writers' Walk' along the East Circular Quay promenade, but that beauty she raves about will probably have you so mesmerised you'll step right over it. Circular Quay doesn't look quite like it used to though – small brass plaques mark the undulating water lines of 1788 and 1844 – far from the geometrical U-shaped quay of today. In more recent years, civic battles have been fought over the shape of the skyline, and the erection of the derogatorily named 'toaster' building, with its multi-million dollar apartments, boutique hotel and designer shops. But the Quay has always been an unfinished piece of work (Bennelong Point was once a tram and ferry terminus branded an eyesore). All the while hawkers peddle harbour cruises offering more views than you can take in in a day, and Japanese school contingents pose for photos in front of Utzon's backdrop.

CITY

Map 3 A3

Validated parking at night only (Chifley Plaza)

Wheelchair access

Arakawa
Japanese

☎ 9229 0191
Level 1, Chifley Plaza,
2 Chifley Square

Five years into its life as one of the city's top Japanese restaurants, the restless Matsukaze, a past master at tempura and sushi, has changed its name, had a design makeover and reoriented itself as a sleek contemporary temple of the set course menu. The private rooms (still ideal for an intimate dinner à deux) remain untouched, but who wants to hide there when the sophisticated deep purple and wood interior, where soft lights create perpetual dusk, is so appealing? Lunch is dominated by city suits, who know a good deal (not to mention good food) when they see it. So tuck into one of the bento ($38.50-$42.50), expertly presented dishes, such as a meaty grilled ocean perch in miso, succulent chicken teriyaki, or the crispy prawn and vegetable tempura, nestling in black lacquer boxes. The only thing off the mark was the tuna carpaccio, fresh juicy fish smothered with cloying mayonnaise.

starter: dinner only
$7.50-$18
main: dinner only
$18-$27.50
dessert: lunch $9.50,
dinner $13.50
Set menu lunch $36-$54
or dinner $60-$100

AE BC DC JCB MC V

Open: Mon-Fri from noon, Mon-Sat from 6pm; reservations advisable (especially for lunch); licensed, no BYO

Map 3 E2

Nonsmoking tables available

Bambini Cafe Bar
Italian/modern Australian

☎ 9264 9550
262 Castlereagh St

The wait for lunchtime service at this chirpy city cafe can seem as long as the menu is short. Perhaps that explains all the executive-class silk ties and patent leather heels – no one here is watching the clock. But when the meals do arrive, they turn out to be mostly bright and tasty dishes to power you through the rest of the working day: smoked salmon roulade ($14), pan-fried tuna ($15) and huge toasted focaccias ($12). Slices of striped char-grilled veal are the foundation of an excellent squat stack that's bolstered and contrasted with beetroot purée, beans and pancetta ($17). Ravioli was less successful – the tomato sauce was fresh and tangy but the pasta was waterlogged ($15). The spare, spacious look is from the pages of *Vogue* circa 1997, with classical silver water jugs and vases of fresh lilies. Bambini is a good business-like choice.

main: $12-$17
dessert: $8
AE BC DC MC V

Open: Mon-Fri 7am-6pm (breakfast: Mon-Fri 7am-11.30am); reservations advisable; licensed, no BYO

Bambini Trust Cafe
Italian

☎ **9283 7098**
St James Trust Building, 185 Elizabeth St

Map 3 D2

 Nonsmoking tables available

Milan or Melbourne? It's not your typical Sydney eatery but a slice of Italy in the CBD. The clientele is made up of oh so groovy lasses that lunch by day and tourists by night. The wood panelling and subdued lighting certainly have the required European-ness and the food is *almost* there. Spaghetti vongole ($18) with clams is tasty with just the right amount of chilli. Penne with cotechino* ($18) is warming and creamy – perfect comfort food for a wintry day. Popular mains include a chicken breast stuffed with prosciutto and porcini ($23.50) and crisp-skinned salmon resting on charred radicchio and artichokes ($24). For dessert lovers, the raspberry crème brûlée ($10) is worth coming for alone – lots of cream and vanilla but not too sweet. Early birds stop in for breakfast for fabulous fruit, yoghurt and muesli combinations ($5-$8.50), eggs any way you want them ($8.50-10.50) and excellent coffee.

starter: $17-$19
main: $19-$24.50
dessert: $10

AE BC DC MC V

Open: Mon-Fri 7am-11.30am, noon-3pm, 5pm-10pm; reservations advisable; licensed, no BYO

Banc
Modern French

☎ **9233 5300**
53 Martin Place

Map 3 B2

 Smoking after 2.30pm and 10.30pm only

With its subtle lighting, plush banquettes, green marble pillars and imposing mirrors, Banc has the feel of an ultra-exclusive European gallery – only here the art comes delivered on the plate. We begin with the vibrantly colourful expressionism of the assorted vegetarian starters ($25) – a bold circle of tomato and basil here, a square of goats cheese tortellini on a bed of diced peppers there. Call it a Picasso. The tender quail on a platform of potato and mustard with shaved truffle ($26) is reassuringly earthy, just like the squab breast ($39), splayed like a roasted heart, on risotto – basically Constable country. The mini desserts ($20) – a mango glacé trimmed with delicate milk bubbles, the champagne jelly quivering and rosy, the lemon tart simply sensational. A Gainsborough perhaps? We mull over the possibilities, sipping the wine expertly suggested by the sommelier, enjoying the utter elegance and professionalism of it all.

starter: $22-$28
main: $36-$39
dessert: $18-$20
Degustation menu $85 or $95.

AE BC DC MC V

Open: Mon-Fri noon-2.30pm, Mon-Sat 6.30pm-10pm; reservations essential; licensed, no BYO

I want to be Alone

Eating alone should always be a pleasure, allowing your full attention to be given to the experience of dining. But too often restaurants can make lone diners feel less than comfortable. To combat this we have compiled a list of places where even the most novice soloist will feel at home.

Bambini Trust Cafe St James Trust Building, 185 Elizabeth St, City ☎ 9283 7098
Open all day, you can hide behind the dark wood panels in the corners of this cafe and have all the cups of coffee, wines by the glass and Italian sweets you like – without anyone telling you to get back to work (see review p 27).

Chatswood BBQ Kitchen 377 Victoria Ave, Chatswood ☎ 9419 6532
The laminex table-sharing in this small room means no one knows where one group ends and the next group begins – so you'll just blend into the scenery, leaving you to concentrate on choosing one of the 100 cheap, but always good, Chinese meals (see review p 186).

Cinque 261a King St, Newtown ☎ 9519 3077
The bookstore next door thoughtfully provides customers with stools to sit on, a bench to lean on and a window into the cafe so you can order a cappuccino and cake while you flick through the latest cookbook or peruse the latest trash lit release (see review p 117).

GPO Food Court No 1 Martin Place, City ☎ 9229 7704 Map 3 B1
Despite talk to the contrary, you can get food here at a reasonable price from the greengrocer, the baker or the sushi-maker. Or eat alone at the Westin Hotel – everybody else does.

Iku 25a Glebe Point Rd, Glebe ☎ 9692 8720 Map 10 E6
The atmosphere's always calm, and you can mix with like-minded macrobiotic-loving souls perched on high stools at the wooden benches – or keep to yourself in the small but pleasant leafy courtyard.

Kazbah on Darling 379 Darling St, Balmain ☎ 9555 7067
With glossy mags to flick through, friendly staff to chat to and big plates of baked eggs, spicy sausage and haloumi to get through, you'll hardly notice you're alone (see review p 99).

Longrain 85 Commonwealth St, Surry Hills ☎ 9280 2888
Just because it's one of the coolest spots around doesn't mean you shouldn't enjoy it when you're solo. High stools and generously sized bar benches mean you too can sample the betel leaves and beer (see review p 79).

Mother Chu's Vegetarian Kitchen 367 Pitt St, City ☎ 9283 2828
Laminex tables, no alcohol and plenty of other lone diners so you won't feel conspicuous (see review p 34).

Newsbar Mezzanine, Grace Bros, Pitt St Mall, City ☎ 9238 9460
Right next to the footwear section is a place to rest your shopper's feet. In a heritage corner of the Grace Bros department store, Newsbar will make you a pasta or risotto to get you back on your feet for the afternoon shopping leg (see review p 34).

Sushi Bar Makoto 119 Liverpool St (Cnr Liverpool and Pitt Sts), City ☎ 9283 6767 Map 4 A3
Fresh, simple Japanese fare in fresh, simple surroundings (black, white, and a brick-red feature wall). Sit on one of the comfy black pod stools around the sushi train.

CITY

BBQ King
Chinese

☎ 9267 2586
18-20 Goulburn St

Map 4 A2

 Nonsmoking tables available

This is Chinatown at its most authentic, from the wiped-down laminate tables to the efficient, verging on abrupt, service. You might just as well be in Kowloon. Frequented by top-notch chefs and exhausted waiters seeking solace in the wee hours, the food is uncomplicated, fresh, tasty and plentiful. Don't stress about ploughing through the extensive menu, unless you're determined to sample pigs' intestines or chicken feet. Try the house special platters of roast meats: will it be the barbecued duck with a lemony soy sauce ($12.80), the tender, juicy soy-sauce chicken ($11.60) or the roast pork with crunchy crackling ($12.80)? If you get stuck, there are combination platters. Add a huge plate of steamed Chinese broccoli ($8), and perhaps some velvety eggplant in black-bean sauce ($9.50), and you've got a huge feast for two. Tables are nearly always full, but turnaround is fast and the wait is never long.

starter: $4-$8
main: $8-$17.80
Set menu $19-$25/person (min 6 people)

AE BC DC MC V; Eftpos

Open: daily 11.30am-2am; reservations accepted (large groups only); licensed & BYO (corkage $2/person)

Edna's Table
Modern Australian

☎ 9267 3933
204 Clarence St

Map 2 D5

 Nonsmoking tables available

With its clean lines and soaring ceilings, the dining room at Edna's Table makes the perfect backdrop for the Kershs' warm hospitality and innovative ways with native Australian flavours. Seated on plush, high-backed terracotta chairs at white-draped tables are an assortment of tourists, escapees from inner-city workplaces and good-time groups, all seduced by fine dining free of pretensions. Asian influences are apparent in the sugar snap pea and sea parsley salad, with a tangle of soba noodles ($14.50/$24) (from the separate vegetarian menu), and in the tender twice-cooked duck with Balinese red rice, enlivened by tart rosella buds ($28.90). For the full event, the degustation menu runs the gamut of lemon aspen oysters, crocodile and corn swagbag with native mint pesto, ocean trout baked in paperbark, roasted emu fillet and Raymond's signature kangaroo fillet. A trio of ice creams ($12.50), including dreamy strawberry with cracked pepperberry and zingy pear, makes a refreshing finale.

starter: $10.50-$16.80
main: $19.90-$28.90
dessert: $11.90-$13.50
Degustation $75

AE BC DC MC V; Eftpos

Open: Mon-Fri noon-2.30pm, Tues-Sat 6pm-10pm; reservations essential; licensed, no BYO

CITY

Map 3 A3

Chifley Square $10

Wheelchair access

Smoking after 2.30pm, and 10.30pm only

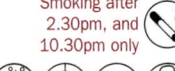

Forty One
Modern Australian

☎ 9221 2500
Level 41, The Chifley Tower, 2 Chifley Square

Forty One occupies a penthouse position, high above the twinkling lights of Sydney. It's an eye-popping location, with fine food – including an inventive vegetarian menu – and an encyclopaedic wine list to match. The courteous, friendly waiters expertly negotiate the Titantic-style swirling staircase, linking Forty One's two levels. To start, plump for the prawns in potato waistcoats, a too cute trio of juicy wrigglers, and the smoked, cured and raw salmon plate with a very Russian chaser of vodka. Full-on gamey mains of wild hare and venison cutlet both display elegant lengths of bone, the deer paired up with cromesquis – an upmarket spring roll stuffed with melting foie gras. Don't tax yourself over the dessert choice – just go for variations on a theme, a platter of everything, including a luscious sauterne custard with lychees, that's a sweet tooth's dream come true.

starter: lunch $25
main: lunch $35
dessert: lunch $15
Set menu $85 or $95,
degustation $110

AE BC DC MC V

Open: Sun-Fri noon-2pm; Mon-Sat 6pm-9pm; reservations essential; licensed, no BYO

Map 4 A2

Smoking throughout

Pavement tables

Grand Taverna
Spanish

☎ 9267 3608
**557 George St
(cnr Liverpool St)**

The stretch of tapas bars that line Liverpool St evoke the most passionate of arguments: which is the best, which the most authentic, where can you get a table, who offers free flamenco lessons. While maybe not first choice, Grand Taverna is almost *everyone's* second. Stripped of gimmicks and pretension, it's noisy, the menu is limited and the service somewhat brusque, but it induces that communal conviviality that is typical of a real Spanish taverna. While there are single dishes available, nearly everyone orders either the mixed tapas platter, or the paella, both of which are priced at $38-$50, depending on the size. The mixed tapas features large samples of, among others, chorizo in tomato and garlic, mushrooms in garlic, garlic prawns, wonderfully tender calamari, and scallops in olive oil and tomato, all served steaming hot from the oven. Another jug of sangria ($15) and, in typical Spanish fashion, all arguments are cast aside.

main: $10-$37
dessert: $4-$5
AE BC MC V; Eftpos

Open: daily noon-3pm, 5.30pm-10pm; reservations accepted (lunch only); licensed, no BYO

Hyde Park Barracks Cafe
Modern Australian

☎ 9223 1155
Queens Square, Macquarie St

Map 3 C3

Wheelchair access

 Nonsmoking tables available

 Courtyard seats

The barracks were built to house convicts after dark in a bid to stop crime. The walls now serve the much less retributive function of creating a buffer against the Macquarie Street traffic. In the courthouse, with its soaring ceilings and ivy peeping through the door, you can enjoy fine food that the previous inhabitants couldn't have dreamed of. Mains expertly combine many contrasting, satisfying arrays of flavours. Roasted lamb comes with a sweet caramelised onion gravy and a tangy yoghurt and mint tzatziki ($25.50). The barbecued flavours of a char-grilled chicken ($24.50) are wonderfully set off by the sweet and smoky tastes of grilled eggplant, ever-so-slightly bitter radicchio, a tart grape juice sauce and fresh figs. A flourless chocolate cake has the same texture as the accompanying double cream ($9). On the weekends the menu's pared down, with fruit and nut breads ($5.50), steak sandwiches ($16.50) and fish and chips ($15.50).

starter: $11.50-$16.50
main: $24.50-$27
dessert: $9-$12
Set lunch $25.50 or $30
AE BC DC MC V

Open: Mon-Fri 8am-3pm, Sat & Sun 10am-3pm; reservations advisable; licensed, no BYO

Inside
Modern Australian

☎ 9241 1978
133 Macquarie St

Map 3 A3

 No smoking inside

 Pavement seating

In an era of downsizing and subdividing, Inside is appropriately squeezed into what was once the basement kitchen of a Victorian sandstone terrace built for pastoralist and politician George Oaks. Politicians from the nearby NSW Parliament House may still moonlight as pastoralists, but the closest they're likely to get to meat is a plate of Inside's char-grilled scotch fillet with new potatoes ($25.50). Though when busy they may prefer the baguettes with capers, salmon and pesto fillings ($4-$8). The three egg-white omelette ($8.50) will no doubt please the Macquarie St medical crowd. A sticky duck risotto ($19) was rather ordinary but a haloumi, tomato and basil salad, presented in a geometrical stack ($6.50), is much better. By 2pm it's almost all over as staff pack up and put away berry tarts with macadamia and mint pesto ($10.50). But an undisclosed boutique coffee blend and just-chewy-enough chocolate brownies ($3) keep going all afternoon.

breakfast: $5.50-$14.50
main: $17-$25.50
dessert: $10.50
AE BC DC MC V

Open: Mon-Fri 7am-7pm; reservations accepted; licensed, no BYO

Bodhi (p 41)

Map 3 C1
Wheelchair access

J.P. Bastiani
Mediterranean

☎ 9238 7088
**Merchant Court Hotel,
Level 8, 68 Market St**

For those who like to dress up and eat in style J.P. Bastiani, on the eighth floor of the new Merchant Court Hotel above the Grace Bros city store, is a charmed location. Romantic tinkles waft across from the piano bar, accompanying an ambitiously smart set menu of two or three courses. Sink into your plush dining chair to sample an entree of fresh harbour prawns on sweet red capsicum and cucumber with flying fish roe dressing. Then on to mains such as pan-seared salmon topped with smoked duck-breast slices on thyme potatoes, wilted spinach and a red-wine butter sauce. Desserts are as rich, chocolate ganache tart with rhubarb compote and King Island cream for example. And seafood lovers can enjoy a buffet ($38) on Friday and Saturday nights. Of course, if you do over do it, there's always a five-star room awaiting you above.

Set menu: lunch $29 or $38, dinner $38 or $48
AE BC MC V; Eftpos

Open: Mon-Sat noon-3pm, Sun-Thurs 7pm-10.30pm, Fri & Sat 6pm-10pm (breakfast: Mon-Fri 6am-10am, Sat 6.30am-11am, Sun 11am-3pm); reservations advisable; licensed, no BYO

CITY

Lam's Seafood Restaurant
Chinese

☎ **9281 2881**
35-37 Goulburn Street

Map 4 A2

 Smoking throughout

Lam's Seafood Restaurant, located as it is near a Cantonese cinema, looks like the sort of place where cop movie antiheroes take a break from knuckle-grazing shenanigans with the mafia, triads or yakuza. There are tanks full of fish and monstrous lobsters, wide round tables and swift, confident waiters in bright white shirts. In keeping with the size of the restaurant, the menu offers 140 dishes, from steamed Tasmanian scallops at market price to the congee with pig blood jelly for $6. Not surprisingly, they serve a first-class Peking duck ($15.50) – the type that sweats flavour – accompanied with a hot marmalade of a lemon sauce. The pippies with XO chilli sauce ($15.80) arrive in a bountiful pile and are as fresh as you could hope for. With Lam's open every night 'til four am, you'll be able to bring the whole vice squad, but leave your .38 at the door.

starter: $3.60-$16.80
main: $2-$42
Set menu $35/person
  (min 8 people)

AE BC DC MC V

Open: daily noon-4am; reservations accepted; licensed & BYO (corkage $2/bottle)

MoS Cafe
Modern Australian

☎ **9241 3636**
**Museum of Sydney,
cnr Bridge & Phillip Sts**

Map 1 E4

 No smoking inside

 Pavement tables

Look, we like a rocket leaf as much as the next guy, but when the little buggers constitute almost half of an entrée, something has to give. Our taleggio ravioli surrounded by melt-in-the-mouth Balmain bugs ($16) came with a heap of foliage that did nothing to add to the dish. In fact, MoS Cafe seemed to have a predilection for camouflaging its dishes with mounds of superfluous salad leaves. All those business-men supping and sunning themselves at the forecourt tables didn't seem to mind though, and neither did the ladies-who-lunch perched under the imposing, sandstone colonnade, nor the groovers sitting at the communal table. Green stuff aside, we thought the millefeuille of crispy wonton sheets layered with sandcrab, crunchy snake beans and drizzles of palm sugar ($18) imaginative and brimming with flavours. The oversized parfait glass cradling shards of meringue, summer berries and champagne mousse ($11) is swooningly sensational.

starter: $13.50-$19.50
main: $24-$28.50
dessert: $11-$13

AE BC DC MC V

Open: Mon-Fri 7am-10pm, Sat & Sun 8.30am-6pm (breakfast: Mon-Fri 7am-noon, Sat & Sun all day); reservations advisable

CITY

Map 4 A3

Mother Chu's Vegetarian Kitchen
Chinese vegan

☎ 9283 2828
367 Pitt St

Tofu-lovers take note, in a neighbourhood more renowned for its Peking duck and honey prawns, Mother Chu's is heaven in a tempeh-laden claypot. The room's cloying, 1980s-style mushroom pink interior may not be much, but it's easy to forgive the daggy design when there's so much bountiful beancurd and glorious gluten to concentrate on. For a full-on tofu hit, start with the mixed entrée platter ($4.50). Laden with vegetarian spring rolls, curry puffs and slices of stir-fried gluten, it's a great selection of soy-based nibbles. Health-buffs beware – we were surprised when our plate of honey pumpkin ($9.50) came fritter-style, surrounded by deep-fried apple and carrot slices. A dish of sizzling eggplant ($9.50) is a more wholesome choice, with peas, carrots and tofu bound in a chilli-infused miso sauce. We found the sweets disappointing though, with a rather dull dish of apricot and boysenberry vegan ice cream ($3.50).

starter: $1.80-$3.50
main: $6.50-$12
dessert: $3.50-$4.50
AE BC MC V

Open: Mon-Sat noon-3pm, 5pm-10pm; reservations accepted (advisable Fri & Sat); unlicensed

---

Map 3 C1
Wheelchair access

Newsbar
Italian

☎ 9238 9460
Mezzanine Level, Grace Bros,
Pitt Street Mall

Newsbar is the mid-range option of Grace Bros' four slick, modern eateries, and the brainchild of restaurateur Steve Manfredi. In a heritage corner of the Pitt St emporium, Newsbar is bright and elegant, with a pressed metal Art Deco ceiling and eye-catching yellow elliptical lamps hanging like stalactites from the ceiling. The antipasto ($12.50), an abundant offering with novelties such as cabbage rolls stuffed with risotto, was let down only by the rather oily frittata and watery roasted tomato. Interesting pastas ($14.50) include orecchiette with Italian sausage and parmesan, and penne with mussels, calamari and fennel. The risotto ($14.50) is a creamy, stocky symphony of meaty field mushrooms and silverbeet with the added sharpness of preserved lemons. Desserts (all $6) include calorific cakes and a not-too-sweet concoction of poached fruit with champagne jelly and honey biscuits.

starter: $12.50-$14.50
main: $14.50-$17.50
dessert: $6
Set lunch $24.50
AE BC DC JCB MC V; Eftpos

Open: Mon-Wed, Fri & Sat 9am-5pm, Thurs 9am-8pm, Sun 11am-4pm; reservations advisable; licensed, no BYO

Cafe Crawl – City

When Sydney's first modern coffee shops opened their doors in the 1950s, young people flocked to sample the new brew. But the sight of so many young women consorting with European men so disturbed some people that they assumed the brown drink was an aphrodisiac and established a parliamentary inquiry. Today, Sydney's love affair with caffeine (and being seen) is as strong as ever. From the frappé to the latte, from the single espresso to the low-fat soy milk decaf, there's a cup for everyone. So join us on a cafe crawl around Sydney, starting here with the central city.

Bar Cupola Ground Level, Queen Victoria Building, York St, City ☎ 9283 3878 Map 2 D6
Under the Queen Victoria Building's dome, Bar Cupola serves a smooth Columbian blend. Then there's an array of teas (earl grey, darjeeling) and cakes (apple and berry crumble, orange syrup cake) that would make Queen Vicky proud.

Bittersweet Coffee Level 5, Grace Bros, City ☎ 9238 9460 Map 3 C1
In the middle of Grace Bros' record and bookstores you can quell a bout of impulse buying with a leisurely perusal of CD covers and dust jackets over Bittersweet's coffee, mini pizzettas, milkshakes and Valfrutta juices. Coming soon: Manfredi (the Versace of Sydney's Italian food scene) will release his latest perfume – his very own signature blend of Piazza D'oro coffee.

Concrete 224 Harris St, Pyrmont ☎ 9518 9523 Map 2 C1
It's an industrial-looking but very sunny, very comfortable and very chic spot in one of Sydney's most up-and-coming suburbs. The Grinders coffee and 15 different breakfast options (including a dozen different ways with eggs) is just a few years new but it's fast becoming an old favourite.

Deli on Market (DoM) 30-32 Market St, City ☎ 9262 6906 Map 2 C5
In a National Trust-classified former wool shed DoM serves up modern meals (baguettes with chicken or salmon, lentil soup and light crepes). Take your meal away or sit with a strong coffee around the communal blond-wood table.

Gumnut Tea Garden 28 Harrington St, The Rocks ☎ 9247 9591 Map 1 C3
Originally home to an Irish convict given a reprieve from the gallows thanks to his blacksmithing skills, this cafe features a large leafy courtyard, smaller rooms for wet weather and reasonably priced lunches.

Macchiato 338 Pitt St, City ☎ 9262 9525 Map 4 A3
It's a big mixed mod Oz menu and a big mixed crowd in a big industrial-chic space – and now there's wood-fired pizzas to boot. Coffee is Portioli ($2.50).

Pavilion on the Park Café 1 Art Gallery Rd, City ☎ 9232 1322 Map 3 D3
This is a tranquil spot in the Domain gardens, in front of the Art Gallery of NSW. There's beer on tap and the menu is more thoughtful mod Oz restaurant than slapdash cafe. Watch the Indian myna birds doing splits on the stainless steel tables as they try to pick up the crumbs.

Map 3 D3
Wheelchair access
Smoking on terrace only
Terrace tables

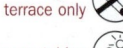

Pavilion on the Park
Modern Australian

☎ 9232 1322
1 Art Gallery Rd

The view from the outdoor tables of Pavilion on the Park is magnificent at night – giant Moreton Bay fig trees are silhouetted against the glowing towers of the city skyline. Free-standing braziers make the lily-fringed terraces popular, while inside a wood-panelled feature wall and terrazzo floor create a warm glow. Our starters barely put a foot wrong: the organic carrot and coriander 'soup', more akin to a puree, is quickly thinned with a mini-carafe of coconut milk. And the roasted flavours of the wild mushroom starter go wonderfully with the accompaniments of sweet pear, slightly sour almond pickle and salty goats cheese. The mains were always going to have a hard time keeping pace, and we found the blue-eye cod pie and gnocchi were disappointing. Coffee and desserts were back on track – with a subtle cinnamon ice cream and red wine sauce.

Set menu $50 or $65
AE BC DC MC V

Open: Sun-Fri from noon, dinner depending on functions at the Art Gallery; reservations advisable; licensed, no BYO

Map 3 B1
Wheelchair access

Post
Modern Australian

☎ 9229 7744
**Lower ground floor,
1 Martin Place**

Like taut, society dowagers, Sydney's public buildings have been undergoing massive facelifts. The GPO, that old Martin Place monolith, has recently been transformed into a smart hotel and a bunch of boutiques, bars and restaurants. Post, located in the building's imposing sandstone basement, is the GPO's snazzy brasserie, with snappy service and well-executed dishes. Start with an oyster orgy. A dozen freshly shucked Tasmanian Pacifics ($29) served with red wine vinegar are fat, supremely juicy and too good to share. The shellfish isn't the only dish to make you feel selfish; flecked with peas and spinach, the risotto ($17) is perfect, enriched with a dollop of mascarpone and a softly poached egg. And in the true spirit of restoration, the warm, gooey, banana pudding ($13) resembles a suitably towering architectural edifice. Judging by the GPO's roaring success, it may not be long before developers plot to re-make Parliament House into a holistic day spa.

starter: $9-$20
main: $16-$35
dessert: $13-$14
AE BC DC MC V

Open: Mon-Fri noon-3pm, Mon-Sat 6pm-10pm, Sat brunch 11am-3pm; reservations advisable; licensed, no BYO

CITY

Restaurant CBD
Modern Australian

☎ 9299 8911
Cnr York St & King St

Map 2 B5

Nonsmoking tables available

While Friday-night rock thuds through the floorboards from the CBD Bar below, unruffled waiters breeze between white-clothed tables in the civilised environs of Restaurant CBD. Situated on a busy city corner, this restaurant is well-known as a business lunch spot. It keeps the hubbub largely at bay with its gentleman's-club trappings of comfortable chairs, elegant paintings, a well-stocked bar and food that is more than respectable. The one-time British leanings of CBD's menu have given way to more international flavours such as the Japanese-inspired marinated Atlantic salmon with tempura mussels ($15.50) and the adventurous coral trout on sauerkraut with shiitake mushrooms and star anise bouillon ($27). Old Dart specials are still on the menu for the traditionalists: try the roast suckling pork rump with ham hock, pancetta and split pea purée ($26.50). For dessert, go troppo and order the sublime lime bavarois with coconut sauce, kaffir lime syrup and roasted fig ($12.50).

starter: $6.50-$16.50
main: $24.50-$27
dessert: $12.50
Set menu $40 or $50

AE BC DC JCB MC V

Open: Mon-Fri noon-3pm, Mon-Fri 6pm-10pm; reservations essential; licensed, no BYO

Slip Inn
Modern Italian

☎ 9299 1700
111 Sussex St

Map 2 B5

Wheelchair access

Entertainment: Thurs night jazz 9pm-11pm

Smoking throughout

Courtyard tables

It looks like just another renovated pub on a busy city corner. But walk through the bar to discover a hidden Italianate courtyard, with babbling fountain and capacious table umbrellas. Lunch is served here, while at night the restaurant moves inside. Dinner in the downstairs Sand Bar (featuring a beautiful old sandstone wall) is a treat, with candle-lit tables and exemplary service. Good crusty bread is served gratis with superb extra virgin olive oil, infused on the premises with parmesan, rosemary and garlic. Swordfish (fish of the day, $22) is well cooked and presented. Even better is an exotic risotto of tender scallops on caramelised leeks ($16.50). Starring for desert, baked panettone with lemon custard ($9) is divinely sponge-like and light. Also served in the restaurant (or at the bar), are their justly popular pizzas, with toppings such as honey-roasted chicken, pumpkin, mascarpone and sage. Bravo!

starter: $12-$16.50
main: $16.50-$24.50
dessert: $9

AE BC DC MC V

Open: Mon-Fri noon-3pm, Tues-Fri 6pm-10pm; reservations recommended; licensed, no BYO

CITY

Map 2 A6
Parking $10 after 5.30pm (Wilson, Bond St)
Wheelchair access
No smoking (dining area); smoking in lobby & bar only

starter: $15-$22
main: $27-$36
dessert: $15-$18
Sun smorgasbord $49 (adults) & $29 (children)
AE BC DC JCB MC V

The Summit
Modern Australian

☎ 9247 9777
Level 47, Australia Square, 264 George St

When the Summit opened in 1968, revolving restaurants were cool. The novelty has since worn off, and it was only in 1998 that this Sydney icon got a makeover. Apparently inspired by Kubrick's *2001: A Space Odyssey*, the tone is millennial-retro with heavy '60s references: the burnt orange/red carpet, the furniture and the food. The Summit serves retro classics like prawn cocktails ($22) and beef béarnaise ($36). Prices being high, one would expect a funky modern twist but the prawn cocktail was mediocre. Stick to the mod Oz choices like grilled snapper with scallops in a lemon butter sauce, or mushroom risotto with watercress ($27). The food is adequate but it's the view you're really paying for (pointing to Sydney's continued obsession with real estate). To enjoy the circular scenic ride it's a place to go at least once or, alternatively, skip the food and head straight for the Orbit Bar next door.

Open: Sun-Fri noon-3pm, daily 6pm-10pm; reservations advisable (essential Fri & Sat evening); licensed, no BYO

Map 2 E5

Degustation lunch: $85/person
Degustation dinner: $130/person
Set menu only
AE BC DC MC V

Tetsuya's
Japanese/French

☎ 9267 2900
529 Kent St

Tetsuya's staff prepare you for your culinary marathon (seven lunch courses and 13 dinner courses) by constantly bringing fresh silver cutlery and white plates as used ones are whipped away. The side table looks like a convention of Alcoholics are Fabulous – covered by glasses from the wine tasting menu ($60/$40). Mainly Australian wine arrives with each course – described in the manner of a formal announcement. In fact, it is like being in class (albeit pleasurable) as the waiter tells you: 'mid-plate is a grilled freshwater eel on sushi rice, to the right, seared scallops with truffle'. 'The Tasmanian ocean trout is served with konbu seaweed and salt to bring out the flavour'. All good educational experiences provide challenges: the tiny discs in the mascarpone and coffee ice cream turn out to be sweet lentils! Tetsuya does morsels of food that come with megabytes of flavour. That's why you might wait six weeks for a dinner booking.

Open: lunch Tues-Sat (arrivals noon-1.30pm), dinner Mon-Fri (arrivals 7pm-8.30pm); reservations essential; licensed and BYO (corkage $10/bottle)

CITY

Wine Banc
French

☎ 9233 5399
Lower Ground Level (entrance Elizabeth St), 53 Martin Place

It's a jazz venue, it's a wine bar and cellar – it's underground. It's not illicit speakeasy territory, but you can imagine illicit affairs going on over martinis in dark corners, while business affairs are consummated over cohiba cigars. The bottles of plonk are stacked up behind glass walls, but what's good wine without good food? Shallow bowls of tomato gazpacho with crab meat ($12), shucked oysters ($13/$24) or roasted chicken with warm mustard potato salad ($20) are good accompaniments to your glass of Tasmanian Pipers Brook riesling ($6.50) or bottle of '93 Louis Roederer Cristal ($310). We didn't begrudge one cent of the $20 for a tart of buttery pastry topped with an arrangement of caramelised, baby-sized onion halves covered with a mound (or was it a cloud?) of creamy goats cheese. Lemon tarts and sorbets are for dessert, if you're not onto the scotch by then.

Open: Mon-Fri noon-3pm, 5pm-midnight, Sat 6pm-midnight (supper menu 10pm-midnight); reservations accepted for lunch only (advisable); licensed, no BYO

Map 3 B2

Entertainment: live jazz Tues from 9pm, Thurs-Sat from 10pm

Smoking throughout

starter: $12-$18
main: $18-$24
dessert: $12-$14

AE BC DC MC V

COCKLE BAY

blackbird
Modern Australian

☎ 9283 7385
Cockle Bay Wharf, Balcony, 201 Sussex St

Filling the gap between Cockle Bay's food-hall style outlets and pricier sit-down restaurants, blackbird has attitude. It's good, not bad. The vibe is funky: colourful furniture, local artwork, TVs in the toilets and a showy central bar. Over in the corner is a groovy 'chill' space, a '70s-style lounge arrangement complete with games (Mastermind anyone?). The staff are trendsetter-types, and the service is generally switched-on. And the food? On a cool day, the red lentil dahl ($8.90) with hot rock bread and salsa is a hearty stomach-warmer; spinach and ricotta ravioli with rocket pesto ($11.90) also hits the spot. Baked coffee and chocolate ricotta cake ($5.50) is too much to finish. Punters can also go for hot-stone pizzas and breakfast lasts until 4pm. It's not top-notch nosh but portions are hefty and the menu changes every three months. Considering the location and views, blackbird is good value and good fun.

Open: daily 8am-1am (breakfast: daily 8am-4pm); reservations taken for lunch only, Mon-Sat; licensed, no BYO

Map 2 D4

Wheelchair access

Smoking throughout

Balcony tables

starter: $8.90
main: $6.90-$12.50
dessert: $2.50-$5.50

AE BC DC MC V

COCKLE BAY

Map 2 D4
Valet parking $20
(Wheat Rd at Cockle Bay Wharf)
Wheelchair access
No smoking inside
Terrace tables

starter: $5-$8
main: $12-$25
dessert: $6.50
Banquet $30, $34
or $38/person
(min 4 people)
AE BC DC MC V

Chinta Ria... The Temple of Love
Malaysian

☎ 9264 3211
Cockle Bay Wharf,
Roof Tce, 201 Sussex St

Behind the genuine temple doors at Chinta Ria lies a giant big bellied Buddha dressed in a necklace of flowers. Bunches of joss sticks and fruit offerings sit in front of him, while prayer flags hang from the ceiling. In this temple to gastronomy, black garbed staff with shaved heads seat you at '50s retro chairs. Creamy laksa ($12/15) makes an ideal lunch for travellers and hordes of workers from neighbouring skyscrapers. Recommended too are noodle stir-fries ($12/15). On our most recent visit, roast duck bok choy ($13/$16) seemed a little dry and was served with one measly leaf of green. Safer choices appear on the upmarket specials list: whole squid ($20) is tender, lightly battered and served with an excellent tamarind sauce. You'll leave the Temple of Love feeling as content and swollen bellied as Mr Bo-tree himself.

Open: daily noon-2.30pm, Mon-Sat 6pm-11pm, Sun 6pm-10.30pm; reservations accepted for lunch only; licensed & BYO (corkage $5/bottle)

DARLING HARBOUR

Map 2 D3
No smoking inside
Terrace tables

starter: $10-$16
main: $14.50-$26.50
dessert: $7-$10
Set menu $39.50 or
royal thali (silver platter)
menu $70
AE BC DC MC V

Zaaffran
Indian

☎ 9211 8900
Level 2, 345 Harbourside

A refined Indian restaurant in Darling Harbour – that leisure park precinct where the steak and seafood basket has always reigned supreme – makes Zaaffran an oddity. The music and décor is an oddity too: somewhere between a five-star hotel and the Peter Sellers movie *The Party*. You won't find a 'standard' curry here, and diners seeking palate-shattering spiciness will be disappointed. But you're better served appreciating the array of subtle flavours, typical of traditional Indian cuisine. Starters are uniformly excellent. Baked mushrooms are stuffed with a cacophony of harmonising ingredients such as ginger, dill and yoghurt ($12). Seafood is another speciality. A seafood sampler ($36) provides a taste of everything, or try a barramundi pan roasted with chilli and cloves ($16/$28) – the creamy, smooth raita is an almost necessary foil to this pungently garlicky, salty creation.

Open: Tues-Sun noon-2.30pm, Sun-Thurs 6pm-9.30pm, Fri & Sat 6pm-10pm; reservations advisable (essential weekends); licensed, no BYO

HAYMARKET

Bodhi
Chinese/vegetarian

☎ **9212 2828**
Shop 10, Ground Floor, Capitol Square, 730-742 George St

Map 4 B2

Some fans are still mourning Bodhi's move from its first floor Haymarket heritage loft to its current Capitol Centre home (a venue that proves the phrase 'upmarket food hall' isn't necessarily oxymoronic). But the basic principles remain the same. There's the smattering of families and the odd couple, but the yum cha is best enjoyed with a large support group. The vegetarian 'Peking duck' ($15), steamed buns ($3.80) and plump dumplings filled with mushroom and cabbage or barbecue-flavoured gluten ($3.80) are almost universally loved, but much of the rest depends on your taste. The 'deep-fried mango coconut surprise' ($15) had our opinions divided but we did concur over the honeyed 'Japanese' pumpkin – thin glazed slices scattered with toasted sesame ($8.50). Preservatives, MSG, garlic and onions are all no nos (they unbalance the body's five elements: air, earth, fire, mineral and water). Flavours therefore veer between disarmingly delicate to barely there.

Open: daily 9am-midnight (yum cha 9am-5pm, dinner from 5pm); reservations advisable for large groups; licensed & BYO (corkage $1.50/person)

starter: $5-$6.50
(yum cha $3.80 per serve)
main: $8-$15
dessert: $3.80

cash only

Chinese Noodle Restaurant
North-western Chinese

☎ **9281 9051**
Prince Centre, 8 Quay St

Map 4 B1

It's unlikely that the queues of eager diners patiently loitering outside this Haymarket hole in the wall are here for the geographically confused décor: green plastic grapes hanging from the ceiling, and walls covered with Middle Eastern carpets. More likely they've come for some bargain tucker. If you're hungry, try a hearty and spicy Xinjiang lamb noodle soup ($8.80) or an overflowing plate of stir-fried noodles ($8.90). If you're *really* hungry start off with dumplings ($6), such as pan-fried gou tie stuffed with pork, greens and spices, or traditional steamed pork buns. Spicy chicken salad, crispy fried pork and scrambled eggs with zucchini (a tasty omelette north-western-Chinese-style) are also on offer. Watching the noodle men pull, pummel and roll dough into long, thin, slippery strands is part of the entertainment. It's hard to get a grip on the noodles armed only with chopsticks. Perhaps that's why the staff sit down to their meals armed with forks.

Open: daily 9.30am-6pm; reservations accepted; unlicensed

starter: $6-$8
main: $6-$10

cash only

HAYMARKET

Map 4 B1
Validated parking (Wilson Parking under Market City)
Nonsmoking tables available

Kam Fook Shark's Fin Restaurant
Cantonese

☎ 9211 8388
Level 3, Market City,
9 Hay St

Kam Fook is the ultimate yum cha experience. Though take heed, on a Saturday or Sunday it's suggested that you arrive at 10am or after 2pm or you'll find yourself, ticket in hand, and a stomach loudly reminding you of the passing of time. What a feeling, when finally you're weaving your way past the stylish slimline fish tanks and through the 800 chattering and clattering diners. Service is fast. Ask what's in the steamer on the laden trolley, and if your Cantonese isn't good, hope that a fellow diner might assist. Most of the chubby dumplings and assorted fried rolls and buns speak for themselves, though. Look for the deep green of the spinach or garlic chive dumplings showing through the rice flour wrapping. Then there's shark's fin with coriander, glutinous rice sheets filled with salted turnip and water, and chestnut or spicy pork with vegetables in mashed taro root wrapping.

starter: $4.50-$18.80
main: $10-market price seafood
dessert: $3.80
Banquet menu $28 or $35

Open: daily 10am-5pm for yum cha, Sun-Thurs 5.30pm-11pm, Fri-Sat 5.30pm-midnight; reservations accepted (dinner only); licensed, no BYO

Map 4 B2
Wheelchair access

passionflower
Modern Australian desserts

☎ 9281 8322
Level 1, Capitol Square,
730-742 George St

passionflower is a unique east meets west dessert bar and the shopfront for Serendipity ice cream, which is served in many of the city's top restaurants. After a Chinatown feast it's a perfect pit stop to soothe the stomach with a green tea and a ginger ice cream ($5). Or, if you don't know what's good for you, you can skip dinner altogether and devour a K2 ($24). This mountain of ice cream features a choice of flavours – papaya, lychee, black sesame (amazing), durian (smells funny, tastes sensational), wasabi (very interesting), guava, lemon and adzuki bean. Traditionalists can still get rum and raisin, strawberry, chocolate and banana, but it is the Asian flavours you should really indulge in – exotic combinations like rising sun or black pearl ($9.50 each). The extensive menu includes Belgian waffles, crepes, milk shakes, frappés ($5.50), frozen virgin cocktails ($6.50) and cakes. Prepare your sweet tooth – and warn your dentist! *Also at 291 Harbourside, Darling Harbour;* ☎ *9281 8022*

dessert: $4-$35
MC V

Open: Sun-Thurs 10am-midnight, Fri & Sat 10am-1am; reservations not accepted; unlicensed

On Your Plate **Chinese**

No longer do we say 'let's eat Chinese'. Now its 'let's have yum cha, noodles, dumplings, duck, hot pot, congee, barbecue'. We can pronounce Sichuan and Xinjiang. What's more, we know the difference. Chinese cuisine has come of age in Sydney over the past decade. Thanks to healthy migration from the mainland, Taiwan and Hong Kong, Sydney's Chinese restaurants are catering more to discerning Chinese tastes. The food has to be better. And it is.

We may not be at the stage of liking our snake baked or our dog boned, but we'll have slivers of eel in spicy sauce and roasted pigeon with the pointy beak. Chinese communities are concentrated, though not exclusively, in certain parts of town. Yum cha can be devoured in Hurstville and Castle Hill as well as in the bustle of Chinatown. A venture to Ashfield will satisfy those with a yearning for lighter Shanghai cuisine, though there are also some northern stunners hidden away like Great Wall (see review p 95).

Chatswood is where Hong Kong and Taiwanese food dominate. Neutral Bay has the tastiest Shandong flavours. Great Beijing-style hotpot spots are dotted all around – try the Grape Garden in Willoughby (see review p 205). The Cantonese character of yesteryear still dominates Chinatown, although increasingly there is choice a plenty of other Chinese cuisines in this historic precinct. Bursting with places to eat, satisfaction can sometimes be about knowing where to look. Our picks include Mother Chu's and Bodhi (see reviews pp 34, 41) for the best vegetarian; Kam Fook and Silver Spring (see reviews pp 42, 44) for yum cha; Sea Bay and the Chinese Noodle Restaurant (see reviews pp 52, 41) for northern fare; barbeque at BBQ King; and seafood and great late night congee at Golden Century (see reviews pp 29, 52).

Fusion puts a contemporary spin on the traditional and orthodox cuisine. It's providing delights such as dumpling fillings of water chestnut & egg or spanish mackeral & coriander at fu-manchu and the irresistible Asian antipasto at Watermark (see reviews pp 134, 182).

Sydney's cooks and diners are spoilt with the amazing range and quality of fresh vegetable and fish market produce. This includes locally cultivated Asian herbs and Asian-style cuts of seafood. The import and local production of ingredients such as bean starch products, varieties of tofu, preserved vegetables and spicy sauces has improved markedly in response to restaurant and home-kitchen demands. Traditional culinary skills are also widely celebrated, and we hardly bat an eyelid at the performance art of noodle throwing, the creation of those ever-lengthening strands of light, white streamers.

If nostalgic, there are still some establishments where sweet and sour prevails. Next door though, you might discover somewhere serving slivers of potato lightly stir-fried in a piquant Sichuan peppercorn infused oil. (See glossary p 254 for a guide to regional cuisine styles).

Margaret Bourke

Margaret is a Sydney-born freelance writer who has been commenting on Chinese cuisine since her return from a 4-year sojourn in China. Her writing has appeared in numerous publications including Australian Good Taste *magazine and the* Sydney Morning Herald *.*

HAYMARKET

Map 4 B2
Wheelchair access
Nonsmoking tables available

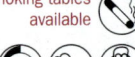

Silver Spring
Cantonese

☎ 9211 2232
477 Pitt St (cnr Hay St)

Silver Spring holds its own in the old part of Chinatown, near Central Station, away from the busy hub of Dixon Street. Yum cha here is consistently above average. That they accept bookings at weekends has always been a big plus and now it's even possible to book on-line. Vegetarian and seafood dumplings, steamed broccoli, sliced barbecued meats and rice porridges are recommended from the yum cha trolley, usually working out at between $10-$15 per head. Custard tarts are delectably flaky and the mango pudding never disappoints. Silver Spring's à la carte menu is very good too. It's a pleasant place to dine at night for a quiet change from the yum cha crowd. Signature dishes include sautéed boneless chicken or diced fillet steak hotpots ($12.80), pan fried shredded beef with assorted vegetables in a taro nest ($15.80) and a chilli fish fillet or prawns, served with poached vegetables ($18.80).

starter: $6-$13.80
main: $12.80-$24.80
(seafood market price)
dessert: $4
Banquet menu $25, $30, $35/person
(min 8 people)
AE BC DC MC V

Open: daily 10am-3pm, 5pm-11pm (Sat & Sun 9am-3pm); reservations advisable for yum cha; licensed & BYO (corkage $5/person)

Map 4 B1
Smoking throughout

Xic Lo
Vietnamese

☎ 9280 1678
215a Thomas St
(cnr Ultimo Rd)

Forget red-flocked wallpaper and glitzy lanterns, Xic Lo's clean contemporary design, all shiny metal surfaces and sharp angles, is as modern as they come around Chinatown. Lunchtime sees suits and city shoppers squished up close, savouring the egg noodle soups and vermicelli salads, and sipping their soybean drinks. Nights make for more relaxed eating, and allows the opportunity to make a mess over a bowl of pho ($5.50) without too many witnesses. Just *try* to get through that aromatic soup of slippery rice noodles, beanshoots, fragrant basil and beef without slurping. The generous portion of crispy-skin chicken ($6.50) is attractive and medicinal, arriving with a piping-hot bowl of flu-busting chicken broth. And not content with plating up mere spring rolls, modern Xic Lo also lists winter, autumn and summer rolls. The latter are the tastiest, oversized rice paper bundles teeming with sliced pork, prawns and shredded mint ($6).

starter: $5-$6
main: $5.50-$7.50
dessert: $3
cash only

Open:Tues-Sat 11am-11pm, Sun & Mon 11am-10pm; reservations advisable (especially lunch); BYO (no corkage)

PYRMONT

Furusato
Japanese

☎ 9660 0477
48 Harris St

Map 2 E1

Courtyard tables

Way down the end of Harris street, in fact, so far that most Sydneysiders have forgotten it exists, there's a thriving little community of pubs and restaurants. And at the furthest end is Furusato, a charming Japanese restaurant on what was once called Land's End. For starters, try the beef sashimi ($5), ridiculously thinly sliced raw beef, mixed at the table with plumped bean sprouts and a raw egg – don't let the raw bit put you off; it's one of the chef's favourites, and with good reason. For mains, the donburi (beef, onions, sesame seeds, fragrant sauce and rice, $11), or barbecue pork (served sizzling with miso soup and rice, $12) are as good as you'll find in many other, more expensive Japanese restaurants. Like a lot of out-of-the-way places, the food is well worth the trip (two minutes to the tram station – it's not that far, *really*).

starter: $4-$6
main: $13-$39
dessert: $3
Set banquet $22-$25

MC V

Open: Mon-Sat noon-3pm, daily 5pm-10pm; reservations accepted; BYO (corkage $3/bottle)

Kokum
Indian

☎ 9566 1311
2 Scott St

Map 2 E1

No smoking inside

Pavement terrace tables

The subtleties of subcontinental food in Sydney are often lost in over salting and too much pure heat, but at Kokum the dishes are delicately, deliberately and deliciously flavoured. Mushrooms are slow roasted with fenugreek ($9.90), tender, skinless chicken is cooked with ground poppyseed paste ($12.90) and a subtly sweet orange sorbet is flecked with coriander ($4.90). Claiming to be the only Goan restaurant in Sydney, it serves up traditional staples like 'sannas' – rice dumplings the size of a small alarm clock – for soaking up curry juices. Meanwhile dishes like 'porco empregado' (pork stir-fried with ginger and capsicum, $13.90) tell the story of Goa's history under Portuguese rule. In a renovated eighteenth century cottage (the bricks were made by convicts) Kokum sits in a post-modern cityscape between Star City Casino, the new harbourside apartment suburb Jackson's Landing, and the low-lying Water Police headquarters. Kokum's cuisine is a welcome addition.

starter: $3.90-$9.90
main: $9.90-$19.90
dessert: $4.90-$6.90
Set menu $24 and $29
  (min 4 people)

AE BC DC MC V; Eftpos

Open: daily 6pm-10.30pm , Mon-Fri noon-2.30pm; reservations essential Thurs-Sat; BYO (corkage $2/bottle)

PYRMONT

Masuya
Japanese

☎ 9566 2866
261 Harris St

Map 2 D1
Smoking throughout
Pavement tables

This more humble branch of Masuya – a hop, skip and a jump from the fish markets – is a relaxed and economical option. The light, simply decorated interior is appealing – there's even a tiny counter, if you care to sit and watch the chefs at work, and outdoor tables for sultry nights. Vegetarians are well served by a special platter of vegetable tempura, sautéed tofu and fried noodles ($12.80), or starters such as the huge brick of creamy tofu with wakame seaweed ($5.50). The deep-fried Tasmanian oysters ($8.50) are excellent as is the chicken fillet in a tangy miso and garlic sauce ($12.90). The sushi here is very acceptable too, but if you want a bit more variety try their latest operation, Sushi Bar Makoto, on the corner of Liverpool and Pitt Sts – one of Sydney's few decent sushi train restaurants.

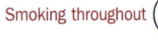

starter: $5.50-$8.50
main: $12.50
dessert: $3.80
Set menu: lunch $12.50-$17.50, dinner $19.80-$23.50
AE MC V

Open: Tue-Sun noon-2.30pm, 6pm-10pm; reservations accepted; licensed & BYO (corkage $2/person)

Yoshii
Japanese

☎ 9211 6866
Ground Floor, Mercure Apartments, 50 Murray Street

Map 2 C2

Attention to detail is everything at Yoshii, an elegant enclave within the architectural Disneyland that is Darling Harbour. Discerning sushi lovers will already be familiar with chef Yoshii Ryuichi's stylish way with this quintessential Japanese cuisine; we were particularly bowled over this time by the marine flavour infused, souffle-like omelette, wrapped around sushi rice. Tantalising elements of the $60 dinner course, such as the tiny fried quail leg in a blue cheese and miso sauce, appear in the cheaper set lunches, but do yourself a favour and go for the full banquet. Portions might be small, but your tastebuds will certainly thank you after trying dishes such as the sea urchin in consommé, served in an egg shell with a sprinkle of gold leaf for good luck on top. The traditional ceramics are chosen with as much care as the ingredients.

starter: $10-$17
main: $20-$35
dessert: $10
Set menu: lunch $20-$30, dinner $60
AE BC DC JCB MC V

Open: Tue-Fri noon-3pm, Mon-Sat 6pm-10.30pm (last orders 2.30 and 10pm); reservations advisable, essential for sushi bar; licensed, no BYO

THE ROCKS

CENTRAL SYDNEY

bel mondo
Italian

☎ 9241 3700
Level 3, The Argyle Stores, 18-24 Argyle St

With its stunning converted warehouse interior and open kitchen (one of Sydney's first), bel mondo has style – and money – written all over it. One glimpse at the prices on the wine list (featuring many lesser known labels) tells you that. On the food front, things start well. In a greedy lifetime of antipasto sampling we've never seen anything more beautiful than bel mondo's eight delicious morsels arranged on a rectangular plate ($25.50). Linguini topped by juicy bug tails laced with chilli and garlic ($28.50) is fantastico, and a rich ragu of pungent wild mushrooms with light (yes really!) polenta could be straight from the Dolomites. But our main events were disappointments. Barbecued duck ($39.50), a signature dish, we found fatty and rubbery and the roast pheasant was dry. Complaints revealed that owner/chef Steve Manfredi had a night off. The verdict? Go (if someone else pays) and make sure Manfredi's cooking.

Open: Mon-Fri noon-2.30pm, daily 6.30pm-late; reservations essential; licensed, no BYO

Map 1 C3

Entertainment: live jazz at Antibar on Fridays 5.30pm-7.30pm (winter only)

Smoking after 2.30pm (lunch) and 10.30pm (dinner)

Balcony tables

starter: $23.50-$29.50
main: $26.50-$45.50
dessert: $16.50
Degustation $95

AE BC DC MC V

THE ROCKS

Map 1 D3
Non-smoking tables available

Boulders at The Rocks
Modern Australian

☎ 9241 1447
143 George Street

Will someone *please* give that man a raise! Or a valium. Or a brandy. Or something. What, between taking orders, serving drinks, taking bookings, making coffee, totalling bills and friendly banter, just to watch the waiter is tiring; and yet he doesn't even raise a sweat. Swerving nimbly through the lunching crowd of the CBD, he delivers the entrée and is showing some new diners to a table before the Cajun smoked trout ($14.50) atop tangy lemon cream spinach has stopped wobbling. But that's not to suggest inattentiveness or brusqueness. Indeed, on inquiring if the barramundi ($26.50) is fresh, the assurances come complete with the fish's bloodline and family history. Enough to convince us it was worth trying. Settle back and enjoy the continuing pantomime over coffee ($4) and flourless almond and chocolate mudcake with mango purée ($8): after all this vicarious exercise, you deserve a break.

starter: $12.50-$16.50
main: $19.50-$26.50
dessert: $8
Tapas menu served from 6pm
AE BC DC JCB MC V

Open: Mon-Fri noon-2.30pm, daily 6pm-10.30pm (breakfast: daily 7am-10am); reservations accepted (advisable Fri-Sun); licensed, no BYO

Map 1 C1
Wheelchair access
Smoking throughout

Lord Nelson Brewery Hotel (Bistro)
Modern Australian

☎ 9251 4044
19 Kent St

Imagine an acoustically unfriendly sandstone pub, full of men of somewhat spurious disposition who haven't had a beer for 50-odd years: Gawd! That was 1841, and the Lord Nelson has been soothing Sydney's parched throats ever since. Thankfully, some things change. While your first beer in 50 years must taste pretty bloody good, it's difficult to imagine that the first frosted pint was a patch on the Nellie's newer, award-winning ales from their in-house brewery. And while early Europeans almost starved to death through their refusal to eat the local seafood, had they been tempted by grilled perch on scalloped potatoes with lemon buerre blanc and snow pea leaves ($15), surely the colonial meat-and-potatoes paradigm could have been avoided. Team it with a couple of Trafalgar pale ales ($4.50) and you're on your way to experiencing the fabled Sydney sandstone glow.

starter: $7.50
main: $9.50-$15
dessert: $6.50
AE BC DC MC V

Open: daily noon-3.30pm, 6pm-9.30pm; reservations advisable, especially weekends; licensed, no BYO

THE ROCKS

MCA Cafe
Modern Australian/ seafood

☎ 9241 4253
Museum of Contemporary Art, 140 George St

Map 1 D3

Wheelchair access

No smoking inside

Deck tables

The chairs on the balcony of the MCA cafe face either the Cahill Expressway atop Circular Quay Railway Station, the contemporary art museum that houses the cafe, or the Opera House across the water: we wonder who should pay the bill? The cafe is a self-declared fish specialist, so we were disappointed with a starter of five scallops in their shells and served on sea salt ($14.50). They were the colour of the Opera House sails and we thought lacking in flavour. A marlin steak ($24.00) is somewhat tastier, with vinegar onions barbecued just so. Pork and fennel sausages and a lamb dish covers the other meat groups on the day of our visit. Vegetarians are well-catered for with a light-enough gnocchi tossed in a just-cooked tomato and parsley sauce ($14.50). Desserts are often the best part of the meal deal – whether simple honeyed mascarpone and hazelnut biscuit wafers ($5), or old-fashioned rhubarb pie ($8).

starter: $12-$15
main: $19-$24
dessert: $5-$8
Set menu $40 or $50

AE BC DC MC V

Open: Mon-Fri 11am-3.30pm, Sat & Sun 9am-3.30pm (breakfast: Sat & Sun 9am-11.30am); reservations advisable for outdoor seating; licensed, no BYO

Rockpool
Modern Australian

☎ 9252 1888
107 George St

Map 1 D3

No smoking inside

Rockpool's pre-eminent reputation means that even if you aren't in the mood for dessert, not even for the passionfruit soufflé ($18), you're going to order it – because you're insanely curious about what the kitchen will produce. With its golden beret-shaped top and fluffy underbelly, the soufflé rises to the usual Rockpool heights. Rockpool, as the name suggests, deals mainly in fine seafood dishes – and the odd serving of lamb with a heady truffle mayonnaise. Sydney's best produce is combined with some of the best techniques in Chinese, Thai, Italian, French and even Indian cooking. A jew fish, for instance, comes with a garam masala-flavoured laksa sweetened with basil and tomato and served with semolina noodles; an unforgettable, sensational combination. Free-standing lights are reminiscent of a movie set, with low slung, rose-patterned sofas and an undulating ramp like a catwalk. It's all pure theatre – with one waiter to handle the sour dough, another the cutlery, and yet another the witty repartee.

starter: $31-$35
main: $42-$45
dessert: $18-$21

AE BC DC MC V

Open: Mon-Fri noon-2.30pm, Mon-Sat 6pm-11pm; reservations advisable; licensed, no BYO

THE ROCKS 49

THE ROCKS

Map 1 C3

Separate smoke-free dining available (lunch); smoking at bar only (dinner)

Terrace tables

Sailors Thai
Thai

☎ 9251 2466
106 George St

Sailors Thai's professional yet approachable staff make their entrance from behind a curved silver partition like actors in a play, bearing creations that dazzle the eyes and tease the nose. Start with chicken and fresh coconut salad ($17), a delicate combination of slivers of silky coconut flesh, poached chicken and peppery Thai basil. Rabbit and bean curd braised with oysters and Chinese broccoli ($29) is a perfectly judged symphony of tastes and textures: tender white rabbit meat, creamy oyster flesh and the chlorophyll hit of the Chinese greens. A more challenging, fiery dish is spicy red curry of pork, green beans, crispy fish and salty duck eggs ($28). It's a pungent creation, packing a powerful punch at every bite. Finish off with the soothing pastel shades and gentle flavours of tea sorbet and coconut ice cream ($11) and depart the Victorian sandstone Sailors Home building for a romantic stroll along Circular Quay.

starter: $15-$18
main: $16-$30
dessert: $10-$12

AE BC DC MC V

Open: Mon-Fri noon-2pm, Mon-Sat 6pm-10pm; reservations advisable (essential Fri & Sat); licensed, no BYO

Map 1 C3

No smoking inside

Balcony tables

Sailors Thai Canteen
Thai

☎ 9251 2466
106 George St

The Sailors Thai Canteen is a modern conversion of the upstairs room of the 'Sailors Home'. The main décor feature is the long communal stainless-steel table. Like the more expensive Sailors Thai downstairs the Canteen serves up food that sparkles – from simple dishes like pad thai ($13) to a warm salad of chicken mince, threaded through with thin glass noodles and awash with fresh mint, finely shredded onions and lime juice ($15). Other dishes, such as pineapple prawn curry ($20) and papaya salad ($16) are probably the most flavour-filled lunches you'll find in this corner of Sydney. A dessert plate that includes egg custard and Thai jelly ($10) is large enough to share – hopefully by this stage the crowds will have whittled down enough to allow you one of the few balcony seats, with a glimpse of Circular Quay's blue waters.

main: $13-$20
dessert: $10

AE BC DC MC V

Open: daily noon-8pm; reservations not accepted; licensed, no BYO

THE ROCKS

Unkai
Japanese

☎ 9250 6123
ANA Hotel Sydney, Level 36, 176 Cumberland St

Map 1 D2

Validated parking ($5 in hotel's car park)

Wheelchair access

Nonsmoking tables available. No smoking at sushi bar

Unkai's restaurant and separate sushi bar are generally recognised as among the pinnacles of Japanese fine dining in Sydney. High above Circular Quay with panoramic harbour views, the food and service needs to grab your attention. Unkai's chefs work hard at this, adding decorations such as butterfly-shaped carrot slices to sushi and sashimi, or a square of white radish to float above the fluffy prawn dumpling in clear bonito and konbu soup. Both these dishes are part of the kirara lunch set menu ($49.50) and the kaiseki dinner banquet ($90). But you don't need to spend a fortune to sample what Unkai does best. The tempura gozen ($32.50) lunch of cooked tuna salad, sashimi, tempura and chawan-mushi, is excellent. For privacy and the full Japanese experience, complete with waitress in kimono, book one of the two tatami rooms.

starter: $10-$19
main: $15-$68
dessert: $4.50-$9.50
Set menu: lunch $35-$50, dinner $60-$90

Open: daily 6.30am-10am, 6pm-10pm (sushi bar last order 9.30pm), Sun-Fri noon-2.30pm; reservations essential; licensed, no BYO

AE BC DC JCB MC V

WALSH BAY

hickson one
Modern Australian

☎ 8298 9912
Pier One Parkroyal, 11 Hickson Rd

Map 1 A3

Wheelchair access

Smoking throughout

Pier tables

Eating at an upmarket hotel doesn't have to be pricey or formal, as proved by hickson one at the Pier One Parkroyal. It's a classy waterside cafe/wine bar, with the menu covering wide tastes. There's Italian (fettucine with smoked salmon, $15), Asian (tempura prawns, $22), Middle Eastern (Moroccan spiced lamb, $20) and old faithfuls (fish and chips, $14). The decor conveys casual chic – wooden floor, metal-topped tables, subtle marine colours and folding glass doors swept back for an open-air feel. The outside seating has harbour views over to Blues Point and Lavender Bay. The food is mainly successful. Tomato and basil soup ($6.50) is smooth and flavourful; grilled tuna steak ($24) is tasty, if slightly overdone, and served on a tower of char-grilled vegetables; mud cake ($7.50) is suitably solid. A welcome escape from the tourist hordes at the Rocks.

starter: $4-$9.50
main: $14-$24
dessert: $7.50-$8.50

Open: Wed-Sat noon-10pm, Sun noon-4.30pm; reservations accepted; licensed, no BYO

AE BC DC JCB MC V

Back for More

Golden Century
393-399 Sussex St, Haymarket ☎ 9212 3901 Map 4 A1
To get to your seat at the Cantonese-style Golden Century, you have to walk past tank after tank of fish on death row (lobsters attempting a break-out thrash and futilely splash water over the side). It must be the only restaurant in Sydney so big it needs its own escalator to connect the two huge floors.

Sea Bay Restaurant
372 Pitt St, City ☎ 9267 4855 Map 4 A3
Sea Bay's sesame shallot pancakes, noodles and dumplings (steamed, boiled and fried) are among Pitt St's culinary highlights. The floor-to-ceiling mirrors give it a fun park hall-of-mirrors effect, and make this northern Chinese cuisine seem even more popular than it is (which is very popular indeed).

✱ *Write to us:* We think we've got Sydney well-covered – even so, there are always new places to try. Our tastebuds will travel, so let us know which restaurants, cafes and bars you think we should include. Write to us or email us (see p 11 for details) and the best suggestions will receive the next edition free.

INNER EAST

Darlinghurst

East Sydney

Elizabeth Bay

Kings Cross

Potts Point

Redfern

Surry Hills

Woolloomooloo

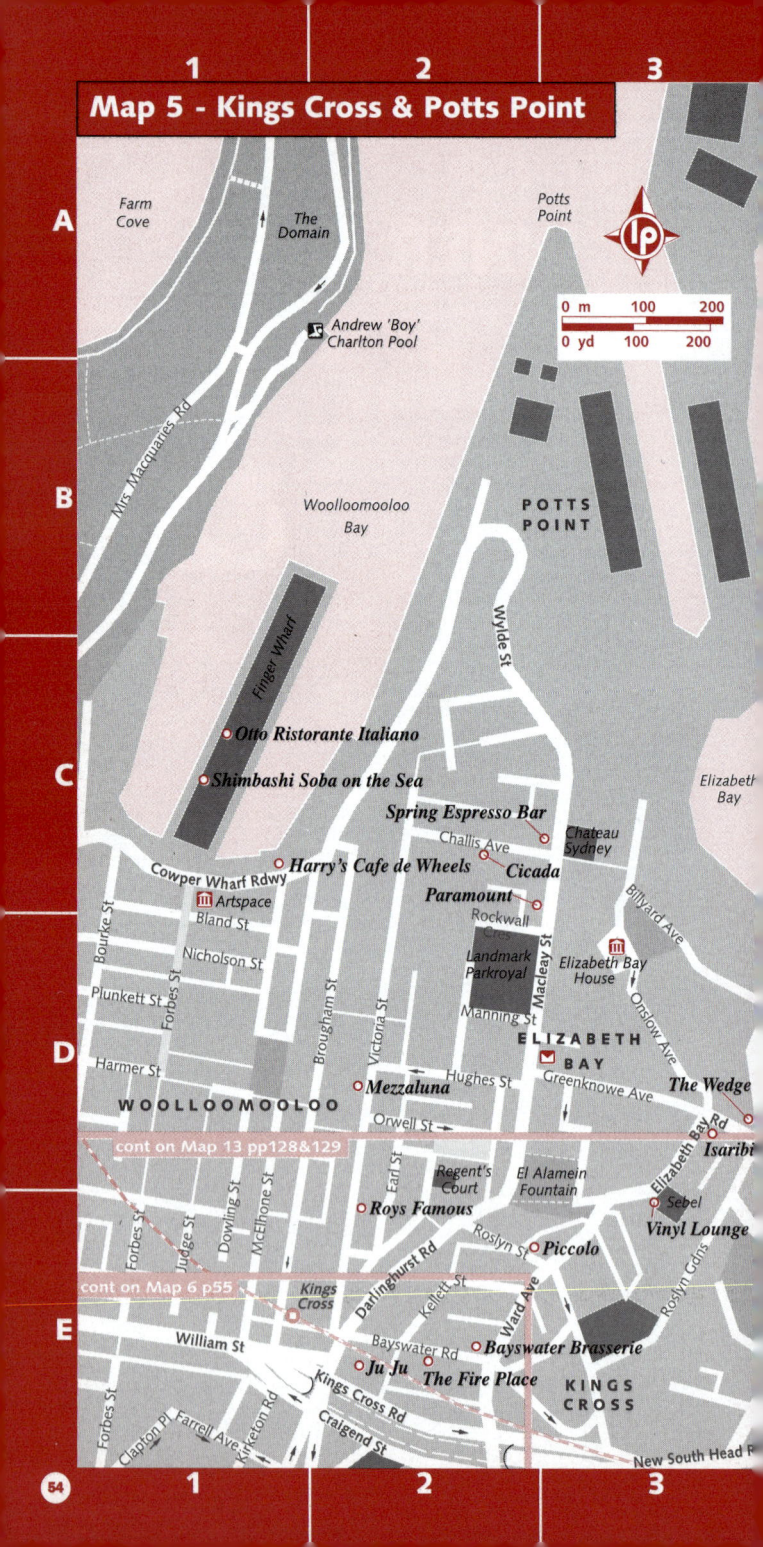

Map 5 - Kings Cross & Potts Point

Map 6 – East Sydney & Darlinghurst

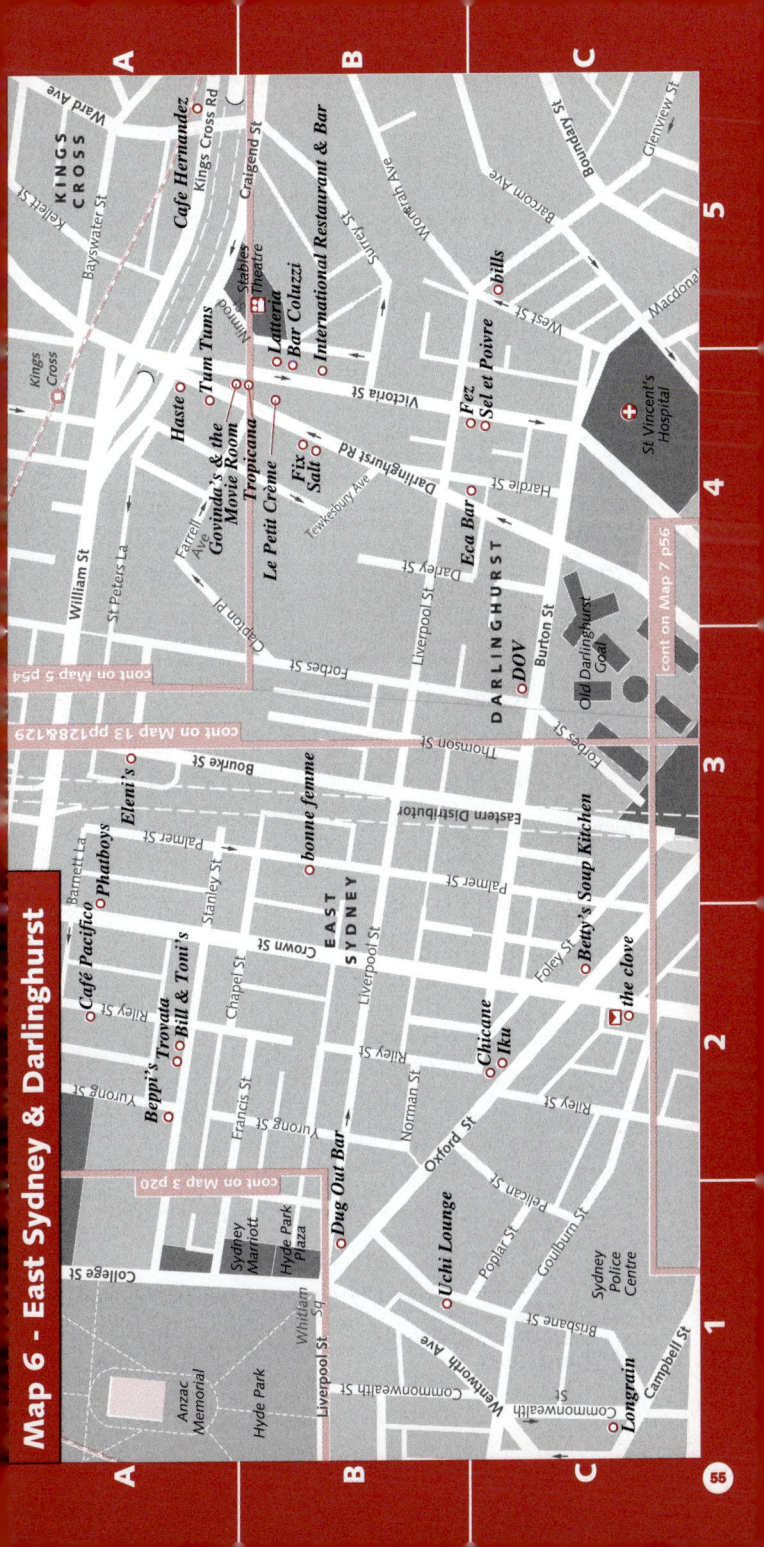

- Cafe Hernandez
- Café Pacifico
- Phatboys
- Eleni's
- Beppi's Trovata
- Bill & Toni's
- Haste
- Tum Tums
- Govinda's & the Movie Room
- Tropicana
- Le Petit Creme
- Stables Theatre
- Latteria
- Bar Coluzzi
- International Restaurant & Bar
- Fix
- Salt
- bonne femme
- Fez
- Sel et Poivre
- hills
- Eca Bar
- Dug Out Bar
- DOV
- Uchi Lounge
- Chicane
- Iku
- Betty's Soup Kitchen
- the clove
- Old Darlinghurst Gaol
- St Vincent's Hospital
- Longrain

KINGS CROSS
EAST SYDNEY
DARLINGHURST

cont on Map 3 p20
cont on Map 5 p54
cont on Map 13 pp128 & 129
cont on Map 7 p56

Map 7 – Inner East & South

cont on Map 6 p55

- Mykonos on Crown
- Campbell St
- Reservoir St
- Taylor Square
- Darlinghurst Court House
- Cafe 191
- ARQ
- Balkan Seafood Restaurant
- Angkor Wat
- Albury Hotel
- Victoria St
- Darlinghurst Rd
- Sturt St
- Oxford St
- Academy Twin
- Verona
- Mali Cafe
- Crown St
- Denham St
- Riley St
- Little Riley St
- Ann St
- Flinders St
- Taylor St
- Chisholm St
- Sims St
- Short St
- Hill St
- Hannam St
- Napier St

SURRY HILLS

- Albion St
- Billy Kwong
- Marque
- Fitzroy St
- Bourke St
- Nichols St
- Hutchinson St
- South Dowling St
- Albion Ave
- Church St
- Foveaux St
- Hopetoun
- Fitzroy St
- Seymour Pl
- Collins St
- Norton St
- Richards Ave
- Prasit's Northside on Crown
- Clock Hotel
- Marshall St
- Bennett St
- Prospect St
- Moore Park Rd
- MG Garage
- fuel
- Riley St
- Alexander St
- Phelps St
- Arthur St
- Tudor St
- Rainford St
- Piment Rouge
- Nepalese Kitchen
- Davies St
- Brett Whiteley Gallery
- Arthur St
- cont on Map 13 pp128 & 129
- Moore Park
- Anzac Pde
- La Passion de Fruit
- Devonshire St
- Nobbs St
- Tabou
- Matsuri
- Crown St
- Nickson St
- Bourke St
- South Dowling St
- Eastern Distributor
- La Persia
- Cossie's Cafe-Restaurant
- Mort St

STRAWBERRY HILLS

- Erciyes Restaurant
- Maya Sweets Centre
- Ridge St
- Sushi Suma
- Cleveland St
- Baptist St
- Alio

REDFERN

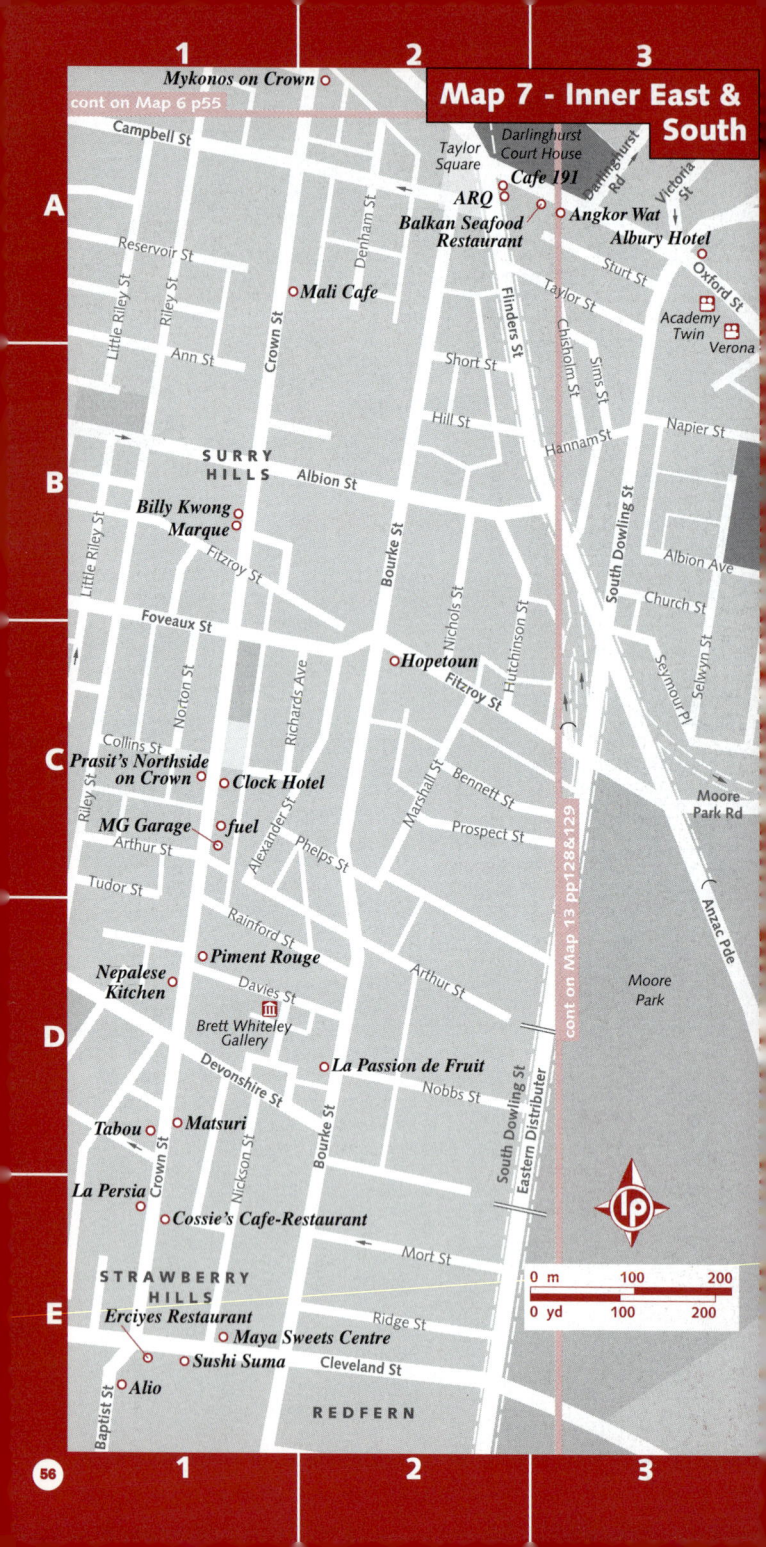

0 m / 100 / 200
0 yd / 100 / 200

BEST

- **Billy Kwong**
  Chinese for the new millennium

- **bonne femme**
  A French favourite

- **Chicane**
  Let yourself be seduced

- **Marque**
  Intimate dining with Gallic charm

- **Tum Tum's**
  As good as a night in Bangkok

Inner East

The colourful inner-east, some might say, is the area that is most expressive of the true essence of Sydney. At Woolloomooloo Wharves, Greenpeace inflatables have intermittently battled with nuclear-loaded warships. While most everyone else has had a pie from the legendary Harry's Cafe de Wheels van in Cowper Wharf Rd (Map 5 C1) on the harbour foreshore (including, reputedly, a young Sophia Loren). Rising above Woolloomooloo are the art deco apartments, designer restaurants and designer lifestyles of Potts Point, which in turn give way to the seedier terraces of Kings Cross's red light district. Bisecting the region is Oxford Street, home of the rainbow coloured Mardi Gras. Each year millions line the route to cheer bare-breasted dykes on bikes and marching boys executing perfect point turns while keeping strategically-placed pieces of lamé in position. In Surry Hills and Darlinghurst the colour is provided by artists' studios, galleries and boutique frock shops. You'll find a little Italy in Stanley Street, while Cleveland Street, Redfern is home to a little Lebanon and little India strip. Redfern has also been the centre of colour issues of another kind: in the 1970s it was the birthplace of the first indigenous housing, legal and medical services organisation.

DARLINGHURST

Map 7 A3
Smoking throughout

Angkor Wat
Cambodian

☎ 9360 5500
227 Oxford St

Outside of Cabramatta, Cambodian restaurants are very thin on the ground in Sydney. This isn't why Angkor Wat stands out from the Oxford St crowd – that's down to the super-friendly service and the deliciously different food, spicier than Vietnamese and less complex than Thai. Beneath strings of colourful flags jazzing up the already sprightly yellow walls, we wet our appetites on krouch chien ($5.50), succulent legs of marinated, deep-fried quail. The smoked salmon soup ($6) is a meal in itself and shows that the restaurant isn't afraid to chuck non-Cambodian ingredients into the pot. You couldn't get more authentic, though, than the banana blossoms with prawns ($16), several subtle flavours jostling in a light broth. The brandy seafood ($16), served with blue flames flickering around a generous pile of scallops, mussels, prawns and squid, is more flash than substance. Simpler is better, as proved by the yummy banana and sago pudding in coconut milk ($4.50).

starter: $5.50-$7.50
main: $9.50-$17
dessert: $3.60-$4.50
Banquets $20-$25

AE BC DC MC V

Open: Sun, Tues-Thurs 5.30pm-10.30pm, Fri & Sat 5.30pm-11pm; reservations advisable (especially Fri & Sat); licensed & BYO (corkage $2/person)

Map 7 A3
Smoking throughout

Balkan Seafood Restaurant
Seafood

☎ 9331 7670
215 Oxford Street

Popular with the Croatian community and seafoodies in general, Balkan Seafood is a block up from Taylor Square. Hectic and free of affected hipness, it's decked out in a trusty ocean motif and has an accommodating buzz that appeals to all comers. Despite the name, there are in fact eighteen meat dishes on the menu, but you'll probably want to check out the blackboards to see what marine goodies are on offer. The seafood platter for two ($51.80) is the best bet for the indecisive, stacked with pink calamari, enormous grilled prawns and octopus, and hearty fillets of scampi and flathead. Included are a batch of Tasmanian mussels, poached in their green shells with a rich Croatian sauce. The only 'dessert' was a bowl of sweet, cold strawberries ($5), which, as the management well knows, is the ideal way to finish off this generous harvest from the seas.

starter: $8.80-$16.80
main: $5-$26
dessert: $5

AE BC DC JCB MC V

Open: Tues-Fri 6pm-11pm, Sat & Sun 6pm-midnight; reservations advisable; BYO (corkage $2/bottle)

DARLINGHURST

bills
Modern Australian
☎ 9360 9631
433 Liverpool St

Map 6 C5

Put simply, bills does some of the best breakfasts in Sydney. No, scrap that, make it New South Wales. In fact, it's hard to think of a better place in Australia to greet the day. Excessive praise? Dig into a plate of fluffy ricotta hotcakes with banana and honeycomb butter ($12.50) and try arguing. Still quibbling? Move on to delicate fritters bursting with sweetcorn and sided by bacon and roast tomato ($12.50). Need a bit more convincing? Dive into the moist Birchermüsli with fresh fruit ($8.50). All this goodness is served up in the simplest of rooms. A large blond-wood communal table laden with style magazines and newspapers is the cafe's centrepiece, seating an ever-changing array of Darlinghurst darlings. bill's status is undeniably confirmed by the number of people prepared to wait patiently for a seat, despite the plethora of Victoria St cafes nearby. So don't linger over your second latte – move on and let others enjoy the spread.

Open: Mon-Sat 7.30am-3pm (breakfast: Mon-Sat 7.30-12.30); reservations not accepted; BYO (no corkage)

breakfast: $4-$12.50
lunch: $10.50-$17.50
dessert: $5

AE BC MC V

Chicane
Modern European
☎ 9380 2121
1a Burton St
(entrance also 52 Oxford St)

Map 6 C2
Wheelchair access

Smoking at the bar and outside only

Terrace tables

For a grand entrance at Chicane use the discreet door on Oxford St, with the industrial chic staircase down into this latest hot date for hipsters. Also wear black – all the waiters, and most of the patrons lounging in the wickedly comfy chairs, do. Over in the intriguingly dark dining room, with its padded booths made for seductions, it's the seriously glam food that's doing the wooing. The affair begins with a trio of creamy goat cheese profiteroles ($14) on a crunchy bed of artichokes, wheatberries and oven dried tomatoes. The tuna tartare ($16), a mound of fine raw fish to be mixed with dabs of pine nuts, pear, quail egg-yolk and chilli, keeps up the pressure. The thick, softly flaking salmon ($26), resting above a divine salad of cucumber, date and fennel, sees resistance crumbling. Cave in under the double assault of a sinful champagne sorbet with macerated berries and a sandwich of mango sauterne jelly and brandy snaps (both $12), and pledge undying love.

Open: daily 6pm-10.30pm, supper Sun-Wed 10.30pm-2am (kitchen closes 1am), Thurs-Sat 10.30pm-3am (kitchen closes 2am); reservations essential; licensed, no BYO

starter: $12-$26
main: $25-$38
dessert: $12

AE BC DC JCB MC V

Map 6 C2

Smoking throughout

the clove
Indian

☎ **9361 0980**
249 Crown St

An Indian restaurant in a deconsecrated church? In Surry Hills, where cars in cafes and clubs in undertakers' rooms are as everyday as property-development applications, anything's possible. Oddly enough, new and old, East and West, streetwise and best-dressed meet harmoniously in the clove restaurant, which manages to preserve much of the integrity of the original building without making a mausoleum of it. Earnest, suited waiters spirit themselves from table to table beneath exposed dark-wood rafters, steaming curries and crispy pappadams in hand. Order a mixed entrée ($14.90) and go to heaven over tender tandoori lamb cutlets, golden vegetable pakoras and ghee-soaked samosas. Mains also present a host of tempting choices. Try the green banana curry with lentils ($7.90) for something mild, or add some spice to your meal with a hot-as-Hades duck vindaloo ($10.50). The clove is a sanctuary for lovers of authentic, affordable Indian food.

starter: $5.50-$15.90
main: $6.90-$12.90
dessert: $2.50-$7.50
Set menu $20 or $22/person
(min 6 people)
AE BC DC JCB MC V

Open: Mon-Fri noon-3pm; Sun-Thurs 6pm-11pm, Fri & Sat 6pm-11.30pm; reservations advisable (especially Fri & Sat nights); licensed & BYO (corkage $1.50/person)

DARLINGHURST

Mykonos on Crown
Greek

☎ 9368 7900
302-308 Crown St

Map 7 A2

Smoking throughout

Balcony tables

Although lacking the patina of age, Mykonos on Crown's simple blue-and-white décor and irrepressible waiters soon signal that you're deep in taverna country here. Not that there's anything wrong with that when you've got an 'ouzo plate' ($8) in front of you – chunks of cucumber, olives, fetta and tomato – and a tumbler of the devilish, milky aniseed drink in your hand. The deep-fried whitebait ($8.50) are amazingly oil-free, convincingly fishy and sublimely crunchy all at the same time, while char-grilled eggplant ($6) is griddle-marked and softly oozing, accompanied by a garlicky skordalia. Dinner took a nose-dive with a gluggy, bechamel-heavy moussaka ($15.50) that even lashings of retsina (well, at $15 a bottle, why stint?) couldn't salvage, but all was forgiven when the lamb kleftiko ($16.50) made its grand entrance. This hunk of fall-apart tender meat comes in a parcel of foil, and is surrounded by savoury potato chunks sitting in a puddle of juice fragrant with lemon and oregano.

Open: Mon-Sat 6.30am-3pm, Sun 6.30am-noon, daily 5pm-late; reservations advisable; licensed & BYO (corkage $1/person)

starter: $6.30-$12
main: $16-$19
dessert: $6-$8.20

AE BC MC V

Phatboys
Thai

☎ 9332 3284
118 Crown St

Map 6 A3

Smoking throughout

Pavement tables

At Phatboys everything's presented with style and fresh floral flourishes, so while it may not be the cheapest Thai in town, the extra cents make sense. Whole coconuts are filled with drinks (and the odd curry), while an entrée of betel leaves is arranged like a flower and topped with mounds of coconut, ginger, peanuts and fish sauce ($8.50). The duck curry sounds a little like fruit salad – what with pineapple and grapes – but it's a satisfying dish ($16.50). Chicken marinated in red wine then wrapped in pandan leaves and deep-fried is another excellent choice ($9.50). In contrast to the food, the décor couldn't be simpler: polished floors and bright white walls, with one featuring a floor-to-ceiling mirror. At the far end of the room a letterbox-shaped slit allows for peeping between cooks and clients, while a golden reclining god looks on magnanimously from above.

Open: Mon-Fri lunch from noon, daily from 6pm; reservations advisable on weekends; licensed & BYO (corkage $3/person or $7/bottle)

starter: $8.50-$10.50
main: $13.50-$23.50
dessert: $6.50-$7.50

AE BC MC V

Cafe Crawl – Inner East

If you want your coffee with a touch of French style, a dash of Italian tradition or a cup full of Darlinghurst cool – leaning on chrome bars or sinking into cosy couches – the inner east is the place to crawl.

Cafe 191
191 Oxford St, Darlinghurst ☎ 9360 4295 Map 7 A2
If you've just arrived and you're wondering which Oxford St subculture to cosy up to, Cafe 191, at the crossroads of Taylor Square, is *the* spot for people-watching. Boy couples love that their pet dogs get priority treatment with complimentary bowls of water, while the rest of Oxford St's diverse life is bound to make an entrance at some point in the day.

Cafe Hernandez
60 Kings Cross Rd, Potts Point ☎ 9331 2343 Map 6 A5
It might be a 24-hour opener in Kings Cross, but the owners say they like to maintain a respectable 'family atmosphere' where everyone's welcome. Taxi drivers refuelling with a coffee or two, post-shift waiters from the nearby cafes and restaurants, and stage actors after a night on the boards – everyone's there to catch a bit of the theatre of life that's always on show.

DOV
Cnr Forbes & Burton Sts, Darlinghurst ☎ 9360 9594 Map 6 C3
It looks like a sparkling silver railway rest-house of the future – which is appropriate for a cafe at the crossroads of Darlinghurst culture. Everyone here seems to be on the fast track to somewhere else – art school students, business minds and Mardi Gras marching crews all call this inviting cafe their second home.

Eca Bar
128 Darlinghurst Rd, Darlinghurst ☎ 9332 1433 Map 6 C4
Eca and Bar are two words that keep coming up in our best coffee in Sydney surveys: a wedge-shaped slice of cool-as-chrome Darlinghurst life. This place is best for those who like sharp clothes, sharp haircuts and smart talk. If not, stick to your instant coffee with two sugars and full-cream milk, sweetie.

La Passion de Fruit
633 Burke St, Surry Hills ☎ 9690 1894 Map 7 D2
This is the Carmen Miranda of cafes. The aerobic fruit person portraits could be inspired by the chirpy customers who sip endless frappés here, but both the young and old come for the excellent coffee. Going strong for over 20 years, you might feel a little out of place if you don't know the staff personally.

Latteria
320 Victoria St, Darlinghurst ☎ 9331 2914 Map 6 B4
The name may have changed, but this skinny cafe is the same old formula: Sydney's schmooziest and coolest would rather queue here (leather jacket casually slung over the shoulder) than sit at an empty seat a few doors away. Even the milkcrates have been upgraded to designer tree-stumps.

Le Petit Crème
118 Darlinghurst Rd, Darlinghurst ☎ 9361 4738 Map 6 B4
The elder statesman of the Darlinghurst cafe-clique, and as popular as ever. Doctors, nurses, solicitors and lawyers share the limited air space with actors and the odd curious tourist, tucking into eggs benedict, omelettes and baguettes baked on-site.

Mali Cafe
348a Crown St, Darlinghurst ☎ 0414 730 248 Map 7 A1
It's all warm, soft edges, in this charming cafe, like a friend-of-a-friend's kitchen. The aim is to make you feel at home with home-made cakes and couches that are practically beds. It's a formula that works for numerous French tourists and armies of young women practising meaningful expressions to reflect their meaningful lives.

Piccolo
6 Roslyn St, Kings Cross ☎ 9368 1356 Map 5 E2
'Since 1950 BC', says the postcard, and Piccolo doesn't look like it's had a touch-up since it opened (the same could probably be said for most of the patrons). Piccolo's coffee has passed the lips of Sammy Davis Jr, Marianne Faithfull and Frank Sinatra. Piccolo is for those who like their coffee with a large dose of history (there's a wall full of photographs of patrons past) and a lung full of smoke. As the postcard says: 'If you've got nowhere else to go, you could go to Piccolo'.

Piment Rouge
536 Crown St, Surry Hills ☎ 9331 3452 Map 7 D1
Piment Rouge means 'red chilli', and it boasts one of the hottest cafe menus in town (you may need to ask for a side order of a glass of milk). The black, white, red and chrome look hints at salacious overtones, but it's all pretty tame really.

Roys Famous
176 Victoria St, Potts Point ☎ 9357 3579 Map 5 E2
Melburnians visiting Sin City can calm any anxieties with a cup of Grinder's coffee (a blend from their home state). Roys Famous is popular with both locals and tourists finding their bearings. They also have evenings of live jazz once a month.

Sel et Poivre
263 Victoria St, Darlinghurst ☎ 9361 6530 Map 6 C4
French toast, baguettes, croissants, omelettes and a French waitress: a cafe for Francophiles on a budget (but we have to ask, why the Tuscan red walls?).

Spring Espresso Bar
65 Macleay St, Potts Point ☎ 9331 0190 Map 5 C3
It's on the international map thanks to *wallpaper** magazine dubbing it the place for Sydney's biggest, hippest breakfast. So you'd think they could upgrade the pavement milk crate chairs! Go while your bottom can still find a vacant patch of concrete to perch on.

The Wedge
70 Elizabeth Bay Rd, Elizabeth Bay ☎ 9326 9015 Map 5 D3
Compact, sleek and classy, it's the miniature mobile phone of Sydney cafes. Another one of Sydney's best cups of coffee (strong, with real full cream milk). Snacks include toasted schnitzel sandwiches.

DARLINGHURST

Map 6 B4
Valet parking (evening)
Wheelchair access

Salt
Modern Australian

☎ 9332 2566
Kirketon Hotel,
229 Darlinghurst Rd

More than simply a restaurant, Salt is a gourmet's (or gourmand's) recreation centre, with a champagne bar and Fix, a wine and cigar bar, to complement the main restaurant. From the frosted mauve to the monochrome clientele, it's almost too groovy for it's own good. In the end, however, it pulls it off with spectacular panache. The service is attentive without being cloying; the food, the best of Australian produce with French and Asian influences. The roasted barramundi ($32.50) is tender, moist and beautifully complemented by the lemon and basil risotto. The curried loin of roasted lamb, served slightly rare with cauliflower purée and mustard fruits is typical of the culinary magpie-ism Salt dabbles in, with perfect results. And if your legs aren't yet wobbly from the extensive wine list, then desserts such as star anise panna cotta and saffron pear ($15.50) will certainly make you weak at the knees.

starter: $16.50-$23.50
main: $32.50-$33.50
dessert: $15.50
Business lunch Mon-Fri $40-$45 or degustation dinner $90 or $115
AE BC MC V

Open: Mon-Fri noon-3pm, daily 6pm-late; reservations advisable; licensed, no BYO

Map 6 A4

Tum Tum's
Thai

☎ 9331 5390
199 Darlinghurst Rd

As Tum Tum's tongue-blasting jungle curry ($7.50) started its assault on our mouths, we felt like cartoon characters with steam pouring out of our ears and noses. We tried to remember the last time we'd had such a wonderfully fiery creation, maybe somewhere near Chiang Mai but never anywhere near Darlinghurst. Until now. Like all the best meals eaten at street stalls in Thailand, Tum Tum's focus is solely on the food. Operating chiefly as a takeaway cafe, the undecorated room is tiny – try and wrangle a spare seat and order away. Two deep-fried chicken wings ($4) power-packed with garlic, noodles and mince are dumbfoundingly good. As is the chicken salad ($8.50), with tangles of skinny vermicelli noodles encasing chicken, chilli and fragrant coriander. But if your palate has been on hiatus, the jungle curry, crowded with sweet basil, chicken and a truckload of fresh chillies, is the kick-in-the-mouth, wake-up call you've been waiting for.

starter: $1-$2
main: $6-$13
cash only

Open: daily 11am-11pm; reservations not accepted; unlicensed

EAST SYDNEY

Beppi's
Italian

☎ **9360 4558**
Cnr Yurong & Stanley Sts

Map 6 A2

P Valet parking $15

Smoking after 10pm

You can't judge a book by its cover but you *can* judge a good Italian restaurant by its gnocchi. Feather-light spinach and ricotta dumplings ($16) would have floated out of the bowl had we not gobbled them greedily. Our crab-stuffed ravioli ($18) in a creamy tomato sauce disappeared almost as fast. Beppi's, Sydney's benchmark Italian restaurant, is still going strong after 45 years. Ma certo, the salmon-pink walls and white-aproned waiters are as far from hip and groovy as Sydney is from Rome, but how many trendy restaurants boast a cellar you can eat in where dusty bottles of Grange rub shoulders with fine Italian wines? Traditional Italian menu staples include carpaccio, prosciutto with melon, a couple of risotto and eight pasta dishes, as well as veal every-which-way. A tender, just-salty-enough veal saltimbocca ($28) didn't 'jump in the mouth' – it melted. If you're still going by dessert you can tuck into torta di marscapone (tiramisu in disguise, $14.90) or a rich choccie cake dripping with zabaglione ($11.50).

Open: Mon-Fri noon-3pm, Mon-Sat 6pm-11.30pm; reservations advisable (essential for tables in the cellar); licensed, no BYO

starter: $16-$18
main: $19-$29
dessert: $10.50-$14.90

AE BC DC JCB MC V

INNER EAST

EAST SYDNEY

Map 6 B3

bonne femme
French

☎ 9331 4455
191-193 Palmer St

The buzz on bonne femme has cooled since its initial days of pot rattling in the kitchen behind the chic minimalist dining room, a palate of soothing chocolate and grey. The cooking – French with a lighter touch – is no less assured, though. It's still not a place for vegetarians; the only option on the regularly changing menu was a fine starter of smooth-as-silk goat's cheese mousse, partnered with crunchy walnuts and firm beetroot ($12). A similarly inspired marriage was the yolky poached egg on a crisp smoked trout tart doused in lemon butter ($15). Our mains – tender lamb drizzled with zesty pesto ($25) and veal with that old standby, kipfler potatoes, and the more unexpected plump sour capers – were practically faultless. Looking like a toasted iceberg in a sea of blood plums, the Valrhona chocolate bombe ($10) provided a suitably dramatic, if overly sweet, climax to a relaxed evening.

starter: $11-$16
main: $21-$24
dessert: $10
AE BC DC MC V

Open: daily 6pm-late (kitchen closes 11pm); reservations advisable (especially weekends); licensed, no BYO

Map 6 A2

Smoking throughout

Café Pacifico
Mexican

☎ 9360 3811
1st floor, 95 Riley St

Here's a riddle: Why did the Mexican push his wife off a cliff? Okay, before the accusations of misogyny flood in, let it be noted that this is merely quoted from the mirror on the wall. That being said, it does offer a keen insight into the tongue-in-cheek flair that typifies Café Pacifico. Fitted out in Tex Mex kitsch, other gems of enlightenment adorning the walls offer '1.5 million margaritas served so far' (how many patrons subsequently swung the night away in the bar-side hammock isn't mentioned), and numerous allusions to the parallels between chilli and viagra. The menu offers few surprises choice-wise, the standard canteena fare of fajitas ($17.50) and cerviche ($9.50) – though the swordfish fajitas ($19) are a delicious exception. But once you get over the fact that the mod Oz coriander twist just doesn't suit Mexican food, you'll be thankful for its simple but delicious authenticity. And the answer to the riddle? The mirror, alas, left it hanging.

starter: $5-$9
main: $12.50-$19
dessert: $5-$6.50
Set menu $30
AE BC DC MC V

Open: Mon-Thur 6pm-10.30pm, Fri noon-2.30pm, Fri & Sat 6pm-11pm; reservations advisable (especially weekends); licensed, no BYO

EAST SYDNEY

Eleni's
Modern Greek

☎ 9331 5306
185a Bourke St

Map 6 A3

When that groovy gaggle of Greek gods – Dionysus, Aphrodite and Bacchus – decamped from Mt Olympus they sped straight to Sydney's best mod Greek restaurant. Tiny as a Santorini sun-baking patch, Eleni's unpretentious white interior is a suitably simple backdrop for chef Peter Conistis' rich and complex creations. His twice-cooked fetta and zucchini soufflé ($16) is benchmark material. A warm, wobbling dome of sharp cheese tempered by a sweet roast tomato sauce, it's moan-out-loud good. Mains elicit similar exaltations. A rabbit and black olive filo pie ($28) is a hearty affair, and the roasted lamb loin wrapped in vine leaves is a real show stopper. Served pink and sided by a potato and lamb shank tart, it's a flesh-lover's fantasy. The crispy nougat tartlet ($12), studded with candied pistachios and topped with fluffy Iranian fairy floss, is good enough for the gods (and all us mortals).

starter: $13-$19
main: $27-$29
dessert: $12

AE BC MC V

Open: Fri noon-2.30pm, Mon-Sat 6.30pm-11pm; reservations advisable (especially Thurs-Sat); BYO (corkage $3/bottle)

Trovata
Italian/Mediterranean

☎ 9361 4437
76 Stanley St

Map 6 A2

Smoking throughout

Pavement tables

Leichhardt may make legitimate claim to being the 'Little Italy' of Sydney, but Stanley St in East Sydney must run a close second (albeit on a much smaller scale), with the same mix of alfresco dining and convivial atmosphere that draws people back again and again. Trovata has established itself over the years as one of Stanley St's most popular. Tuck into some bruschetta ($4.50) and contemplate the extensive menu, while enjoying the sun afforded by the pavement tables. Even in winter, the sun pours in and, with generous mains and a great wine list, it's easy to find yourself suddenly and pleasantly dozing, whiling away the hours in a most Mediterranean fashion while your spaghetti with sardines and sun-dried tomatoes ($16.50), or your chicken and kumera risotto ($15.50) remains half-eaten, awaiting your second attempt. And with desserts such as the wonderfully coffee-rich tiramisù ($7.50), you may find lunch slowly but surely creeping towards dinnertime.

starter: $7-$15
main: $11.50-$20
dessert: $7.50

AE BC DC MC V

Open: Mon-Fri 11.30am-late, Sat & Sun 9am-late (breakfast until 2pm); reservations accepted; licensed and BYO (corkage $3.50/bottle)

ELIZABETH BAY

Map 5 D3

Isaribi
Japanese

☎ 9358 2125
41 Elizabeth Bay Rd

Isaribi is trailblazing the robatayaki style of Japanese cooking and eating in Sydney. Entranced diners sit around huge grills and feast on a selection of morsels plucked from the glowing coals, garnished and presented to them on a wooden paddle. If you don't want to be in the thick of it, you can still get a bird's-eye view of proceedings from the mezzanine tables. About three or four dishes per person is a good starting point and icy-cold glasses of sake make the perfect accompaniment. A bowl of agedashi tofu ($5) and spinach with sesame ($4.50) are a good foil for the meaty chicken balls ($5), which are not what you might fear but rather small and deliciously crispy meatballs with a hint of teriyaki. Grilled fishcake ($5) turns out to be a grill-seared patty of white fish paste cut into slices, with a small pyramid of grated ginger on the side, while plump Tasmanian oysters ($10) arrive comfortably nestled on a bed of salt and lime wedges.

starter: $4-$14
main: $4-$10
dessert: $4.50
AE BC DC MC V

Open: daily 6pm-11pm; reservations advisable; licensed, no BYO

Map 5 E3

Smoking throughout

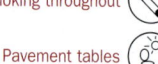

Pavement tables

Vinyl Lounge
French/modern Australian

☎ 9326 9224
1/17 Elizabeth Bay Rd

With a shoebox-sized shop next door displaying collectibles straight out of *wallpaper**, the retro-chic Vinyl Lounge fits right into this section of Lizzie Bay Road. Amid funky furniture and walls covered with teen-idol album covers from the days when vinyl reigned, you can chew on some of the crunchiest baguettes around, served with Hank's jam ($3.50) or eggs ($5.50) for breakfast, or filled with combos such as grilled eggplant, herbed ricotta and cucumber for lunch. If you have a serious low-blood-sugar situation on your hands, try the baked eggs with tomato and basil ($6.80), and maybe a side order of bacon or sausage. For less dire cases, there's semolina with poached dried fruit or muesli with yoghurt – and, as you'd expect from a French-Tahitian team, the coffee hits the spot, too. You'll need to be persistent to score a table here on weekend mornings, when the beautiful people linger longer.

breakfast: $3.50-$6.80
lunch: $5.50-$12

cash only

Open: Tues-Fri 7am-4pm, Sat 8am-4pm, Sun 8am-3pm (breakfast: all day); reservations not accepted; unlicensed

KINGS CROSS

Bayswater Brasserie
Modern Australian

☎ **9357 2177**
32 Bayswater Rd

Map 5 E2

Entertainment: DJ in bar Fri & Sat 8pm-midnight

Nonsmoking tables available

Courtyard tables

Bayswater Brasserie could be praised solely for its longevity. In Sydney's fickle restaurant scene it's an achievement to stay in business for one year, let alone seventeen. However, there are other reasons to applaud this sassy stayer. The interior's timeless appearance, for one – classical French brasserie-style embellishments like deep chocolate leather banquettes, dark wooden tables and a sparkling white tiled floor still look fresh and appealing. Noteworthy too is the restaurant's multiple uses. Feel like an after-work drink? Score a booth in the suitably dark, stylish bar. Romance? Slink into the lush, candle-lit, garden courtyard. Looking to impress? Take a seat in the chic, glass-roofed front room. The menu, brimming with well-constructed dishes at reasonable prices, is worthy of recognition. Succulent, fresh oysters ($2.20-$2.50 each) served on ice are sure-fire winners as are strapping mains like roast quail with a melting red wine risotto ($21). And the warm quince tart ($11) is engagingly sweet and homey.

starter: $8.50-$22.50
main: $16.50-$24
dessert: $7-$11

Open: Mon-Sat noon-midnight; reservations advisable; licensed, no BYO

AE BC DC JCB MC V

International Restaurant & Bar
Modern Australian

☎ **9360 9080**
Level 14, 227 Victoria St

Map 6 B4

Nonsmoking tables available, smoking throughout in restaurant after 11.30pm

It's not every night that you open a leather-bound menu and see that the designers of the waiting staff's shirts, ties and cufflinks have been acknowledged. The International Restaurant & Bar might be swish but it isn't brisk; you're welcomed with comfortable cheerfulness and shown to a seat with billion dollar views. The building's position on a hill above the mean streets gives the impression that you're much higher up than the 14th floor. The dishes are classic and done with real flair – and are seriously photogenic! The slow-roasted muscovy duck breast ($28), with its caramelised endive, is the sort of thing that royal types probably dine on at Christmas. Dedicated roast fans will find their Holy Grail in the herb-crusted rump of lamb ($29). The seared fillet of Atlantic salmon on squid ink noodles ($29) goes further than its minimalist serving suggests. And the chilled fruit and sorbet ($12) provides an impressive finish.

starter: $17-$32
main: $28-$32
dessert: $12-$15

Open: daily bar 5.30pm-11.30pm, restaurant 7pm-11pm; reservations essential; licensed, no BYO

AE BC DC JCB MC V

Bar Brawl

Care for a pre- or post-dinner drink? Sydney is full of great bars, so you can be sure to find a lounge to suit.

The Albury Hotel 6 Oxford St, Paddington ☎ 9361 6555 Map 7 A3
A bunch of blokes in Bonds T-shirts filling an old-style Aussie pub to capacity have never looked this good before ... bring your boyfriend, or, if your name is 'Portio Turbo', 'Mogadonna' or 'Amelia Airhead', bring your best beehive and diamante ensemble. The 'ladies lounge' next door has a somewhat tamer cabaret scene.

Anti Bar at bel mondo Level 3, Argyle Stores, 18-24 Argyle St, The Rocks ☎ 9241 3700 Map 1 C3
It's not strictly a bar (more of a pre- and post-dinner drink venue) but it's nonetheless a great way to sample some bel mondo antipasto without the bel mondo price tag. It's in a restored early 19th century wool store of barn-like dimensions, but the cage elevator, and sweeping bar are more New York (see review p 47).

Aqua Luna Bar Opera Quays, East Circular Quay ☎ 9251 0311 Map 1 D5
You might not be able to afford one of those new East Circular Quay apartments, but you can approximate the experience for the price of a cocktail and a 'Romeo y Julieta' cigar ($20) on the Juliet balcony and lounge chairs (see review p 24).

ARQ 16 Flinders St, Darlinghurst ☎ 9380 8700 Map 7 A2
This is the sort of place where the cast of Starship Troopers might go to unwind after a day of saving the planet: a mega three-level complex of dance floors, leather couches, fluorescent bars, top DJs and a smoke machine working overtime. The mezzanine level overlooks the dance floor, and has pink velvet seats in round cut-out 'pods' – for the mixed, youngish crowd when they eventually tire.

bohem 467 Pitt St, Haymarket ☎ 9211 8777 Map 4 B2
Bohem is located in a 150-year-old building that was once the headquarters of the Australian Gas Light company, and this bar/restaurant/club has made the most of the domed glass roof, oversized white columns and sandstone opulence of the original structure. Chairs are covered in Italian silk and the ambience is an eclectic mix of Moroccan food and music, Victorian grandeur and a little bit of Berlin sophistication. Upstairs its vodkas and whiskies in the lounge area, downstairs at the Gas nightclub, a mid- to late-20s crowd at the house music nights.

Different Drummer 185 Glebe Point Rd, Glebe ☎ 9552 3406 Map 10 D5
Above the bar a pheasant lays an electrically illuminated golden egg – right next to the dancing Coke can with Blues Brothers' glasses, antique brass fire fighter equipment and a TV screening the X-Files. You can order tapas treats at the bar with your glass of beer or sangria, and in the backyard beer garden there is an excellent Spanish bistro: what more could you want in a local bar?

Dug Out Bar Burdekin Hotel, 2 Oxford St, Darlinghurst ☎ 9331 3066 Map 6 B1
A short flight of stairs takes you down to a room with walls tiled like a circa-1930s underground railway station: it's as if someone has miniaturised St James, installed some period polished dark wood benches and a walk-in cigar pantry, strewn a few candles around and topped it all off with a funky jazz soundtrack and mind-bending Martini mixes.

Fix Kirketon Hotel, 229 Darlinghurst Rd, Darlinghurst ☎ 9360 4333 Map 6 B4
Sipping drinks at the very compact Fix is a bit like being inside a builder's orange toolbox. Luckily, the state-of-the-art air-con system sucks out smoke and cigar fumes (cigar lovers note – there's a humidor here), so you don't get too uncomfortable while mixing with visiting celebrities of the fashion, art and design worlds. Although it's attached to the boutique Kirketon Hotel, locals have also taken it to their designer-clad hearts. A classic 'cocktail Fix' is $12.50.

Glenmore Hotel 96 Cumberland, The Rocks ☎ 9247 4794 Map 1 C3
One of the last old-style pubs left in the Rocks. BYO your own schooner from the ground floor bar when you head up to the picnic tables and astroturf carpet of the rooftop 'garden'. The views of Circular Quay are multi-million dollar ones, but the drink prices – and the company – are some of the most down-to-earth around.

Haste 169-173 Darlinghurst Rd, Kings Cross ☎ 9331 0011 Map 6 A4
This restaurant/bar, on the cusp of Darlinghurst and Kings Cross, is a little white-washed slice of La Dolce Vita with its Italianate terrace overlooking the busy William St - Kings Cross Rd junction. A mainly 30s-40s crowd sip classic mixes into the wee hours. There's a short and sweet mod Oz restaurant menu as well as a keep-the-hangover-at-bay bar menu of hot chips, nachos and antipasto.

Hopetoun 416 Bourke St (Cnr Bourke and Fitzroy Sts), Surry Hills ☎ 9361 5257 Map 7 C2
Once the uncontested crucible for every new Australian rock band, the Hopetoun is still a staging point for garage bands on the make. But come Sunday afternoons it transforms itself into a chill-out space full of laid-back DJ's and all-night party creatures having a last nightcap. It's called (what else?) 'Frigid'.

Horizons Bar Level 36, ANA Hotel, 176 Cumberland St, The Rocks ☎ 9250 6000 Map 1 D2
This is one bar where there's no fighting for a view – everyone has one, although while some people get the Opera House and the Bridge, others get Darling Harbour and the West. Staff in bow ties can be a little slow with your order, but complimentary nuts and nibbles keep most complaints at bay.

International Bar Level 14, 227 Victoria St, Kings Cross ☎ 9360 9080
At night the wall-to-wall city views capture showboats trawling the harbour under a black night sky studded with a million glittering city lights. Inside, a million bright, young, glittering things in black keep the bar staff busy with the blender. With funky lights and half-moon booths, it's a hip room-with-a-view (see review p 69).

Kuletos 157 King St, Newtown ☎ 9519 6369 Map 9 A4
Trompe-l'œil walls – fake marble and allusions to classical Greece. With nightly happy hours (6pm-7.30pm) it's popular with university students and Newtown's first-flat buyers who order Toblerones (Baileys, Kahlúa, honey) and red corvettes (Frangelico, grenadine, strawberries and raspberry cordial).

Laundro.Net.Cafe 113-115 Hall St, Bondi ☎ 9365 1211
By day you can wash your clothes and munch on an Elvis or Priscilla burger and email your 50 best friends! By night, this outback-theme bar hosts live acoustic rock, pop or dance/trance music and serves cocktails with names like 'screaming orgasm' and 'sheep shagging farm boy' (see review p 138).

Martini Bar Level 1, 99 Norton St, Leichhardt ☎ 9568 3344 Map 12 B2
The Martini Bar is on the top floor of the industrial-chic building that houses Leichhardt's Palace Cinema – so it's the perfect spot to dissect the movie you've just seen (on the bar stools, perched on the terrace high tables or settling into the deep felt couches). But this bar is also attracting an all-ages crowd throughout the week – many of whom, no doubt, come for the groove/funk/jazz ensemble who have a semi-permanent gig here.

Orbit Bar at the Summit Level 47, Australia Square, 264 George St, City ☎ 9247 9777 Map 2 A6
Yes, it is a revolving cocktail bar, and it is cool – straight out of 'Goldfingerrrr' (or Austin Powers, depending on what stage of the evening we're talking about). It serves up killer cocktails and the flakiest of cheese straws (see review p 38).

KINGS CROSS

INNER EAST

Map 5 E2

Entertainment:
karaoke from 10.30pm

Smoking throughout

Ju Ju
Japanese

☎ 9357 7100
Shop 320, Kingsgate Shopping Centre, Bayswater Rd

Fancy crooning like Elvis or the Spice Girls? Kick off your shoes (you'll have to before they'll let you in) and come on down to Ju Ju, a 'goody and delicious' – their description – fair dinkum izakaya*, where the karaoke fun begins after 10.30pm. In a wooden-lattice booth, snack on meltingly fresh tuna sashimi and avocado ($7), a yummy shabu-shabu beef salad ($7) that is a meal in itself, delectable chunks of juicy chicken in a miso sauce ($7.80), a pair of sweet, crispy pumpkin spring rolls ($5.80) and okonomiyaki* ($8) – a jumble of tastes and textures as assorted as the notes coming out of the singers' mouths. The waiters scurry around attentively, and our only gripe was having to wait so long for a table; we'll know to book next time. In short, a party place with fab nosh that won't break the bank. Now, pass us that mike.

starter: $3.80-$7
main: $9.80-$15
dessert: $4.50
Set menus $9.80-$24

cash only

Open: Sun, Tue-Thu 6.30pm-1am (last order 11.30pm), Fri & Sat 6.30pm-3am (last order 1.30am); reservations advisable (especially weekends); licensed, no BYO

POTTS POINT

Cicada
Modern Australian

☎ 9358 1255
29 Challis Avenue

Map 5 C2

Valet parking

Smoking after 10.30pm

Take an elegant Victorian terrace complete with leadlights and fabulous floor tiles, paint the high-ceilinged dining room a fetching raspberries-and-cream colour, glass in the balcony, serve up some great nosh and you've got one of Sydney's most pleasant restaurant experiences. Commence the Cicada experience with gently steamed zucchini flowers stuffed with herby ricotta ($15) and a tuna fillet ($16) seared on one side only. A Provençal style fish stew ($28) is a piquant symphony of top-quality poached seafood while lamb rib-eye ($26), tender and pink, is paired with earthy roasted mushrooms. Only a magnificent looking nectarine and peach schnapps soufflé ($11) failed to impress. The wine list boasts an extensive local and international selection although prices are a bit top-heavy. Service is attentive but not too rushed. The $25 set menu at lunch or early dinner, designed to attract locals who can't be bothered to cook, is a real bargain.

starter: $11-$17
main: $24-$28
dessert: $8-$11
Set menu $25

AE BC DC MC V

Open: Mon-Sat 6.30pm-10.30pm, Thurs-Sat noon-3pm; reservations advisable; licensed, no BYO

Mezzaluna
Modern Italian

☎ 9357 1988
123 Victoria St

Map 5 D2

Valet parking from 7pm ($20)

Smoking throughout

Terrace tables

Many of the dishes here are flamboyant fancy flights that take off from traditional bases. For example, a starter of double-baked blue swimmer crab and scallop soufflé with steamed vongole ($21.50). More grounded is an osso buco dish – huge and flavoursome veal shanks served with tender saffron risotto ($28.50). The home-made pastas are well worth trying – perhaps braised goat ravioli with sage butter ($18.50). It's all so rich and multi-layered that even a vegetable terrine has a powerful dose of gorgonzola cheese on top of the layer of ricotta. The desserts could afford to be simpler: the gelato/mud cake/Tia Maria soaked sponge range can seem like the redundant icing on the cake ($12). Perhaps it's because the lush environment gives the chef so much to live up to; the space looks like the Brady Bunch lounge-room given a mod makeover and the terrace has glittering city views.

starter: $17.50-$21.50
main: $23.50-$36.50
dessert: $12
Set menu $70 and $85

AE BC DC MC V

Open: Mon-Fri noon-3pm, Mon-Sun 6pm-11pm: reservations advisable; licensed, no BYO

POTTS POINT

Map 5 C2
Smoking in bar area only; no cigars or pipes

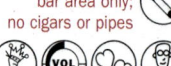

Paramount
Modern Australian

☎ 9358 1652
73 Macleay St

This is a place to make a grand entrance: through the heavy door and into the comfortably contoured space framed by wavy walls of translucent fibreglass. But any lingering concerns about the triumph of style over content evaporate with the first mouthful. Service is thoughtful too, with a shared starter of chilli salt squid, grilled eel and black ink noodles ($28) presented on two plates. Plump for the five-spice duck and shiitake mushroom pie with ginger glaze ($38), or a salad of Sichuan-spiced duck, seared scallops, rocket and lychee ($30). Both are remarkable for their depth of flavour, as is a delicate dessert of grilled peaches on a clotted cream tart ($12), strewn with bittersweet pistachio praline. There's a happy hubbub in the air – the sound of designer diners discussing the merits of dotcom shares, mingling with the unself-conscious merriment of groups of sweat-shirted out-of-towners.

starter: $28-$30
main: $38-$40
dessert: $12-$20
Tasting menus $100 or $150/person
AE BC DC MC V

Open: daily 6.30pm-11pm; reservations essential; licensed, no BYO

REDFERN

Map 7 E1
Wheelchair access
Smoking at bar only

Alio
Modern Italian

☎ 8394 9368
5 Baptist St

Dessert can be the most important part of a restaurant meal and Alio's warm chocolate tart with nutty highlights and biscuit crust base ($9) almost dispelled any of our doubts about what went before. Chef Ashley and his sister Tracey Hughes (co-owners) worked in London's River Cafe, and their ages (mid-20s) are in stark contrast to the majority of people dining amid the hot-pink feature walls. The prices are in the lower figures too, considering the up-to-the-minute, lovely jubbly, modern Italian meals. Take dishes like al dente papadelle with pungent wild mushrooms ($15), or a jew fish whose terrific taste belies the uninspiring khaki-coloured blob of thyme and lentil sauce that accompanies it ($25). Our only real disappointment was a char-grilled sirloin that comes well done rather than the asked-for rare ($24).

starter: $12-$15
main: $21-$25
dessert: $7-$10
AE BC DC MC V

Open: Tues-Sat noon-3pm, Mon-Sat 6pm-10pm; reservations essential; licensed, no BYO

REDFERN

Erciyes Restaurant
Turkish

☎ 9319 1309
409 Cleveland St

Map 7 E1

Entertainment: female belly dancer Fri 8.30pm, 9.30pm, and Sat 8.30pm, male belly dancer Sat 9.30pm

Smoking throughout

Named after the manager's home town in Turkey, this unpretentious restaurant has been running for 10 years and shows no sign of retiring despite a slightly split personality. Dine here on a weeknight and the room (decorated with Turkish travel posters and rustic handicrafts) is usually quiet and uncrowded. Come on a Friday or Saturday night and the place is heaving – belly dancing is the star attraction, and patrons often join in the fun. But either way you'll enjoy the food which is cheap and delicious. Bring a few people to sample a range of the dips and side servings ($4-$10). Don't miss the fried eggplant, covered in yoghurt with a paprika dusting, an addictive mixture of sweet and tangy. Grills and Turkish pizza are other menu staples. Spicy Turkish sausage gives the folded sucuklu pizza ($7) an appetising kick. Kofta ($8), grilled patties of fine, spiced lamb mince, is tender and flavourful. At these prices, you can afford to experience both sides of Erciyes' personality.

starter: $4-$10
main: $7-$15
dessert: $2-$7
Set menu $20-$25

Open: daily 11am-midnight; reservations advisable (a week in advance for Fri & Sat evenings); licensed & BYO (no corkage)

AE BC DC JCB MC V; Eftpos

Sushi Suma
Japanese

☎ 9698 8873
421 Cleveland St

Map 7 E1

Smoking throughout

The green *noren* (sign cloth) hanging outside the door is the only hint that behind this unassuming shopfront, near a late-night garage, lies a little piece of Japan. Here you'll find many a homesick expat – whole families of them – wolfing down some of the most authentic Japanese food in Sydney. At full tilt, which is almost always, the pace of food preparation and delivery is breathtaking. At the open kitchen four chefs whip up platters of chunky sushi ($12.90) and groaning baskets of tempura, while the waiters speedily distribute bowls of miso soup and delicate deep-fried tofu. You'll need to have been on a starvation diet for a week to polish off their set menus; easier on the constitution are the combination meals ($12.90). And if you find the place bursting at the seams, join the steady stream of locals grabbing a takeaway.

starter: $6.80-$8.80
main: $10.90-$14.90
dessert: $3.60
Set dinner $25.90

Open: Tues-Fri noon-2pm, Tues-Sun 6pm-10pm; reservations not accepted; BYO (corkage $1.20/person)

AE BC MC V

INNER EAST

SURRY HILLS

Map 7 B1

Billy Kwong
Chinese

☎ 9332 3300
3/355 Crown St

If your enthusiasm for Chinese food is tainted by childhood memories of orange batter-balled whatnots from the local takeaway, then Billy Kwong may set your palate towards culinary redemption. Chef Kylie Kwong has taken the refreshingly bold step of eschewing the mod Oz approach to authentic Chinese food. The result? Well, the jellyfish on the charcuterie plate ($12.50) may not be to your taste (though it does deserve an attempt), but the rest of the nibblies are just as they should be: delicately sweet, sticky, salty and sour. 'Myriam's sweet braised pork' ($20.50) – crunchy and salty on the outside, tender and pink on the inside – is complemented by a sweet and sour chilli garlic dip that has bite without fire. Decked out like teahouse meets Ikea, the overall effect is surprisingly warm and casual. But it's not a big space, so get there early or be prepared to wait.

starter: $10.50-$12.50
main: $18.50-$20.50
Banquet $40

AE BC MC V

Open: Mon-Sat 6pm-10pm; reservations not accepted; BYO (corkage $3/bottle)

Map 7 C1

Nonsmoking tables available

Balcony tables

Clock Hotel
Modern Australian

☎ 9331 5333
470 Crown St

The Clock Hotel's renovation symbolises the ongoing gentrification of Surry Hills. The modern downstairs bar is light, buzzing and a great place to enjoy a drink while you wait for a table – preferably on the wrap-around balcony – in the appealingly decorated restaurant upstairs (and you may well have to wait). Vegetarians will fare best with starters, such as the crispy deep fried zucchini flowers filled with ricotta and pinenuts ($13.50) well teamed with a pesto sauce, or the rich gnocchi with gorgonzola and baby spinach ($14). From the mains, the Asian spiced pork ($21) is succulent and tender, served on a bed of greens and shiitake mushrooms, while the flesh flakes perfectly off twice-cooked duck ($22) mingling with a crunchy salad of rocket and lentils. Classic desserts, like sherry trifle ($9.50), are revisited with modern touches such as amaretto biscotti and muscatels, but no jelly.

starter: $10-$14.50
main: $14-$23.50
dessert: $9-$10

AE BC DC MC V

Open: Mon-Sat noon-11pm, Sun noon-9pm; reservations accepted (recommended weekends); licensed, no BYO

SURRY HILLS

Cossie's Cafe-Restaurant
Modern Australian

☎ 9699 8482
638a Crown St

Unlike other Crown St stalwarts, there's nothing pretentious about Cossie's, and that's why we like it so much. The staff are friendly, the décor plain wooden, the food delicious and always served in generous portions. A huge blackboard menu dominates one wall, with a tempting range of standard dishes, such as ceasar salad, assorted pastas and a daily risotto. You really can't go wrong with the excellent value two or three course dinner deals at $21 and $25. We're told that the homemade pumpkin ravioli are "big ones" and are not disappointed by the mini-omelette patties of pasta teamed with zesty tomato sauce and perfectly cooked spinach. A main of pan-fried bream rests on mash that's too lumpy for our tastes – but that's small quibbling. This is comfort food like only your mum makes. So, go on, spoil yourself with desserts such as apple and cherry crumble and a decadent, huge helping of sticky date cake.

Open: daily 8.30am-11pm (breakfast: all day); reservations accepted; BYO (no corkage)

Map 7 E1

Smoking throughout

Pavement tables

starter: $8.50
main: $12.80-$14.50
 (lunch $8-$9)
dessert: $6.50
 (lunch $4.50)
Set menu $21 or $25

AE BC MC V

fuel
Modern Australian

☎ 9383 9388
476-488 Crown St

How many restaurants have an Aston Martin for sale at one end and packets of white truffle risotto at the other? Even with three BMWs parked outside, the old school barber shop and supermarket across the road couldn't look less impressed. Surprisingly, the prices are almost within reach of Joan Average – fuel is the lower case, ever-so-slightly lower class restaurant to the upper case stable mate MG Garage. But it's often every bit as good. A rabbit pie ($22) embodies all the best things about traditional English pie: slightly peppery vegetables, hearty meat and a perfectly browned flaky top. A tagliatelle dish with squid takes some getting to know before you can appreciate the subtle lemon, chive, parsley flavourings ($16). A modest-looking mango meringue ($9), meanwhile, is a delightful puff on the outside and just chewy enough on the inside. With that Aston sparkling under movie set lights, you'll probably fantasize about a James Bond-style departure.

Open: Mon-Fri noon-3pm, Sat & Sun 8am-3pm, Mon-Sat 6.30pm-10pm, Sun 6.30pm-9.30pm (breakfast: Sat & Sun 8am-noon, brunch: noon-3pm); reservations not accepted; licensed, no BYO

Map 7 C1

Valet parking at MG Garage next door

No smoking inside

Pavement tables

starter: $10-$16
main: $21-$24
dessert: $9

AE BC DC MC V

INNER EAST

Crown St, Surry Hills

Is there any other street in the world where pint-sized pets prance out of dog grooming shops sporting purple Cher-helmets and tiger spots, while just a few doors along, one of the city's spiffiest restaurants sports leather and chrome fixtures and an MG on the menu (just $45,000)? Will Surry Hills be the next Soho? It *is* one of the most talked about suburbs in one of the world's most talked about cities, and strolling along Crown Street is like reading a history of the suburb's erratic evolution. At one end you'll find a 24-hour gaming den, at the other a theme cafe. In between there's an array of unpretentious Asian eateries, a video store that stocks all the latest epic Bollywood flicks and a person selling 'Alaskan iced fruit tisane' and 'Gippsland shadows of blue' cheese. Renovations continue unabated, thanks in part to the freak hailstorm of '99 that left dozens of lacy terrace houses sporting tarpaulins on their battered roofs. But gentrification is by no means complete. Colourful graffiti marks many a wall, artists' studios (most notably the Brett Whiteley Gallery) and rag traders hide amid the warehouses and low-rise offices. Decades ago some batty local residents set about beautifying McElhone Place. Now it and the surrounding lanes are a peaceful cat haven lined with planter boxes and pot plants backing onto the maddening traffic of South Dowling Street.

SURRY HILLS

La Persia
Iranian

☎ 9698 4355
545 Crown St

Map 7 E1

Nonsmoking tables available

Courtyard and balcony tables

At La Persia, a sky-blue painted terrace tucked in next to the Surry Hills post office, the exotic menu reads like an incitement to indulgence. The staff are happy to suggest the best ways to be led astray, and at these low prices, we were only too willing to follow. The noon-o-panir-o-sabzi ($5.90), a picnic of pitta bread eaten with garnishes of fetta, fresh herbs and walnuts, is a refreshing accompaniment to the aash ($5.90) a thick soup of puréed beans, spinach and noodles, obligingly split into two small bowls to share. The fesenjune ($12.50), meat balls on fluffy rice in a mouthwatering and uniquely different pomegranate, walnut and plum sauce, tastes sensational. Less of a blast was the abgusht ($12.50) – a large lamb shank, in a thin stew with chickpeas and potatos. For a perfect ending go for the duo of delicate rosewater icecream and sorbet ($6.90) washed down with the zesty sundried lime tea ($2.50).

starter: $2-$5.90
main: $9.50-$13.50
dessert: $5.90-$6.90
Banquets $20-$25,
 combination platter $29

Open: Mon-Thu 6pm-10pm, Fri & Sat 6pm-11pm; reservations advisable (Fri & Sat); licensed & BYO (corkage $1.50/person)

AE BC DC MC V; Eftpos

Longrain
Thai

☎ 9280 2888
85 Commonwealth St

Map 6 C1

Wheelchair access

Smoking at bar only

On a balmy summer night everyone's dressed in black: this is Sydney at its most New York. Two communal steel tables run the length of this warehouse conversion, and those designer diners yell to their chums across the tables' expansive girths. Perched on a black bar stool, you'll have a view of the black-clad staff pounding what you imagine is Thai curry paste, but what turns out to be lime for caipiroskas (vodka/ice/sugar). Try one with a cute baby-sized entrée of fresh green betel leaves topped with chicken and Thai spices ($3). A $45 mud crab is Mr Popularity: endless plates of these sizable critters, still in their red armour, march out of the kitchen. Phat thai ($14) and a special of scallops with roe and strips of greens ($30) arrive somewhat haphazardly, while a futuristic-looking dessert plate (coconut curls, hairy swirls of a rambutan and lemon sorbet, $20) will happily change your mind about Asian sweets.

starter: $3
main: $14-$45
dessert: $10-$20
Set menu for banquet room
 (lunch $35 or $45,
 dinner $55 or $65)

Open: Tues-Fri noon-3pm, Tues-Sun 6pm-11pm; reservations accepted (lunch & banquet room only); licensed, no BYO

AE BC DC MC V

SURRY HILLS

Map 7 B1

Smoking in the bar after 10.30pm

Marque
Modern French

☎ 9332 2225
355 Crown St

Forgoing the petrolhead gimmicks of that other Crown St fine dining contender, Marque wins with the less is more approach. An intimate, moodily lit dining space is enlarged by a wall long mirror, and the half-height curtains cause passersby to wonder just what lies beyond. The dishes, silver served by impeccably polite staff, are not too fussy, intensely flavoursome, and often surprising – like the whole beetroot tart ($14) in a creamy horseradish sauce, with the looks of a pork pie, but tasting much, much better. Also the perfectly cooked barramundi fillet with poached oysters ($36), doused in a clear gazpacho, sees the chef experimenting successfully at the Mediterranean limits of French cuisine. Even the boudin blanc ($28) is re-worked as a disc of chicken and pork, rather than the traditional long white sausage. The quivering, silky smooth blancmange banished thoughts of school meals forever, while the delicious mini tarte tatin with vanilla ice cream evoked autumn in Paris.

starter: $14-$20
main: $28-$38
dessert: $12
Degustation $110
AE BC DC MC V

Open: Mon-Sat 6.30pm-10.30pm; reservations advisable (essential weekends); licensed & BYO (corkage $10/bottle)

Map 7 D1

Matsuri
Japanese

☎ 9690 1336
618 Crown Street

Since we last visited, Matsuri has knocked down the wall that separated its smoking section, so you can now enjoy their fabulous sushi and sashimi in a more spacious and smoke free environment. Service is a bit snappier, too, although Matsuri's popularity still means that you should book, especially if you want the stupendous sushi/sashimi platters, (made for two but big enough to feed a whole party). One of the entree specials, teriyaki swordfish ($8) – three meaty, marinated fillets draped languidly over a mound of crisp, cooked beansprouts and slivers of cucumber – is so classy it deserves to be a main course. Everything else remains the same – the sushi still beautifully displayed, the cuts of fish excellent and vegetarian options, such as the sweet omelette and avocado topped nigiri-zushi, available. The special lunch menus, including a range of teriyaki and tempura dishes from $7.50, remain cracking value, too.

starter: $5-$8.50
main: $12.50-$25
dessert: $3-$4.50
sushi & sashimi boats $32-$43
AE BC DC MC V

Open: Mon-Fri noon-2.30pm, Mon-Sat 6pm-11pm (last order 10pm); reservations advisable (essential at weekends); licensed & BYO wine only (corkage $1.50/person)

SURRY HILLS

Maya Sweets Centre
Indian

☎ 9699 8663
468-470 Cleveland St

Map 7 E1

The strip lights, bare floors and bench seats in this basic vegetarian cafe are soon forgotten when you realise it's virtually impossible to spend more than $10 on a meal. During the week, daily specials give you the chance to try earthy, home-style Indian dishes, such as Punjabi mustard greens and spinach, served with pan-fried corn bread and white butter ($7). Lovers of dosas, those lacy, crispy crepes made from rice and mung-bean flour, should look no further than the masala dosa ($6.50). Filled with potatoes and cashews flavoured with onion, curry leaves and mustard seeds, this comes with a dish of fresh coconut chutney and a bowl of fiery sambar on the side. And, if you can't manage a bowl of sticky gulab jamun or a few pistachio barfis* after all that, make like the steady stream of locals and take a selection home for later.

Open: daily 10am-10.30pm; reservations not accepted; BYO (no corkage)

starter: $2-$3.50
main: $5.20-$9
dessert: $1-$3
South Indian or Punjabi thali
 (3 curries and dessert, $9)

BC MC V

MG Garage
Modern Australian/
Mediterranean

☎ 9383 9383
490 Crown St

Map 7 C1

Valet parking $15

Wheelchair access

Smoking tables available for lunch, no smoking at dinner

We must have been the only ones to arrive courtesy of State Rail for our dinner at MG Garage – a showroom of sexy cars and jazzy food. The interior is as plush as the inside of a Porsche and it's filled with those from Sydney's fast tracks. Even the chocolate cake is so rich it comes with a 24-carot gold leaf ($10). The menu features the familiar – oysters, lobster, sweet breads – and the far-from-familiar – sea urchin sauce for the baked barramundi ($36), liver faggots (bundles) and chickweed salad. The only disappointing thing about the clay-baked guinea fowl ($62 for two) was that it wasn't broken open at the table: pink, tender flesh is served on plain old barley made beautiful with currants and morel mushrooms. Just as at more conventional car yards, staff are quick to swoop, but here they only have your best interests in mind. And don't leave that marshmallow-like nougat with toasted hazelnut which comes with your coffee – eat it.

Open: Mon-Fri noon-2pm, Mon-Sat 6.30pm-10pm; reservations essential; licensed, no BYO

starter: $19-$26
main: $34-$38
dessert: $10-$15

AE BC DC MC V

The Joy of Food

When stories started filtering through that a French chef was slipping Viagra into his soup, we knew the era of gastro-porn had reached its apotheosis. These days it's not enough to be a great chef, you have to be a naked chef, performing your moves from open-plan kitchens in front of salivating diners.

Dinner Dates

Chris Manfield's 'The Chef Who Shagged Me' dinner
At its November 1999 debut, guests in flares, blue eye-shadow and white lipstick (and that's just the boys) were served angels on horseback, chicken kiev and peach melba. It's set to be an annual event (see Paramount review p 74).

Tetsuya's 'St Valentine's Day for Singles'
Tetsuya Wakuda, arguably Sydney's most famous chef, is so occupied by his passion for food at his eponymously named restaurant that we wonder when he finds the time for a love life. Sydney singles rushed to pay $200/head for his Valentine's Day degustation dinner in 2000 (see Tetsuya's review p 38).

Tony Bilson's 'Menu Erotic'
On St Valentine's 2000 the Ampersand menu got stuck into food full of pheromones (chemicals said to stimulate sexual activity); truffles, sea urchins, oysters and chocolate praline were all on the menu.

Sydney's Sexiest Staff

If you see a bevy of beautiful boys in angelic white eating dinner at the odd hour of 5pm on Campbell Pde, you've spotted the staff of Hugo's. As gorgeous as Bondi Beach ... as are most of the celebrity diners.
Hugo's 70 Campbell Pde, Bondi ☎ 9300 0900 Map 14 B4

Sydney's Sauciest Dish

Prasit's 'yum condom' salad (tiger prawns, lime juice, chilli and latex-like sheets of rice paper) has to be one of the most stylish ways to drop an innuendo to your dinner date. If that doesn't work, Prasit's suggestive staff will inject a bit of spice into your night (see Prasit's Northside on Crown review p 83).

Deli Delectables (from erotica to exotica)

The sweets display at jones the grocer reminds us of those shops that sell bliss bombs made of fruit, massage bars masquerading as chocolate and other edible love-aids. At jones you can collect a set of karma sutra chocolates ($6 for a six-pack) and wrap your lips around red chocolates shaped like Salvador Dali's kisses. As your relationship develops, you can pick up 'I love you' chocolates, Turkish delight and rocky roads. For juices ($4.90), try a 'citrus smack', or a 'low cut berry bikini'.
jones the grocer 36 Campbell Pde, Bondi ☎ 9130 1100 Map 14 C4
(branch also at 68 Moncur St, Woollahra)

Best Food to Break Up With

Thai Jaroen means 'good fortune'. If you're hoping for better luck in love next time around, break up here and you can blame the fiery food for any tears that show up on the night.
Thai Jaroen 234 King St, Newtown ☎ 9519 4716 Map 9 B3

SURRY HILLS

The Nepalese Kitchen
Nepalese

☎ 9319 4264
481 Crown St

Map 7 D1

Smoking throughout

Courtyard seats

This Crown St gem oozes class, from the elegantly rustic furniture and traditional artifacts decorating the walls, to the authentic and wide-ranging menu of Nepalese dishes. It's almost always packed (and can get quite loud), but service remains charming and unflustered. The food is milder and less greasy than that of Nepal's subcontinental neighbours, and is jazzed up with achars (spicy relishes), including soothing ginger-flavoured tomato or fiery red chillies with garlic. From the starters we wolfed down the plump chicken dumplings ($6) and enjoyed the glistening char-grilled baby eggplant ($5.50). The nine-bean curry ($8) is a main for hardcore veggies; it was upstaged by the masu ko-pulau ($11.50), an exotic rice, nut and currant mix topped with a chunky lamb curry. Desserts include rice or semolina puddings flavoured with raisins, coconut and orange peel – all pleasant diversions on this trek through the heights of Himalayan cuisine.

starter: $4.50-$6
main: $8-$12
dessert: $4.50
Banquets $20 or $22
AE BC DC MC V; Eftpos

Open: daily 6pm-11pm (last order Sun-Thurs 10pm); reservations essential; BYO (corkage $1/person)

Prasit's Northside on Crown
Thai

☎ 9319 0748
413 Crown St

Map 7 C1

Smoking after 10pm

Prasit's walls are a princely purple and its Thai cuisine is fit for a king. Appropriately, a crown of roast lamb cutlets is the centrepiece of a massaman curry ($25). A creamier, subtler version of your local takeaway's massaman, this dish is marred only by too many fatty pieces in the lamb. Other rich offerings include 'girlfriend's stuffed swimmer crab' ($15.50) – the meat is steamed, minced and deep-fried before the shell's top is replaced. Then there's crayfish, lobster, quail, spatchcock. Grab a Singha beer or two from the Clock Hotel just over the road and seat yourself by the upstairs concertina windows for a view of the street life and grassy park below. The view inside is good too: that waiter with the arched eyebrows looks like he's just been reading the menu's purple prose. *Also at Prasit's Northside Takeaway at 395 Crown St,* ☎ *9332 1792, and 77 Mount St, North Sydney,* ☎ *9957 2271.*

starter: $14.50-$18.50
main: $15.50-$25.50
dessert: $10
Set menu $45
AE BC MC V

Open: Thurs & Fri noon-3pm, Mon-Sat 6pm-10pm; reservations essential; BYO (corkage $2/person)

SURRY HILLS

Map 7 D1

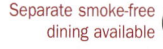

Separate smoke-free dining available

Tabou
French

☎ 9319 5682
527 Crown St

If you've got the formula right, why change it? Tabou's frilly curtains, white paper over tablecloths, Gallic chanson music and down-the-line brasserie food delivered with a jaunty 'bon appetit' are French to the tricolour core. A loyal following packs the place out every weekend, but the waiters moving smartly between the cramped tables retain their cool delivering homemade goodies, such as the meltingly divine pâtés and chunky andouillette sausage ($20). Swoon over the soft lamb, steeped in thyme jus and given a garlic kick with aubergine caviar ($24), but the duck confit ($22) we found a trifle dry. You'll have no complaints, however, over the candied lavender pear ($8), its sweetness cut by the tart yoghurt ice cream. So what has changed, since we last visited? Well, there's a bar upstairs, but keep it quiet otherwise it'll get as busy as the small slice of Paris below.

starter: $10-$15
main: $16-$24
dessert: $8
Set menu $25 or $30
AE BC DC MC V

Open: Mon-Fri noon-3pm, daily 6pm-1am (supper menu 10.30pm-1am); reservations essential; licensed, no BYO

Map 6 B1

Smoking throughout

Uchi Lounge
Japanese

☎ 9261 3524
15 Brisbane St

Since our last visit, Uchi Lounge's restaurant has moved upstairs into the former gallery space, while downstairs is now a bar area with comfy chairs to, well, lounge around in. The atmosphere is more sophisticated – the gauze room dividers/lights are a particularly stylish touch. Thankfully, the cooking remains as refreshingly different and appealing as before. The salty-sweet grilled eggplant with miso and parmesan ($10) is a nod to mukokuseki (no-nationality cuisine), a style of food found at the trendiest of Japan's izakaya. The char-grilled baby octopus in a salad of avocado and translucent white crunchy fungus ($7) has an intriguing mix of textures, and there is zen simplicity in teriyaki grilled eel and salmon on snow pea sprouts ($14). Uchi's modest range of desserts, including white chocolate cheesecake and three berry tart ($6), is a huge improvement on the depressing brevity and predictability of those available at rival establishments.

starter: $2-$8
main: $10-$14
dessert: $6
AE BC MC V

Open: Mon-Sat 6pm-10.30pm; no reservations; licensed & BYO (corkage $2/person)

WOOLLOOMOOLOO

Otto Ristorante Italiano
Italian

☎ 9368 7488
8 The Wharf,
6 Cowper Wharf Road

The in-situ wool-bale elevators at the Woolloomooloo finger wharf were used to load ships in the early 1900s; now the only boats are yachts and speedsters owned by residents in the new wharf apartments. And while the spot welcomed European migrants in the 1950s, now they have taken over the restaurants – and the meals are as brilliant as the deck-side sunshine. Try twisting your tongue around Otto's 'salad of quail saltimbocca with grilled pear and treviso radicchio' ($19), or 'swordfish with anchovies, green beans and eggplant in saor' ($26). Antipasto ($17) comes in artful, flavourful mouthfuls and with an espresso cup of creamy asparagus soup. A dish of upright pasta cylinders filled with ricotta and pumpkin and served on a burnt sage butter puddle ($17/$22) is a multi-flavoured sensation. Desserts ($15) of gelato, cassata, espresso and liqueurs included a very good, modern take on rice pudding: a stunning blueberry risotto.

Open: Tues-Sat noon-midnight, Sun noon-10pm; reservations necessary; licensed, no BYO

Map 5 C1

Wheelchair access

Smoking at bar and outside only

Tables on wharf boardwalk

starter: $16-$26
main: $22-$33
dessert: $15
Set menu $55-$75

AE BC DC MC V

Shimbashi Soba on the Sea
Japanese

☎ 9357 7763
6 The Wharf,
Cowper Wharf Road

You'd be hard-pressed to find better soba and udon noodles in Sydney than those served here, prepared by a highly experienced Japanese soba chef. Already this new branch (the original outlet is in Neutral Bay) is attracting a steady stream of Japanese tourists and those in search of good-value dining on this glitzy strip of wharf. Shades of jade, charcoal and dark wood make for a harmonious interior and create a feeling of calm, enhanced by the lapping waters and bobbing boats just beyond the board walk. Salty, grainy soba chips ($3) make a fine accompaniment to an Asahi beer. Order chilled tofu ($6), squares of chalky-fresh tofu, variously topped with grated ginger, spring onions and bonito shavings – very refreshing on a steamy Sydney day. A bowl of tempura udon ($16) pairs creamy-white, deliciously fat noodles swimming in a savoury broth with a platter of crispy tempura of fish, prawn, pumpkin, capsicum and mushroom.

Open: Tues-Sat noon-2.30pm, 6pm-10pm; reservations advisable (essential Fri & Sat); licensed, no BYO

Map 5 C1

Non-smoking tables available

Terrace tables

starter: $3-$18
main: $9-$17
dessert: $4-$6
Set lunch $16 (Tues-Fri only)

AE BC DC JCB MC V

Back for More

Betty's Soup Kitchen
84 Oxford St, Darlinghurst ☎ 9360 9698 Map 6 C2
It's Darlinghurst's giant communal kitchen for locals suffering from fancy food fatigue: fish fingers, eight varieties of soup (including potato, lentil, carrot and ginger, and gazpacho), lamb stew, bangers and mash, and bread and butter pudding. The dollar prices for most items can be counted on one-and-a-bit hands.

Fez
247 Victoria St, Darlinghurst ☎ 9360 9581 Map 6 C4
Affordable mod Oz/Mediterranean/North African food in a funky modern Arabian-looking room. Warm, sweet apple and cinnamon Turkish tea and Moroccan mint tea are sipped into the late evening hours.

✱ *Write to us: Where do you go to eat time and time again? Is it fabulous food, divine décor, great service, or a place to do business that brings you back? Write or email us (see p 11 for details) and the best suggestions will receive the next edition free.*

Annandale

Ashfield

Balmain

INNER WEST

Camperdown

Chippendale

Drummoyne

Dulwich Hill

Enmore

Erskineville

Glebe

Haberfield

Leichhardt

Marrickville

Newtown

Petersham

Rozelle

Map 8 - Inner West

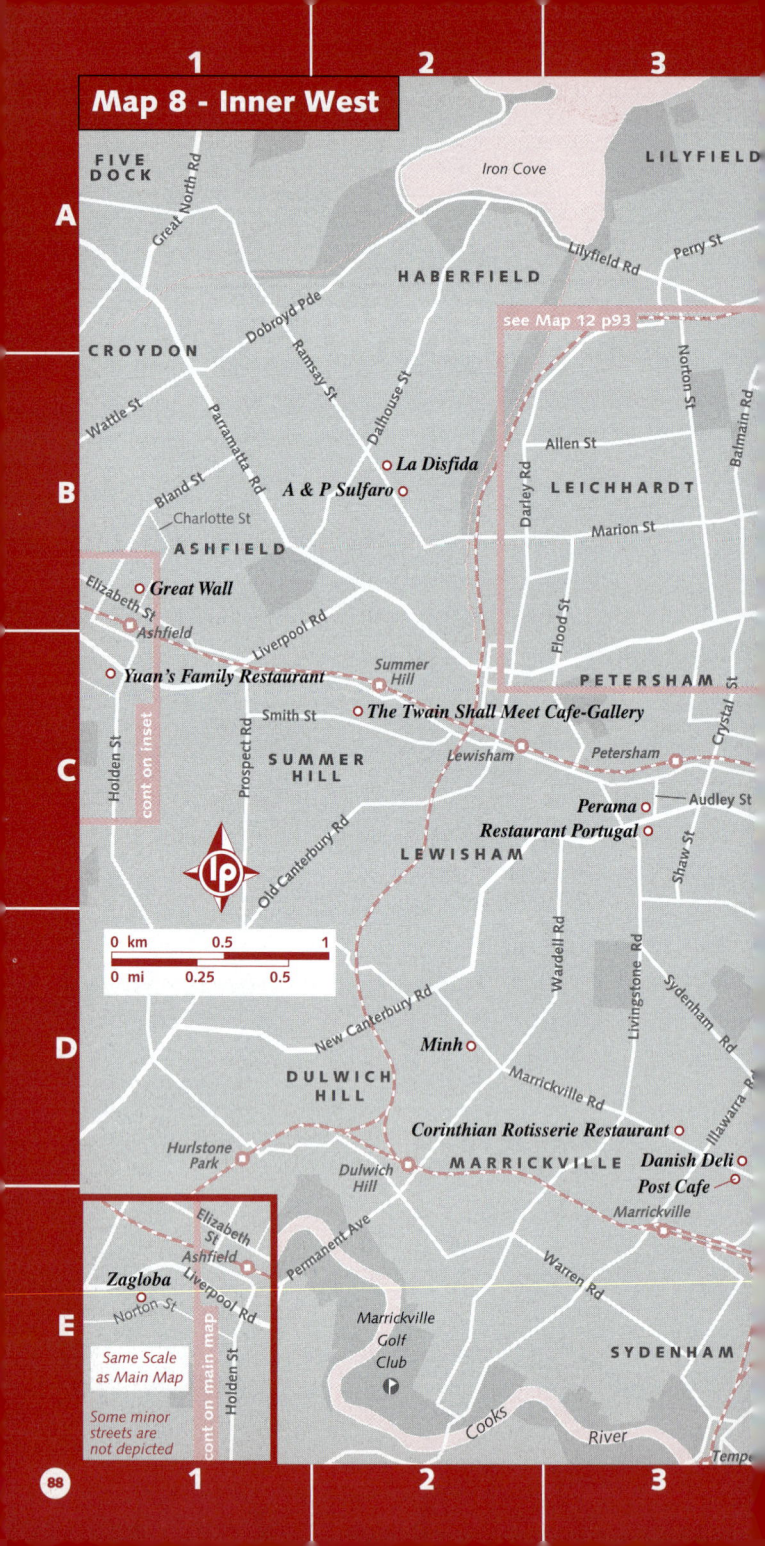

Map Locations

A (grid 4-6):
- ROZELLE
- PYRMONT
- Balmain Rd, Brenan St, Harris St, Pyrmont St
- Sydney Maritime Museum Restoration Site
- Rozelle Bay, Glebe Point, Blackwattle Bay
- Anzac Bridge
- Fish Market Sushi Bar
- The Boathouse on Blackwattle Bay
- see Map 11 p92
- cont on Map 2 pp18&19

B (grid 4-6):
- ANNANDALE
- GLEBE
- ULTIMO
- Moore St, Catherine St, Booth St, Young St, Johnston St, Nelson St, Wigram Rd, Glebe Point Rd, Ferry Rd, St Johns Rd, Wattie St
- Harold Park Raceway
- Bridge Rd
- Valhalla
- Hoyts
- see Map 10 p91

C (grid 4-6):
- STANMORE
- CAMPERDOWN
- DARLINGTON
- EVELEIGH
- Salisbury Rd, Parramatta Rd, Missenden Rd, Kingston Rd, Liberty St, Carillon Ave, King St, Wilson St, Abercrombie St, City Rd, Henderson Rd
- Stanmore, Trafalgar St
- side-on café
- Sydney University
- The Rose Hotel
- Seymour Theatre Centre
- Macdonaldtown
- see Map 9 pp90&91

D (grid 4-6):
- ENMORE
- NEWTOWN
- ERSKINVILLE
- Addison Rd, Enmore Rd, Edinburgh Rd, Edgeware Rd, King St, Sydney Park Rd, Mitchell Rd, McEvoy St, Huntly St
- Newtown, Erskineville, St Peters
- Sydney Park

E (grid 4-6):
- ST. PETERS
- ALEXANDRIA
- Bay Tinh
- Victoria Rd, Unwins Bridge Rd, Princes Hwy, Canal Rd, Burrows Rd, Alexandra Canal, Euston Rd, Bourke Rd, O'Riordan St, Gardeners Rd, Coward St
- Sydenham
- SRA Cooks River Rail Freight Terminal

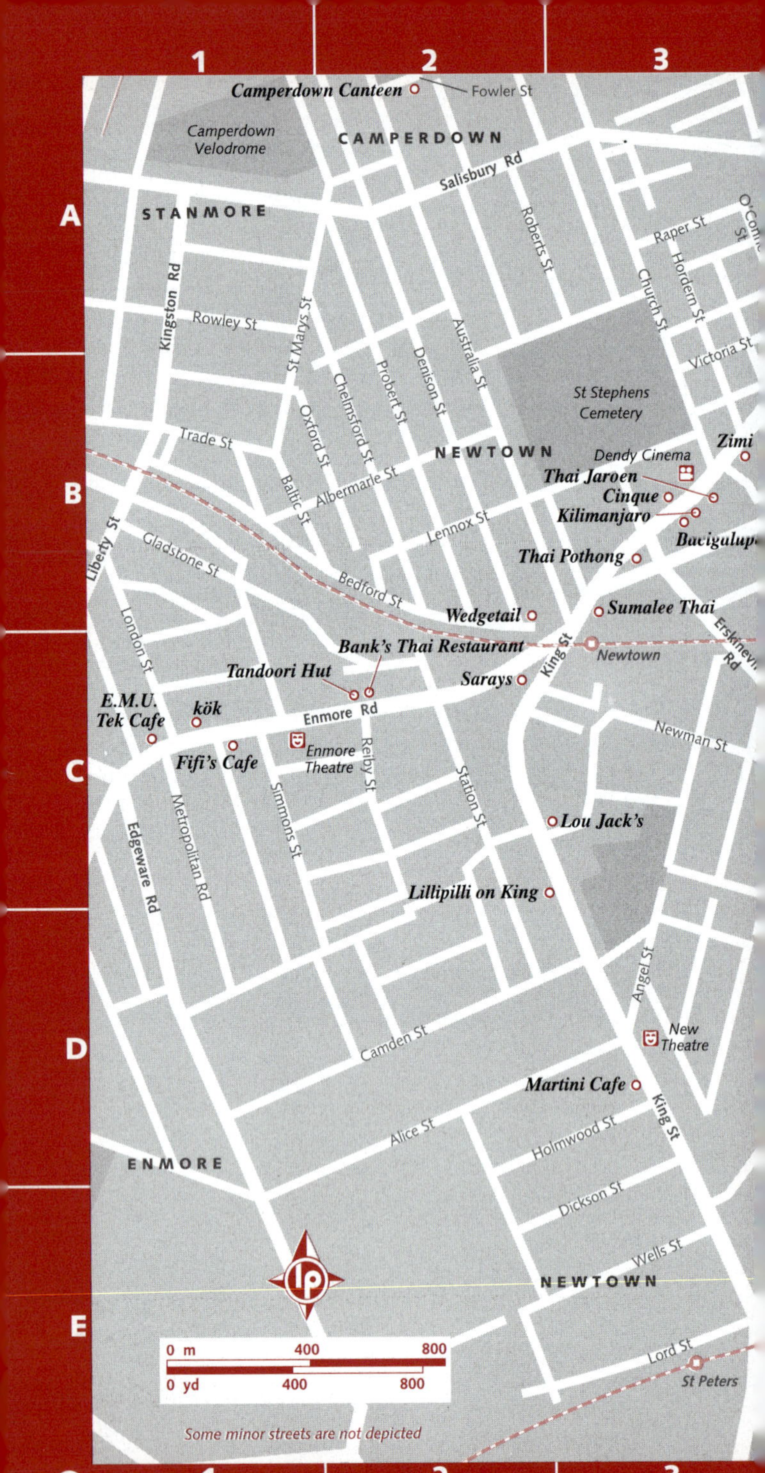
Camperdown Canteen
Fowler St
Camperdown Velodrome
CAMPERDOWN
Salisbury Rd
STANMORE
Roberts St
Raper St
O'Connell St
Hordern St
Church St
Kingston Rd
Rowley St
St Marys St
Australia St
Denison St
Probert St
Chelmsford St
Oxford St
Victoria St
St Stephens Cemetery
Trade St
NEWTOWN
Dendy Cinema
Zimi
Thai Jaroen
Cinque
Kilimanjaro
Baltic St
Albermarle St
Lennox St
Bacigalupo
Liberty St
Gladstone St
Bedford St
Thai Pothong
Wedgetail
Sumalee Thai
Erskineville Rd
Bank's Thai Restaurant
King St
Newtown
London St
Tandoori Hut
Sarays
E.M.U. Tek Cafe
kök
Enmore Rd
Newman St
Fifi's Cafe
Enmore Theatre
Reiby St
Station St
Simmons St
Metropolitan Rd
Edgeware Rd
Lou Jack's
Lillipilli on King
Angel St
Camden St
New Theatre
Martini Cafe
King St
Holmwood St
Alice St
ENMORE
Dickson St
Wells St
NEWTOWN
0 m 400 800
0 yd 400 800
Lord St
St Peters
Some minor streets are not depicted

Map 9 - Newtown & Enmore

Map 10 - Glebe

Map 11 - Balmain & Rozelle

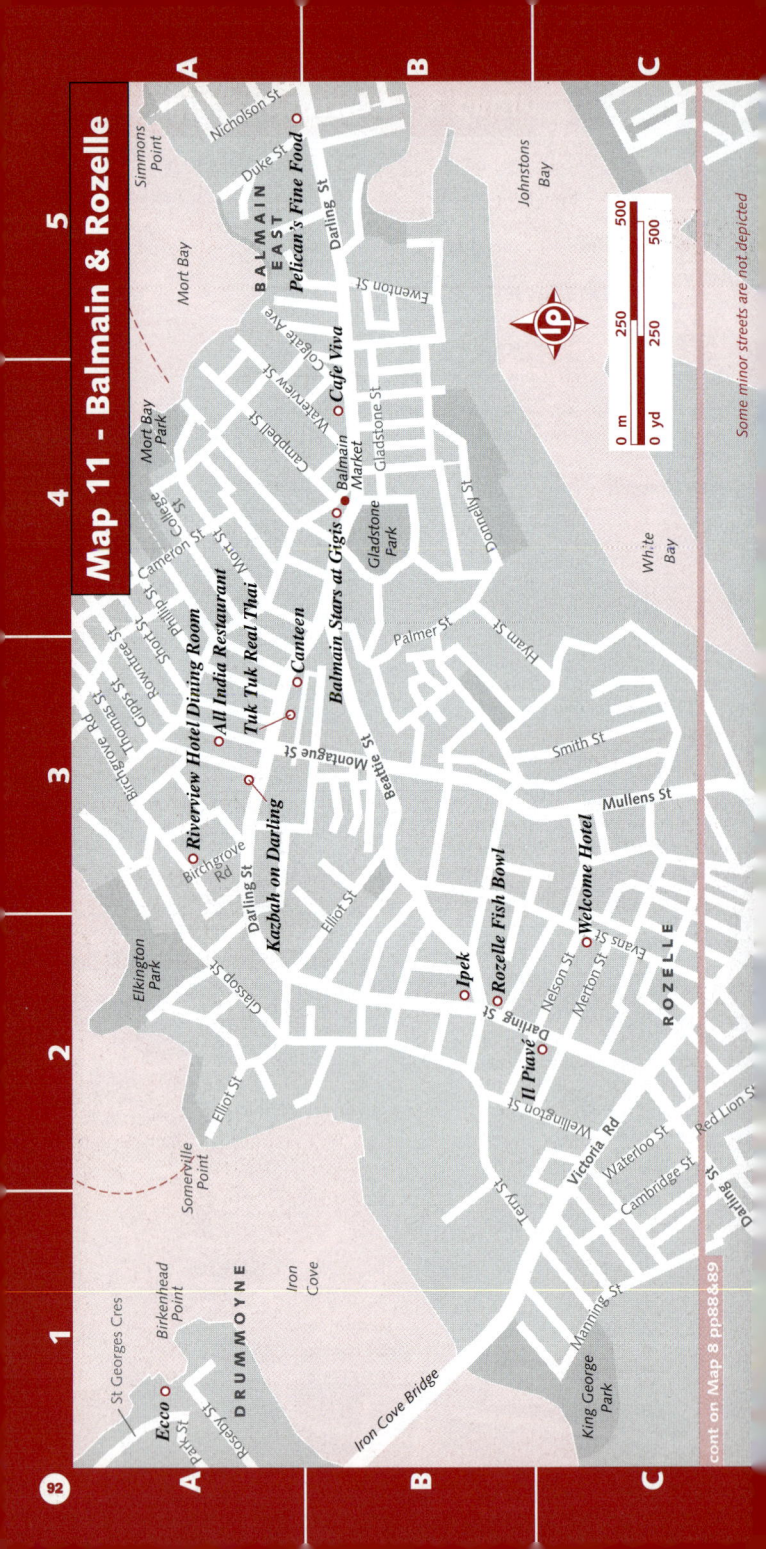

- Ecco
- Pelican's Fine Food
- Café Viva
- Riverview Hotel Dining Room
- All India Restaurant
- Tuk Tuk Real Thai
- Canteen
- Balmain Stars at Gigis
- Kazbah on Darling
- Ipek
- Rozelle Fish Bowl
- Welcome Hotel
- Il Piavé

Some minor streets are not depicted

cont on Map 8 pp88&89

Map 12 - Leichhardt

LEICHHARDT

- Grappa
- Bar Italia
- Elio
- Uno 53
- Portofino
- Café Barzu
- Frattini
- La Crimerai
- Palace
- Martini & Martini Bar
- Dante
- Surjit's Indian Restaurant
- Caffe Sport
- Rick Damelian Centre
- Globe

PETERSHAM
- Camo's on the Park

Streets: Darley Rd, Flood St, Allen St, Macauley St, Carlisle St, Marlborough St, Foster St, Short St, Norton St, Wetherill St, Balmain Rd, Moore St, Styles St, Marion St, Lords Rd, Tebbutt St, Renwick St, Railway St, Catherine St, Young St, Annandale St, Parramatta Rd

0 m 200 400
0 yd 200 400

Some minor streets are not depicted

BEST

- **The Boathouse on Blackwattle Bay**
  Fabulous seafood on the port side

- **Grappa**
  Italian favourites with innovative style

- **Il Piavé**
  Charming service and antipasto to remember

- **Minh**
  Vietnamese stayer with a warm welcome

- **Safari**
  Happy Indonesian will have you smiling

- **Tanjore**
  Culinary tour of India

Inner West

The old boat shed at Glebe's Blackwattle Bay is being razed to clear the way for another batch of little inner city apartments with big harbour views. While the advertising blurbs might euphemistically dub these pads artists' studios, the old boat shed was, until recently, home to *real* artists and a kooky cafe. Before that it was just one spot on a long stretch of docklands, wool stores and furious ferry activity that dominated Glebe, Balmain and Birchgrove throughout the early- to mid-1900s. This mini-history says much about the changing face of the inner west. At the beginning of the 20th century, beer and trouble brewed in pubs on practically every corner of these harbourside suburbs. Some of the bloodiest battles between the Unemployed Workers Movement and police were fought here with iron bars and guns during the depression years, when slum landlords tried to clear their property of poverty-stricken tenants. In the 1970s, 'green bans' saved parks and whole suburbs from over-development, while women's libbers set up the first refuges to help Sydney's battered women and children. Today the narrow leafy streets and Victorian terraces in the suburbs surrounding Sydney University are routinely described as 'renovators' dreams'. Chocolate factories are being turned into chic flats that are gobbled up by investors and first-apartment buyers. The always more middle-class areas of Strathfield and Summer Hill, meanwhile, are prized for their Federation homes. But the inner west has firmly retained its multicultural colours – with a visible Portuguese presence in Petersham, the Chinese cafes and restaurants of Ashfield and the African, Thai and Polynesian quarters of Newtown. Leichhardt has even combined the inner-city apartment boom with a piazza theme in the new 'Italian Forum'.

ANNANDALE

Surjit's Indian Restaurant
Indian

☎ 9569 8884, 9564 6600
215 Parramatta Rd

Map 12 B3

Smoking throughout

Indian batsman and national hero Sachin Tendulkar raves about Surjit's 'jumbo' tandoori prawns ($8.90). And early on a hot Monday night, soon after his team have flown the country, there's still a scattering of diners and a steady stream of takeaway orders for the big shrimp. This place's appeal can't be the function room décor (pink chairs, white fan serviettes). Perhaps it's the quirky menu? It describes a mutton dish ($10.90) as inspired by the 'dancing girl that almost stole the Moghul throne', delivers a super-condensed history of Indian cooking and pledges 'our motive is to satisfy you'. We were fairly bowled over by Sachin's prawns – peppery-hot and served with smooth raita. Rich, slightly oily roti breads ($2) are served straight from the glass-walled tandoor oven, but the samosas ($4.90) won't keep you awake at night pining for their pedestrian pastry. A giant white board provides the entertainment: try deciphering which Indian player's signature goes with which scrawl.

starter: $4.90-$13.90
main: $8.50-$14.90
dessert: $4.90

AE BC DC MC V

Open: daily 5.30pm-11pm; reservations accepted (advisable weekends); licensed & BYO (no corkage)

ASHFIELD

Great Wall
Chinese (Northern)

☎ 9798 6930
11 Charlotte St

Map 8 B1

Smoking throughout

Great Wall is a quaint, down-market restaurant hidden away in a cul-de-sac on the undeveloped side of Ashfield Station. Reminiscent of the little cafes dotting the entry point of *the* Great Wall, it's no misnomer. Owner and chef Fan Ju is eager to please. You can call on him if you'd like to know about the dishes that are listed in Chinese characters and pasted on the wall. The modest menu has a great selection of northern-style dishes, characteristically hot, sour or salty. You can't go wrong with a dish of fried slivers of potato with green chilli ($5.50), hot and sour pork and capsicum ($8.50) or dumplings, boiled or braised ($6). Good to see the dumpling-rolling table in use at the back – a pack of 22 frozen dumplings to take home is great value at $4. A cosy place to try lamb hotpot, especially in the depths of winter ($9.80).

starter: $3-$9.50
main: $5.50-$12

cash only

Open: Wed-Mon 12.30pm-3.00pm, daily 5.30pm-10.30pm; reservations accepted; BYO (no corkage)

INNER WEST

ASHFIELD

Map 8 C1

Smoking throughout

Yuan's Family Restaurant (Yuan Zhong Yuan)
Chinese (Shanghai)

☎ 9798 9411
184-186 Liverpool Rd

Yuan's Family Restaurant has a following of regulars so enamoured of the atmosphere and karaoke opportunities that when a new owner and chef came on board recently, nothing changed on the Shanghai-style menu – not even the 'sharp's fin chicken soup'. One can encounter quiet family meals or raucous, rice-wine swilling parties in full swing. Cold cuts of sliced soyed beef ($7), deep-fried vegetarian goose ($8.80) and spicy Sichuan diced chicken ($7) are always good for starters. Stir-fried snow-pea leaves ($9.80) have that genuine Shanghai taste. Dumplings ($4), steamed or pan-fried, are great instant fillers and popular with the young. If you'd like to put an unfortunate giant crab out of its misery, you'll get it for a good market price. Other favourites include shredded pork with chilli, sour and garlic sauce ($8.80) and the 'sizzle at your table' combination seafood with deep-fried bubble rice ($13.80).

starter: $3-$8.80
main: $7.80-$19.80
dessert: $3.50-$4.50
BC MC V

Open: daily 11.30am-2.30pm, 5.30pm-11.30pm (later on weekends); reservations accepted; licensed and BYO (corkage $1/person)

Map 8 E1

Smoking throughout

Zagloba
Polish

☎ 9716 9119
73-75 Norton St

Zagloba is found on Ashfield's Norton St – parallel to the main drag of Liverpool Rd – and is incorporated into the Polish Community Club. Named in honour of author Henryk Sienkiewicz's beery folk hero, the walls feature portraits of his foppish characters and, of course, jolly Zagloba himself, tankard in hand. The menu attests to a sensibility that is not so much parochial as regionally Eastern European. A good start are the chumpy, saltwater-fresh herrings 'à la Hungarian' ($7) and a coffee cup of enlivening beetroot soup with a roll of croquet bread ($5). The ravioli 'à la Russian' is cheesy and cut twice the size of its Italian cousin. Likewise, the potato dumplings in champignon sauce ($9) resemble jumbo-sized gnocchi. The popular and generous pork hock ($12) requires washing down with a strong pilsener. Beer fans will appreciate the club-priced range of imported Polish beers.

starter: $5-$8
main: $6-$14
dessert: $1.50-$8.50
cash only

Open: Wed-Sat noon-3pm, Wed-Thurs 5pm-9pm, Fri 5pm-10pm, Sat 5pm-11pm, Sun noon-9pm; reservations accepted; licensed, no BYO

INNER WEST

BALMAIN

All India Restaurant
Indian

☎ 9555 8844
'The Bijou',
2a Rowntree St

In any other Indian restaurant, ordering Balmain bugs would surely count as living dangerously. Not here – the Goan-style dark, shiny sauce of bugtail balchao ($15.80) is a delicious muddle of homemade fresh onion pickle, and fresh herbs and spices that doesn't overwhelm the succulent bug meat. The light tangy yogurt-based sauce of chicken vadi rasewala ($12.80) makes a pleasing contrast, although the dried lentil dumplings hiding in the sauce are crunchy and bear an unnerving resemblance to Cheerios. On the side, aloo paratha ($3.50) is stuffed with golden potato flecked with black mustard seeds, and the steamed rice is fluffy and plentiful. It's gratifying to see forays into regional Indian cuisine here, with a Nepali spinach and lamb curry and South Indian dosas. And, if you've developed a taste for living on the edge, try Sunday brunch on the veranda or in the earth-hued dining room. There are filled parathas, masala omelette and other Anglo-Indian delicacies, all washed down with, chai, lassi or (if you must) espresso.

Open: daily 6.30pm-10.30pm, Wed-Fri noon-3pm, Sun 9am-3pm; reservations advisable (especially weekends); BYO (corkage $1.50/person)

Map 11 A3

No smoking inside

Veranda tables

starter: $7.80-$10.80
main: $8.80-$15.80
dessert: $5-$6.80
Banquet from $24.50/person

AE BC DC MC V

Balmain Stars at Gigis
Italian

☎ 9818 2170
229 Darling St

A taste of old-style, salt-of-the-earth Balmain, this is the quintessential family restaurant. On a typical Saturday night, tables are occupied by grandparents placating their charges with pizza and coke, groups of teens refuelling as a prelude to a big night, and dressed up middle-aged couples rekindling romance over champagne and scaloppine. The menu is a crowd-pleaser, too, with an element of whimsy in its suggested pizzas for each of the twelve star signs – fussy Virgos get four different corners, while flamboyant Leos get tomato, cheese and 'the lot' ($11.90-$17.90, depending on size). There's the usual trattoria dishes of pasta ($10.50-$12.50) and veal or chicken every which way, as well as gourmet pizzas – the minimalist parmigiana with grilled eggplant and parmesan is a treat. Kids get a free lollipop while the bill is settled and everyone leaves happy.

Open: daily noon-10.30pm; reservations advisable (essential weekends); licensed & BYO (corkage $1/person)

Map 11 B4

Smoking throughout

Pavement tables

starter: $2-$12
main: $8-$18.90
dessert: $6.80-$8

BC MC V

BALMAIN 97

Pizza and Pide to Go

Everyone has a favourite pizza joint. Here are ours:

Arthur's Pizza 260 Oxford St, Paddington ☎ 9331 1779 Map 13 C2
This place is so popular you can't even guarantee a free seat if you rock up early on a Monday night. The popular pizzas epitomise the new fad of fusing the traditional pizza with the 1990s gourmet versions. 'Mamma' comes with olives, anchovies, capers and sun-dried tomatoes, while 'Tosca' is roasted vegetables and goat's cheese.

The Australian Hotel 100 Cumberland St, The Rocks ☎ 9247 2250 Map 1 D2
Gourmet pizzas with unusual toppings (emu, kangaroo, crocodile) and a good range of vegetarian pizzas. Expensive, but worth it just to watch the Americans pulling disgusted faces at the menu that Australians should eat 'roo.

Bar Italia 169-171 Norton St, Leichhardt ☎ 9560 9981 Map 12 A2
While the rest of Norton St has been getting a starched linen tablecloth makeover, Bar Italia has stuck to the reliable old formula of waiters in old T-shirts, cheap pastas ($7-$8.50) and budget focaccias ($5-$6). The courtyard is always busy with orders for spaghetti marinara or the Bar Italia 'special pasta sauce' of prawns, chilli and bacon (see also p 141).

Bill & Toni's 72-74 Stanley St, East Sydney ☎ 9360 4702 Map 6 A2
So it's not pizza, just great value pasta. Upstairs it's $7 spag bol and $13 schnitzel and pasta combos. Osso buco and other mains go for just $10.50. Green salad, white bread and orange cordial are complimentary. You're always guaranteed a colourful meal deal here.

Efes Turkish Pizza 124 King St, Newtown ☎ 9516 4276 Map 9 A4
The Saracoglu family has been perfecting these pizzas (golden crispy on the outside, hot and juicy on the inside) for nigh on 11 years. The cheese is a memorable melted blend of mozzarella, fetta and haloumi. The traditional kusbasili (lamb pizza) is highly recommended.

Izmir Turkish Pizza and Kebab 253 Bondi Rd, Bondi ☎ 9130 4170 Map 14 C3
Big, succulent Turkish pizzas for a really good price. We think the vegetarian pizzas are their best: try the potato, tomato, garlic and mint version.

Ipek 570 Darling St, Rozelle ☎ 9810 6411 Map 11 B2
Cheap and authentic Turkish pizza, fresh dips and tabouli – with the added bonus of seriously extended opening hours of 11am-4am.

La Botte da Ercole 608 Willoughby Rd, Willoughby ☎ 9958 6785 Map 18 B2
Traditional Italian pizzas and pastas alongside modern antipodean ingredients like NZ whitebait, WA scampi and Tasmanian salmon. An excellent local, with owner Ercole adding his own brand of Italian enthusiasm to the proceedings.

La Disfida 109 Ramsay St, Haberfield ☎ 9798 8299
You'd have to go to Rome to find pizzas more authentic than these thin-crusted beauties (see review p 110).

Sarays 18 Enmore Rd, Enmore ☎ 9557 5310 Map 9 C2
A constantly refreshed stock of soft, warm ovals of Turkish bread, some of Sydney's spiciest vine leave rolls (they add plenty of chilli), tastiest eggplant salad and beetroot dips ... and then there's the near-perfect Turkish pizzas.

BALMAIN

Kazbah on Darling
Middle Eastern/ modern Australian

☎ 9555 7067
379 Darling St

Map 11 A3

Smoking after 2pm and 10.30pm only; no cigars or pipes

Pavement tables

A soothing vista of white linen and tapestry-cushioned window seats welcomes you to the Kazbah. On weekend mornings Balmainites browse through magazines, chatter, and casually breastfeed their babies plucked from designer buggies. Try a leisurely Sunday brunch, the menu ranging from a delightful Birchermüsli ($8.50) scattered with seasonal berries and toasted pistachios, to a terracotta dish of baked eggs with chunks of spicy 'sucuk' sausage and haloumi ($8.50) and served with Turkish toast. For those with hangovers there's a plate of hummus with minced lamb and pinenuts on pita bread ($9.50). Water comes scented with mint and lemon, and there's a choice of rockmelon, watermelon or orange juice. Dinner strays further into mod Oz territory, but echoes of the Middle East linger in chicken bisteeya*, kalamata olives and white bean mash ($22) and whole roasted baby snapper, with carrot-steamed couscous and walnut parsley dressing ($22.50).

Open: Tues-Fri 6.30pm-10.30pm, Sat & Sun 9am-3pm, 6.30pm-10.30pm; reservations advisable (essential Fri & Sat evenings); licensed & BYO (corkage $2/person)

starter: $12-$14.50
main: $19.50-$23
dessert: $10-$14.50

AE BC DC MC V

Riverview Hotel Dining Room
European

☎ 9555 9889
29 Birchgrove Rd

Map 11 A3

Nonsmoking tables available

Climbing the stairs from the bustling bar into the light, airy dining room is like entering another world. Service is relaxed and charming and chef Richard Moyser's produce-driven menu emphasises stylish comfort food. The beef and Guinness pie ($15) – a velvety beef stew encased in crumbly pastry – is so hard to resist that he's never been allowed to take it off the menu. Skate wrapped in prosciutto and served with a piquant salad of artichoke and capsicum ($18) is a lighter but equally tasty choice. Desserts range from nursery classics with a twist to fresher flavours, such as passionfruit parfait with caramelised figs ($12). There's even a separate cheese menu – one cheese $6, selection of four $12 – that does justice to fine cheeses from home (the Hunter Valley) and away (England and France). This is pub dining at its best.

Open: Fri & Sun noon-2.30pm, Tues-Sat 6pm-10pm; reservations advisable; licensed, no BYO

starter: $10-$14
main: $16-$21
dessert: $8-$12

AE BC DC MC V

INNER WEST

BALMAIN

Map 11 A3 — Nonsmoking tables available — Pavement and balcony tables

Tuk Tuk Real Thai
Thai

☎ 9555 5899
350 Darling St

Tuk Tuk's headset-wearing staff in their jaunty orange T-shirts combined with the frenzied action in the open kitchen leave you in no doubt that this is a tightly run operation. In the softly lit upstairs dining room, on the wide balcony and across the pavement, acid-yellow chairs surround dark-wood tables. Inside at street level, those who didn't think to make a reservation chow-down on their noodles from bar stools clustered around stainless steel tables. And what tasty chow it is, too. Banana flower salad ($15.50) is a tongue-tingling medley of shredded lemongrass, kaffir lime, mint and chilli, soothed by the silken texture of poached chicken in coconut milk. And the golden-coloured rich and nutty massaman lamb ($11.50), has achingly tender meat with chunks of potato. There's little reason to stint on the side dishes, either. Try pad phak tong ($10.50), a scramble of sweetly charred pumpkin with egg, tofu, shallots and coriander.

starter: $2-$9.50
main: $10.50-$18
dessert: $5.50
BC MC V

Open: Tues-Sun noon-3pm, 5.30pm-10pm; reservations advisable (essential Fri & Sat evenings); BYO (no corkage)

CAMPERDOWN

Map 9 A2 — No smoking inside — Pavement tables

Camperdown Canteen
Modern Australian

☎ 9557 4106
15 Fowler St

On a leafy cul-de-sac facing the local cricket oval, the Camperdown Canteen is one of those bijou cafés that you just want to keep to yourself. The always jolly, sometimes delightfully ditzy, staff are guaranteed to get your day off to a good start. The all-day breakfast is a godsend for late risers: Vienna toast, coffee and an assortment of jams, or mushrooms, or even the rather fancy grilled ricotta, avocado and tomato is a bargain at $7, the full works $9.50. Weekday lunch sees the place teeming with cognoscenti from nearby Sydney Uni, tucking into one of the chunky, no-nonsense salads, such as the niçoise or the tandoori chicken ($8.50). The lox bagel ($8.50) is swamped with lettuce, but also has delicious touches such as plump capers and horseradish as a dressing.

main: $6.50-$9.50
dessert: $2
cash only

Open: Mon-Sat 7.30am-3pm; reservations accepted; unlicensed

CHIPPENDALE

The Rose Hotel
Modern Australian

☎ 9318 1133
52-54 Cleveland St

Map 8 B6

Smoking throughout

Courtyard tables

The Rose is where the inner east meets the inner west and the inner city: patrons span the slick and seedy, the flannel-ettes and the fashion-ettes. Not surprisingly the menu tries to satisfy all comers – from a vegetarian risotto ($13.90) to pizzas ($11.90 for plain old ham and pineapple, $15.90 for fancy goat's cheese and eggplant varieties). There's even a Thai green curry. But stick to the roasts and steaks (averaging $16) – excellent cuts of meat with mod Oz flourishes (purée, jus) that you'd pay much more for elsewhere. Or try pies with huge flaky pastry caps and french fries and dips on the side ($13.90 vegetarian/$15.90 beef). Sit in the ivy-decorated courtyard under cupid lamps, surrounded by trompe-l'oeil walls and Sydney inner-city society. You can have a game of bocce out the back, a game of pool out the front, or a nip or two in the little cocktail lounge.

starter: $7-$10
main: $13-$18
Set menu $25

Open: Tues-Fri noon-2.30pm, Mon-Thurs 6pm-10pm, Fri & Sat 6pm-10.30pm, Sun 12.30pm-4pm, 5.30pm-9pm; reservations advisable (essential Sat & Sun); licensed, no BYO

BC MC V; Eftpos

INNER WEST

DRUMMOYNE

Ecco
Italian

☎ 9719 9394
Drummoyne Sailing Club,
2 St George's Crescent

Map 11 A1

Private parking (yacht club carpark)

Smoking throughout

Like a phoenix out of the ashes, Ecco has risen to new heights after being turfed out of its previous home to make room for poker machines. It is packed to bursting every night with loyal old customers and those who've had their ear to the ground. The cooking falls somewhere between simple home-style and grandstand variety. Home-made pappardelle are cooked to perfection, coated in an almost-too-rich mascarpone, artichoke and prosciutto sauce ($16.50), while a love-me-tender salmon carpaccio ($14.50) dressed with basil and olive oil just disappears on the tongue. Fat, juicy prawns marry well with Sicilian caponata ($26.50) and a tasty boned and stuffed spatchcock ($23.50) smells wonderfully of sage. They're keen on desserts in this part of town and Ecco takes the prize for Sydney's richest chocolate mousse ($8.50). Think of the inside of a Lindt ball, double it, and you get the idea.

starter: $13.50-$22.50
main: $18-$34.50
dessert: $6.50-$8.50

Open: Wed-Fri & Sun noon-3pm, Tues-Sat 6pm-10pm; reservations essential; licensed, no BYO

AE BC DC MC V

DULWICH HILL

Map 8 D2

Smoking throughout

starter: $3.50-$8.90
main: $3.50-$22.50
AE BC DC MC V

Minh
Vietnamese

☎ 9560 0465
506 Marrickville Rd

'It all sounds so good, I can't choose,' though clichéd, is genuinely valid at Minh. A simple establishment in a low-key suburb, it has been well-regarded for its sixteen years and has a hefty menu. And it doesn't just sound good; the crispy pancake entrée ($6.50) has a superior, toasty taste, while the beef grilled in betel leaves ($5.90) and prawn paste on sugar cane ($8.90) are like magic tricks that perform in your mouth. As for mains, the Minh duck salad ($8.80) takes you somewhere tropical and leaves your mouth clean with its juicy basil/aniseed finish. The grilled king prawns ($15.90) are big enough to have been shot. Soups such as bon gai da (vermicelli noodles in a shrimp paste, $6.80) are complex and invigorating in all seasons. Bring a big group here – the fridge is loaded with Vietnamese beer and the manager, Mrs Tinh, is a cheerful character with a welcoming laugh.

Open: daily 10am-10pm; reservations accepted; licensed & BYO (corkage $1/bottle)

ENMORE

Map 9 C1

Smoking throughout

starter: $5
main: $5-$7
dessert: $3
Banquet $18
AE BC DC MC

Fifi's Cafe
Lebanese

☎ 9550 4665
158 Enmore Road

The menu for Fifi's Cafe is superimposed over a sepia photo of Beirut in 1949, the year that Fifi Fudda – arguably Newtown/Enmore's finest Lebanese cook – was born there. The prices on the menu are not at all what you'd expect from a place that looks like this; a definitively modern, clean and sharp design with a measure of Orientalism suggested by some gold-framed prints. Lebanese meals are often served as spreads, and so the banquet dishes are an appropriate choice and are budget-priced at $18 per person. It's promising from the start with two mezze (dip) dishes, the smoky baba ghanoush and creamy hummus, followed by vine leaves oiled in lemon butter sauce, minty cabbage rolls and tabouli fresh from the chopping board. The meaty, wheaty kibbe shells are Fifi's speciality, and the lamb kebabs and chicken skewers are served with a concentrated, white-hot garlic sauce.

Open: daily 5.30pm-10.30pm; reservations accepted; BYO ($1/person)

Enmore Rd, Enmore

The almost Dickensian decay of Enmore Rd has always been part of its appeal: shop windows are crammed full of old jugs, mangled microwaves and dressmaker dummies destined never to pose again. The new clothes stores feature mannequins wearing sequined belly dancer ensembles and black bustiers for designer Goths. They're a sign of Enmore's newer face, along with Polymorph body piercers and The Wild One sex aid store ('wear it like you mean it'). Sales staff no doubt lunch at that perennial Enmore Rd resident, the Little Devil Temptation cake shop. The grey-haired army at the Cat Protection Society doesn't seem the slightest bit phased though – the green pussy logo is still standing its ground. As are Marie Louise and George Mehzer, owners of the eponymous pink and purple beauticians that's a time capsule from the 1950s. In the middle, centrestage, is Enmore Theatre. A hundred touring posters testify it's been host to a thousand genuine pop stars, the odd protestor and the occasional poseur: Billy Bragg played here, as did Marianne Faithfull, Siouxsie and the Banshees and Ani di Franco. And ever since it got its own swag of Thai restaurants a few years ago, Enmore Rd has been a pretender to the King St throne. With the recent addition of a set of slightly swankier eateries, like kōk and Fifi's, it might just be about ready for a coronation.

ENMORE

Map 9 C1
Wheelchair access
Smoking after 11pm

kök
Modern Australian

☎ 9519 0555
143 Enmore Rd

kök (pronounced shirk, and meaning kitchen in Swedish, the chef's native language) is about as suave as Enmore gets. The super starchy napkins are in direct contrast to the friendly staff and soothingly quiet ambience, jazz tootling away in the background. The starters poke around Asia for inspiration, taking in Thai and Vietnamese dishes; we play it safe with Peking duck ($15) – fun finger food and another example of the restaurant's relaxed attitude – and a chilli hot Balmain bug-meat salad on a sweet potato and corn fritter ($16). From the mains, the chestnut and mushroom pie ($23) is a beauty, the fish dishes – roast snapper in a heady bouillabaisse sauce ($28) and the peanut-crusted blue-eye cod ($24) – equally satisfying. All the desserts are tempting, none more so than the saucy chocolate sponge pudding with cherries ($10). Endearing touches, such as olives on arrival, petits fours with the bill, and wine suggestions with every dish, all add to the creation of a special night out.

starter: $10-$19
main: $23-$28
dessert: $10-$12
Degustation $75
AE DC MC V; Eftpos

Open: daily 6pm-11.30pm; reservations advisable (especially weekends); licensed, no BYO

Map 9 C2
Smoking throughout

Tandoori Hut
Indian/Pakistani

☎ 9519 8140
93 Enmore Rd

Tandoori Hut is situated in the middle of Enmore Road, five minutes walk from Newtown Station. The décor is quite plain, save for Indian Tourist Board posters of young women smiling welcomes at you from the subcontinent. However, the 'Hut' offers well-loved numbers prepared with remarkable balance and richness. The lamb chop entrée is soaked in a heady, aromatic marinade and their malai kofta ($6.50), cottage cheese dumplings as soft as butter and served in a complex cashew sauce, deserves a prize. Most of the dishes tend to be on the mild to medium end of the thermometer – rogan josh (lamb), beef, chicken and seafood masala – but for those who favour a bit of gunpowder in their curry dishes, the management will heat things up a bit. Try out the mango lassi drink freshly prepared from fruit and yoghurt – it makes a creamy accompaniment to the spicy sauces.

starter: $2.90-$11.90
main: $5.50-$12.90
dessert: $2
AE MC V

Open: daily 5:30pm-midnight; reservations accepted; BYO (no corkage)

INNER WEST

ERSKINEVILLE

Caffeine
Mediterranean

☎ 9516 4207
128 Erskineville Rd

Map 9 C4

Entertainment: live jazz band Sun 4pm-8pm

Smoking throughout

Pavement tables

Caffeine's corner store position and wrap-around plate glass make sitting inside here like looking out through the eyes of Erskineville, observing the village going about its business. On weekends, all day breakfasts of bacon and eggs are served up to a steady smattering of locals, while lunchtimes and evenings see Greek, Lebanese and Indian meals happily keeping company on dinner tables. Specials might include a Russian fish stew ($12) or Indonesian gado gado ($6). Felafel plates ($5) come with a mountain of hummus, and there's no stinting on the tender lamb souvlaki skewers either ($5.50). Bakes such as prawns in tomato ($12) and veal moussaka ($11) are other likely menu items. The walls host a rotating exhibition: when we last visited, the beaded, bejewelled mannequin busts could be described as Mexican rococo meets Mardi Gras. The 'Don't touch our balls' sign is just another piece of Caffeine's off-beat humour.

starter: $5.50-$6
main: $6-$12
dessert: $4.50-$5

cash only

Open: Tues-Sun 10am-10pm (breakfast: all day); reservations advisable on weekends; BYO (corkage 50c/person)

Spanish Tapas (p 107)

GLEBE

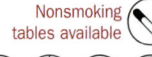

The Abbey
Italian

☎ 9660 4792
156 Bridge St

Map 10 D4

Nonsmoking tables available

It's difficult to know what to make of the Abbey's atmosphere. It's either a kitsch and camp masterpiece, or a confused marketing ploy from another era. But the food is first-rate, and the service friendly and attentive: when 'Sir' ordered an out-of-stock bottle of wine, a better wine was offered (with a conspiratorial wink) at the same price. Dishes include baby octopus salad ($15.90), and veal slices with a creamy paprika and capsicum sauce ($25.90). The desserts are wickedly sinful. The crema pasticiera and raisin pancakes served with créme de cacao sauce ($10.90) demands penance, but alas, it seems the confessional has been converted into the gents. The decidedly racy Richard Claderman is piped from the organ loft and, with another conspiratorial wink, patrons are enjoined to dance. 'A rose for the lady' on the way out confirms it's all tongue-in-cheek. And with that in mind, it's an absolute hoot.

starter: $16
main: $25
dessert: $10
AE BC DC MC V

Open: Mon-Sat 6pm-midnight; reservations advisable; licensed, no BYO

The Boathouse on Blackwattle Bay
Modern Australian/seafood

☎ 9518 9011
End of Ferry Rd

Map 8 A6

Valet parking $15

Wheelchair access

Smoking at the bar only

The Boathouse on Blackwattle Bay is Sydney on a stick – it perches on piers sunk deep into the harbour foreshores. Water-skimming city views, a relaxed, urbane atmosphere and the freshest food available make this restaurant a showcase for the many foods and flavours that represent Australian cuisine at its best. The Boathouse is primarily a fish restaurant, and with the fish markets a mere stone's skip across the bay, the restaurant is fortuitously placed to procure good produce. The menu changes daily to accommodate what's in season. We devoured three enormous, barely-seared scallops ($19) drizzled with a citrus sauce that happily complemented the scallops' fresh flavour. The monkfish wrapped in nori and served tempura-style with a salad of finely shredded seaweed ($28) is the star of the mains' menu, but the passionfruit ice cream with coconut syrup and sago ($14) outshone all. Its imaginative presentation is on a level pegging with its sunburst flavours.

starter: $16-$22
main: $25-$32
dessert: $14-$18
AE BC DC MC V

Open: Tues-Sun noon-3pm, 6.30pm-10pm; reservations essential; licensed, no BYO

GLEBE

Spanish Tapas
Spanish

☎ 9571 9005
28 Glebe Point Rd

Map 10 E6

Entertainment: flamenco dancing Thurs-Sun night

Smoking throughout

Spanish Tapas, which began modestly on Darlinghurst Rd, is now at home in Glebe. What with whitewashed walls, gaudy Spanish-themed paintings, and a steamy flamenco trio setting the floor afire, the ambience would be rollicking Costa del Sol, if not for the distinctly Sydney parade passing outside its huge, open windows. On busy nights you may spend a long time waiting for the various paella (from $30 for two people, including a hearty vegetarian version). If your appetite just can't be contained, the zarzuela de marisco ($36) – piles of seafood simmered in a rustic tomato wine sauce – is faster, the sauce going down very nicely with a basket of bread. There are 24 tapas to choose from; we liked the deep-fried butterfly sardines ($7), the rotund meatballs ($7.50) and the mussels steamed in onion, garlic and white wine ($10.50).

starter: $5-$12.50
main: $14.50-$36
dessert: $4.50

AE BC DC MC V

Open: Mon-Fri noon-3pm, daily 5.30pm-11pm; reservations advisable (especially Fri & Sat night); licensed & BYO (corkage $2/person)

Tanjore
Indian

☎ 9660 6332
34 Glebe Point Rd

Map 10 E6

Smoking throughout

Sydney may be a long way from the East End of London but for any Brit (or anyone else for that matter) on a perennial quest for the great curry house, Tanjore comes pretty close. The food mercifully bobs in its sauce, rather than drowns, allowing the wonderful flavours typical of Tamil cooking to come through. Their tandoori dishes, such as the rack of lamb (barrah kebab, $11.90) and prawn tandoori ($14.90) warrant special mention, as does the beef do piazza ($10.90). But the standout is unquestionably Bombay fish ($14.90), with wonderfully moist ling fillets bathed in subtle spices and coconut milk. The décor is a bit ad hoc – Glebe grunge meets Bombay teahouse – but there's something warm and comforting in that. Though the service is attentive, no one seems to be in any particular hurry, so bring *two* bottles of wine: as EM Forster said, 'India is best left unhurried'.

starter: $4.90-$13.90
main: $10.90-$15.90
dessert: $5.50
Banquet $20
(not offered Sun)

AE BC DC MC V

Open: Tues-Fri noon-2.30pm, Sat & Sun noon-3pm, Mon-Wed & Sun 5pm-10.30pm, Thurs-Sat 5pm-11pm; reservations advisable (especially weekends); BYO ($2/person corkage)

INNER WEST

GLEBE

Map 10 D5

No smoking inside

Thai On Wok
Thai

☎ 9660 9011
193 Glebe Point Rd

Where outside Bangkok are you going to find a spanking fresh Thai lunch for $6 ($8 for seafood), including rice? At Thai On Wok, unassumingly sandwiched between Gleebooks and Sharky's burger joint. Here, huddled around laminated tables and spilling onto the street, hungry students and jaded workers wait for their number to come up. Favourites include the crisp-tender vege stir-fries teamed with chilli jam, fresh ginger or the intriguingly named prik khing sauce. There are also hearty bowls of red and green curry, smoky-tasting wok-charred noodles and minced meat or seafood salads, spiked with lemongrass, chilli, lime juice and coriander. You could do a lot worse than refuel here before taking in a movie at Hoyts on Broadway. Prices are only a few dollars more in the evening and you can start with a fishcake or a cluster of BBQ octopus for $1.80 apiece. It's got to be better than popcorn and choc-tops for dinner.

starter: $1-$6.50
main: $7-$12
cash only

Open: daily noon-11pm; reservations not accepted; BYO (no corkage)

Yak & Yeti

GLEBE

Well Connected Café
Cafe fare

☎ 9566 2655
35 Glebe Point Rd

Can the geek-to-groove paradigm shift any further? First we're told Bill Gates is quite the philanthropist; and now, it seems, the IT geek stereotype is far more likely to be a Saba-wearing hip young thang, sipping short blacks while downloading some new mp3. Exaggeration? Well, maybe that bit about Saba-wearing. But if you like your email with a raspberry and mango frappé and a liberal dose of Rae and Christian, then Well Connected is a large slice of groove beyond the typical Internet cafe. And, if you're not cool enough to be a techno geek, never fear: walk past the computer terminals, up the stairs and onto the street-side, sun drenched verandah where, amid market bazaar retro furnishings, you can relax over a delicately spiced vegetable pot pie ($8.90) or a lavash wrap ($7.90) and watch the ever-entertaining Glebe street scene pass by to a soundtrack of dub and Northern Soul.

Open: Mon-Sat 8am-11pm, Sun 10am-11pm; reservations accepted, advisable Sunday evening; BYO (no corkage)

Map 10 E6

Entertainment: DJ Roger and friends (dub, techno, Northern Soul) Sunday 7pm onwards

Smoking throughout

Patio tables available upstairs

starter: $3-$8.90
main: $7.90-$8.90
dessert: $2-$5.90

BC MC V; Eftpos

Yak & Yeti
Nepalese

☎ 9552 1220
41 Glebe Point Rd

Travellers to Nepal often return with glowing tales of incomparable scenery and a vibrant culture; mention food, however, and a grimace born of high altitude Delhi belly usually brings the conversation to a grinding halt. Determined to overcome the stereotype, Yak & Yeti brings traditional Himalayan favourites such as momos* ($5.90) and achars* ($4.90-$5.50) to an initially curious clientele who, in turn, become stalwart regulars. Indian-influenced but nonetheless individual, Yak & Yeti is a cut above the somewhat mundane Sydney-Indian scene. Though it sounds unlikely, khasi masu (goat, $12.90), is an absolute must, being surprisingly tender and delicately spiced with chilli, coriander and fenugreek. Similarly, mis-mas ($9.90), a vegetable and coriander curry, and aloo tama ra bori ($10.90), a bamboo, potato and bean mix from Kathmandu, are dishes unlikely to be found elsewhere. And that keeps regulars coming back to the prayer flag-laden rooms for a bit of Nepalese culture and Nepalese tea ($2.50).

Open: Mon-Fri 5.30pm-10.30pm, Sat & Sun 5.30pm-11pm; reservations advisable (especially weekends); BYO (corkage $2/person)

Map 10 E6

Nonsmoking tables available

starter: $4.90-$12.90
main: $11.90-$15.90
dessert: $4.20-$4.90
Banquet menu $20.90, $23.90 or $25.90

BC MC V

INNER WEST

HABERFIELD

Map 8 B2
Smoking throughout

La Disfida
Italian

☎ 9798 8299
109 Ramsay St

You can have whatever you want here – just so long as it's pizza. And, take our word for it, you really *do* want this pizza – thin-crusted, charred and bubbled from the fiery oven – and slice-swapping is obligatory. Toppings are authentically meagre, but full of fresh flavour – wafer-thin prosciutto, silvery flashes of anchovy and pungent olives, all on a tomato sauce that actually tastes of tomato. With a good bottle of red, this is as close to Neapolitan heaven as you're likely to get. When it's busy (which is always), you might want to order some bocconcini speck ($6) – springy morsels of mozzarella wrapped in prosciutto and briefly crisped in that same brick oven – and bruschetta ($4), to tide you over. Come early or be prepared to loiter outside while you wait for a table. Oh, and dress lightly – the warm, yeasty breath of the wood-fired oven soon permeates the small dining room.

starter: $4-$6
main: $13
dessert: $5-$7
BC MC V

Open: Tues-Sun 6pm-10.30pm; reservations not accepted; BYO (no corkage)

LEICHHARDT

Map 12 A2
Nonsmoking tables available
Pavement tables

Café Barzu
Italian/modern Australian

☎ 9550 0144
121 Norton St

Let's talk about cakes: banana, carrot or orange and poppyseed; chocolate mousse cake, chocolate mud cake, chocolate cheesecake, chocolate date cake; lemon cheesecake, baked cheesecake; pecan pie and tiramisù. Fancy something savoury instead? No problem. Italian regulars such as focaccia, pizza and bruschetta, and hearty salads are on offer throughout the day. The dinner menu includes pasta, risotto and traditional meat dishes served with seasonal vegetables. Some dishes are more successful than others. Our open prawn ravioli ($13.30) incorporated onions, semi-dried tomatoes, smoked ricotta and lemon, but the pasta and prawns – got lost, and the caesar salad ($8.90/$12.90) was let down by stale croutons. But then there's the cakes. Café Barzu is a hip, modern eatery and deservedly popular. On hectic nights the covered courtyard is quieter.

starter: $6.90-$13.30
main: $13.10-$19.60
dessert: $6.50
Set menu $28-$31
AE BC DC MC V

Open: Sun-Thurs 11.30am-11.30pm, Fri & Sat 11am-midnight, (kitchen closes one hour before closing time); reservations advisable (Fri & Sat evenings); licensed and BYO (corkage $2/person)

LEICHHARDT

Dante
Italian

☎ 9550 0062
**Italian Forum,
Shop 39, 23 Norton St**

Map 12 B2

Validated parking (Italian Forum parking)

Wheelchair access

Entertainment: live music some weekends

Nonsmoking tables available

Pavement tables

If the buildings were a few centuries older and the paint was peeling Leichhardt's Italian Forum could *almost* pass for the real thing. Dante is one of its more upmarket eateries where lunching ladies and shiny suits (who wouldn't look out of place sporting violin cases in Palermo) sit at tables under the loggia. Pasta dishes arrive with alarming speed, but the pasta is cooked better here than at many Italian eateries about town. An unusual sugo of zucchini, prawns and a dash of olive paste makes penne Beatrice ($13.50) a good choice. Involtini* with prosciutto, cheese and asparagus ($18.50) indicate that the chef has a way with veal. Seafood starters and mains feature and the grill gets a workout – calf's liver and bacon ($16.50) is especially popular. Gelato lovers could eat here six times before exhausting the ice cream desserts and moving onto the ubiquitous tiramisù and (strawberry flavoured) zabaione.

starter: $8.50-$14.50
main: $16.50-$23.50
dessert: $6.50-$9.50

AE BC DC MC V

Open: Sun-Fri noon-2.30pm, daily 6.30pm-10pm; reservations advisable; licensed, no BYO

Elio
Modern Italian

☎ 9560 9129
159 Norton St

Map 12 A2

Smoking after 10.30pm (no pipes or cigars)

Courtyard and balcony tables

Elio's waiters really know their stuff. Just before service starts, they all sit down to dine at a long table laden with platters of pasta, risotto and salads. Strolling past the floor-to-ceiling windows, it can be hard to wait your turn. Later in the evening, excited chatter bounces off the bold feature walls of scarlet and turquoise, making an upstairs or courtyard table a wise move for a more tranquil dining experience. The wood-fired bread, with its chewy, charred crust, is perfect for mopping up peppery green olive oil or the burnt thyme butter and semi-dried tomatoes that garnish the irresistible potato and garlic ravioli ($14). Mains range from a serious steak, served with gorgonzola butter and wilted spinach ($24) to the more delicate grilled scampi with saffron and chive risotto ($21). A mound of balsamic-tinged rocket salad makes a perfect accompaniment, topped with slivers of perfectly nutty, aged parmesan. Afterwards, a glass of vin santo, with biscotti for dunking, is a civilised choice.

starter: $12-$17
main: $14-$24
dessert: $8-$10

AE BC DC MC V

Open: Mon-Sat 6pm-11pm, Sun noon-10pm; reservations essential; licensed & BYO (corkage $3/bottle)

INNER WEST

On Your Plate **Italian**

The beauty of Italian food is its simplicity. This means that you don't have to eat posh for good Italian nosh. Prosciutto and figs can be equally good if it costs $7 and is served on a laminex tabletop or if it costs three times that amount and comes complete with a white-jacketed waiter and a sparkling harbour backdrop. With Italian food, style will never triumph over substance.

Since the 1950s and '60s, Leichhardt has been regarded as Sydney's Little Italy, although Stanley St in East Sydney has its own Italian flavour. There's a sense of self-propagation in Sydney's Italian eateries, and many newer restaurateurs have been trained under the watchful eye of more established ones.

Now Sydney-ites can enjoy eating Italian all sorts of ways; modern or orthodox styles of cooking; upmarket city restaurants or traditional home-style eateries – they're all abundantly available.

Australians are far more adventurous in their eating habits than Italians who stick rigidly to the antipasto, primo (pasta/rice), secondo (meat/fish) and dolce formula. We'll eat pasta as a main course, or as an accompaniment to meat, and we've almost grown to expect innovative 'mod Med' dishes (perhaps roast chicken, stuffed with preserved lemon and couscous) on a trattoria menu above the faithful veal saltimbocca.

The regional nature of Italian cooking is defused in the Australian context, leading to greater range and variety across menus as well. You'll often find both northern-style polenta and risotto dishes featured side-by-side with seafood pastas and tomato-based vegetable dishes from the south. This has been influenced by the abundance of fresh ingredients available in Sydney. As good as they are, Italy's fishmongers and butchers cannot come close to the quality, variety and value of Australia's seafood and meat.

As for pizzas, we can enjoy authentic Italian style pizzas (if you want the minimalist margherita with a charred doughy base), or we can go for inventive 'gourmet' ones. Using Australian ingredients many of these work well but tandoori chicken and baba ganoush toppings score as low on the authenticity meter as the old shredded ham and pineapple variety.

Given these eclectic geographical tendencies, we need to go back to that key element of Italian cooking – simplicity. Look for pastas and risottos with a couple of key ingredients (rather than the everything-in-the-pantry variety), grilled fish, slow cooked stews served with polenta, and roasted meats. But for a taste of the exotic, if imported buffalo mozzarella is on the menu, try it; the unique salty, milky flavour is unforgettable.

Sally Webb

Sally Webb is a self-confessed Italian food snob, thanks to 5 years living and eating in Italy. She writes for various publications including Gourmet Traveller *and* Vogue Entertaining. *She has also worked on many LP guidebooks, including those to Rome and Italy.*

Grappa
Italian

☎ 9560 6090
1/267-277 Norton St

When a restaurant's clientele is made up of the chefs and waiting staff of Leichhardt's eateries, you know you're onto a good thing. Despite its ugly exterior, Grappa's recent arrival has given the 'wrong' end of Norton St a new lease of life. The minimalist interior is decked out in soothing neutral tones with snazzy artwork on the walls and a beehive-shaped pizza dominating one end. The menu combines traditional Italian favourites with innovative takes on the same. Zucchini flowers stuffed with mozzarella and anchovies are deep fried to perfection in the lightest of batters ($13), while figs and prosciutto served with melted blue cheese ($15.50) will have your tastebuds tingling. Scampi ravioli ($17.50) is good, although too fishy for the delicate burnt butter sauce, and the grilled tuna steak ($24.50) was overpowered by its olive tapenade. Alcohol-marinated strawberries with zabaione ($9.50) is a refreshing dessert. Grappa lovers have a choice of 17 varieties. Maybe that's what the chefs *really* come for.

Open: daily 6pm-10pm, Tues-Fri & Sun noon-3pm; reservations advisable; licensed, no BYO

Map 12 A2

Private parking
Wheelchair access
Smoking throughout
Balcony tables

starter: $10.50-$21.50
main: $14-$29
dessert: $9.50-$11

AE DC MC V

Martini
Italian

☎ 9568 3344
99 Norton St

Martini has mod Oz written all over it with its over-designed interior, sleek lines, moulded white chairs and corrugated tin roof. An innovative Italian eatery, it marries tradition with experimentation. The menu is particularly strong on appetizers (such as vegetable soufflé, marinated barramundi, garfish and red wine terrine) and pasta dishes. The tang of the gorgonzola is a perfect foil for salty bresaola* ($13). Fat ravioli stuffed with sweet pumpkin ($14) is rich and good but its sultana and pine nut sauce somehow just misses the correct sweet/savoury balance. Zuppa di fagioli* ($12) is plate-moppingly good – rich, thick and full of flavour as only true peasant food can be. Steak, venison, liver, trout and quail battle it out for mains attention. For a sweet finale try the creamy panna cotta drowning in amaretto sauce ($9) or the shortcrust pastry tulip filled with mascarpone ($9) – Martini's waist-padding tiramisù.

Open: Mon-Fri 6pm-midnight, Sat & Sun noon-3pm, 6pm-3am; reservations advisable; licensed, no BYO

Map 12 B2

Wheelchair access
Nonsmoking tables available
Balcony tables

starter: $12-$24
main: $19-$26
dessert: $9-$14

AE BC DC MC V

LEICHHARDT

Map 12 A2
Nonsmoking tables available
Balcony tables

Portofino
Italian

☎ 9550 0782
166 Norton St

A stalwart of Leichhardt's 'spaghetti strip', the stylish but informal Portofino is bustling, noisy and always full. The starters were the highlight of our meal; tasty char-grilled calamari ($13) on a bed of rocket splashed with lemon juice, and a delicious carpaccio di manzo ($13) – slivers of tender raw beef surmounted by shavings of parmesan, drizzled with olive oil. Pastas range from the basic spaghetti al ragu to a more exotic linguini con granchio (with crab, lemon zest and cream) but are on the whole too elaborate for this cucina italiana purist. The penne pesce spada ($16) is an interesting marriage of swordfish with semi-dried tomatoes, capers and olives, but the pasta would have benefited from less cooking time and more salt. The extensive menu features veal, chicken and seafood mains as well as pizza. Desserts ($8.50) are of the share-or-despair variety, including a wicked raspberry crème brûlée. The staff are friendly and efficient, and the prints and hand-painted plates on the wall add a nice touch.

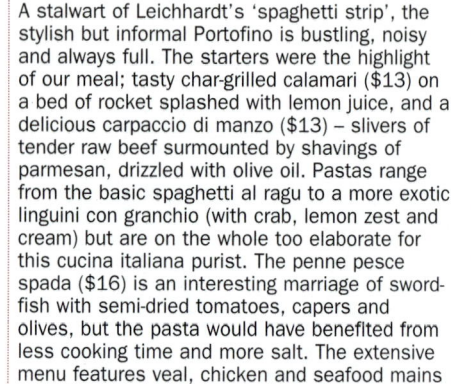

starter: $4.50-$13
main: $13-$26
dessert: $8.50
AE BC DC MC V; Eftpos

Open: Wed-Sun noon-3pm, daily 6pm-midnight; reservations advisable (especially Fri, Sat & Sun); licensed & BYO (corkage $4/bottle)

Map 12 A2
Wheelchair access
Smoking in the bar only
Balcony tables

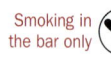

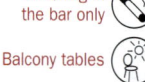

Uno 53
Mediterranean

☎ 9572 8992
153 Norton St

In a dining market awash with wilted rocket, rotolos of goat's cheese and macerated elderberries, it's refreshing to read a menu that features such classics as cotechino (Italian sausages), albóndigas (Spanish meatballs) and moussaka (Balkan lasagne). The hip and hopping downstairs bar is one of Uno 53's attractions, but if Mediterranean dining is your pleasure, you'll be drawn to the upstairs dining area with its exposed rafters and breezy outlook. Spiedini, grilled skewers of bread and mozzarella ($6.90), are great when shared tapas-style with escalivada, a roasted vegetable salad ($6.90). The pan-fried chicken livers with risotto ($15) confirm the restaurant's unspoken declaration that simple ingredients are nothing to be ashamed of. In fact, they can be a knockout! Finish with another winner: banana pancakes with chocolate and caramel sauce ($8).

starter: $6.90-$12.90
main: $12.90-$15
dessert: $8-$8.90
AE BC DC JCB MC V; Eftpos

Open: Sun-Wed 5pm-11pm, Thurs-Sat 5pm-midnight; reservations advisable (essential Fri & Sat evenings); licensed, no BYO

MARRICKVILLE

Bay Tinh
Vietnamese

☎ 9560 8673
316-318 Victoria Rd

Map 8 D4

Smoking throughout

Marrickville is not about showiness, but it has real pace and colour. So too the town's Bay Tinh restaurant, the simple but jaunty vehicle for the cuisine of Mr Tran Tinh, former chef to the President of South Vietnam. Slide open the heavy door and you'll be greeted with two rooms of tightly-packed red and white tables. The use of space is economical; be ready for a bustle, as what's on offer here is the best around. It's worth going just for the entrée of cubed beef ($4.20) – seared tender and served with a tart, silt-like sauce of lemon juice, salt and pepper. The tight, plump prawn rolls laced with fresh mint are also a good choice. For mains, the bonfire dishes of either prawn, chicken or beef (around $11) are a big attraction here, arriving in a moat of lighter fuel which is ignited into lapping blue flames. It's hands-on as a traditionally dressed waitress instructs the table on how to wrap the stewed contents into rice paper rolls.

starter: $3.20-$5.20
main: $6.80-$11.70
BC MC V

Open: Fri & Sat 5.30pm-10.30pm, Sun-Thurs 5.30pm-10pm; reservations accepted; BYO (corkage $1/bottle)

Corinthian Rotisserie Restaurant
Greek

☎ 9569 7084
283 Marrickville Road

Map 8 D3

Smoking throughout

The Corinthian Rotisserie is a stalwart Marrickville favourite that's been going strong for thirty-seven years – twenty of them under the current management. Family photos spanning four decades tell a proud story, and this sense of lifelong commitment translates into you being welcomed as if into their home. With its walls swathed in Grecian pastoral scenes, the Rotisserie is everything you'd expect. Not recommended for those who prefer to pick, the serves are rich and hearty, starting with entrees such as the spicy sausage ($7), chunky and slightly sour, and the skordalia ($5), tangy garlic and mashed potato that you gather up on hunks of bread. Cook and patriarch Frank Giannakelos occupies the front of the restaurant, whacking great handfuls of octopus onto a hissing grill, (served with chips and salad, $14). Along with the goat stew ($12), the lamb head is popular here; the stack of meaty skulls in the front kitchen is an occult sight, but they are a Giannakelos speciality.

starter: $5-$8
main: $11-$17
dessert: $2-$5
cash only

Open: daily noon-3pm, 6pm-3am; reservations accepted; licensed & BYO (corkage $3/bottle)

MARRICKVILLE

Map 8 D3

Danish Deli
Danish

☎ 9572 7988
181 Marrickville Road

The Danish Deli brings a healthy, smoky Nordic flavour to Marrickville, and why not – just about every other ethnic group is represented in this marketplace of a town. Operating as both a traditional takeaway delicatessen and a sit-down eatery, it makes for an ideal Saturday morning brunch, offering weekend papers, over 15 different teas and coffees and freshly squeezed juices. The open Danish sandwiches ($3.80) are bigger than hamburgers and laden with fine cured ham, rare roast beef or chicken and what are possibly the world's best scrambled eggs. There is real skill in the preparation, not surprising when you learn that in Denmark the training for the deli game is extensive and culturally respected. The platter dishes give you a chance to try nearly all the good stuff: Danish frikadels meatballs, marinated vegetables, Danish potato salad, bocconcini and plenty more.

starter: $2.50-$6.95
main: $2.50-$12.50
dessert: $3.95-$6.95
cash only

Open: Mon-Fri 8.30am-6pm, Sat 8am-4pm; reservations accepted; unlicensed

NEWTOWN

Map 9 A4

Nonsmoking tables available

Asakusa
Japanese

☎ 9519 8530
119 King St

With its wood floors and matching furniture, tasteful prints of kabuki actors, jolly lanterns, and fine traditional china and lacquerware, you'd expect Asakusa to be on the pricey side. That it's not is just one of the pleasures of this perennially popular restaurant, well known for its good value 'hot pot' platters (from $19 for two), where you cook a stew of chicken, beef or seafood at your table – lots of fun and very filling. Our tastebuds were immediately tingling over the edo-mae salad ($4.50), tidy piles of cucumber, pickled ginger and seaweed slivers, liberally laced with a vinegar dressing and a dash of wasabi. After trying the tuna and salmon sushi and sashimi in the Fuji lunch box ($15), we understood why locals rave about the quality of the fish here. The only bum note was the large, but stodgy chawan mushi ($6), a savoury egg custard, with a way too solid texture.

starter: $1.50-$12.50
main: $12.50-$17.50
dessert: $3.50
Lunch boxes $6-$15,
Party menus $19-$29.50
AE BC MC V

Open: Mon-Fri noon-2.30pm, Sun-Thurs 6pm-10pm, Fri & Sat 6pm-11pm; reservations advisable (especially Fri & Sat evenings); licensed & BYO (corkage $2/bottle)

NEWTOWN

Cinque
Modern Australian

☎ 9519 3077
261a King St

Map 9 B3

Wheelchair access

Smoking throughout

Cinque's one-size-fits-all noshery reflects Newtown's 'one big happy family' philosophy: clucky mums and dads, the pierced and pretty crowd and the serious cinephiles heading to the Dendy theatre behind. There's pasta or focaccia, a mod Oz prime cut with purée, and even a special of lime and mango bread ($3.50). And OK, the gazpacho ($5.50) could be a little more puréed, the chicken quesadilli ($10.50) could do with a lot less cheese and a little more chilli, and the gnocchi could taste a touch more home-made ($10.50). But it's cheap, it's open for breakfast, lunch and dinner and – perhaps most importantly – the staff are as chilled as the jazz soundtrack. Cinque is a tables-and-chairs-spilling-out-onto-the-street sort of affair (with a window bench and stools for those perusing possible purchases in the adjoining bookstore). And if the visual melange of the passing crowds isn't interesting enough, check out the marble-effect glass above the kitchen.

starter: $6-$7.90
main: $11-$16.90
dessert: $7

cash only

Open: daily 7.30am-11pm; reservations not accepted; BYO (corkage $1/person)

Kilimanjaro
African

☎ 9557 4565
280 King St

Map 9 B3

Don't be surprised if, upon entering, you're politely asked to choose from the blackboard menu and wait outside: there are only ten-or-so tables here so a bit of al fresco banter with other similarly 'shunned' diners is more or less inevitable. But the wait is unlikely to be lengthy, and once you're ushered to a cozy table with carved wooden bowls, any feelings of neglect quickly evaporate among the aromas of saffron and other spices, and a cheery and intimate atmosphere. Whether you're new to African food or not, heeding the editorial commentary on the menu will set you straight. Yassa (chicken on the bone with spices and steamed onions, $8): 'Very Tender', says the blackboard. Saussou-Gordiguan (tuna baked with spice and tamarind, $9.50): 'Very Tasty'. So concise. So accurate. No dessert on offer here, but it's not missed as the servings are surprisingly filling. Instead of wine, try washing it all down with a traditional African drink such as bissap or ginger ($1.50).

starter: $5-$5.50
main: $8-$9.50

cash only

Open: daily noon-3pm, Mon-Thurs & Sun 6pm-10pm, Fri & Sat 6pm-11pm; reservations not accepted; BYO ($1.50/person)

Cafe Crawl – Inner West

Whether you're writing a film script, a poem or have yet another essay deadline, visit one (or many) of our favourite western cafes for some caffeine inspiration.

Bacigalupo
284 King St, Newtown ☎ 9565 5238 Map 9 B3
It's Newtown's little literati scene, where scribblers and lap-top tappers work on word counts and readers flick through the latest glossy mags hanging from the counter. Look for the pressed metal ceiling and the mosaic of metal olive oil containers decorating the façade. It's unpronounceable, so just call it 'kiss of the wolf' (that's what it means).

Badde Manors
37 Glebe Point Rd, Glebe ☎ 9660 3797 Map 10 E6
The feeling's all olde worlde, but Badde Manors attracts new age types and eager new students from that university down the road. Chai and loose-leaf herbal teas are the latest go, but the special Robert Timms coffee blend has been going strong for 19 years.

Cafe Viva
Shop 5, 189 Darling St, Balmain ☎ 9810 9569 Map 11 B4
When they ripped out the booths and funky amoebae-shaped tables and replaced them with boring square brown numbers, one of the few bits of originality in the all-too-often sterile look of hyper-designed Sydney cafes disappeared. Thankfully the menu is still as colourful as ever: try Dr Seuss-inspired green eggs and ham and 'LSD' coffee.

Caffe Sport
2a Norton St, Leichhardt ☎ 9569 2397 Map 12 B2
The perfect antidote to the glitzy new Norton St eateries: fading sports posters on the walls (from Ferrari racers to the Sydney Flames – the women's basketball team), old-timers swapping statistics and sipping coffees in the corner, and budget focaccia ($4.50) and pasta ($6.50).

Camo's on the Park
Cnr West and Station Sts, Petersham ☎ 9568 4644 Map 12 B1
Home-made preserves and museli, fresh muffins, eggs florentine, 'Nim's eggs' with bacon, banana chutney, rocket pesto and a parkside possie: it's just about all you want on a lazy Saturday morning. Serves are as large as the ceiling-to-floor Pollack-inspired artworks. Come back the next day for the Sunday roasts.

Canteen
Shop 332 Darling St, Balmain ☎ 9818 1521 Map 11 A3
Canteen's permanently in progress renovations matches the half-finished homes of the young DINK couples that do coffee here, while the occasional movie producer will drop by during another day of scouting the peninsula's famous vistas.

digi.kaf
174 St Johns Rd, Glebe ☎ 9660 3509 Map 10 D4
A multifunctional environment for multimedia moguls on the make and musical whiz kids. You'll also find local business types doing lunch and backpackers doing their emails home. Breakfast (home-made baked beans, frittatas and eggs cooked with a chef's flair) can be very slow in coming, but the results are usually well worth the wait.

E.M.U Tek Cafe
149 Enmore Rd, Enmore ☎ 9557 4577 Map 9 C1
It's DIY culture, from dropping in and logging on to the Internet terminals lining the walls to the do-it-yourself ordering. Plant yourself at one of the kidney-shaped tables with your breakfast of soy smoothie ($3.50), sourdough bruschetta ($6) and short black ($2).

Iku
25a Glebe Point Rd, Glebe ☎ 9692 8720 Map 10 E6
Macrobiotic and vegan puddings, laksas, burgers and nori rolls might not sound like your typical fast food, but it's an established Sydney vegetarian chain store. The ideal place to plonk yourself down when you're on your own, on the go, or on the mend. And now, the first Iku franchise: 62 Oxford St, Darlinghurst, ☎ 9380 9780.

Martini Cafe
529 King St, Newtown ☎ 9557 7756 Map 9 D3
Whisk & Pin museli, Hank's jam, Segafredo coffee, bruschetta with roast tomato, haloumi, basil and poached eggs, sausages soaked in champagne, stainless steel fittings and Christine Keeler chairs: the classic, cool Sydney cafe.

Pelican's Fine Food
81 Darling St, Balmain ☎ 9810 1966 Map 11 A5
Everything is made on site in this takeaway coffee shop: the owner/pastry chef turns out sweets like brownies and blueberry cheesecake daily, pies in winter and savoury tarts in the warmer months.

Post Cafe
274 Marrickville Rd, Marrickville ☎ 9572 9339 Map 8 D3
Aussie Post has been moved to a little building out the back, and this slick cafe has taken over the heritage-listed room. With soaring ceilings, arched windows and paintings dripping from the walls, it's like a boutique art gallery that serves excellent coffee and Mediterranean-flavoured snack foods and sweets.

Satelite Expresso
80 Wilson St, Newtown ☎ 9557 8698 Map 9 B4
You can switch between David Bowie LPs and Tammy Wynette CDs in the turntable corner (next to the white vinyl lounge, where an Absolut vodka bottle harbours nothing more sinister than H20). The standard double-strength 'explosive' coffees are more than enough buzz for the part-time DJs, short-film auteurs and plucky poets who look for inspiration here. See their output at Thursday film and performance nights.

The Twain Shall Meet Cafe-Gallery
116 Smith St, Summer Hill ☎ 9716 5190 Map 8 C2
Established by an Australian/Korean couple, and now run by a Greek/English couple, this cafe is keeping the village-like Summer Hill happily harmonious. Choose from a few dozen different teas (ginseng, Japanese, Korean and earl grey varieties), 'mega-short blacks' and 'mega-hot chocolates', and snacks like 'The Twain Shall Meet' Greek salad with Turkish bread.

NEWTOWN

Map 9 C2
Wheelchair access
Smoking throughout

Lillipilli on King
Native Australian

☎ 9516 2499
441 King St

Newcomers to what has been dubbed 'native Australian cuisine' may think the tag a tad euphemistic once confronted with slices of Skippy on a plate. But through sheer quality of produce and presentation, even the most skeptical of patrons quickly overcome such prejudices, tucking into an array of native flora and fauna with epicurean abandon. Few symbols of our national identity are spared. Start with skewered kambara (crocodile) with a wild rosella sauce ($14), or the vegetarian-friendly kanpuka salad ($16) – native water lily buds drizzled with a bunya nut and warrigal green pesto. Try a dilly bag-style buru (kangaroo) steak, stuffed with oysters and mushrooms and smothered with pepperberry jus ($22.50). For those with fonder memories of Ranger Matt and co., choose from emu fillets ($22.50) to paperbark-baked barramundi ($22.50) and lemon myrtle fettuccine ($18). The tiered glacé trio ($7) of eucalyptus, lillipilli and macadamia flavoured ice cream is a must for dessert.

starter: $9-$14
main: $18-$23
dessert: $7
AE BC MC V; Eftpos

Open: daily 6pm-late; reservations advisable (especially weekends); BYO (corkage $1.50/person)

Map 9 C3
Entertainment: live Greek alternative music Friday night only (taverna night)
Smoking throughout
Courtyard tables

Lou Jack's
Greek

☎ 9557 7147
420 King St

For most of the week, Lou Jack's is a groovy Newtown cafe, offering yummy breakfasts, grilled haloumi as an option with everything, meze and pasta in a friendly, relaxed atmosphere. Friday night, though, is 'Taverna night', and it's a hoot, with live entertainment and a degustation ($25/person) that just keeps coming ... and coming ... and coming. Stuff yourself senseless with taramasalata (*real* taramasalata – not that pink, low-rent substitute), tzatziki, melitzanosalata (grilled eggplant dip), and baskets of pide. Then there's marinated olives and dolmades. Followed by kefte (spiced meatballs), marinated octopus, souvlaki and grilled haloumi. And on it goes for more than one-and-a-half hours until the red sofa looks about as far as you can make it without collapsing. Which is a pretty popular option, and a great vantage point to chill out and enjoy the live music and marvel at the stamina of some of the more energetic among us as they dance and stamp their way into the night.

starter: $5.50
main: $5-$9.50
dessert: $1.50-$5.50
Meze platter $27,
degustation $25
cash only

Open: Mon-Fri 8am-5pm, Thurs & Fri 8am-10.30pm; reservations essential Friday nights; BYO (no corkage)

NEWTOWN

Mio
Mediterranean

☎/fax 9519 5328
105 King Street

Map 9 A4

Smoking after 10pm

Mio, née Brio, has undergone a facelift and a change of focus, from American/vegetarian to modern Mediterranean. But the commitment to fresh produce, innovation and generous servings remains. If you're in the habit of 'leaving room for dessert', leave *a lot* of room. In fact, don't even think about sides... though the bruschetta and olive tapenade ($9) is deservedly tempting. And think very seriously indeed about the feasibility of a starter... though the grilled haloumi salad with roasted capsicum strips and balsamic ($8) is tasty enough to advise pushing your luck. And mains? Well, you have to have a main; a beautifully moist seafood risotto ($19) or a vegetarian-friendly globe artichoke ravioli ($18), perhaps. But the mudcake! Three contestants, a single serving, and, after five attempts, the mudcake unconquered, the challengers in a dozy state of too-much-to-eat lethargy. Great coffee and a convivial atmosphere makes for a delightful defeat.

Open: Tues-Fri 6pm-10.30pm, Sat & Sun 11am-10.30pm; reservations advisable, especially weekends; licensed & BYO (corkage $2/person)

starter: $3-$10
main: $15-$22
dessert: $9

AE BC JCB MC V

Safari
Indonesian

☎ 9557 4458
22 King Street

Map 9 A5

Smoking throughout

Just down from Bob Gould's famously disordered bookstore, Safari has a similarly eclectic interior. Indonesian parasols and fountains, Grecian columns, a statuette of Toad of Toad Hall... or maybe there's more to the Indonesian Happy Drink ($2.50) than milk and rose syrup? While the signage is captioned 'Seafare', there's lots here for vegetarians and non-seafood eaters, such as terong kipas – deep-fried eggplant with chilli dipping sauce ($5.90) – and dangang balal ($10.90), tender, spice crusted beef with a chopped chilli garnish. That being said, the seafood is the house speciality. The barbecued sea bream with lemon and chilli ($15) is swimming in Safari's homemade secret soy blend and garnished with birdseye chillis (have water handy), baked onions and a drizzle of lemon. Like the décor, the service can be a tad erratic, but once you've settled in, there is an ever-smiling, homey feel that has locals coming back again and again.

Open: Mon-Thurs 6pm-10.30pm, Fri & Sat 6pm-11pm; reservations accepted; BYO (corkage $1.50/person)

starter: $3-$6.90
main: $6.90-$15
dessert: $3-$3.50
Indonesian banquet ($20/person)

AE BC MC V

INNER WEST

Map 9 B3

Nonsmoking tables available

Thai Pothong
Thai

☎ 9550 6277
294 King St

This huge 280-seater is often overlooked on a street where the small restaurant rules. But it's one of the best-lookers, despite the sprawl. The décor is classic King of Siam – golden statues of soldiers and royalty flicker as waiters pass by bearing dishes alight with flames. It's a wonder the ceiling fans – which are working so hard you'd think they were competing in the air-con Olympics – don't blow those fires out! Your food will also tend to be low on chilli heat. Entrées include curry puffs ($7.20), of course, but also a dish that's like an Indonesian gado gado ($11.90) – vegetables with peanut sauce. An oily duck curry ($15.90) is as rich as promised. The flowers on the tables are a nice touch, but service can be as distant as those diners at the other side of the room. The menus are very user-friendly, particularly for large groups, with beer-, wine- and chef's suggestions-of-the-month.

starter: $6.90-$8.90
main: $11.90-$23.90
dessert: $5.90-$8.90
AE BC DC MC V; Eftpos

Open: daily noon-3pm, 6pm-11pm; reservations essential (Fri & Sat evenings); licensed & BYO (corkage $2/person)

NEWTOWN

Wedgetail
Italian (pizza)

☎ 9516 1568
1a Bedford St

Map 9 B2

Pavement tables

In a world of haute minimalism this place is a relief: Wedgetail gives you terracotta tones, pots and pans hanging from the ceiling and a bowl of lemons next to a basket of art-directed twigs. A wall sculpture of old oven dials saves it from being too twee – as does *The Godfather* soundtrack on high rotation. Situated in the closest thing Newtown has to a piazza, this thin crust pizza purveyor has stood the test of the suburb's Thai takeover. There are many variations on a couple of themes (vegetarian, seafood) and a daily special or two. Pasta is relegated to a tiny menu corner, but antipasto should not be overlooked – it's more of a hybrid salad with touches like fresh rocket and figs. Thankfully the sweet pizzas have made way for the likes of a blueberry tart with cinnamon-infused anglaise ($7.50). Requests for a vegan pizza or less cheese on a seafood pizza are no problem.

starter: $6.50-$15
main: $10-$22
dessert: $7
Set menu $20

cash only

Open: Tues-Sun 6pm-10pm, Fri & Sat 6pm-11pm; reservations advisable (essential weekends); BYO (corkage $1.50/person)

Zimi
Italian/modern Australian

☎ 9519 4044
224 King St

Map 9 B3

Wheelchair access

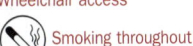

Smoking throughout

Zimi was once the smartest-looking queen of King St. A modern minimalist madam on a strip that looked like it would never wipe the smear of grunge from its face. One or two other slick sisters have joined her now, but she's still winning all the popularity prizes. It's mainly pasta and pizza, with excellent extras like salads doused in above-average dressings of walnut oil and fresh citrus flavours. There's a structural soundness to the creamy but not too-heavy risotto – try the chicken and basil version, topped with freshly-shaved parmesan ($12.50). There are also meaty mains like lamb cutlets with a three-cheese polenta mash ($17). Sometimes the pumpkin in your tortellini might be a little lumpy and your pizza might have a slightly soggy crust, but none of this seems to matter. You're not paying a queen's ransom – but if your wallet *is* stretched, the 'Money Lent' hoc shop is right opposite. Some things about King St will never change.

starter: $6-$7.50
main: $9.50-$17.50
dessert: $1.50-$6

AE BC DC MC V

Open: Mon-Fri 5pm-late, Sat & Sun 11am-late; reservations not accepted; BYO (corkage $1/person)

INNER WEST

PETERSHAM

Map 8 C3
Smoking throughout

Restaurant Portugal
Portuguese

☎ 9564 1163
102 New Canterbury Road

Although this is a classic venue for couples, gentlemanly proprietor Manuel Duarte really likes to see this burly fare enjoyed as it is in his native Lisbon – with cheery company and generous amounts of red wine. The menu, revolving around pork and seafood, isn't big, so turn up with a party of six and you can try just about everything. After an entrée of sharply flavoured chourico sausages ($8) and saucy clams bulhao pato ($14), the tour continues with some Portuguese sardines, their silver skins blackened almost to ash, char-grilled octopus (both $13.50) and the pork alentejana ($14), gravy-ladled chunks of pork spliced with baby clams. These are meals you'd knock back between pirate voyages around the Med, but they're pretty good on a Friday night out as well.

starter: $1.80-$14
main: $11.50-$17.50
AE BC MC V

Open: Tues-Thurs 5pm-9:30pm, Fri & Sat 11.30am-10pm, Sun 11:30am-9pm; reservations accepted; licensed & BYO (corkage $2/bottle)

ROZELLE

Map 11 C2
Wheelchair access
Courtyard tables

Il Piavé
Italian

☎ 9810 6204
639 Darling St

The brainchild of former soccer player Robert Enzo Martin and his sister Vanessa, Il Piavé is a winner from the start. If the perky service does not charm you, the sleek design and the courtyard shaded by a huge eucalypt will. And that's before you get swept away by the vast bowls of homemade pasta and gnocchi. An antipasto to die for has borlotti beans, green beans, roasted capsicum, pickled eggplant, prosciutto and other cured meats with shavings of parmesan ($12.90). Which makes us grateful we settled for one main of quail with polenta slices drizzled with truffle oil ($19.90) and an entrée-size char-grilled seafood ($15.90). This precarious mound of claws and shells includes huge mussels, clams, crab, squid and a giant skewered prawn. With such sticky-finger-inducing food, request a finger bowl. In the face of such generosity and good intentions, no wonder it's booked-out on a Tuesday just weeks after opening.

starter: $9.50-$15.90
main: $15.50-$28.90
dessert: $6.90-$8.90
AE BC DC MC V; Eftpos

Open: Thurs, Fri & Sat noon-2pm, Sun noon-3pm, Tues-Sat 6.30pm-10pm; reservations advisable; licensed & BYO (corkage $3/bottle)

ROZELLE

Rozelle Fish Bowl
Seafood/modern Australian

☎ 9555 7302
580 Darling St

Map 11 B2

No smoking inside

Pavement tables

Relax at one of the blond-wood tables at this friendly neighbourhood restaurant or, for a ringside view of how it's all done, perch on a plush magenta stool at the counter. The seasonally changing menu of Asian- and Mediterranean-inspired dishes is supplemented by daily specials, which might include quick-fried Hawkesbury River calamari with chilli or grilled scallops served with a dollop of creamy, smoky baba ghanoush and drizzled with sweet red capsicum butter (both $14.90). A vast, steaming bowl of fragrant saffron seafood risotto ($19.90), replete with scallops and mussels, betrays the European heritage of chef Xavier Deslis. If it's comfort food you're after, you need look no further than the beer-battered or grilled fish of the day, served with a peppery mixed-leaf salad, thick-cut chips and lemon myrtle mayonnaise ($14.90). And the tangy, velvety lemon and lime tart ($8) might still entice you to indulge, even after all those chips.

starter: $14.90
main: $14.90-$19.90
dessert: $7.50-$9

AE BC DC MC V

Open: Tues-Thurs 6pm-9.30pm, Fri & Sat 6pm-10.30pm (two seatings: 6pm & 8.30pm); reservations essential; BYO (corkage $2/bottle)

Welcome Hotel
Modern Australian

☎ 9810 1323
91 Evans St

Map 11 C2

Nonsmoking tables available

Courtyard tables

In this genuine neighbourhood pub, you can choose your spot in the stylish dining room or in the magical courtyard shaded by palms and ferns, both cleverly shielded from the rowdy bonhomie that prevails in the bar. Crostini with tomato and chilli jam ($10) are topped with a tasty mishmash of sun-dried tomatoes and mild goat's cheese. For mains, the baked stuffed lamb with garlic and spinach on braised red cabbage and gratin potatoes ($18.50) is comforting, if a little ordinary, but a light dish of papardelle with fresh prawns ($12.50) drizzled with lime-and-ginger-infused olive oil has more zing. Although the overall experience is a pleasant one, the combination of restaurant prices and bar service jars a little. The need to traipse back to the counter to order dessert is particularly galling, and for each course you have to stand in line and pay in separate transactions.

starter: $8.50-$14.50
main: $15.50-$22.50
dessert: $8-$11

AE BC DC MC V; Eftpos

Open: daily noon-3pm, 6pm-10pm; reservations advisable (essential weekends); licensed, no BYO

INNER WEST

Back for More

Bank's Thai Restaurant
91 Enmore Rd, Enmore ☎ 9550 6840 Map 9 C2
From the candle-lit shadow puppets casting some South-East Asian ambience on the walls, to the plastic grapes and fairy lights in the courtyard, to that scrumptious chilli and garlic crocodile stir-fry, Bank's Thai just keeps getting bigger and better.

Frattini
122 Marion St, Leichhardt ☎ 9569 2997 Map 12 B1
The linen service and lovingly made traditional Southern Italian food all smacks of a place in the next price bracket up the scale – but Frattini's popular whitebait fritters, deep-fried spinach and ricotta dumplings and veal parmigiana all come at incredibly reasonable prices.

Perama
88 Audley St, Petersham ☎ 9569 7534 Map 8 C3
Perama's modern Greek food – fresh Australian produce and a touch of Asian flavours – is almost a case study in what's so fine about Australian dining. We recommend the delightful and not-too salty haloumi and pretty much anything barbecued.

Simply Thai
186 King St, Newtown ☎ 9565 5111 Map 9 B4
The laksas are still some of the very best we've ever tried, and we're even getting used to the Scandinavian-feel décor.

Sumalee Thai
Bank Hotel, 324 King St, Newtown ☎ 9565 1730 Map 9 B3
It's a mega-beer garden decked out like a Thai island resort. The birthday groups and work parties are banquet sized and the servings are generous, so don't worry about the big price tags on the mains – you won't need starters or desserts, which rarely feature on the blackboard menu. This food's for sharing. (Ask for a table under one of the gas heaters in winter).

✱ *Write to us:* *We think we've got Sydney well-covered – even so, there are always new places to try. Our tastebuds will travel, so let us know about suburbs where there's more to discover. Write to us or email us (see p 11 for details) and the best suggestions will receive the next edition free.*

EASTERN SUBURBS

Bellevue Hill

Bondi

Bondi Junction

Bronte

Double Bay

Moore Park

Paddington

Rose Bay

Vaucluse

Woollahra

Map

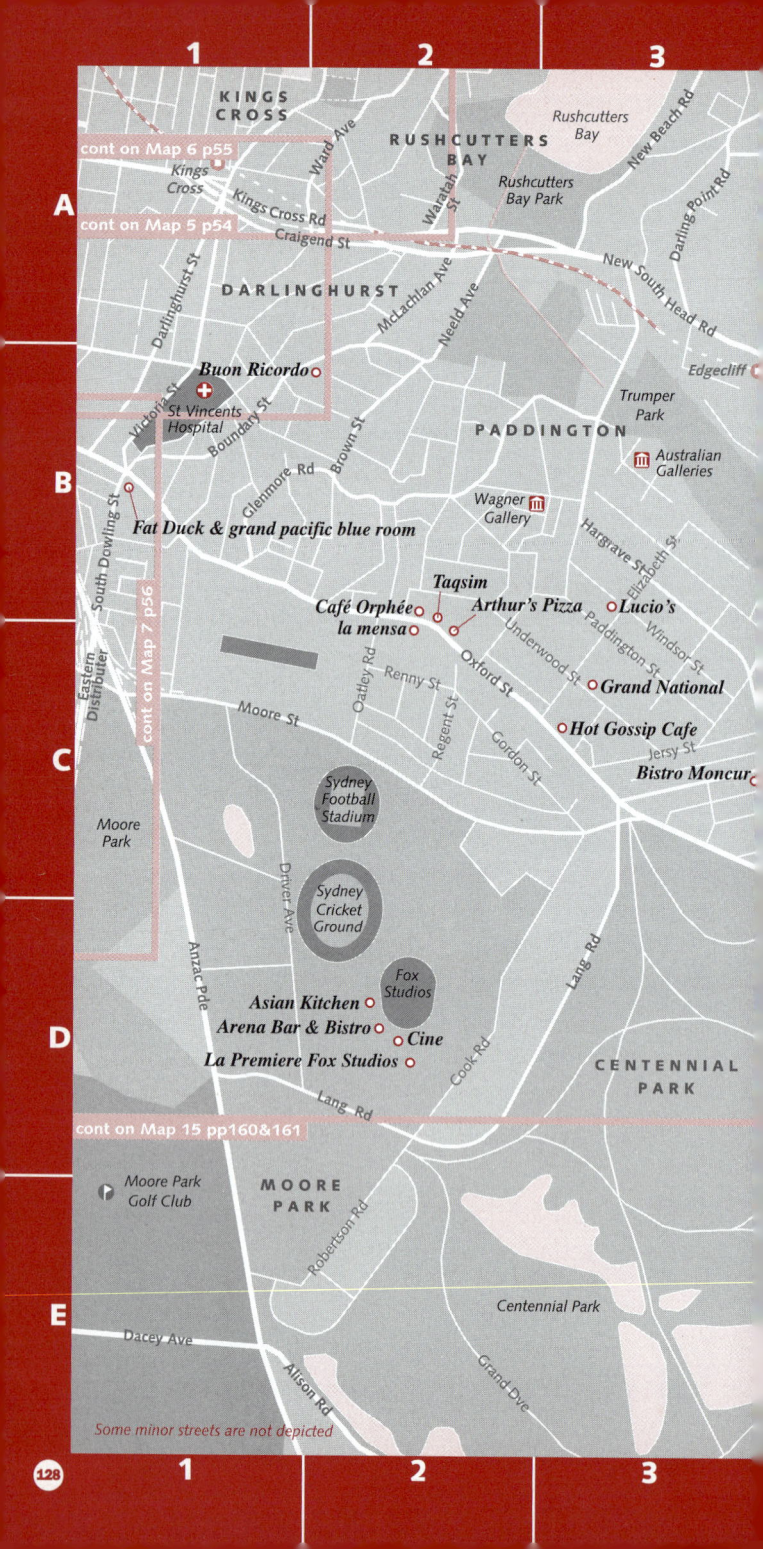

KINGS CROSS
- Kings Cross
- Kings Cross Rd
- Ward Ave
- cont on Map 6 p55
- cont on Map 5 p54
- Craigend St

RUSHCUTTERS BAY
- Rushcutters Bay
- Rushcutters Bay Park
- Waratah St
- New Beach Rd
- Darling Point Rd
- New South Head Rd

DARLINGHURST
- Darlinghurst St
- McLachlan Ave
- Neeld Ave
- Boundary St
- Brown St
- Victoria St
- **Buon Ricordo**
- St Vincents Hospital
- Edgecliff
- Trumper Park

PADDINGTON
- Glenmore Rd
- Wagner Gallery
- Australian Galleries
- Hargrave St
- Elizabeth St
- Paddington St
- Windsor St
- **Fat Duck & grand pacific blue room**
- South Dowling St
- Eastern Distributor
- cont on Map 7 p56
- **Café Orphée**
- **la mensa**
- **Taqsim**
- **Arthur's Pizza**
- **Lucio's**
- Oatley Rd
- Renny St
- Regent St
- Oxford St
- Underwood St
- Gordon St
- **Grand National**
- **Hot Gossip Cafe**
- Jersy St
- **Bistro Moncur**
- Moore St
- Moore Park
- Anzac Pde
- Driver Ave
- Sydney Football Stadium
- Sydney Cricket Ground
- Fox Studios
- **Asian Kitchen**
- **Arena Bar & Bistro**
- **Cine**
- **La Premiere Fox Studios**
- Cook Rd
- Lang Rd
- **CENTENNIAL PARK**

cont on Map 15 pp160&161

MOORE PARK
- Moore Park Golf Club
- Robertson Rd
- Centennial Park
- Dacey Ave
- Alison Rd
- Grand Dve

Some minor streets are not depicted

Map 13 - Paddington & Woollahra

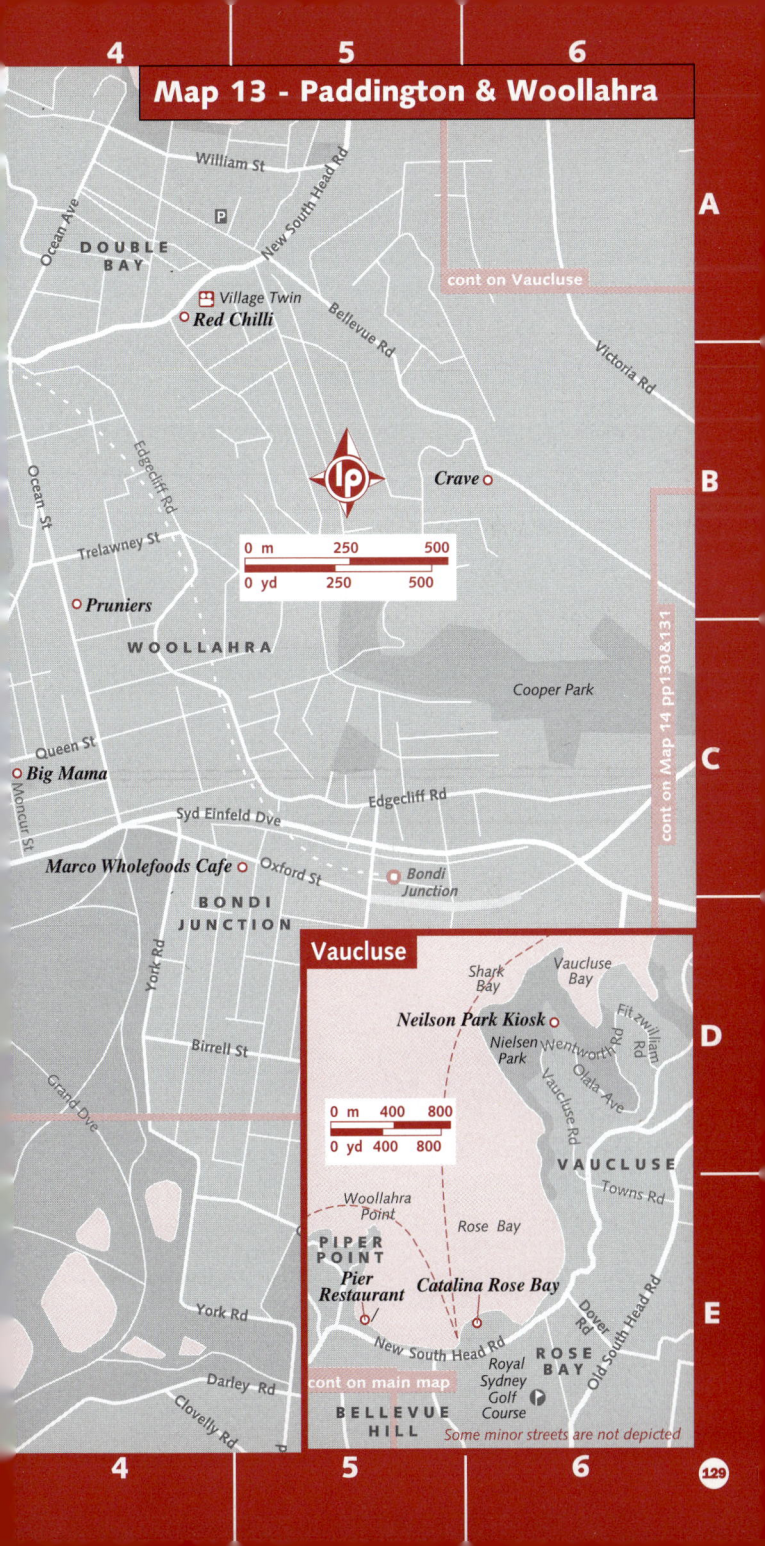

Map 14 - Bondi

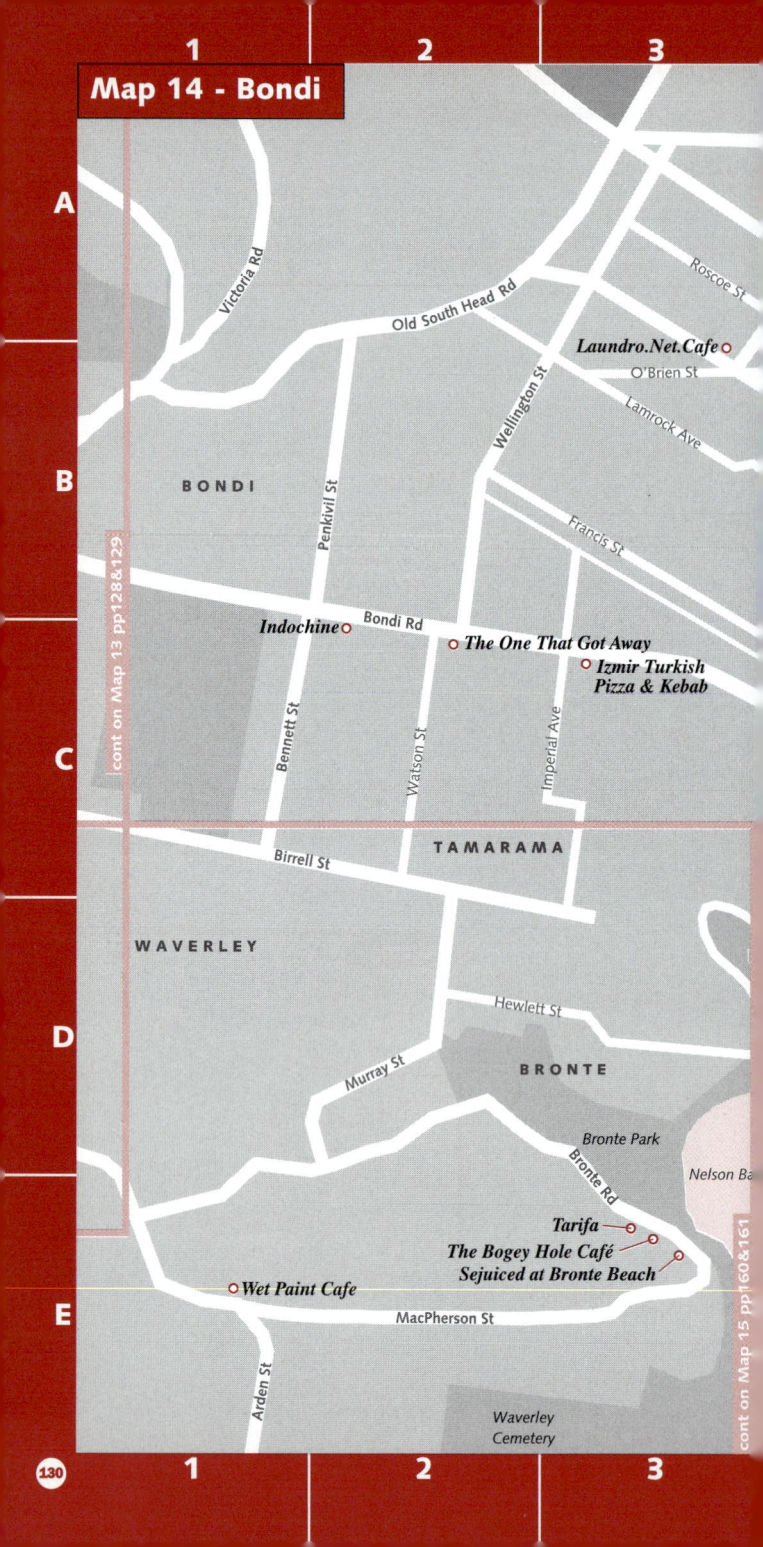

- Laundro.Net.Cafe
- Indochine
- The One That Got Away
- Izmir Turkish Pizza & Kebab
- Tarifa
- The Bogey Hole Café
- Sejuiced at Bronte Beach
- Wet Paint Cafe

BONDI
TAMARAMA
WAVERLEY
BRONTE

Victoria Rd, Old South Head Rd, Roscoe St, O'Brien St, Wellington St, Lamrock Ave, Penkivil St, Francis St, Bondi Rd, Bennett St, Watson St, Imperial Ave, Birrell St, Hewlett St, Murray St, Bronte Park, Bronte Rd, Nelson Ba, MacPherson St, Arden St, Waverley Cemetery

cont on Map 13 pp128&129
cont on Map 15 pp160&161

130

Map: Bondi Beach area

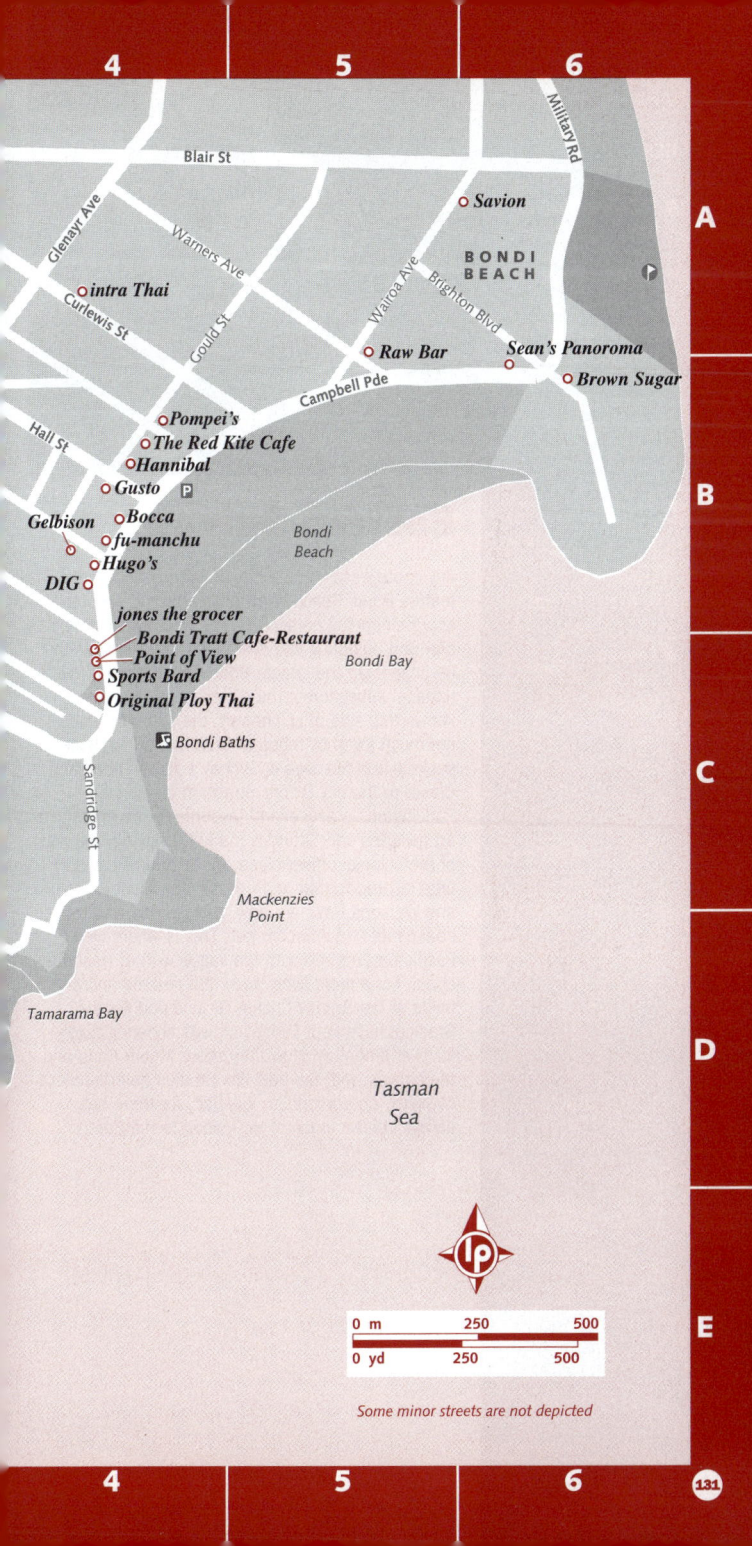

Streets and locations:
- Military Rd
- Blair St
- Glenayr Ave
- Warners Ave
- Curlewis St
- Gould St
- Wairoa Ave
- Brighton Blvd
- Campbell Pde
- Hall St
- Sandridge St
- Bondi Beach
- Bondi Bay
- Mackenzies Point
- Tamarama Bay
- Tasman Sea

Listings:
- Savion
- intra Thai
- Raw Bar
- Sean's Panoroma
- Brown Sugar
- Pompei's
- The Red Kite Cafe
- Hannibal
- Gusto
- Gelbison
- Bocca
- fu-manchu
- Hugo's
- DIG
- jones the grocer
- Bondi Tratt Cafe-Restaurant
- Point of View
- Sports Bard
- Original Ploy Thai
- Bondi Baths

Scale: 0–500 m / 0–500 yd

Some minor streets are not depicted

131

BEST

- **Catalina Rose Bay**
  Sydney dining at its most divine

- **grand pacific blue room**
  Cosy or happening – whatever your mood

- **Sean's Panaroma**
  Simply perfect creations, relaxed attitude

- **Taqsim**
  Eat like an Egyptian

Eastern Suburbs

Any photo essay on the city of Sydney will always feature Bondi Beach. With its celebrated spectacle of wave-hopping horseplay, lazy, coconut-oiled sexuality and posturing lifesaver culture, it demands to be filmed. Off the beach, Bondi is a parade of multinational subcultures; the pizzerias are the best known this side of Leichhardt, the summery pubs are much loved by tribes of British and Irish backpackers and the area is Sydney's Jewish heartland. Closer to the city Oxford Street, in fashionable Paddington, is a weekend favourite for its boutiques, art galleries and Saturday market. Originally the digs of the colonial officer class, the exclusive bay suburbs located further north (Rose Bay, Double Bay and Watsons Bay), are now synonymous with the boat-pants and intercom set. This is where clean Pacific breezes mix with the vague waft of wealthy ennui. For a more lively pace, the revered sporting fields of the Sydney Cricket Ground and Football Stadium have kept Sydney crowds cheering madly for over a century. Now they share Moore Park, and the crowds, with the new Fox Studios entertainment complex. An appropriate location, for there has always been a touch of Hollywood to the East.

BELLEVUE HILL

Crave
Modern Australian/
New York deli

☎ 9327 1670
98G Bellevue Rd

Map 13 B6

No smoking inside

Pavement tables

We've been known to plan a weekend around visits to Crave in suburban Bellevue Hill, where the clan who started up Bondi's famous Gusto weave their New York deli-cum-cafe magic. Chase off the night-before demons with one of Sydney's finest caffè lattes and a ricotta and jam-slathered bagel. Return at lunchtime for a fabulous toasted focaccia with goat's cheese, roast pumpkin and caramelised onion ($6.50), a to-die-for chicken pie ($4.95) or one of the three daily salads. Greedily, slink back for a reviving fruit whip ($4.50) – berries and banana blended into a frenzy – then take away some pasta and a Crave sugo before heading off to the tailor to get your clothes let out! Jewish ladies in tennis gear rub shoulders with journalists as they perch on stools at the bar, while people in-the-know pick up sandwiches, home-made chutneys and jams, wicked biscuits and fudge.

main: $5-$10
dessert: $5.50

Open: Mon-Fri 8am-7.30pm, Sat & Sun 8am-5pm; reservations not accepted; unlicensed

AE BC DC MC V; Eftpos

BONDI

Bocca
Modern Australian

☎ 9130 8611
84 Campbell Pde

Map 14 B4

No smoking inside

Pavement tables

Sandwiched between two good, inexpensive eateries – Il Puntino and fu-manchu – and only a volleyball's strike from the pricier but ever-popular Hugo's and Sports Bard, Bocca needed a strong nerve to enter the Campbell Pde food stadium. Visually it makes the grade: rigorously simple and elegant. For service too it scores the necessary points. And the food at Bocca cleans up with intricately constructed, original meals. Skip the too-fussy oyster ravioli and brave the pigs' trotter terrine ($17.50), an ensemble of quail, veal sweetbreads and pigs' hooves. The braised snapper with roast potatoes, zucchini and tapenade ($23.50) is pleasantly subtle after so much richness. While the pineapple carpaccio ($8.90) with lime and pearls (that's tapioca by any other name) knocks spots off the entire meal with its mix of sweetly sharp and spicily warm flavours. With unasked-for appetisers punctuating the meal, order modestly.

starter: $13.80-$17.50
main: $22-$24.50
dessert: $8.90

Open: daily 6.30pm-11.30pm; reservations accepted; licensed & BYO (corkage $4/bottle)

AE BC DC MC V; Eftpos

EASTERN SUBURBS

BONDI

Map 14 B4

Smoking throughout

Pavement tables

DIG
Modern Australian

☎ 9365 6044
56 Campbell Pde

Wear your sunglasses, bite through the thick slices of sourdough bread, and sit your dog down on your patch of pavement. The weekend breakfast is the most important meal of the week in Bondi, and there are a number of ways to take it. Organic porridge ($5.90) is one, so is tofu with snappily fried button mushrooms ($7.50). DIG pours generous serves of creamy hollandaise over poached eggs (organic, of course, $9.50). Order a 'Bondi Mermaid' ($10.90) and the eggs come with crêpes and 'champagne' ham. At night, candles and white tablecloths are whipped out and dishes like a seafood medley ($19.50), grain-fed sirloin ($19.50) and Atlantic salmon ($21.50) are whipped up. If Campbell Pde has an uptown end, this is it – all polished wood, white walls, and corner seating. While you're playing at being posh, open up the weekend paper and find that ideal million dollar apartment just down the road.

starter: $11.50-$15
main: $16.50-$23.50
dessert: $9.50

AE BC DC MC V; Eftpos

Open: daily 7am-midnight; reservations advisable (Thurs-Sat evenings); licensed, no BYO

Map 14 B4

No smoking inside

Balcony tables

fu-manchu
Chinese

☎ 9300 0416
Level 1,
80 Campbell Pde

The main room at fu-manchu in Bondi is reminiscent of the restaurant's Darlinghurst outlet; slick Hong Kong chic with steel tables for two and digital artworks on the wall. A smaller room features a rosewood Chinese banquet table for groups, but the best seats are the plastic chairs on the balcony. This is one of the few first floor eateries on Campbell Pde, at the southern end of Bondi Beach. If you've been skating, surfing or just schmoozing with the sun-washed masses below, you'll probably have a healthy appetite for the much-loved vegetarian steam buns ($4.50) or the large chicken and prawn laksas ($12.50). We love the chilli salt prawns ($14.50), cooked in a crispy tempura batter with spring onions peeking through and chilli flakes and fine onion strips tossed on top. We're not so taken with the tofu with shrimp mince ($5.50). But most of your forays into this pan-Asian menu are likely to be well rewarded.

starter: $4.50-$9.50
main: $9.50-$16.50
dessert: $6.50

cash only

Open: daily noon-3pm, 5.30pm-10.15pm (last orders); reservations accepted; licensed & BYO (corkage $2/person)

Campbell Pde, Bondi

The Irish, English, Canadian, German and Japanese accents heard up and down Campbell Parade are probably all saying the same thing: 'Which way to Utopia?' The promised antipodean land isn't on the northern end of Bondi Beach, where even the grand hotel palisades can't disguise the seedier side of Bondi – the pubs and pokie machines, the 24-hour adult video services in hotels where no-one checks in under their real name. The smells of souvlaki, Royal Copenhagen ice cream and battered, deep-fried Mars Bars (the surfer's snack) all make up the distinct Bondi scent. Everyone's strutting their stuff here – rollerbladers, rappers and Brazilian street dancers treat the esplanade as a stage. Bare-breasted grandmothers frolic in the surf while short-film directors convene in the Bondi Pavilion (which, like the people in Bondi, has a permanently peeling skin). Being in Bondi inevitably means tottering on that brink between having the best time and the worst trip of your life (watch your step). There's always been an element of carelessness and undercurrents of violence. During the week, surfheads wage a war of the waves, while on weekends, petrolheads take over the streets. But Bondi has, also, long been a home to a tribe of privileged trust-afarians, and by the late 1990s the rest of Sydney society had discovered Bondi. Magazine-empire princes and their bikini model wives bought up the prime real estate. The gourmet providers moved in with them, of course, turning the southern end of the Parade into a Paddington-by-the-beach. Even the crumbling Bondi Icebergs, where a club of swimmers brave the sea baths during even the coldest winter snaps, is gearing up for a complete refit and an 'international' restaurant. No wonder the annual nude surfing comp had to go.

BONDI

Map 14 B4

Smoking throughout

Pavement tables

Gelbison
Italian

☎ 9130 4042
10 Lamrock Ave

Within a stone's throw of the trendy cafes and slick apartments along the southern stretch of Sydney's most famous beach lies one of Bondi's most steadfastly authentic eateries: Gelbison (better known to spooneristic locals as 'Mel Gibson's'). This unpretentious pizzeria, frequented mostly by in-the-know locals, has been serving up thin-crusted pizzas, rich-sauced pastas and other traditional Italian dishes for 15 years. Cheap, crowded, bright and noisy, this has always been the place to come for the incredible zingaro ($13.50), a fresh tomato pizza heaped high with zingy rocket leaves, or the fettuccine stracciatella ($9.50), a full-flavoured pasta smothered with a creamy pea, mushroom and bolognese sauce. Gelbison makes every dish memorable by keeping things simple. There's a subtle eccentricity about the place too. The faux marble finish on the walls is at odds with the jolly Italian aphorisms nailed to them, and the service is sometimes capricious. But who cares? Gelbison isn't about appearances, it's about food.

starter: $6.90-$13.50
main: $5-$17.90
dessert: $5.50-$6.50

cash only

Open: daily 5pm-midnight; reservations accepted; BYO (corkage $2/table)

Map 14 B4

Entertainment: belly dancer on Fri & Sat at 9.30pm

Smoking throughout

Hannibal
Lebanese

☎ 9130 4605
82-86 Gould St

Hannibal has red Arabic carpets on the walls, red-carpeted floors and red-hued lighting so low vegetarians need to be vigilant to ensure they don't confuse a meatball for a mushroom. It's a long way from the Bondi beach culture, but back street Hannibal is a handy haven for locals. Birthday groups spread out on floor cushions and share a hookah, or perhaps a mixed starter of chef's specials (hummus, tabouli and what is not too extravagantly dubbed 'the best felafel in the world', $17). Try Lebanon's national dish, kibee nayeh ($13), slightly glutinous raw meat and crushed wheat seasoned with olive oil and lemon (wrap it in pita bread with a mint leaf on top). Thumbs up to the spinach and pine nut pie ($7.50). The house wine has a very high quaffability quotient, but watch that the hookah pipe finale doesn't send you reeling back and staring at the silver moon and stars on the ceiling.

starter: $7-$12
main: $7-$17
dessert: $2-$3
Set menu $20 or $24/person (min 2 people)

AE BC DC MC V

Open: Sun-Thurs noon-11pm, Fri & Sat noon-midnight; reservations essential for large groups; licensed & BYO (corkage $2/person)

BONDI

Indochine
Vietnamese

☎ 9387 4081
99 Bondi Rd

The décor hasn't changed – artificial plants, lacquered mother-of-pearl landscapes and a poster of Catherine Deneuve in (what else?) *Indochine*. In the few years this Vietnamese restaurant has been plying its trade on Bondi Rd, the food hasn't changed much either – that is something to be grateful for. Fans still queue for fresh rice paper rolls with a sweet peanut sauce ($6) and Vietnamese pancakes bursting with pork, prawns and bean sprouts ($7.20). Braised scallops with ginger ($14.40) are a perennial favourite. Their warm, juicy flavours are a good complement for the smoky sweetness of minced prawns wrapped around grilled sugarcane sticks ($12.50). A simple accompaniment to a meal – or a dish to enjoy on its own – is the steamed fresh asparagus with oyster sauce ($8.90). If you've got room for anything else, finish with sugar bananas cooked in coconut milk ($4.20). They're amazingly sweet!

Open: daily 6pm-10pm; reservations advisable (especially Fri & Sat evenings); BYO (no corkage)

Map 14 C2

Smoking throughout

Courtyard tables

starter: $5.60-$7.20
main: $7.50-$19
dessert: $4.20-$6

AE BC MC V

---

intra Thai
Thai

☎ 9130 3324
88-90 Curlewis St

intra Thai has an almost temple-like calm that's a world away from the glitzy Thai restaurant-cum-nightclubs just a few hundred metres away. Bondi locals seem to prefer intra Thai's chintzy chandeliers and single-carnation-in-vase vibe. Or perhaps it's the goldfishes' fascinating fish tank shenanigans – God only knows what the carved wooden deities resting above are thinking! The staff bring you chilled water without asking, servings are generous and the flavours are complex and distinct. Minced tofu larb ($9.50) is a wonderfully salty, coriander, lime foil to dishes such as the sizzling seafood platter ($12.90). 'Volcanic chicken' ($10.90) is a spatchcock marinated in rum, encased in an armour of aluminium foil and delivered to your table in flames: it's tender, sweet, crispy on the outside and the meat falls off the bone. Add to all that interesting flavours, such as grapefruit sauces, and you'll wonder why you would queue to go anywhere else.

Open: daily 5.30pm-10.30pm; reservations advisable; BYO (no corkage)

Map 14 A4

Nonsmoking tables available

starter: $4.40-$6.40
main: $7.90-$16.90
dessert: $3-$4
Set menu $19.50/person
 (min 4 people)

AE BC MC V

EASTERN SUBURBS

BONDI

Map 14 B3

Entertainment:
live jazz/rock and DJ venue
Mon-Sat 7pm-11.30pm,
Sun 4pm-11.30pm

Smoking throughout

starter: $4.50-$5.50
main: $6.50-$12.50
dessert: $2.50-$5.50

cash only

Laundro.Net.Cafe
International

☎ 9365 1211
**113-115 Hall St
(cnr Glenayr Ave)**

This place tries to be all things: a laundromat, an internet centre, a bar, a music venue, an eatery. Amazingly, it works. Laundro.Net.Cafe judders with dancing washing machines, drumming computer keyboards and the spin cycle of acid jazz/rock. From sud-resistant cement floor to industrial lampshaded ceiling, it's a place with groove. But you don't have to be hipper-than-thou to eat here. Playfully titled dishes like the buddha burger (tofu burger with Asian greens, $7.90) and the fat snag (sausages and mash with tomato chutney, $7.90) aren't a disguise for indifferent food, either. The nachos desperados (small, $6.90) is a mountainous plate with plenty of jalapeños. The luciano ($6.50) describes itself as a pesto and goat's cheese crostini, and while the goat seemed absent from our serving, the thick, home-made pesto and smoky, juicy chunks of tomato compensated. Swilled down with well-priced beers and wines, a meal at Laundro.Net.Cafe is an alive-and-kicking experience.

Open: daily 11.30am-11.30pm (breakfast: daily 11.30am-2pm); reservations not accepted; licensed, no BYO

The One That Got Away
Seafood

☎ 9389 4227
163 Bondi Rd

Map 14 C2

Bondi wouldn't be Bondi without a fish and chips shop but a takeaway of this calibre is a surprise. The One That Got Away was the winner of the 1999-2000 Sydney Fish Market Seafood Award for the best large seafood retailer, and it's easy to see why. Attention to detail is evident everywhere: in the blue terrazzo floor studded with starfish, in the painted fish swimming across the ceiling, and, most of all, in the feast of seafood on display. If dining in (at bar stools), choose from 12 types of fish ($7.90-$13.90) and a range of shellfish ($5.90-$12) and have them grilled, barbecued, steamed or poached. Snack on exquisite sushi ($1.50-$2.50 each), or feast on the mixed platter for two ($39) and enjoy scallops, prawns, octopus and a whole blue swimmer crab. If all this sounds too fancy for you, don't worry – you can still get your classic battered fish and chips ($5.80).

Open: daily 10am-9pm; reservations not accepted; BYO (no corkage)

starter: $1.50-$4.90
main: $5.90-$14.90

AE BC MC V; Eftpos

Original Ploy Thai
Thai

☎ 9300 6604
8 Campbell Pde

Map 14 C4

Separate smoke-free dining available

The name might seem misleading – how can this be the *original* Ploy Thai when two other restaurants of the same name have blazed trails of delectableness before it? Confusion vanishes when you learn that the other restaurants have gone, to be replaced with this Ploy Thai restaurant alone. Original Ploy Thai is a delight in many ways. First, there's the price: it's cheap. Second, there's the service: quick, unobtrusive and polite. Last, there's the food: a plethora of fresh, tasty Thai dishes. Deep-fried taro ($1.80 each), a Medusa-like nest of taro shreds, makes a great starter. For mains you can't go past the duck larb* ($12.50), a sweet-and-sour, hot-and-spicy combination of mint, lemon juice, chilli and cashews. For a simpler taste sensation, try the barbecued prawns with a pungent fish sauce ($12.50). Forgive the throwaway plastic containers, just as you forgive the Mediterranean décor (left behind from the previous owners), and sample the desserts ($3.50) – coconut and taro feature strongly.

Open: daily 11am-10pm; reservations essential; BYO (no corkage)

starter: $1.80-$8.50
main: $4-$12.50
dessert: $3.50

AE BC MC V

BONDI

Map 14 C4

Nonsmoking tables available

Pavement tables

Point of View
Modern Australian (Tapas)

☎ 9365 5166
1/34 Campbell Pde

Point of View's self-styled acronym – PofV – looks like a chemical symbol at first glance. However, PofV is more about artistry than chemistry. Its menu of modern Australian tapas dishes is startling, for it juxtaposes cuisines and flavours with seemingly no regard for theme or consistency. And it works. From the balsamic grilled mushrooms with goat's cheese ($8.50) to the richer flavours of quesadillas with spiced chicken, roasted sweetcorn and smoked cheddar ($13.50) or the tangy surprise of saffron prawns with pickled pepper and rocket ($13.50). From the freshness of giant Vietnamese rice paper rolls ($8.50) to the medley of warm Mediterranean flavours on the vegetarian mez plate ($13.50). Imagination and confidence inspirit every dish. If tapas doesn't appeal try the à la carte menu. All this originality, combined with a comfy interior, personable waiters and a spectacular view of Bondi Beach, combines to make PofV a stunner.

starter: $8.50-$15.50
main: tapas $8.50-$13.50,
á la carte $13.95-$22.50
dessert: $9.50
Set menu $25, $29, $35 or $40

AE BC DC MC V; Eftpos

Open: daily 5pm-midnight; reservations advisable (especially Fri & Sat); licensed, no BYO

Map 14 B4

Smoking throughout

Outdoor seating

Pompei's
Italian

☎ 9365 1233
126-130 Roscoe Street

Located off Bondi's main beachfront strip, Pompei's open design gives the impression that the local carnival of sun-tendered Brits, stringy surfers and stately Jewish mothers are somehow moving right through it. Proud of authenticity in all stages of its pizza production, Pompei's offers 27 regional Italian stylings at prices cheaper than your local ham & pineapple merchants. The Quattro Formaggi ($13.50) is like a full day's cheese tasting in every slice. By contrast, the Rossa ($7.50) is a stripped-down combination of tart tomato paste, garlic and basil. Pompei's cool and bright citrus colour scheme is unlike your average pizzeria, but then again this place is also a gelataria of note. Behind the glass counter, the gelato lies in great molten folds, under a mist of refrigeration, like a carefully-monitored exhibit. Among the treasures are the white milk chocolate gelato, the vanilla with warm raspberries, and the good old strawberry which is shockingly tasty.

main: $7.50-$13.50
dessert: $3.50-$10.50

AE BC MC V

Open: Tues-Sun 11am-midnight; reservations accepted; BYO ($1/person)

Lick It Up

Things have moved on since the scoop of Streets from the local milk bar, but our love of ice cream remains. Now we indulge in sorbet and gelato in exotic flavours. Here is a list of our favourites. Tip – rock hard ice cream anaesthetises the taste buds so let your scoop begin to melt before you start licking.

A & P Sulfaro 119 Ramsay St, Haberfield ☎ 9797 0001 Map 8 B2
This ice cream is made in the traditional Italian way with fruit syrups. Try hazelnut, torrone (nougat) or chocolate with a real cocoa flavour. Buy by the cone, the cup or containers of up to five litres.

Angkor Wat 227 Oxford St, Darlinghurst ☎ 9360 5500
For an exotic selection of imported ices, including durian – the pungent South-East Asian fruit that is certainly an acquired taste (see review p 58).

Bar Italia 169 Norton Street, Leichhardt ☎ 9560 9981 Map 12 A2
You'd think the gelato was being scooped out for free, judging by the constant counter crush here. One taste of the hazelnut, pistachio or zabaione gelato, or the tropical-flavoured sorbets and you'll understand why Bar Italia's blends have more fans than the Italian soccer team (see also p 98).

Bravo Trattoria Gelato & Coffee Bar 6-8 Falcon St, Crows Nest ☎ 9906 6630 Map 17 A1
Gelato comes in all the traditional flavours (Tia Maria, coffee, zabaione) as well as a few less traditional ones such as guava, and white chocolate hazelnut. You can try a scoop of each of the 16 flavours here by ordering your own gelato mountain, but you'll need help to conquer this *Coppa Mondiale* (World Cup).

La Crimerai 2/106 Norton St, Leichhardt ☎ 9564 1127 Map 12 B2
Luigi De Luca has worked with indigenous groups to come up with his 'bush tucker' wattleseed and lemon myrtle gelato. And his 'bommeralia' ice cream won first prize at the National Italian Gelato Makers Association competition in 2000.

La Persia 545 Crown St, Surry Hills ☎ 9698 4355
Their rosewater ice cream and sorbet has a taste that conjures up 1001 nights (see review p 79).

Paramount 73 Macleay St, Potts Point ☎ 9358 1652
Chris Manfield's tropical tutti frutti (pineapple, star anise, candied ginger ice cream sandwich with nougatine wafers) is a knockout (see review p 74).

passionflower Shop G12, 730-742 George St, City ☎ 9281 8322
Go to passionflower for exotic flavours such as green tea and azuki bean, durian, and wasabi, as well as the classics like rum and raisin, strawberry and chocolate (see review p 42).

Pompei's Cnr Roscoe and Gould Sts, Bondi Beach ☎ 9365 1233
The glass gelataria cabinet from Italy features 24 flavours made with cream, milk and organic fruit. Try nougat, mango sorbet, panna cotta, tiramisú and – their own invention – the pear and ginger gelato (see review p 140).

BONDI

Map 14 A5

No smoking inside

Pavement and mini-balcony tables

Raw Bar
Japanese

☎ 9365 7200
Cnr Warners & Wairoa Aves

The skimpily-dressed Bondi set have been known to queue for an hour to get in here. As the sun goes down, goose bumps pop up on their arms as if in synchrony with the lights popping up in windows on the south Bondi headland. It's that stunning aspect across the water that tempts people past the jet-black awnings and grassy green exterior of Raw Bar, into its bento box-sized dining room. For while the sushi can be very good, it can also be very average. Bondi babes who are so totally now can sit picking at sashimi ($8.80/12 pieces) that is so five hours ago. But when the cook is on form, the gyoza ($7.80) are great. A bento box ($29/$16 vegetarian) feeds two regular people (five Bondi bods). Bean curd and dipping sauces ($8.50), california rolls (4 pieces/$7.50) and chicken teriyaki ($12.80) are other options. Did someone say dessert? They're not too familiar with the concept around here.

starter: $2.80-$10.80
main: $10.80-$29
AE BC DC MC V

Open: daily noon-10pm; reservations advisable; BYO (corkage $2/person)

Map 14 A6

No smoking inside

Pavement tables

Savion
Kosher

☎ 9130 6357
1/38 Wairoa Ave

Savion's kitchen looks like it hasn't been refurbished since the turn of the century – the *previous* century – but its food seems to please today's palates. You'll find chicken schnitzels in pita with salad ($6), generous baskets of chips ($2.50, $5 or $8), and mini felafel rolls ($4.50) stuffed with more felafels than you can poke a menorah at. Hefty wooden tables, Star of David wall murals and authentic, simple food are the hallmarks of this popular Jewish eatery. But don't forget to scrape your plate into the bin at the meal's end, and don't ask, as we did, for a squeeze of lemon juice on your chicken if you spy wedges garnishing other dishes in the bain-marie. Jewish law decrees that it's terefah (forbidden) to eat certain products together. However, friendly waiters may oblige you with a ritually fit lemon obtained from somewhere out back.

main: $2.50-$8
cash only

Open: Sun-Thurs 9am-9pm, Fri 9am-3pm; reservations accepted; BYO kosher wine only (no corkage)

BONDI

Sean's Panaroma
Modern Australian

☎ 9365 4924
270 Campbell Pde

The term 'modern Australian' often means a wine list longer than the menu and mains priced at a very modern $30 plus. At least at Sean's Panaroma (say it slowly) it's all served up with a casual Australian attitude: pots and pans hang from the ceiling, postcards perch above the stove and miniature blackboard menus swing in the breeze. The miniature chairs, meanwhile, look like they've been kidnapped from the Bondi primary school. They're so small it's hard to believe those who sit on them actually eat the roasted, buttered organic chicken ($26), or pâté and truffle creations in front of them. Moist and tender barramundi ($30) in a shallow bath of tomato and peas impresses, as does the only vegetarian main – a simple linguine with rocket, chilli and lemon ($16). A sorbet of mango, papaya and banana ($10) is as sweet as it needs to be and in colours to match your bikini.

Open: Thurs-Sun noon-3pm, daily 6.30pm-9.30pm; reservations advisable (especially weekends); licensed & BYO (corkage $2.50/person)

Map 14 B6

No smoking inside

Pavement tables

starter: $11-$18
main: $16-$32
dessert: $10

BC MC V

BONDI JUNCTION

Macro Wholefoods Cafe
Modern Australian/vegetarian

☎ 9389 7611
Cnr Oxford & Ruthven Sts

Come to Macro Wholefoods Cafe and experience what goodness and flavour are all about. The macropie ($7, with two salads of your choice) is a fine place to start. Cut through the thick wholemeal crust to the potato, corn and mushroom filling and delight in a sweet and savoury mouthful. The burgersaurus ($6) is a dish to enlarge your mind. Macro serves up an exotic burger of tempeh, tofu, shiitake, tamari and more, topped with a pile of pickles and greens on a sourdough bun. For a snack at any time of the day, have a bowl of miso broth ($3), or charge yourself up with a freshly squeezed organic fruit juice ($3.50/$4.50). Macro is more micro than anything in size, but in its sunny interior there is always space for the newly converted health nut.

Open: Mon-Fri 8am-8pm, Sat 8am-7pm, Sun 9am-6pm (breakfast: Mon-Fri 8am-12pm, Sat & Sun until 3pm); reservations not accepted; unlicensed

Map 13 C5

Pavement benches

main: $3-$9
dessert: $1.50-$4

AE BC MC V; Eftpos

EASTERN SUBURBS

BRONTE

Map 14 E3

No smoking inside

Pavement tables

Sejuiced at Bronte Beach
Modern Australian

☎ 9389 9538
487 Bronte Rd

This knockabout cafe with rough wooden floors, plate-glass windows and a fine view across Bronte Beach does a healthy trade, rehydrating barefoot sunbakers and salt-blasted surfers with freshly squeezed juices. The separate juice menu has plenty of suggested combos, as well as lassis and smoothies (both $4.50). Cosmic concoctions such as the spirulina rush ($4.50) – orange, apple and pineapple juice blended with banana, spirulina and ice – give a nutritious jump-start to the day, although coffees also flow freely for those times when only caffeine will do. The food sits comfortably between 'healthy' and regular cafe fare, ranging from breakfasts of porridge with dates and caramelised sugar ($5.50) to strangely bland eggs any style ($6), with your choice of extras, including golden kumara hash cakes ($2). Later in the day, try baked ricotta on toast with spinach, watercress, pine nuts and almond dressing ($7) or a salmon bagel with lemon and dill cream cheese ($8.50).

main: $2.50-$10
dessert: $5.50
cash only

Open: daily 6.30am-6.30pm (kitchen closes 5pm); reservations not accepted; unlicensed

BRONTE

Tarifa
Modern Australian

☎ 9386 9456
471 Bronte Rd

Map 14 E3

No smoking inside

Pavement tables

Tarifa calls itself 'a mostly healthy cafe', and in a place like Bronte, where trim-and-terrificness is the preoccupation of the morning, it's sure of a constant stream of patrons. You have to be up pretty early to get the best seat in the house – a place on the long bench facing out to sea. Sit and watch the day brighten over the waves of joggers passing across the beach. Grilled strawberries with honey- and cinnamon-spiced ricotta on sourdough toast ($6.50) are a suitably vivid accompaniment to the colours of the morning. So too are the range of juices ($2.80 small, $3.80 large). Shape up the latter part of the day with a lavish roll-up stuffed with avocado, cucumber, egg, tomato, and tahini dressing ($7.50), or pizzettes loaded with roast pumpkin, spinach and pine nuts ($10). Tarifa is Bronte's best place to go for the nosh-up before the push-up.

main: $3-$9
dessert: $3-$6

Open: daily 7am-5pm (breakfast: all day); reservations accepted; unlicensed

cash only

Wet Paint Cafe
Modern Australian

☎ 9369 4634
50 Macpherson St

Map 14 E1

No smoking inside

The paint's not so wet – this restaurant has been around for close on four years. Early in 2000 new owners moved in, but the change of management did nothing to deter the crowds, who still pack themselves in between the dark green and mustard walls. Dining at the Wet Paint Cafe is like having a meal – a very *good* meal – in someone's kitchen. The fact that the cooking area is in full view has something to do with this. So does the cosy junk-style interior (check out the corrugated iron 'curtain' over the window). The seafood chowder ($8.50) is a hearty starter, while the Creole grilled chicken ($15) takes meat and three veg to new heights with its rosemary, garlic and lime-marinated chicken breast, juicy corn cob and fried potatoes soaked in mustard sauce. For dessert, the berry grumble ($7, and that's no typo) is as country-kitchen scrumptious as you could wish.

starter: $5-$9.50
main: $12.50-$19
dessert: $7

Open: Tues-Sat 6pm-10pm; reservations essential; BYO (corkage $1.50/person)

cash only

EASTERN SUBURBS

DOUBLE BAY

Map 13 A4

Red Chilli
Thai

☎ 9328 2558
338 New South Head Road

In between signing leases for $900 per week units and stocking up on the locally popular leopard skin and zebra striped décor to deck out your new digs, you might want to kick back at Red Chilli for a reliable Thai dish served up in double-quick time. With ingredients all brightly displayed behind the counter, Red Chilli offers over 50 Thai variations and a few other favourites like Malaysian laksa ($8-$9.50) and Vietnamese crêpes ($12-$13.50). The chilli basil pipis ($15.50) are a good balance of those complementary flavours and you might want to ask for an extra helping if you're sharing. The spicy calamari salad ($13.50) is lemon-sweet and soaks up nicely into a plate of jasmine rice. Invigorated, you can waltz off to find that faux white tiger rug, fanged head and all, that you've been wanting.

starter: $1.50-$5
main: $7.50-$15.50
dessert: $4.50
cash only

Open: Tues-Sun noon-2.30pm, 5.30pm-10.30pm; reservations accepted; unlicensed

MOORE PARK

Map 13 D2

Fox Studios' car park **P**

Wheelchair access

Smoking outside & at bar only

Patio tables

Arena Bar and Bistro
Modern Australian

☎ 9361 3930
212 Bent St,
Fox Studios

Bent St is a maze of megastores, movie houses and marketing opportunities for Fox Studios. The new Arena Bar and Bistro is like a studio film that's in the middle of being audience-tested. The current formula stars a cast of popular characters – shucked oysters ($13/$19), a Thai curry ($17.50) and white chocolate ice cream ($7). Good reviews go to the freshly-made tzatziki and baba ghanoush dips ($11.50), to the pillow of creamy potato mash under the lamb sausages ($16.50) and to the fresh fish with crispy thin beer batter ($16.50). The small open kitchen is the scene for occasional moments of dramatic tension when weekend trade guarantees a full house, but waiters in backstage black are unobtrusively professional and focused. Even the room looks like a movable set: a wall of adjustable wooden vertical blinds that folds away, and seating that gradually merges and transforms like an Escher painting.

starter: $11-$16
main: $14.50-$18.50
dessert: $7-$15
Set menu $40
AE BC DC MC V

Open: daily noon-3pm, 6pm-10.30pm; reservations accepted (groups of 10 or more); licensed, no BYO

MOORE PARK

Asian Kitchen
Chinese

☎ **9358 4488**
**220/888 Bent St,
Fox Studios**

Put out an independent box-office hit and the big studio players are bound to want a piece of you. That's what happened to the Chinatown institution Golden Century when Fox Studios bosses installed the proven brand name in a blockbuster-sized new space on Bent St. Perhaps the Fox bods had been to one too many multiplexes, because the Kitchen's initial Pan-Asian cuisine (Indian, Japanese, Malaysian and Chinese) didn't make for a sharing dining experience. Fortunately the Kitchen's settled back into what it does best: shark fin soups ($16.80), a couple of pages worth of live fish (lobster sichuan, mud crab done a dozen different ways), and the odd addendum of Peking duck, barbecued chicken ($13-$38), and Singapore noodles ($12.80). All very lazy Susan-friendly meals. At the budget pavement tables downstairs you can order a roast duck soup and egg noodles ($8.50) with a glass of Toohey's beer or Lindemans chardonnay ($4.50).

Open: Sun-Thurs noon-11pm, Fri & Sat noon-midnight; reservations advisable (essential on weekends and for late night bookings); licensed & BYO (corkage $5/person)

Map 13 D2

- Fox Studios' car park
- Wheelchair access
- Smoking in lounge area only
- Pavement tables downstairs

starter: $4-$16.80
main: $7-$28.80
dessert: $6
Set menu $30, $40 or $50/person

AE BC DC MC V

Reel to Reel Meals

Food and film are two of life's most pleasant activities and in Sydney it's becoming increasingly easy to combine these addictions. Here are just a few of Sydney's most cinematic scenes for dining and drinking.

Short films and short blacks

Bar Coluzzi
322 Victoria St, Darlinghurst ☎ 9380 5420 Map 6 B4
Bar Coluzzi has featured in a Tropfest film – a story about a cowboy coffee-maker coming to the big city and falling in love with a sweet Italian waitress. The scene at Bar Coluzzi is always a bit of a performance: television executives, star footballers, and writers pitching their latest comedy script hold forth at this Victoria St stalwart, while paparazzi shots of celebrity visitors make up a continually growing wall-collage. The food range is limited, but satisfying and sweet.

Tropicana
227b Victoria St, Darlinghurst ☎ 9360 9809 Map 6 B4
It's almost a decade ago that actor/director John Polson and a few of his mates got together to screen their short films in this Darlinghurst cafe. Now every cafe on the strip has a corner TV, screening the winning entries of the Tropfest competition. Every year more than 50,000 gather in the Sydney Domain to watch it all on the big screen, while in Melbourne and Adelaide they converge in cafes to watch the show (and there are plans to broadcast it to London and New York in 2001). The Tropicana is still Victoria St's giant casting cafeteria, where drama school graduates drum up fruitful collaborations with first-time film directors, while in the opposite corner nonchalant locals pretend not to stare at minor TV stars.

Munching movie stars

bills
433 Liverpool St, Darlinghurst ☎ 9360 9631
Tom Cruise, Nicole Kidman and Julia Roberts have all partaken of the bills breakfast – which is almost as famous as they are. When the Tropicana-ites (see above) become more celebrity and less wannabe, they're bound to be found toasting themselves over breakfast at bills as well (see review p 59).

Sejuiced at Bronte Beach
487 Bronte Rd, Bronte ☎ 9389 9538
If Gidget and the Big Kahuna were still stomping around in the surf and sand today, they'd be slurping on Sejuiced's 'juice of the day' or 'power smoothie'. This Bronte Beach cafe is a popular venue for power-breakfasting actors and directors downing wheatgrass shots and 'hypertension healer' blends (see review p 144).

Blockbuster on Bent St

La Premiere Fox Studios
Moore Park ☎ 9266 4887 Map 13 D2
The multiplex cinema at Fox studios now has a 'champagne' class lounge, where you can settle in to watch your flick in plush seats for two, with a private table, wine bottle holder and access to a licensed bar. Tea, coffee and popcorn are complimentary, and a cheese platter comes with each bottle of wine ordered. Tues $16, Mon, Wed, Thurs & before 5pm Fri $21, after 5pm Fri and Sat & Sun $25. Pre-booking is advised. See also reviews of Arena Bar and Bistro (p 146), Asian Kitchen (p 147) and Cine (p 150).

Low-budget productions

Govinda's and the Movie Room
112 Darlinghurst Rd, Darlinghurst ☎ 9380 5155 Map 6 A4
Who said the Hare Krishnas don't have fun? The seating in the upstairs movie room is more like bedding (taking off your shoes is *de rigueur*). Downstairs is a smorgasbord of ghee-laden curries, pappadams, pastas and perhaps an eggless chocolate mousse (the movie & meal deal is $14.90, desserts are $3.50 extra).

side-on café
83 Parramatta Rd, Annandale ☎ 9516 3077 Map 8 B4
Don't be put off by the clubby bohemian ambience – join in. Australian and international short films are screened on Monday and Tuesday for $5 ($10 for special screening nights). Seating ranges from regular cinema pews to beanbags. A $10 pasta buffet opens at 6pm, films start at 8pm.

The restaurants that made the movies

We were going to choose Bondi – Sydney's Beverly Hills – to take out the award as Sydney's most cinematic eating out location (there's so much posing and theatrics on the street it's a wonder show biz agents aren't running around charging tourists shouldering camcorders for appearance fees). But we chose Erskineville instead. The two great stereotypes of Australian film – the acid-tongued drag queen (see *The Adventures of Priscilla, Queen of the Desert*) and the down-on-his-luck working class man (see *Idiot Box* and *Erskineville Kings*) are alive and kicking up their heels in Erskineville's eating and watering holes. The Imperial Hotel (tel 9519 9899) launched Priscilla on her road trip to the Red Centre, and it still hosts some of the best drag shows in town. These days Erskineville's village-in-the-inner-city lifestyle is so sought after that you almost need to be a film star to afford to live there.

Aroy Thai
61 Erskineville Rd, Erskineville ☎ 9519 0044 Map 9 C4
The smart design is more Paddington than Erskineville, but the prices and food are more Bangkok than Sydney: a place that deserves its long-running show of success.

Cafe Brontosaurus
110 Erskineville Rd, Erskineville ☎ 9550 6652 Map 9 C4
With Camptosaurus, Lesothosaurus and Heterodontosaurus burgers, the gimmick never seems to run out of steam. Nor does the window display, complete with stuck-on 3-D glasses for viewing the dinosaur drama publicity poster, and a bunch of rubber monsters that look like the entire marketing output of *Jurassic Park*.

She Bistro at the Rose of Australia Hotel
1 Swanson St, Erskineville ☎ 9565 1441 Map 9 C4
Downstairs it's the classic Australian pub, complete with Art Deco bar for beer guzzling lads and local bands performing on Sunday night. But the upstairs Italian bistro is a new chic look altogether, with a lounge room, bookshelves and pool table.

MOORE PARK

Map 13 D2

Fox Studios' car park

Smoking at bar & outside only

Patio tables

Cine
Italian

☎ 9332 1409
Shop 211 Bent St,
Fox Studios

Cine is a little bit Mary Quant, a little bit Barbarella – not that you can see much on weekends, when party groups yell over the Ricky Martin videos. You can't miss the black and white poster of a young Sophia Loren though, her armpits growing wild and free. The luscious Italian would even look good filling her face with Cine's yeasty, bubbly woodfired pizzas ($12.50-$16.50). The 'Pizza alla Bent St' ($13.90) is covered in cubes of tender lean chicken, fresh avocado, fetta and mozzarella – it's a great dish for two. We thought the barbecued king prawns over iceberg lettuce ($19.90) and an antipasto platter ($9.90) were a bit like the Fox empire: some perfectly pleasing content, but ultimately a triumph of size over substance. Staff sing out 'have a nice day', but we didn't mind when our waitress came bearing a creamy, oversized cheesecake and a wobbling, tottering fruit-topped pav ($6.90).

starter: $4.90-$13.90
main: $13-$21.90
dessert: $6.50-$6.90
Set menu $35 or $39/person (min 10 people)
AE BC DC JCB MC V

Open: daily noon-11.30pm; reservations advisable on weekends; licensed, no BYO

PADDINGTON

Map 13 B2

No smoking during meal times

Buon Ricordo
Italian

☎ 9360 6729
108 Boundary St

Quintessentially Italian, complete with faux Venetian palazzo exterior and a gracious, timeless interior, Buon Ricordo is a far cry from Sydney's slick dining scene. It's usual to find the place packed on midweek evenings. Starters include a fennel and artichoke salad ($18) and risotto with taleggio and pear ($20). Pasta is perfectly cooked and served with clams, cherry tomatoes and a dash of chilli ($19.50) or with a salty peasant-style sugo of pancetta, broccoli and pecorino ($19). Mains include beef, veal, lamb, or all of the above crumbed, fried and served with battered vegetables ($33.50), and fish, like tender John Dory fillets in parmesan batter floating in pea purée ($33.50). Fans of Italian wine will be happy even though the less-than-generous wines by the glass will leave you still thirsty. And service was lacking on this visit. Nice touches are the complimentary bruschetta and petit fours as pre- and post-meal nibbles.

starter: $18-$20
main: $29.50-$35.50
dessert: $13
Degustation $80
AE BC DC MC V

Open: Fri & Sat noon-2.30pm, Tues-Sat 6.30pm-11pm; reservations essential; licensed, no BYO

PADDINGTON

Fat Duck
Modern Australian

☎ 9380 9838
1 Oxford St
(cnr Oxford & Sth Dowling Sts)

Map 13 B1

Nonsmoking tables available

Pavement tables

The Fat Duck was once a cloakroom for the grand Art Deco venue above, but that was when cloakrooms were as large as today's inner city apartments. This V-shaped nook feels like a modern chapel, with its slender windows, arched glass door and pew-like banquets. But then you notice the rubber duckies on the wall. The Peking duck salad (the mascot dish?) is a tongue-tingling tangle of glass noodles, roasted duck, a little chilli oil and squirts of lime ($9.50/$15). And at a time when so much mod Oz can be boring and bland, a grilled tuna – served with a lime wedge, olive tapenade and a bean puree with more garlic than bean – couldn't have been more welcome ($16). Fresh mixed antipasto plates are served for lunches and dinner, while breakfast is looked after by the likes of stewed fruit ($5.50), poached eggs, smoked salmon – even Vegemite soldiers.

starter: $7-$10
main: $9-$16
dessert: $3-$3.50

AE BC DC MC V; Eftpos

Open: Mon-Sat 8am-10pm; reservations accepted; licensed, no BYO

Grand National
Modern Australian

☎ 9363 4557
161 Underwood St

Map 13 C3

Wheelchair access

Nonsmoking tables available

Chick peas and sardines ($12.90) don't normally spring to mind when you think 'pub food'. But when the chick peas come in a lightly spiced fritter-cake that's covered in a hot pink beetroot sauce, with the little silver fishes forming a star-shape on top, it's a welcome sight on our plates any day. The Grand National Art Deco dining room – white columns, white linen and a curvy dark wood bar – is at the forefront of Sydney's pub revolution. Mediterranean (baba ghanoush with baby octopus, $12.50), Indian (tangy dhal with marinated kingfish and baby eggplant, $25.90) and Australian flavours (char-grilled beef fillet with red pepper and chipotle relish, $25.90) all have their menu moments. The wine list is comprehensively antipodean. Perve on all food preparation in the reflective window above the kitchen; or you can ask for 'Valhrona chocolate decadence' ($11.50) and a schooner in the old-style pub bar next door.

starter: $9.50-$18.50
main: $17.50-$25.90
dessert: $9.50-$13.50
Set menu $45 or $52.50

AE BC DC MC V; Eftpos

Open: lunch Wed-Sun from noon, dinner Tues-Sat from 6pm; reservations advisable; licensed, no BYO

EASTERN SUBURBS

PADDINGTON

grand pacific blue room
Modern Australian

☎ 9331 7108
Cnr Oxford & South Dowling Sts

Map 13 B1
Entertainment: live DJs & bands Thurs-Sat 10pm till late
Nonsmoking tables available

Unlink your shirt cuffs, slide into a serpentine banquette and enjoy a cocktail. May we suggest Caipiroska ($9) – vodka over crushed lime, muddled with ice and sugar? Like the music, the menu changes with the seasons and is an interesting fusion of influences. Entrées are particularly seductive: a ring of griddled scallops circling a mound of warm pea purée with a mint vinaigrette ($15) and a generous pile of duck spring rolls with cucumber and chilli relish ($8.50), hot but subtly flavoured. The goat's cheese gnocchi from the mains selection ($19) is tasty, sitting in a tomato and herb vinaigrette with well dressed rocket on top. Share, if you must, the chocolate plate ($15). A huge mirror enables diners to spy on the swinging lounge area Thursday through Saturday. Or go earlier in the week when it's more cosy than cool.

starter: $8.50-$14
main: $19-$24.50
dessert: $9-$15
AE BC DC MC V

Open: restaurant Tues-Sun 6pm-11pm, bar Sun, Tues & Wed until 1am, Thurs-Sat until 3am; reservations advisable (Thurs-Sat); licensed, no BYO

Hot Gossip Cafe
Modern Australian

☎ 9332 4358
438 Oxford St

Map 13 C3
Smoking throughout
Courtyard tables

Hot Gossip is a world away from the minimalist mod Oz cafe. With original milk-bar style booths, deco wooden tables and hordes of collectibles, it has been satisfying locals and visitors for around 17 years. Chef/owner Celina recommends the daily specials – she makes up the huge Woodstock-style spinach pie and meatloaf ($11) fresh each morning. A breakfast-all-day menu suits the clientele of students, artists and alternative types, with the vegetarian fare also popular. It may be Hot Gossip, but the booths allow privacy so who knows what creative endeavours have been hatched over eggs ($7), a macho nachos ($9) or cheesy-topped baked potato ($10). Servings are generous and service is swift and down-to-earth. Hot Gossip deli next door serves lighter deli-style snacks, couscous, quiche and legendary pikelets.

starter: $3-$9
main: $8-$15
dessert: $4-$7
BC MC V; Eftpos

Open: daily 7.30am-11pm (breakfast: all day); reservations accepted; BYO (no corkage)

EASTERN SUBURBS

PADDINGTON

Lucio's
Italian

☎ 9380 5996
47 Windsor St

Map 13 B3

Separate smoke-free dining area

Is it a restaurant or an art gallery? With walls hidden behind fabulous oils, watercolours and prints by John Olsen, Tim Storrier and others, and an Eastern Suburbs art world clientele, you might well wonder. It's a hard act to live up to, and the food aims to do justice to the surroundings. The char-grilled octopus ($18) is superbly tender, with cute morsels of steamed veggies among the tentacles. The green tagliolini with blue swimmer crab ($18.80) is justifiably renowned. A traditional Italian dish of calf's liver ($26.80) is cooked to perfection, while the boned quail ($27.80), though sitting on a rather muddy purée of eggplant and leek like a plucked bird stuck in a bog, tastes good. The sweet finale, a sensuous panna cotta, is served with sublime strawberry gelato. The service is professional (though we found it rather stiff) and the wine list includes a good selection of Australian and Italian wines.

starter: $18-$18.80
main: $27-$29
dessert: $15

AE BC DC MC V

Open: Mon-Sat 12.30pm-3pm, 6.30pm-11pm; reservations essential; licensed, no BYO

Cine (p 150)

Map 13 B2

No smoking inside

Courtyard tables

Taqsim
Egyptian

☎ 9361 6001
210 Oxford St

A meal at Taqsim can be as heady as a hot night in Cairo. The interior is classy, decorated with cushions, arty photos and clay table lamps. The courtyard draped with grapevines and trailing bougainvillea is equally inviting. With warmed Turkish bread we greedily mop up the beetroot bungar ($6.50), a peppery, minty, yoghurty concoction that sets our tongues tingling. The mushy ful medames ($14.50), the Egyptian national dish of spiced and olive oiled fava beans and chick peas, is blander, but still good, while the samaq malfouf ($19.50), a pink Atlantic salmon fillet parcelled in charred vine leaves and infused with herbs is excellent. Wildly ambitious is the peach stuffed with ground lamb, pinenuts and mint, encased in crisp pastry ($17.50) – a dish fit for a Pharaoh. Try, also, exotic desserts ($7.50) like poached wild figs and slushy iced sherbets of rosewater or hibiscus.

starter: $6.50-$18.50
main: $9.50-$19.50
dessert: $7.50
AE BC DC MC V

Open: Sun-Thurs 6pm-9pm, Fri & Sat 6pm-11pm; reservations accepted; BYO (corkage $2/person)

EASTERN SUBURBS

ROSE BAY

Catalina Rose Bay
Modern Australian

☎ 9371 0555
1 Sunderland Ave, Lyne Park

Map 13 E6

- Valet parking ($20)
- Nonsmoking tables available
- Balcony tables

For the John Laws of this world, Catalina is just one of those places you do lunch. To the rest of us it's an extra special indulgence, where, if nothing else, you're guaranteed a harbourside view – yachts tacking, seaplanes zooming by, a pelican perched on the balcony wall – that confirms Sydney as one of the most glorious places in the Universe. Then the food arrives, delivered by angelic waiters, and you *know* you're in heaven. Go for a starter of marinated quail ($23); the tender meat's marriage with wild rocket and grilled figs in a lemon sauce is inspired. Mains of snapper fillet with potato and garilc purée ($36) and brioche crumbed veal cutlet ($34) are more straightforward, letting the quality of the ingredients speak for themselves. As for the fresh-from-the oven lemon tart with a super zesty lemon sorbet ($14) – it's big enough to share, but not if you're dining with us.

starter: $21-$28
main: $32-$38
dessert: $14-$15

AE BC DC MC V

Open: noon-late; reservations advisable (especially weekends); licensed, no BYO

Pier Restaurant
Modern Australian/seafood

☎ 9327 6561
594 New South Head Rd

Map 13 E5

- No smoking inside during meal times
- Deck tables (for drinks & smoking only)

On a gusty autumn's day, when squalls race across Rose Bay and slap rain against the generously sized windows of this pier-propped restaurant, you can be guaranteed of a dining experience as pleasing as any a sunny day could dish up. For, come rain or shine, Pier Restaurant nourishes with fine food, a quietly attentive waiting service and a streamlined, comfortable interior. Order a glass of wine while you peruse the lengthy menu. A lightly spiced lobster medallion with the surprising accompaniment of a caramelised pork hock ($29) makes a satisfying starter. Scrape the sea salt off the top of your crispy-skinned fillet of snapper and enjoy its luscious flavour gently enhanced by a truffle vinaigrette ($30/$39). A banana tart, ice cream and choc-dipped banana trio ($16) makes a decadent dessert. The Pier is a restaurant for all seasons.

starter: $22-$38
main: $28-$39
dessert: $16

AE BC DC JCB MC V

Open: daily noon-3pm, Mon-Sat 6pm-10pm, Sun 6pm-9pm; reservations advisable (especially Thurs-Sat evenings); licensed, no BYO

EASTERN SUBURBS

VAUCLUSE

Map 13 D6
No smoking inside
Porch tables

Nielsen Park Kiosk
Italian

☎ 9337 1574
Greycliffe Ave,
Nielsen Park

There is no finer place to 'do' lunch in Sydney on a fine day than at the Nielsen Park Kiosk, darling. A gentle breeze blows through the pretty Edwardian pavilion with its coloured leadlights, wooden floors, sun-dappled tables and stained bentwood chairs. The outlook is almost cliched Sydney idyll – a sparkling harbour peppered with yachts, tanned bodies swimming in the sea, children splashing in the shallows and Italian mamas picnicking on the shore. But who wants a picnic when they can have divine mozzarella di bufala* (the real thing imported from Italy – milky and salty) followed by al dente bavette* with clams, mussels and just the right amount of chilli ($17.50), or juicy red snapper fillets and scallops piled high and laced with ginger. Yum. Live dangerously and dive into naughty desserts such as zuccotto ($14.50) – a big, rich ball of white chocolate semifreddo.

starter: $13-$24
main: $17.50-$29.50
dessert: $14.50
AE BC DC MC V

Open: Tues-Sun noon-4pm, Fri & Sat 6pm-9.30pm, (Sun breakfast: 8.30am-11am); reservations essential; BYO (corkage $2/person)

WOOLLAHRA

Map 13 C4
Nonsmoking tables available
Courtyard tables

Big Mama
Italian

☎ 9328 7629
51 Moncur St

Big Mama has all the ambience and double the chaos of a hectic Italian trattoria. Tables are tightly jammed between muralled walls and a huge old bar, in the front rooms of a Woollahra terrace. Upstairs is more spacious but less atmospheric; the leafy courtyard the only place to be in summer. Antipasto ($13) is a predictable but tasty overture, the zucchini with mint adding a bit of zest. Big Mama's pasta sughi are refreshingly simple; penne siciliane ($15), with tomato, eggplant, mozzarella and basil is delicious. Veal and chicken dominate the mains. Piccata al limone ($19) is tender although not quite lemony enough. The service was lackadaisical; we were tucking in before we discovered the existence of a board of specials. Desserts include tiramisù and crème caramel. Go there for a pasta fix but don't expect miracles: this is mama's kitchen not haute cuisine.

starter: $11-$16
main: $10-$20
dessert: $7
AE BC DC MC V

Open: Tues-Sun 6pm-10.30pm; reservations advisable; licensed, no BYO

WOOLLAHRA

Bistro Moncur
Modern French

☎ **9363 2519**
116 Queen St

Map 13 C3

Smoking from 10pm

Verandah tables

For Sydney, Bistro Moncur is something of an oddity. While the rest of the food scene went crazy for Asian-influenced mod Oz, Bistro Moncur remained steadfastly French; while others grovelled to the calorie counter, it yelled 'more cream'; and when the narcissistic glare of stainless steel was the yardstick for style, it remained, cosily and comfortably, a bistro. This is what Bistro Moncur's popularity is built on, as well as the robust, warm, wintery food. Think Parisian bistro in December: French onion soufflé gratin ($15), chicken liver paté ($16), prime fillet steak with bernaise ($29.50). The sort of comfort food that makes you *wish* it was snowing outside so you can claim your rapidly expanding girth a primordial biological function, rather than a simple inability to say 'no'. And for those who fancy themselves made of sterner stuff, pit yourself against the lavender créme brulée ($11) as a test of self-control.

starter: $14-$19.50
main: $22.50-$29.50
dessert: $10.50-$12.50

AE BC DC MC V

Open: Tues-Sun noon-3pm, daily 6pm-10.30pm; reservations not accepted; licensed, no BYO

Pruniers
European

☎ **9363 1974**
65 Ocean St

Map 13 B4

Nonsmoking tables available

Courtyard tables

With its terribly tasteful furnishings, acres of crisp linen and a ringside seat on Chiswick Gardens, Pruniers is pure Noel Coward. In culinary terms it's Two Fat Ladies-land – rich food for rich people. Dishes such as poached cod with parsley sauce ($28) and beef strogonoff ($37) feature on a menu of what the restaurant likes to call 'liberated classics'. Sensing a heavy time ahead, we go easy with a starter of rocket, parmesan and tomato salad ($8). The sautéed prawns 'Oscar Wilde' ($30) are plump and juicy in a creamy Pernod and capsicum sauce, the beef fillet ($29), a perfectly cooked round of meat lifted by a mustardy bois boudrain sauce and caper butter. Our hearts swoon when the dessert trolley rolls up; the combination of Valrhona chocolate mousse, summer pudding bursting with fruit, and prune and armagnac custard (tastes of all for $15) will send you into raptures.

starter: $16-$28
main: $28-$30
dessert: $14-$15
Set menu: lunch $35,
  dinners $35-$37

AE BC DC JCB MC V

Open: daily noon-3pm, Mon-Sat 6pm-10pm; reservations advisable (especially Fri & Sat); licensed, no BYO

EASTERN SUBURBS

Back for More

Bondi Tratt Cafe-Restaurant
34 Campbell Pde, Bondi ☎ 9365 4303 Map 14 C4
All views in Bondi are pretty special, but the views at Bondi Tratt tend to be more special than most. There's an interpretation of the Last Supper on the wall above the kitchen, and some people wouldn't be too disappointed if their last supper was at the Bondi Tratt. Mains average of $19 and entrées $12.50.

Sports Bard
32 Campbell Pde, Bondi ☎ 9130 4582 Map 14 C4
From ocean trout with pesto and puff pastry to crispy battered fish, it's generally top food at the top end of Bondi. Feed yourself at the cushioned wooden benches and top the night off with a game of pool in the back room.

✱ *Write to us: Where do you go to eat time and time again? Is it fabulous food, an authentic atmosphere, great service, or a welcome for the kids that brings you back? Write or email us (see p 11 for details) and the best suggestions will receive the next edition free.*

SOUTH EASTERN SUBURBS

Brighton Le Sands

Coogee

Cronulla

Eastlakes

Kingsford

Maroubra

Randwick

Map

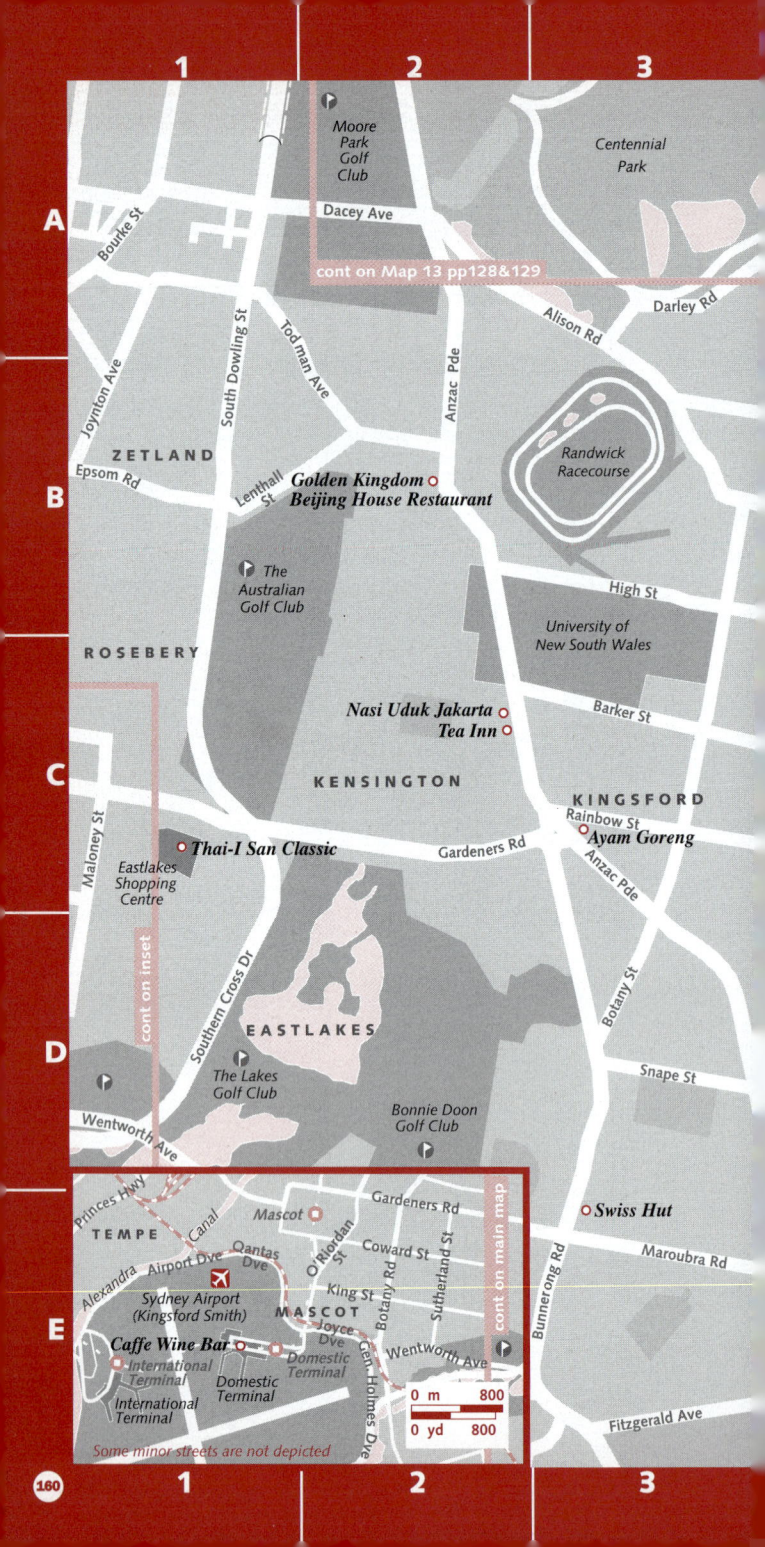

1 **2** **3**

A
- Moore Park Golf Club
- Centennial Park
- Bourke St
- Dacey Ave
- cont on Map 13 pp128&129
- Darley Rd
- Alison Rd

B
- South Dowling St
- Tod man Ave
- Anzac Pde
- Joynton Ave
- ZETLAND
- Epsom Rd
- Lenthall St
- ○ Golden Kingdom
- Beijing House Restaurant
- Randwick Racecourse
- The Australian Golf Club
- High St
- University of New South Wales

C
- ROSEBERY
- ○ Nasi Uduk Jakarta
- ○ Tea Inn
- Barker St
- KENSINGTON
- KINGSFORD
- Rainbow St
- ○ Ayam Goreng
- Maloney St
- ○ Thai-I San Classic
- Eastlakes Shopping Centre
- Gardeners Rd
- Anzac Pde
- Botany St

D
- cont on inset
- Southern Cross Dr
- EASTLAKES
- The Lakes Golf Club
- Bonnie Doon Golf Club
- Snape St
- Wentworth Ave

E (inset)
- Princes Hwy
- Alexandra Canal
- TEMPE
- Mascot
- Gardeners Rd
- ○ Swiss Hut
- Maroubra Rd
- Bunnerong Rd
- Airport Dve
- Qantas Dve
- O'Riordan St
- Coward St
- King St
- Sutherland St
- Sydney Airport (Kingsford Smith)
- MASCOT
- ○ Caffe Wine Bar
- International Terminal
- Domestic Terminal
- Joyce Dve
- Gen Holmes Dve
- Wentworth Ave
- cont on main map
- Fitzgerald Ave

0 m 800
0 yd 800

Some minor streets are not depicted

160

Map 15 - South-East

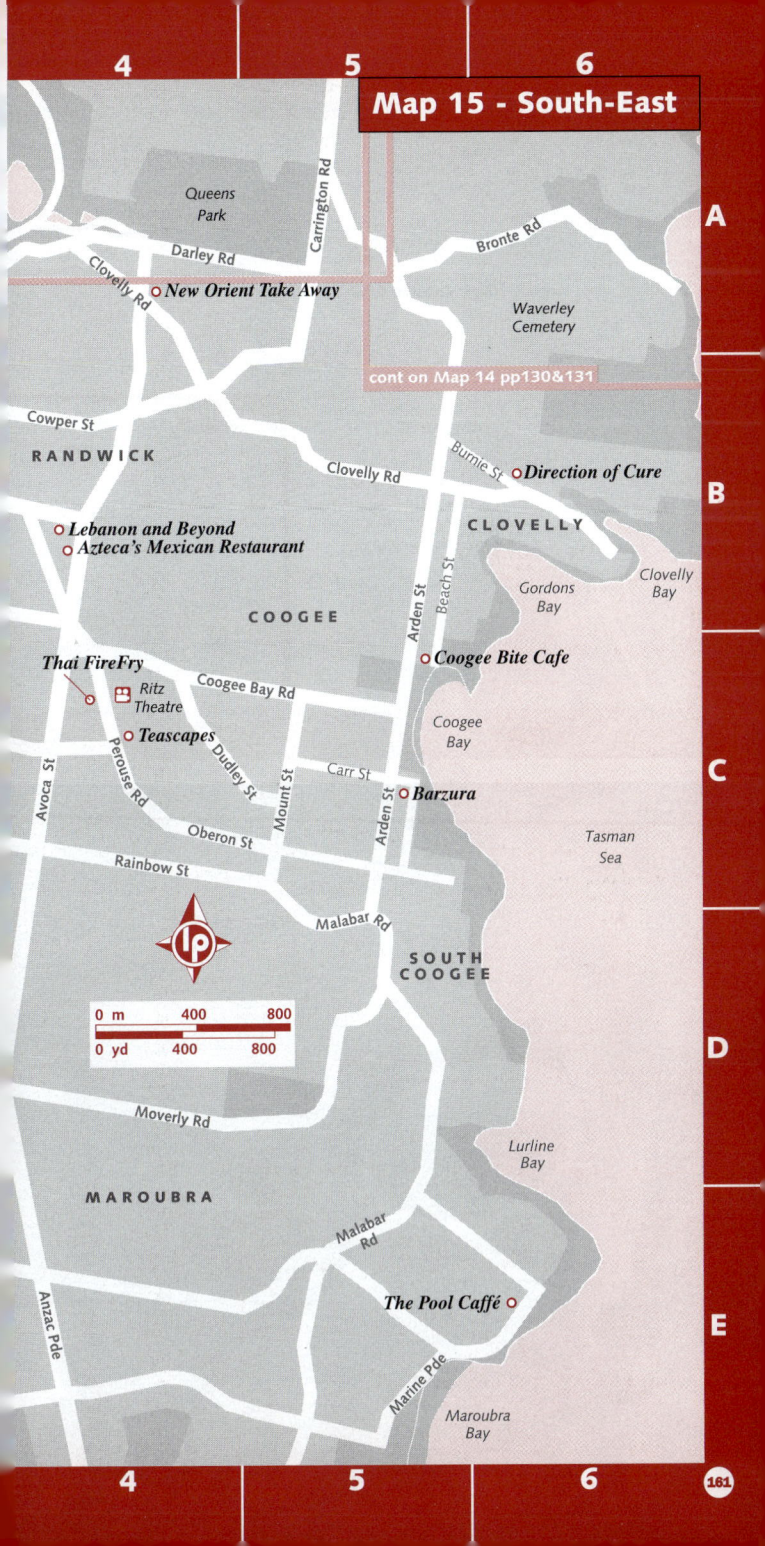

A
- Queens Park
- Carrington Rd
- Darley Rd
- Bronte Rd
- Clovelly Rd
- New Orient Take Away
- Waverley Cemetery

cont on Map 14 pp130&131

B
- Cowper St
- RANDWICK
- Clovelly Rd
- Burnie St
- Direction of Cure
- CLOVELLY
- Lebanon and Beyond
- Azteca's Mexican Restaurant
- Arden St
- Beach St
- Gordons Bay
- Clovelly Bay
- COOGEE

C
- Thai FireFry
- Ritz Theatre
- Coogee Bay Rd
- Teascapes
- Perouse Rd
- Dudley St
- Mount St
- Carr St
- Coogee Bite Cafe
- Coogee Bay
- Barzura
- Arden St
- Tasman Sea

D
- Avoca St
- Oberon St
- Rainbow Rd
- Malabar Rd
- SOUTH COOGEE
- 0 m 400 800
- 0 yd 400 800
- Lurline Bay

E
- Moverly Rd
- MAROUBRA
- Anzac Pde
- Malabar Rd
- The Pool Caffé
- Marine Pde
- Maroubra Bay

161

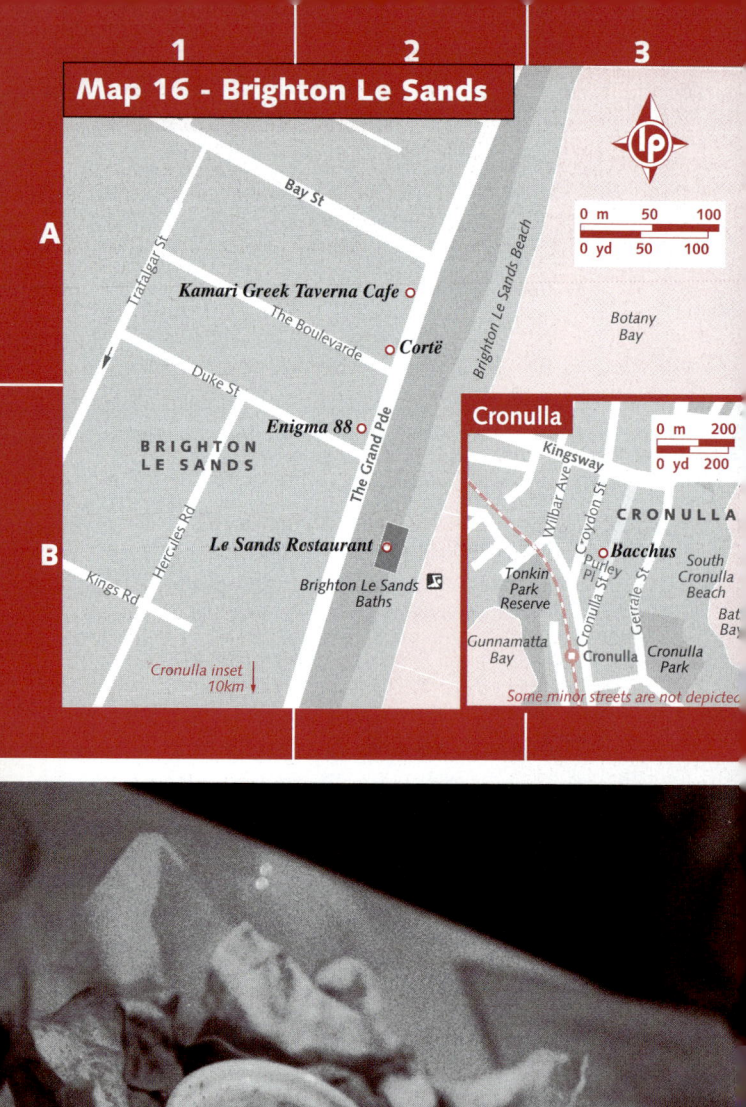

Map 16 - Brighton Le Sands

A

Bay St
Trafalgar St
Kamari Greek Taverna Cafe
The Boulevarde
Cortë
Duke St
Brighton Le Sands Beach
Botany Bay

0 m 50 100
0 yd 50 100

Enigma 88
The Grand Pde
BRIGHTON LE SANDS

B

Le Sands Restaurant
Brighton Le Sands Baths
Hercules Rd
Kings Rd

Cronulla inset 10km

Cronulla

0 m 200
0 yd 200

Kingsway
Wilbar Ave
Croydon St
Purley Pl
Cronulla St
Gerrale St
CRONULLA
Bacchus
South Cronulla Beach
Tonkin Park Reserve
Gunnamatta Bay
Cronulla
Cronulla Park
Bat Bay

Some minor streets are not depicted

BEST

- **Azteca's Mexican Restaurant**
  Authentic, colourful night out

- **Tea Inn**
  Tea and health food Taiwan style

Le Sands Restaurant (p 176)

South Eastern Suburbs

The Sydney's south-eastern region has had a long and sometimes rocky road of settlement – it's home to the Malabar Mansion (Long Bay Jail) and during the 1930s it hosted the optimistically-named tent city 'Happy Valley', home to the Depression's many victims. Today's homes range from the brick and wood bungalows of the purpose-built 'garden cities' of post-WWII, to the ostentatious flats and condominiums that line Anzac Parade. They're a long way from the bucolic grassy neighbourhoods that tempted a wave of settlers in the 1920s, when the tramline opened up the southern beaches and sea baths of Coogee and Maroubra. In 1929 a shark-proof bathing enclosure was opened at the Coogee Ocean Pier, but today the scene's more VB beer and British backpackers. Topping off the region is Randwick, with its raffish racecourse and plethora of single-men's boarding houses undercutting its more genteel pretensions. 'The Spot' – the Art Deco Randwick Ritz cinema and a strip of shops (Spot on Noodles, Spot the Magic Dragon fancy dress, Spot the Look hairdressers) – is one new eating out spot to watch. And back along Anzac Parade (the spine of the south-east) you'll find dozens of budget Indonesian eateries catering to homesick international students from the UNSW.

BRIGHTON LE SANDS

Map 16 A2
Wheelchair access
Nonsmoking tables available
Courtyard tables

Cortë
Modern Australian

☎ 9597 3300
86 The Grand Parade

Sandwiched between a bustling cafe and a seafood/steak house, chic-as-hell Cortë's striking white room is pure 'now'. With its undulating ceiling and watermelon feature wall it looks like an interloper from the eastern suburbs. The kitchen also seem to have their sights set closer to Darlinghurst. Cortë's menu is full of bold descriptions and good intentions, though the food sometimes overshoots the mark with disparate flavours and surplus ingredients. But every unfocused meal is matched with one that works. Witness the ripping entrée of Coffin Bay scallops ($10.50). The chubby little crustaceans sit on towers of jasmine rice, wearing caps of mango-ginger confit. If only our spatchcock ($17.50) had been as well done. Crusted with sage and salt, the over-seasoned bird was accompanied by underwhelming sweet potato gratin and baby olives. And an assiette of desserts ($15) see-sawed between the bland (a chocolate marquis) and the brilliant (rich honey ice cream).

starter: $9.50-$18
main: $14.50-$19.50
dessert: $8.50-$15
AE BC DC MC V; Eftpos

Open: Mon-Thurs 6pm-11pm, Fri-Sun noon-11pm; reservations accepted; licensed and BYO (no corkage)

Map 16 B2
Private parking
Smoking throughout

Enigma 88
Greek

☎ 9556 3611
88 The Grand Parade

A colourful sample plate of meze – plump grilled octopus, golden-fried haloumi, marinated eggplant and a dolmades – is almost like an advertisement for Enigma 88's wares ($10). A plate of piping hot, baby-sized spanakopita is another good introduction to the quality food on offer ($7). Mains follow a traditional Greek path, with choices like the whole crispy-skinned snapper ($22) and spit-roasted lamb cut into a small pile of rough, juicy strips served with tzatziki ($17). They're honest meals served mostly unadorned. The floor is run like a tight ship. On a busy night it might be hard to get staff attention, but when you do have it you'll get patient descriptions of the fine distinctions between, say, a bougatsa ($8) and a galaktoboureko ($6). The former is a dazzling warm custard wrapped in buttery, flaky pastry dusted with cinnamon and sugar, while the latter is a similar dessert that's served sliced and cold.

starter: $7-$12
main: $11-$24
dessert: $6-$8
Set menu $22 (lunch & Monday nights) or $28/person & $35/person (min 10 people)
AE BC DC MC V

Mon-Thurs 11.30am-3pm, 6pm-10.30pm, Fri 11am-3pm, 6pm-11pm, Sat & Sun 11am-late; reservations essential; licensed and BYO (corkage $2/person)

Grand Parade, Brighton Le Sands

Save for an old cannon, impotently aiming out into the Pacific, and a stylized iron sculpture of a tall ship, there aren't many reminders of the Botany Bay made famous by Captain Cook and the gentlemen of His Majesty's Navy. The expansive inlet is now a hectic showpiece of modernity – Port Botany's distant loading towers look like an alien cityscape across the water and endless jumbo sorties arc into Sydney Airport. The traffic belting up and down the Grand Parade hasn't dissuaded restaurateurs from staking major claims along the street facing out across the mouth of the bay and Brighton Le Sands has a substantial concentration and range of eateries. This is a hardcore Greek and seafood town with a number of deluxe fish and chip shops and fishmongers as well as a constantly packed souvlaki bar at the corner of Bay St and Grand Parade. Despite Brighton's waterfront location, it's most popular as a night-time destination, due in part to its essentially suburban feel and also because the largely Greek-descended local community favour late carousing with no apparent time limits. Even in the wee hours of winter, the coffee and Marathon Beer are coming fast and the gelato and ice cream are still pounded into cone after cone.

BRIGHTON LE SANDS

Map 16 A2

Smoking throughout

Kamari Greek Taverna Cafe
Greek

☎ 9556 2533
82 The Grand Parade

Kamari's open frontage, bang in the middle of the Brighton Le Sands seafood strip, looks out beyond a row of beach pines across the expanse of Botany Bay and a sky that's alive with jumbo jets coasting in and out of Sydney Airport. The rough white walls, pastel frescoes and bazouki music chiming in the background lends it a classical taverna feel with modern design that makes it popular with everyone from strolling families to late night cafe fiends. It's a great place for mezedes – light, shared dishes – such as the generous whitebait in parsley vinaigrette ($9.90) and the baked cheese-stuffed mushroom yemista* ($8.50). Mains include gourmet Hellenic specialities such as lamb atlantis (baked lamb with cherry tomatoes and garlic – $20.50) and the pan-fried seafood pilaf. They also make a mean and muddy Greek coffee. Though the staff had a cockiness about them, the vibe is relaxed and cool and the sand-blown vista strangely impressive.

starter: $7.50-$12.50
main: $15.50-$20.50
dessert: $6.50-$8
AE BC DC MC V

Open: Mon-Fri noon-3pm, 6pm-midnight, Sat-Sun noon-midnight; reservations accepted; licensed, no BYO

COOGEE

Barzura
Mediterranean/ modern Australian

☎ 9665 5546
62 Carr St

Map 15 C5

No smoking inside

Pavement tables

You can't miss Barzura – you can spot its industrial-strength signage halfway down Coogee's main drag. It's overkill, really. The bayside location of this cafe/ristorante is inducement enough. But going to extremes seems to be Barzura's doctrine – long opening hours, extensive menus and more-than-good food. Buzzy waiters scud from kitchen to tavern-like dining area with dish after dish: couscous with poached pears and yoghurt ($7.50) and beef burgers with bacon and beetroot relish ($11.50). It's after dark, however, that Barzura really shows its mettle. The wine starts flowing and dishes like the lusciously tender squid salad ($10.50) and the char-grilled veal cutlet with an audaciously sweet maple demi-glaze ($16.50) begin to rocket out of the kitchen. After the last spoonful of your hazelnut meringue roulade ($9), raise a glass – and your voice (volume is another thing taken to extremes) – and toast to 'food' and 'wine', Barzura's twin gods.

starter: dinner $9.50-$10.50
main: breakfast $3-$10.50
 lunch $4-$11.50
 dinner $12.50-$17.50
dessert: $9

AE BC MC V

Open: daily 7am-11pm (breakfast: daily 7am-1pm); reservations essential; licensed & BYO (corkage $2.50/person)

CRONULLA

Bacchus
Italian

☎ 9544 3883
83 Cronulla St

Map 16 B3

Wheelchair access

Smoking throughout

If you're in the neighbourhood of beachside Cronulla and want something to eat, head for Bacchus. The attractive décor is an unusual mix of vivid emerald green and imitation bird's-eye marble. The eclectic menu claims to be Italian offering pasta, pizza and meat and seafood dishes. John Dory fillets with a creamy mornay sauce work well, and a filling frittata ($9.90) with potato, beans, capsicum and eggplant could have been made in Spain. Desserts are designed to sink you – try gourmet gelato in a kaleidoscope of flavours. The service is friendly if a little slow. Watch the passing parade of teenagers with boogie boards and surfie chicks straight out of *Puberty Blues*. They take centre stage on Friday and Saturday nights when Bacchus gets pretty lively with hen's nights and compulsory sing-alongs. You have been warned.

starter: $9-$15
main: lunch $10-$16
 dinner $16-$25
dessert: $5.50

AE BC DC MC V

Open: Mon-Fri noon-3.30pm, 6pm-late, Sat & Sun noon-late; reservations accepted (advisable on Fri & Sat evenings); licensed & BYO (corkage $3.50/bottle)

Cafe Crawl – East/South-East

Lazing on the beach (whether in Bondi or Bali) can take it out of you. To recuperate, there's nothing better than a coffee treatment.

The Bogey-Hole Café 473 Bronte Rd, Bronte ☎ 9389 8829 Map 14 E3
Jam, Anzac biscuits, macaroons, melting moments and mixed berry muffins are made on site, kept in big glass cookie jars at the counter and eagerly consumed by many Bronte locals. They seem to prefer the worn floor, warm service and old-fashioned breakfasts, like eggs benedict ($9), over some of the more hyped-up cafes that share The Bogey-Hole's Bronte Beach view.

Brown Sugar 100 Brighton Blvd, Bondi ☎ 9365 6262 Map 14 B6
It's a little spot on a little street away from the big beach, but locals who've just surfaced from the surf like to squeeze in around the big communal table for the 'black stone eggs' (go and find out for yourself) and some of Bondi's best coffee. The sharp scent of vinegar in the air assures you the poached eggs are being well looked after. Or try the medium-thick pancakes with fresh seasonal fruit.

Café Orphée 178 Oxford St, Paddington ☎ 9360 3238 Map 13 B2
A place for French deli delicacies – brioche and baguettes and open sourdough sandwiches. Pick up some imported French flavours – 15 varieties of mustard and 20 jams and honeys – while you're there.

Caffe Wine Bar Kingsford Smith Airport, Departure Level, Domestic Terminal, Mascot ☎ 9699 3434 Map 15 E1
If it wasn't in an airport it would be just another groovy inner-city coffee stop. Wood panelling (with modern cut-out squares) proper pasta and focaccia and real coffee aren't the usual airport fare. A great place to meet that old friend with a Sydney stopover between connections or a spot to calm the nerves when that business flight is delayed, yet again.

Coogee Bite Cafe 126a Beach St, Coogee ☎ 9665 0190 Map 15 C5
The Bite is a busy beachside spot for breakfast and brunches, with butter yellow walls, banquettes, burgers, buttermilk pancakes, bacon and eggs done a few different ways – and the occasional runaway bambini.

Direction of Cure 23a Burnie Street, Clovelly ☎ 9665 5244 Map 15 B6
Locals and girl couples find plenty of sustenance and healing in this cafe which doubles as a homeopathic consultancy. But take note – the caffeine in your coffee is likely to render that herbal hangover cure next to useless.

Gusto 16 Hall St, Bondi Beach ☎ 9130 4565 Map 14 B4
Pull up a milk crate and pick up a Gusto Cajun chicken burrito ($6.50) if you're ready to pit your take on casual cool against Bondi's South American contingent and other beach-blessed locals. Gusto means coffee, coffee and more coffee, with perhaps one of Gusto's 'famous' chicken and cheese melts.

The Red Kite Cafe 95 Roscoe St, Bondi Beach ☎ 9365 0432 Map 14 B4
More hippy-and-trippy than the usual lippy-and-dippy Bondi cafe, the Red Kite is a strangely well-kept secret. The food is vegetarian and respectable and the coffee is not bad at all. But you go there for the sanctuary feel (perhaps it's the Chapel by the Sea, located on the floor above, exerting an influence?).

EASTLAKES

Thai I-San Classic
Thai

☎ **9693 5046**
Shop 86, BKK Eastlakes Shopping Centre

Map 15 C1

🅿 Private parking

We've always thought walls blackened by the lick of stray flames guaranteed a good Thai restaurant. After visiting Thai I-San, we're now on the look out for formica tables, chairs held together with silver gaffer tape, an air-con trolley and a glowing neon 'Insect-o-cutor'. It's in a nondescript shopping hub in a nondescript part of Sydney, but it's the sort of place where you're likely bump into a friend you've never known to venture beyond her beachside suburb. There are the usual curries ($7.50-$8.50) and curry puffs ($4) of your average Thai tuck shop, but the menu's 98 dishes incorporate more authentic choices. Liver or papaya salads ($6.50), 'Thai I-San sausages' ($6.50) and 'crunchy quails' ($11.90) are closely related to Laos cuisine, and flavours can be extremely pungent and fiery. Our deep-fried fish was so garlicky you'd think the neighbourhood was in the middle of a witch plague.

starter: $4-$6
main: $6.50-$11.90

Open: Wed-Mon 11am-9pm; reservations advisable; BYO (no corkage)

cash only

KENSINGTON

Map 15 B2
Private parking
Smoking throughout

Golden Kingdom Beijing House Restaurant
Chinese (Northern)

☎ 9662 1616, 9662 1122
Ground floor, 147 Anzac Pde

Golden Kingdom Beijing House Restaurant is an expansive feel-good place where devotees in large numbers (it seats up to 200) enjoy its generous servings. Waiters, smart in black and white, are helpful and informed about the cuisine. Sliced fillet of lamb with shallots ($12.80) and crispy skin duck with pancake ($16) would satisfy any northerner with cravings for home cooking. Pan-fried meat dumplings aren't greasy while the steamed vegetable dumplings packed with finely chopped carrot, greens and slivers of vermicelli are a pleasing vegetarian choice (both $9 for 10). A room to the side of the entrance, with a back view of the fish tanks is reserved for those with toddlers. The small fry can gaze at their favourite restaurant attraction undisturbed and at close range. It's a treat to find ice cream and fresh strawberries in an old-fashioned sundae glass complete with wafer ($4) to supplement the seasonal fresh fruit 'on the house'.

starter: $4-$16
main: $9-$32
dessert: $3-$12
BC MC V

Open: daily 11am-3pm, dinner 5pm-11pm; reservations advisable; licensed, no BYO

KINGSFORD

Ayam Goreng
Indonesian

☎ **9697 0030**
464 Anzac Pde

Map 15 C3

Smoking throughout

Love do-it-yourself projects? Then Ayam Goreng is the restaurant for you. It's the kind of joint where you open your own beer, set out the cutlery, even write down your order and deliver it to the kitchen. However, it's easy to feel cooperative when all the punchy Indonesian dishes ring in at under 11 bucks. The menu, a small festival of poultry pleasures, is aimed firmly at students and families who want a taste of home without any annoying fripperies. Suitably spiced, the finger-licking house speciality of sweet, curry chicken (ayam goreng) is so popular that you can order it by the piece (breasts and thighs $3.50 each) or whole ($8). Pile your table high with other savoury goodies like pepes, banana-leaf pouches crammed with mixed vegetables and tofu ($2.50), or the whole crispy, trevally, shrouded in slivers of lemongrass, capsicum and spring onions ($10). And, thankfully, they don't expect you to do the washing up.

starter: $1-$5
main: $5-$10
dessert: $3

Open: Tues-Sun 11.30am-9.30pm; reservations not accepted; BYO (no corkage)

cash only

Tea Inn
Taiwanese

☎ **9697 2789**
311-313 Anzac Pde

Map 15 C2

Nonsmoking tables available

Flip cards on the table describe thirst-quenching iced teas served with straws in long glasses: red whis green tea ($3.50) is 'sweet but sour + a little of wine', ginseng tea ($3) is recommended to 'dispel the exogenous factor of wind and cold'. With piped Taiwanese pop music and happy hour specials to go with these cocktails, it's a brightly-lit, teetotalling nightclub for UNSW students. A thousand colour photocopies on the walls demonstrate dishes, from huge bowls of steamed duck in peppery soup with 'long life' noodles ($7) and stir fried beef with rice ($6.50) to dozens of deep-fried dishes like sweet potato and chicken rolls (both $3). In fact, there's so much that's deep-fried the health-conscious claims of 'less oil' and 'no MSG' initially seem disingenuous. But this is self-confessed 'Tawainese-style fast food'. And you don't get much faster than 'peanut or strawberry special thick toast' ($2.50).

starter: $3
main: $6.50-$8
dessert: $3

Open: Sun-Fri 11am-10.30pm; reservations not necessary (advisable Thurs and Fri); BYO (no corkage)

BC MC V; Eftpos

SOUTH EASTERN SUBURBS

MAROUBRA

Map 15 E6

Smoking throughout after 9.30pm only

Courtyard & pavement tables

The Pool Caffé
Mediterranean/modern Australian

☎ 9314 0364
94 Marine Pde

Good mod Oz might be as rare in Maroubra as sea views are plentiful, but the Pool Caffé can boast both. Perhaps because it's a rare breed, the menu covers oodles of ground – Asian noodle salad ($14.90), Sicilian stuffed fish ($14.90) and tortillas with ricotta and rocket ($13.90). The meze plate ($25) features plump grilled octopus and dips, and a generous pile of flat bread and focaccia (a serve that's proportionate to the dips and toasted to crunchy perfection). The curry of the day is another wise choice, judging by the quality of our aromatic lamb and eggplant Moroccan curry ($18.90) served with pickles and freshly made raita with roughly chopped cucumber. The Moreton bay bug risotto ($22.90) was overwhelmingly creamy, however, and served so fast that we shouldn't have been surprised the rice was not quite al dente. Seating is provided by fold-up timber chairs, while fold-away timber windows open up to sea views.

starter: $9.50-$14.90
main: $17.90-$22.90
dessert: $9-$12
Set menu $28.50-$45

AE BC DC MC V

Open: Fri-Sun lunch from noon, Sat & Sun breakfast from 9am, Wed-Sat 6pm-10pm; reservations advisable; BYO (corkage $2/person)

Map 15 E3

Private parking

Wheelchair access

Nonsmoking tables available

Swiss Hut
Swiss/French

☎ 9344 7755
275 Bunnerong Rd

Since when have oysters ($9.70 a half dozen) or mango chicken salad ($6.90) been Swiss? This is one of the little mysteries you can ponder behind Swiss Hut's faux chalet exterior in an elegantly suburban dining room, that's not the least bit Heidi. They don't do fondue, either, but there *is* emmentaler poulet ($15.90), a chicken and cheese combo on a bed of steamed spinach, and the even better caneton melba ($17.50), a juicy leg of duck with a side garnish of peach and strawberry. Your stomach will thank you for ordering the zurcher gschnatzlets ($16.90) – tender veal slices in a cream and mushroom sauce. The rösti ($4.50), a crisp cake of grated potato, is a must and the whopping profiteroles ($5.90) really hit the spot. Healthy options are marked on the menu, service is tiptop and dramas with kids (we were dining en famille) don't faze them either.

starter: $5.90-$10.90
main: $11.90-$17.50
dessert: $5.90-$7.30
Set menu $22.50-$33.50

AE BC DC MC V

Open: Tues-Fri, Sun noon-3pm, daily 6pm-9.30pm; reservations advisable (especially weekends); licensed & BYO (corkage $1/person)

RANDWICK

Azteca's Mexican Restaurant
Mexican

☎ 9398 1020
140 Avoca St

Mr Heinz beware! Azteca's is elbowing in on the bean market. Black-eyed, haricot or pinto, spiced, refried or pot simmered, this restaurant's bean menu is as colourful as the Mexican bric-a-brac that studs its walls. Start your meal with some sangria (take a bottle of red and they'll spice it up for you) and a five-in-one platter of dips ($13.60) featuring guacamole, cheese, sour cream, and hot, hot chillies. Concerned that you don't go hungry, cheery American waitresses may advise you to add the nachos ($11.50/$14.90) to your entrée order. The corn chips are corny and the bean mix deliciously redefines 'three bean', but by the time your mole poblano* ($14.20) arrives, you may be struggling. With your plate of tender chicken fillets swimming in a bitter chocolate sauce, you'll also receive a generous serving of rice, salad, a tortilla and – you guessed it – beans. Dessert is bean-free but uninteresting. Skip it and have a Mexican coffee ($4.50) instead.

Open: Tues-Sun 6pm-late; reservations advisable; licensed & BYO (corkage $2/person)

Map 15 B4
Entertainment: Mexican singer Tues-Sun 8pm

Smoking throughout

starter: $4.20-$13.60
main: $10.50-$17.20
dessert: $3.90-$4.50
Set menu $25
AE BC MC V

Lebanon and Beyond
Lebanese

☎ 9326 5347
Shop 3, 187 Alison Rd

This is the sort of small local eatery where the waitress is helpful and efficient enough to simultaneously refill your water glass, turn down the lights for a birthday cake presentation and write down a takeaway order for a felafel roll. Order almost any of the largish, homely Lebanese dishes: okra with garlic and coriander ($8.50), or perhaps a rich dish of lamb mince, pine nuts and eggplant on a bed of buttery rice ($12.50). A mixed vege platter ($18) is also on the large size, with plenty of tabouli that's as green as the locals' faces whenever they think of their beach neighbours' soaring house values. A curved plate-glass shop front and black and white floor tiles lend a classy feel, as do whitewashed walls decorated with scenes of sea and snow. But the fold-up wooden chairs are the best indication of the low prices – so low you might be surprised that you can BYO.

Open: Sun-Thurs 5pm-10.30pm, Fri & Sat 5pm-11pm; reservations advisable; BYO (corkage $1/person)

Map 15 B4

Smoking throughout

Pavement tables

starter: $5.50-$6
main: $8.50-$18
dessert: $2
Set menu $18/person (min 2 people)
AE BC MC V; Eftpos

SOUTH EASTERN SUBURBS

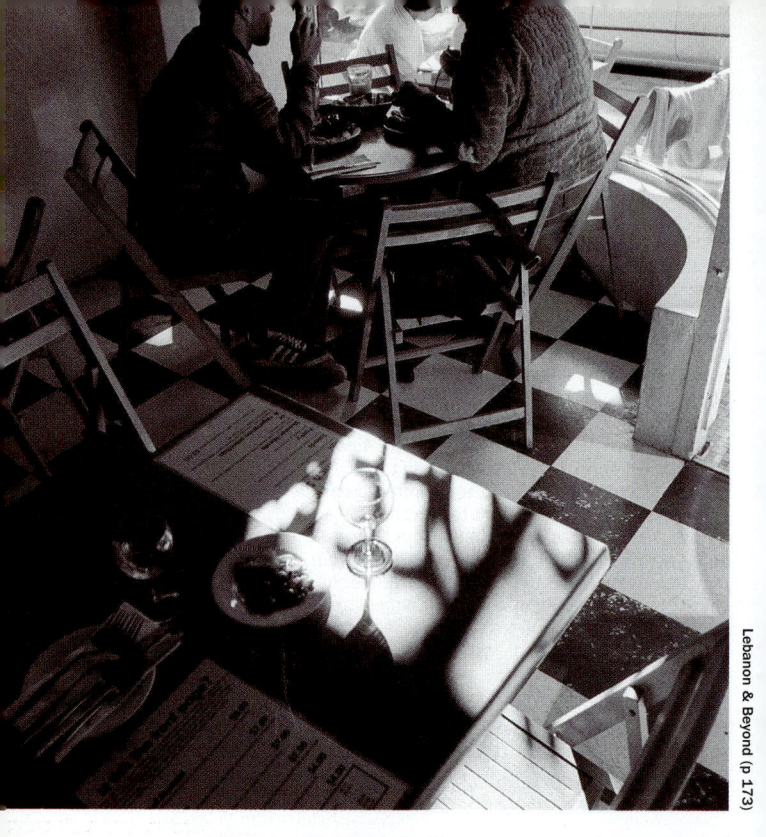

Map 15 A4	**New Orient Take Away**	☎ 9398 6929
	Indonesian	36 Clovelly Road

When the sea breezes are rippling around Randwick, you can smell this tiny kitchen – ensconced on a quiet stretch of Clovelly Road – from blocks away. The New Orient is one of those cheap, spartan places you visit to take the weight off, read the paper and get a dose of something authentic and powerful. On any night except Wednesday, you'll find a cluster of loyal diners drawn from the Indonesian student community. There are only a few dishes and pretty much all of them contain a regionally-distinctive combination of fishcake and egg. The tekwan ($6) is a very refreshing, complex soup with pieces of fishcake and tofu. The pempek lenggang (fishcake omelette, $5.50) is a great big, fluffy frisbee of a thing, afloat in a bowl of high-octane treacle. Likewise, the pancake with peanut chocolate and cheese ($10) seems to hover in a space somewhere between mains and desserts.

main: $1.70-$10

Open: Mon, Tues, Thurs & Fri noon-9pm, Sat-Sun 11am-9pm; no reservations; unlicensed

RANDWICK

Teascapes
Cafe fare

☎ 9398 7994
71 Perouse Rd

Map 15 C4

Nonsmoking tables available

Pavement tables

Kooky, quirky Teascapes is way too much fun for adults. Decorated as part student digs, part curio shop, this is a cafe to bring the kids to, or bring out the kid in you. With its pool table, walls lined with golliwogs and vintage toys and collection of old-school amusements (like Boggle, Pictionary and Pick-Up-Stix), it's a wonder patrons find the time to eat. The food though – styled on your favourite after-school snacks – is well worth interrupting your game of backgammon for. Slurp loudly on a frothy vanilla milkshake ($3), while waiting for a perfectly grilled chicken-cheese melt ($8.50). Served on a wonderfully fresh, toasted baguette and sided by a sprightly little salad, it's a toastie as good as any could be. Fulfil all your childhood fantasies with a gorge-yourself-silly ice cream sundae. The banana melt ($5), smothered in hot chocolate sauce, vanilla ice cream and sprinkles, delights everyone from four to forty.

starter: $2.50-$5.50
main: $6.50-$9
dessert: $5-$6.50

cash only

Open: Mon-Fri 11.30am-late, Sat & Sun 9.30am-late (breakfast: Sat & Sun 9.30-1pm); reservations not accepted; BYO (no corkage)

Thai FireFry
Thai

☎ 9326 4203
20 Perouse Rd

Map 15 C4

Smoking throughout

Pavement tables

There are two real draw cards attracting customers to FireFry: the massive fireball that periodically erupts in the windowfront and is felt across the room, and the generous baskets of complimentary spicy hot prawn crackers. One waitress plonks bowls of curry down on tabletops, while another wanders around scooping out generous rice servings. The whole effect is a little bit mess hall – albeit one where the colour scheme has been devised by Kandinsky on a very happy day. The food, good as it is, is almost an afterthought to these attractions. Seventy-four dishes include delicious battered corn cakes like a plate of Chinese yum cha ($2) while a tom kar gai soup ($5.40), full of plump tender chicken pieces, is thick with coconut cream. A seafood salad ($8) is far from the best we've tried, with a cloying, heavy sauce. It's more gimmickry than subtlety, but locals keep that fireball burning night after night.

starter: $2-$5.60
main: $8-$11.90

($20 min) AE BC MC V; Eftpos

Open: daily noon-11pm; reservations advisable; BYO (corkage $1.50/person)

SOUTH EASTERN SUBURBS

Back for More

Le Sands Restaurant
The Grand Pde, Brighton Le Sands ☎ 9599 2128 Map 16 B2
Le Sands is all about special occasion seafood feasts for the southern suburbs. Ask for a window seat looking out to the softly lit beach and you'll almost forget the oil refinery in the distance.

Nasi Uduk Jakarta
275 Anzac Pde, Kingsford ☎ 9663 4430 Map 15 C2
Rub shoulders with Indonesian expat students in a place that's just like they might find at home: the gado gado, barbecued chicken and fish are all popular, with most mains just $4-$8.

❋ *Write to us:* *We think we've got Sydney well-covered – even so, there are always new places to try. Our tastebuds will travel, so let us know which restaurants, cafes and bars you think we should include. Write to us or email us (see p 11 for details) and the best suggestions will receive the next edition free.*

Balmoral

Berowra Waters

Brooklyn

Castlecrag

NORTH SHORE

Chatswood

Clontarf

Cremorne

Crows Nest

Hornsby

Kirribilli

McMahons Point

Mosman – The Spit

Neutral Bay

North Sydney

Terrey Hills

Thornleigh

Wahroonga

Westleigh

Willoughby

Map 17 - North Sydney

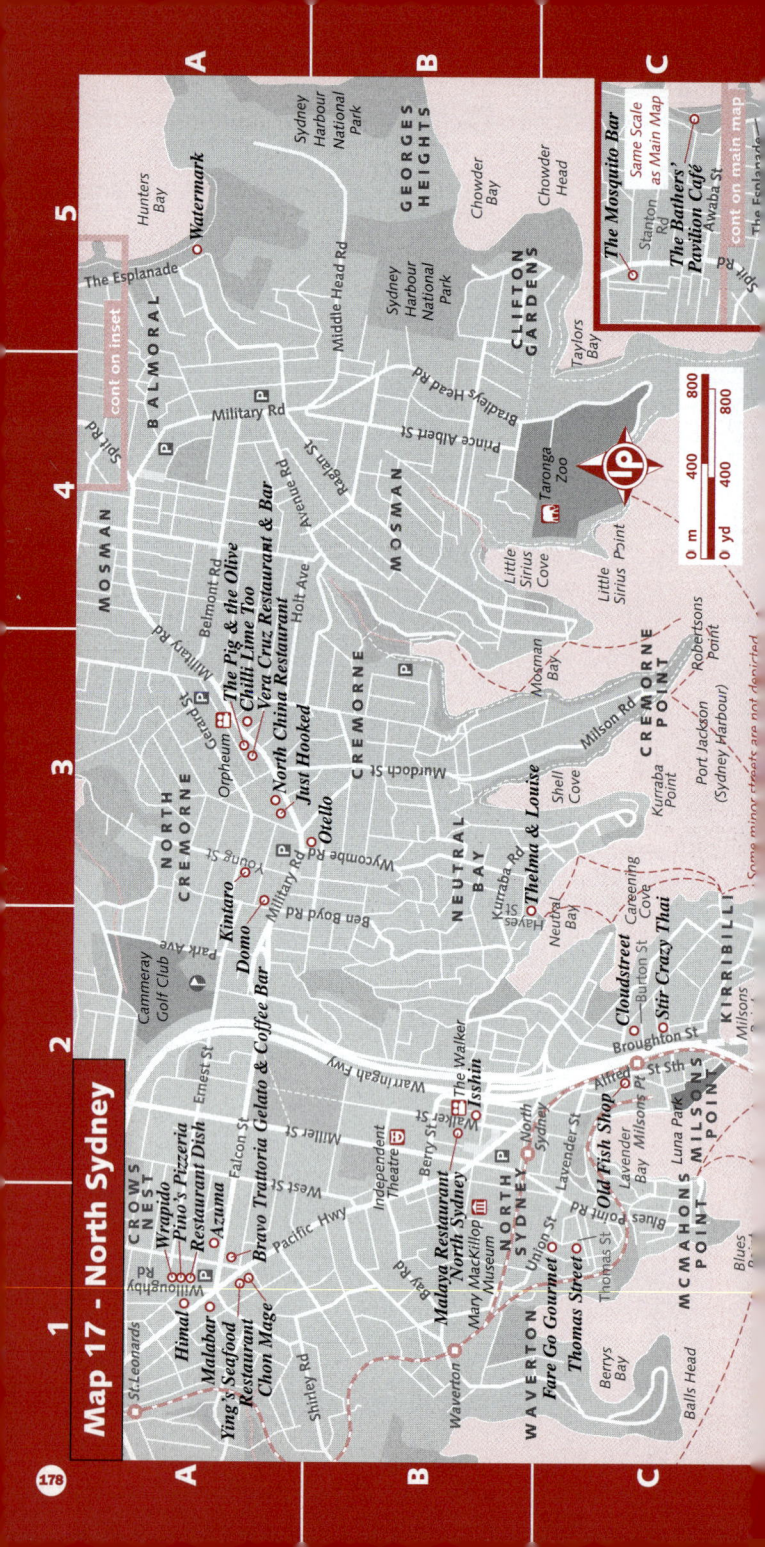

Map 18 - Middle Harbour

Map 19 - Hornsby

Westleigh

- Eucalyptus Dve
- *Scoozi Trattoria*
- Quarter Sessions Rd
- Duffy Ave

Same Scale as Main Map

cont on main map
cont on Westleigh

- Hornsby
- HORNSBY
- Edgeworth David Ave
- *Steps*
- Leonard St
- College Cres
- Waitara
- WAITARA
- Pacific Hwy
- Myra St
- Unwin Rd
- Ingram Rd
- Sydney - Newcastle Fwy
- Millewa Ave
- *Coonabarra Cafe*
- Wahroonga
- WAHROONGA
- Pacific Hwy
- Waitara Ck
- Ada Ave
- Pennant Hills Rd
- Sefton Rd
- Milson Pde
- Normanhurst
- NORMANHURST
- Duffy Ave
- Chilvers Rd
- The Esplanade
- THORNLEIGH
- *Istana*
- Thornleigh
- The Comenarra Pkwy
- Coups Ck

0 km 0.5 1
0 mi 0.25 0.5

Minor streets are not depicted

Map 20 - Outer North

- Marramarra Park
- Hawkesbury River
- *Riverside Brooklyn Restaurant*
- Hawkesbury River
- Brooklyn Rd
- Dangar Rd
- *Anglers Rest Hotel*
- Hawkesbury River
- Muogamarra Nature Reserve
- Ku-Ring-Gai Chase National Park
- *The Restaurant on Berowra Waters*
- *Berowra Waters Tea House*
- Bay Rd
- Berowra Waters Rd
- Pacific Hwy
- Sydney - Newcastle Fwy

0 km 1.5 3
0 mi 1 2

Terrey Hills

- McCarrs Ck Rd
- Yulong Ave
- *Kaiser Stub'n*
- Booralie Rd
- Kanangra Rd
- Mona Vale Rd

0 m 300
0 yd 300

Some minor streets are not depicted. *Terrey Hills inset 6km* *Some minor streets are not depicted*

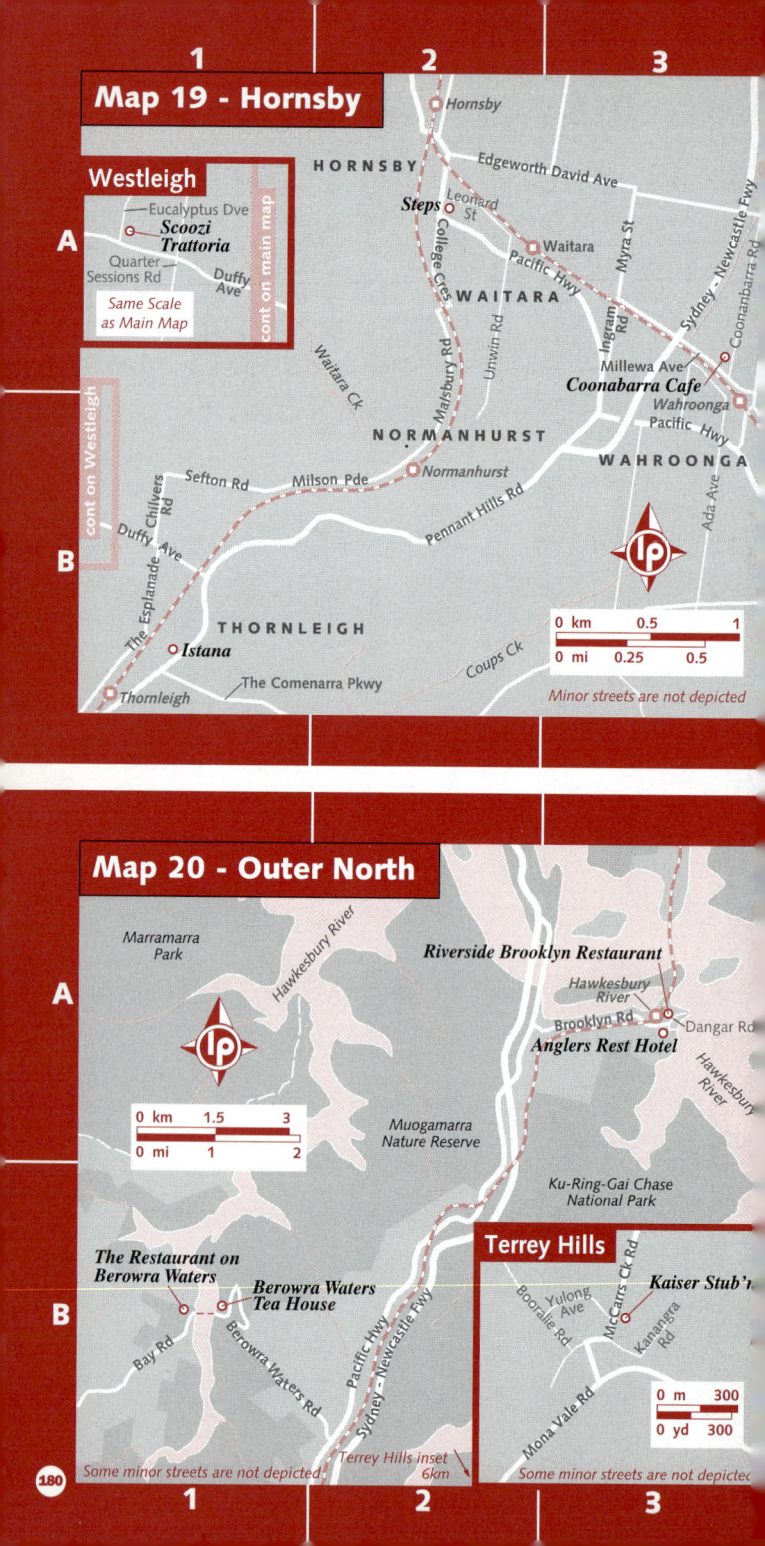

180

BEST

- **Cloudstreet**
  Culinary artistry makes for classy dining

- **Domo**
  Expertly prepared Japanese delights

- **Malabar**
  Delectable dosas and South Indian spice

- **Malaya Restaurant North Sydney**
  Great service at this Asian star

- **Watermark**
  Right setting for that special night

North Shore

Sydney's Harbour Bridge is not merely an architectural icon, it's a psychological one, representing the city's geographic and mental split between north and south. The North Shore covers suburbs north of the harbour to Hornsby and is regarded as Sydney's conservative side, full of dentists, private schools, leafy streets and pristine 4WDs. While not all residents are rich or WASPy, money is certainly evident in the harbourside real estate of Mosman and upper North Shore mansions. One of the first North Shore enterprises was a whaling station at Mosman Bay – now North Sydney is the modern business centre and Chatswood, the main shopping centre. Both have their own eating scenes (Chatswood with a distinct Asian influence). But Crows Nest is the centre of the North Shore's dining universe, packing an impressive range of restaurants into a small area. Elsewhere, Kirribilli has seen a recent rash of openings, and eating establishments line Blues Point Road, McMahons Point. Running through Neutral Bay, Cremorne and Mosman, Military Road also offers a wide spread. The North Shore's culinary presence is not as defined as south of the harbour, but it definitely has its rewards if you know where to look.

BALMORAL

Map 17 C5
Wheelchair access

The Bathers' Pavilion Café
Modern Australian/Italian

☎ 9969 5050
4 The Esplanade

After a recent extensive renovation, this white-washed beauty of Balmoral Beach has retained her faded character. Textures are interwoven with crushed eggshell-effect tops on glossy white tables aside worn wooden tables. Intricately patterned carpets and old model ships are scattered around in eclectic chic. An ancient '20c locker hire' sign is one of the few remnants of the building's change-room days. The menu features delectable dishes like pumpkin and prosciutto pizza ($16.50-$18.50) and fish stew ($22.50). Lamb shanks are served up with a suitably creamy apple risotto – rings of half-dried apple decorating it all ($19.50). Some of the food can be bland: a 'fennel sausage' spag bol and an eggplant gnocchi (both $18.50) were sadly uninspiring. Mussels in wine and garlic, on the other hand, are top notch ($19.50). The best place to sit? Definitely the sunroom, with its views of the neighbouring park's rotunda and statue of Billy, the 'street sweeper's canine friend'.

starter: $9-$16.50
main: $16.50-$24.50
dessert: $12

AE BC DC MC V

Open: daily 7am-10.30pm (breakfast: daily 7am-noon); reservations not accepted; licensed, no BYO

Map 17 A5
Wheelchair access
Dress Code: shoes essential

Courtyard tables

Watermark
Modern Australian

☎ 9968 3433
2a The Esplanade

If you are thinking of proposing, then do it at Watermark – starry nights, shimmering moon, bar lounges facing onto the old Balmoral Baths. Go no further than the Asian antipasto ($19.50). The selection of dumplings come in their own steamer, each one thoughtfully smeared with its own sauce. Mains are mostly seafood: Chatham Island blue-eye cod fillets ($34), pan-fried barramundi fillets ($33), NSW coastal yellow fin tuna marinated and crusted in black pepper, served with sautéed Japanese spinach, caperberries and poached yabbie cannelloni ($34). The roast loin of lamb ($32) served with roasted kipfler potatoes, zucchini in wild thyme, apple chutney and lamb jus is just divine. At breakfast, the blues are brighter, the beach view busier. Relish farm-fresh eggs with bacon ($12) or flap jacks ($13) – wholemeal and dairy free – with your Illy coffee or boutique tea. Watermark provides for children with an under-twelves' menu.

starter: $19-$27
main: $32-$38
dessert: $14-$16

AE BC DC MC V
Entertainment Card

Open: daily 8.30am-10.30am, 6.30pm-10.30pm, Mon-Fri noon-3.30pm, Sat & Sun 12.30pm-3.30pm; reservations advisable; licensed, no BYO

Lowdown on Loos

A new Sydney restaurant won't even think about opening nowadays unless a multi-million dollar budget has been spent on a décor overhaul. And sometimes it seems like half of that budget is spent on the boys' and girls' rooms. The question on fashion-conscious lips in Sydney is now 'have you seen that cute loo at X?' Here are some of the best – and a few of the most perplexing – toilets in town.

A loo with a view

Forty One Level 41, The Chifley Tower, 2 Chifley Square, City ☎ 9221 2500
With the glittering city views from these loos, you'll never want to leave – a sofa and chairs are provided so you can settle in and get comfy (see review p 30).

The Fire Place 19 Bayswater Rd, Kings Cross ☎ 9357 3300 Map 5 E2
The toilet walls are made of glass! They're thick and opaque and very chic.

Loos to woo you

blackbird Cockle Bay Wharf, 201 Sussex St, Cockle Bay ☎ 9283 7385
Catch up on the latest news, Judge Judy's latest decision or developments in your favourite soap as you scrub up at the sink (see review p 39).

Cine Bent St, Fox Studios, Moore Park ☎ 9332 1409
It's somewhat disconcerting, squatting down to go about your business only to find U2's Bono belting out 'Sunday Bloody Sunday' from the video screen at your feet (see review p 150).

Loos that confuse

Cafe Sydney Customs House, level 5, 31 Alfred St, Circular Quay
☎ 9251 8683
The cheeky icons on the male (a lighthouse) and female (a buoy) facilities have been known to confuse customers (see review p 23).

MG Garage 490 Crown St, Surry Hills ☎ 9383 9383
The ultra-modern vanities look like fluorescent white goods from an Eskimo's home. Figuring out how to make the water tap work can take longer than decoding the ultra-foodie menu at this ultra-snazzy eatery (see review p 81).

Old loos to new

When each new restaurant and bar that opens its door looks as clean and sparkling and sterile as modern toilets, we shouldn't be surprised when old toilet blocks are overhauled and turned into the hottest new eating and watering hole.

Bar Quattro St James Station, Hyde Park, City ☎ 9267 0299 Map 3 C3
This 1937 brick and sandstone-veneer toilet was built in the days when St James Station was the end of the city rail line and a public convenience was considered a priority. It's gone through some notorious times, but has now been transformed into a restaurant, with outdoor seating looking out onto the old-timers who play chess on the Hyde Park game tables.

The Bathers' Pavilion 4 The Esplanade, Balmoral ☎ 9969 5050
Built in 1928 so bathers could slip into the neck-to-knee costumes of the day, in 1988 it was given a heritage preservation order, saved from demolition and turned into one of Sydney's swankiest eateries (see review p 182).

The Sydney Cove Oyster Bar 1 Circular Quay East ☎ 9247 2937 Map 1 C5
This red brick building on the water's edge at Circular Quay East was built as a toilet for wharf workers in 1906. Now you can sit at the promenade tables, order oysters by the dozen and a bottle of bubbly from the Australian wine list.

BEROWRA WATERS

Map 20 B1
Wheelchair access
Smoking throughout
Verandah tables

Berowra Waters Tea House
International

☎ 9456 1454
end of Berowra Waters Road

It's enthusing to find such a charming getaway so close to Sydney. Berowra Waters Tea House provides sheltered outdoor dining, with coal heaters for use in winter. Gaze through the gums onto the tranquil, intimate Pittwater view. Watch people messing about in boats or catching the car-ferry across to the opposite shore. A hearty breakfast is available on Saturdays and Sundays at a set price of $15.50 with bottomless coffee or tea and bottled orange juice. You can choose from various combinations of eggs – fried, scrambled or benedict – all with generous extras. We witnessed a kookaburra perched for quite some time on the balcony surveying the scene of satisfied diners. For lunch and dinner choices range from Veal Oscar with asparagus ($28.90) to barbequed duck ($25.90). For dessert try the famous Bombe Alaska ($8.90). The staff are friendly and accommodating.

starter: $13.90-$19.90
main: $25.90-$30.90
dessert: $8.90
AE BC MC V

Open: Wed-Sun noon-3pm, Fri & Sat from 7pm (breakfast: Sat & Sun 9am-11.15am); reservations advisable; BYO

Map 20 B1
No smoking inside

The Restaurant on Berowra Waters
Modern Australian

☎ 9456 1027
Berowra Waters Road

As we stepped onto the boat in the dark to be ferried to the Restaurant on Berowra Waters, formerly Berowra Waters Inn, we wondered if it would live up to its famed reputation of old. Elements do, like the sheer novelty of going somewhere only accessible by private ferry, seaplane or yacht. Our picks from the set menu were crispy forest mushroom rolls (a magic combination of eight types of mushroom) and goat's cheese wontons, with a salad of rocket, eggplant and zucchini. Pan-seared swordfish with mango chutney, Chinese broccoli and sautéed kipfler potatoes was one of the lighter options, or there was roasted muscovy duck with dark cherry compote or olive and rosemary seasoned lamb rump served with pepperonata. It was a struggle to do justice to the sticky date and chocolate pudding with butterscotch sauce. A tip on the location: a day trip offers more, when the river is in its full stunning element.

Set lunch/dinner $75,
breakfast $24.50
AE BC DC JCB MC V
Entertainment Card

Open: lunch Fri-Sun from noon; dinner Fri & Sat from 6pm (breakfast: Sun 9am-noon); reservations essential; licensed, no BYO

BROOKLYN

Angler's Rest Hotel
Seafood

☎ 9985 7860
216 Brooklyn Rd

Angler's Rest, off the Sydney to Newcastle freeway, is a sheltered haven for the weary traveller. Cheap, light meals from the snack bar and snazzier restaurant meals can be eaten outdoors, under umbrellas in the courtyard or on the shady verandah, or indoors at clothed tables. Most seafood served is from local Hawkesbury and Central Coast suppliers – great value with oysters at $14.50 a dozen. Jewfish cutlets ($25) are grilled in lime juice and served with steamed seasonal vegetables and chat potatoes, bream is stuffed with seafood ($26), and whiting fillets ($20) sit comfortably in beer batter. The chef's own fettucine with boscaiola sauce ($11) and glazed rack of lamb ($24) are some non-seafood alternatives. Desserts ($8) are made on the premises. We devoured the mudcake with hazelnuts and almonds and the caramel, banana and cream tart. A freshly pulled beer is on tap in the pub section.

Open: Wed-Sun noon-2.30pm, Wed-Sat 6pm-9pm; reservations advisable; licensed & BYO

Map 20 A3

Wheelchair access

Entertainment: live singer/guitarist Sat night & Sun lunch

No smoking inside

Courtyard & verandah tables

starter: $12.50-$16.50
main: $20-$25
dessert: $8
Function menu available $35/person

AE BC MC V

Riverside Brooklyn Restaurant
Modern Australian

☎ 9985 7248
Level 1, Hawkesbury River Marina, Dangar Rd

This recent edition to the Brooklyn dining precinct has a lot going for it – location, relaxed opening hours and a range of prices on the menu. It's the sort of place where you could literally sit for a whole day and observe the busy river scene unfolding. The balcony looks directly across to Hawkesbury River Station, the railway bridge and the ferry wharf to Dangar Island. Tranquillity stretches beyond where pelicans, gulls and fishing birds cruise at their leisure. And there you are, sipping wine and choosing from the array of tapas, maybe jalapeño chillies with guacamole and sour cream ($8.50), pizzetta ($12.90) or more sizeable dishes such as whole baby snapper with red pepper sauce and scallop potatoes ($23.50). Local Hawkesbury oysters ($18 per dozen) are served when available. Desserts are an attraction: we liked the chocolate torte with white chocolate ice cream ($9) and steamed banana pudding with butterscotch sauce and macadamia glass ($9).

Open: daily noon-midnight; reservations advisable; licensed and BYO ($3/bottle)

Map 20 A3

Smoking throughout

Balcony tables

starter: $4.50-$10.50
main: $12-$24.90
dessert: $8.50-$12.50

AE BC DC MC V

CASTLECRAG

Map 18 B3

No smoking inside

Courtyard tables

Lunch
Modern Australian

☎ 9958 8441
The Quadrangle,
5/100 Edinburgh Rd

When respected Sydney chef Annie Parmentier decided to ditch the restaurant regime and open a cafe, she certainly did Castlecrag's shopping centre a big favour – it's not where you'd expect to have an outstanding foodie experience. The ever-changing menu depends on the best produce Parmentier finds on the day. Around 15 selections are written up on whiteboards, and they all sound eligibly edible. The tone is breezy and the service casual (though at times vague). The floor-to-ceiling louvre windows light an airy, stylish interior, but on a warm day, a table under the outdoor umbrella canopy is prime position. Particularly when you're tucking into juicy Thai prawn cakes on a mound of spicy salad ($15.20), or the more delicate asparagus and kipfler potato salad with smoked trout ($15.20). Both the slow-baked cheesecake ($6.50) and the ricotta and quince cake ($7.50) are a treat.

main: $13.20-$19.20
dessert: $6.50-$9.80
BC MC V

Open: Mon-Fri 9am-5pm, Sat 8am-4pm, Sun 10am-4pm; reservations advisable, especially for lunch; BYO (corkage $1/person)

CHATSWOOD

Map 18 A1

Chatswood BBQ Kitchen
Chinese

☎ 9419 6532
377 Victoria Ave

'Vegetarians need not enter'. A written sign is unnecessary – the glazed, headless ducks hanging in the window speak volumes. Sophistication is also not on the menu. The dining area is small, table sharing not uncommon, and the décor includes laminex tables, paper napkin dispensers and fake wood panelling. Enter for a quick, cheap meal of dependably good Chinese food. The menu lists over 100 dishes, but the specialty is easy to guess. A plate of double mixed BBQ ($11.80) allows sampling of two meats. The duck is tender, the skin crisp and sweet while the pork is firm and moist. In contrast, grandmother bean curd ($8.80) is a comforting hotpot of creamy tofu in beef gravy with just enough chilli to bite without burning. Despite the extensive choice, diners are invited to 'please request any dishes not on the menu'. And if something on another table looks appealing, employ the point-and-order method.

main: $5.50-$14
cash only

Open: daily 10.30am-10pm; reservations not accepted; BYO (corkage $1/person)

CLONTARF

Clonny's on the Beach
Modern Australian/seafood

☎ **9948 2373**
Clontarf Reserve, Sandy Bay Rd

Map 18 B5

No smoking inside

Verandah tables

Here's a restaurant where you don't need to consult a dictionary to translate the menu. Unpretentious Clonny's simply relies on good food and a superb location to impress its visitors. Sit back and salivate over the Middle Harbour views before tackling the refreshingly unadorned menu. The home-made potato and leek soup ($10.50) is a perfect prelude to the juicy New York sirloin with horseradish and chunky fries. Or follow tradition and enjoy beer-battered fish and chips by the beach ($17.50). There's no fancy presentation here, so you don't have to feel guilty about spearing your fork into a work of art. For dessert, there's more old favourites, like warm brownies, sticky date pudding with butterscotch sauce or warm pecan pie. Go the whole hog and sample a taste of them all ($17.50 for two). The obliging staff happily provide takeaway containers for any leftover morsels.

starter: $9-$15
main: $17-$23
dessert: $9.50
Degustation $60
 (last Friday of the month)

AE BC MC V

Wed-Sun noon-3pm, Fri & Sat 6.30pm-10.30pm; reservations essential (Fri & Sat); BYO (corkage $1.50/person)

CREMORNE

Chilli Lime Too
Asian

☎ **9909 0882**
Shop 1, 283 Military Rd

Map 17 A3

Doesn't matter what night of the week it is, Chilli Lime Too is always packed. This stylish eatery opened last year in response to the phenomenal success of its older sibling – Chilli Lime (just around the corner). Number 'too' has gone a step upmarket with black and chrome chairs, laminated tables, French doors and rusty-red walls. The open kitchen spits out a range of Asian goodies, including delectable Vietnamese spring rolls and a tasty Malay satay. The Chilli Lime chicken and mango salad ($12.50) is a must-have. Chunky mango and chicken pieces blend perfectly with Asian greens and an awesome dressing with plenty of bang and tang. Hot on its heels is the chicken and king prawns stir-fried in freshly-ground chilli and bean paste. Desserts don't disappoint either. The tapioca in warm coconut milk with lychees is a masterpiece while the sticky date cake almost had us licking the plate.

starter: $4.50-$8.80
main: $10.90-$14.90
dessert: $5.50
Banquet $19

AE BC DC MC V

Open: Mon-Sat 6pm-10pm; reservations essential; licensed & BYO (corkage $2/person)

On Your Plate **Thai**

The essence of Thai cuisine lies in the intricate balance of four flavours: hot (usually derived from chillies); sweet (cane sugar, coconut sugar and occasionally palm sugar); salty (fish sauce and shrimp paste); and sour (kaffir lime). Anyone who has spent time in Thailand is likely to have eye-watering memories of curries and seafood soups served from steaming cauldrons, and very fond memories of phat thai – a tangle of rice noodles, bean sprouts, dried shrimp, egg and tofu, enlivened with chillies, the crunch of peanuts and the tang of lime. It's the fusion of this more earthy cuisine with the rarefied classical tradition that has produced the quintessential stir-fried dishes and coconut milk-based red and green curries which have taken Sydney by storm.

The sumptuous feasts of Royal Thai cuisine once sustained royal families whose members were in the hundreds. Preparation was exacting – coconut cream would be slowly infused with the smoke from a jasmine candle and the perfume from jasmine flowers – and the dishes were adorned with intricately carved fruit and vegetables. During the course of its voyage to the Antipodes, Thai cuisine sacrificed some of its chilli fire and shrimp-paste pungency to accommodate more delicate palates. However, in the more authentic inner-city restaurants, eastern and northern Thai dishes such as minced pork salad (larb) and acridly spicy green papaya salad (somtam) make a welcome appearance. There's also the fearless bandanna-clad wok handlers, prepared to risk seriously singed eyebrows from their stir-frying techniques in order to supply Sydney's seemingly insatiable demand for Thai takeaway.

The great attraction of eating Thai – whether in Thailand or in suburban Sydney – is that its clean, fiery tastes come through just as powerfully in a bowl of deliciously wok-charred noodles as they do in the most refined Thai dishes, with their carefully orchestrated interplay of taste and texture.

Alison Cowan

A Sydney-based writer and editor, Alison Cowan has worked on guidebooks to Australia, Greece, Hong Kong, Italy, Japan, New Zealand and Vietnam. She has travelled extensively in Asia, Europe and the USA, spending the better part of a year in Thailand before becoming inured to the punch packed by birds-eye chillies.

CREMORNE

The Pig & The Olive
Italian/modern Australian

☎ 9953 7512
318a Military Rd

Map 17 A3

Nonsmoking tables available

The tone set by the restaurant's motto 'eat in or pig out' issues a warning – this is *not* the place to bring a first date. It *is*, however, the place for a cheerful, reasonable meal. Try dropping in for a bite any Friday night – tables are full of chattering groups, families and work parties. Food and service fit the atmosphere: bright and quick. The zesty crunch of goats cheese and tapenade crostini whets the appetite nicely. Pasta and modern Australian mains are offered, but the main focus is on gourmet pizza – perfect for sharing. On good crisp thin bases, one pizza is topped with sweet roasted pumpkin, sharp fetta, plus spinach and garlic; another presents plump king prawns pepped up with basil and chilli. Both are delectable. The huge baby spinach salad with light, creamy dressing is an excellent way to eat your greens. Dessert anyone? Oink oink.

starter: $13.50-$19.50
main: $13.50-$23.50
dessert: $8

AE BC DC MC V

Open: Tues-Sun 6pm-10pm; reservations accepted (advisable Fri-Sun); licensed & BYO (corkage $4/bottle)

Vera Cruz Restaurant & Bar
Mexican

☎ 9904 5818
314 Military Rd

Map 17 A3

Smoking after 10pm & in the bar

From the first handful of blue-corn tortilla chips and tangy salsa, you know this is a slightly different Mexican restaurant. The decor is modernist clinical: the floor is polished concrete, and neon crosses and rainbow-coloured woven blankets contrast with stark white walls. Helpful service makes an eclectic menu less daunting – without a little gentle prodding, we'd never have ordered the grilled sweetcorn (too many bad memories of street stalls at carnivals) smeared with Mexican wild fungi ($7), but it is a winner. The evil-looking black paste has a rich, smoky, almost chocolate flavour that marries perfectly with the juicy corn kernels. A piquant sauce spiked with tangy tomatillos, chewy pumpkin seeds and grainy dumplings of masa cornmeal was the best thing about green pork mole ($20), since the cubes of meat were of variable quality. This is a place to throw caution to the wind – especially after a few tequilas!

starter: $10
main: $20
dessert: $9
Set lunch $19 (Fri only)

AE BC MC V

Open: Mon-Sat 6pm-late, Fri noon-2.30pm; reservations advisable (essential Fri & Sat); licensed & BYO (corkage $2.50/person)

CROWS NEST

Map 17 A1

Smoking throughout

Azuma
Japanese

☎ 9436 4066
32 Falcon St

We, along with Sydney's Japanese community, just love Azuma. Off-duty salary-men prop up the bar during the week, sipping from their bottle of sake, leaning over heavy china plates of sashimi and the restaurant's trademark konnyaku – pounded translucent yam jelly with carrot, chilli and spinach ($10). Their place is taken by families and parties at the weekend. Only sushi is missing from the menu, which offers up an extensive range of fish, meat, noodle and vegetarian dishes. For a real treat, splash out on the kaiseki banquet, which at $50 for nine courses is outstanding value, especially considering the high standard of cooking. The fanciness of the appetiser selection, including a marinated chunk of cod and tempura fried eel, or the succulent slices of duck in a plum wine sauce, is neatly balanced against the simplicity of the melt-in-the-mouth savoury egg custard and an honest bowl of unadorned udon noodles – a fine alternative to the traditional rice at the end of the meal.

starter: $6-$12
main: $10-$28
dessert: $5-$6
Degustation menu $50-$100
AE BC DC MC V

Open: daily 6pm-11pm (last order 10.30pm Mon-Sat, 10pm Sun); reservations essential; licensed, no BYO

Map 17 A1

Smoke-free dining room available

Himal
Nepalese (Newari)

☎ 9460 9058
469 Pacific Hwy

The Pacific Highway has little connection to the Himalayas, except at Number 469. Himal means mountain, and this small restaurant aims to 'transport you to Nepal for one evening', at least food-wise. The softly lit surroundings are very pleasant, with double-clothed tables, traditional music and intricate wooden carvings on the wall. The main influence is Newari cuisine from the Newar people of the Kathmandu Valley. Stuffed with spiced chicken, six juicy dumplings ($8.95) are accompanied by our choice of 'sundries' ($3 each): bhatmas achar (grated soybean sauce), manang achar (potato and cucumber) and mustang achar (spicy tomato and coriander sauce). These side dishes also complement the mains. Dolpa pumpkin ($12.95) (lamb in pumpkin purée) is mildly spiced and tender. The tart sauce in the Himalayan Hotpot ($13.95) is like a freshly made sweet and sour, covering a hearty mixture of chicken and vegetables. It's hard to confirm authenticity, but it certainly tastes good.

starter: $4.95-$15
main: $9.95-$15.95
dessert: $3-$5.95
Banquet $30
AE BC DC MC V; Eftpos

Open: Mon-Fri noon-3pm, daily 6pm-10.30pm; reservations advisable (especially Fri & Sat); BYO (corkage 50c/person)

Malabar
Indian (South)

☎ 9906 7343
332 Pacific Hwy

Map 17 A1

Smoking in upstairs lounge

There's no need to notice the awards and reviews on the wall, or the fairly uninspired surroundings featuring fake palm trees. Wilson Varghese's South Indian food speaks for itself. Even on a Monday night, it's busy. At most tables dosas will appear, impressively long, crisp lentil pancakes, to be quickly devoured. This is, after all, 'the dosas palace' – ours is the mini version, filled with creamy, perfectly spiced potato ($6.90). Varghese knows his spices – every dish displays his craft, learned at India's prestigious Taj Hotel group. In a mild lamb varutha curry ($12.40), tender lamb falls apart in a dark, aromatic gravy. Goan prawn curry ($14.90) cranks up the heat, with firm, crunchy king prawns in a hot coconut and tomato sauce. Meat and vegetarian thalis ($15.90) are offered Sunday to Thursday (lunch & dinner) and Friday (lunch only); Sunday specials include biryani and idli. With ever-courteous waiters, this is one of Sydney's best Indian meals.

starter: $3.90-$12
main: $10.90-$14.90
dessert: $3-$5
Banquet $26.50/person (min 2 people)

AE BC DC MC V

Open: Mon-Fri & Sun noon-2.30pm, daily 6pm-10pm; reservations advisable (especially Fri & Sat); BYO (corkage 70c/person)

Pino's Pizzeria
Italian

☎ 9439 2081
49 Willoughby Rd

Map 17 A1

Smoking throughout

Pavement tables

In a smart piece of interior design, the pizza oven at Pino's is right near the front door, so a heady smell wafts into the street. This olfactory stimulus is only a small part of the restaurant's appeal, confirmed by the many regulars. Qualifying for the term 'institution', Pino's has been serving up traditional Italian fare since 1973. The décor appears not to have changed much in that time: terracotta tiles, posters of Italy, rafia-cased Chianti bottles and cheery red and green tablecloths. Fortunately the food is fresh, the service friendly and attentive. Tempting bowls of steaming pasta sweep by, but the specials on the board win out. A slab of nicely grilled swordfish is accompanied by a melting mango salsa. The char-grilled quail with a zingy lemon and white wine sauce is just the right size to allow for dessert. Too much cream envelops the tiramisù, but the coffee is great. All in all, a relaxed, happy establishment.

starter: $6.80-$10.50
main: $9.50-$18.50
dessert: $4.50-$5.90
Set menu: lunch $15, dinner $21-$25

AE BC DC MC V; Eftpos

Open: Mon-Fri noon-3pm, Mon-Wed 6pm-10.30pm, Thu-Sat 6pm-11pm, Sun 5.30pm-9.30pm; reservations advisable; BYO (no corkage)

CROWS NEST

Map 17 A1

Pavement tables

Restaurant Dish
Modern Australian/French

☎ 9906 2275
47 Willoughby Rd

There's something elusively different about this mod Oz restaurant. Hmm, what is it? Good grief, it's got carpet! Not a polished floorboard or terracotta tile in sight. And very nice it is too, with plain cream walls, white tablecloths and classic wooden chairs. The waiter, dressed in the compulsory long white apron, is attentive and amusing – Dish feels like somewhere special without being stiff. The food is certainly special. A brown paper bag on a plate, when torn open, reveals a generous stash of plump, juicy mussels en papillot ($13.50) with a white wine sauce. Gorgeous. Chargrilled Atlantic salmon is a meltingly pink main. The braised pork neck ($22) was slightly stringy but the flavour is good and smoky. Dessert is essential. The voluptuously creamy vanilla panna cotta ($8.50) is studded with chunks of fresh mango; the incredibly rich flourless chocolate gavache ($8.50) is for card-carrying chocoholics only.

starter: $13-$13.80
main: $22-$24.50
dessert: $8.50-$9

AE DC MC V

Open: Mon-Sat noon-3pm, 7pm-11pm; reservations advisable (especially Fri & Sat); BYO ($1.50 corkage/person)

Map 17 A1

No smoking inside

Pavement tables

Wrapido
Cafe fare

☎ 9438 4946
55 Willoughby Rd

Join the suit and tie brigade at Wrapido and experience Sydney's love affair with tortilla wraps. Packed full of gourmet fillings, these creations put the old ham and cheese sandwich to shame. The Thai spice variety is a meal in itself – marinated spicy beef served with grilled eggplant, a fresh herb, cucumber and green leaf salad and a soy chilli and kaffir lime dressing… highly recommended for those who like a bit of a bite to their food. Also on offer are chicken, seafood, lamb and vegetarian options, plus a range of salads. The orange zinger frappé ($4.50) is as snappy and sharp as Wrapido's interior. It's a tangy mix of orange juice, strawberries, blueberries and pineapple sorbet, blended with ice. After such a vitamin hit you're entitled to gorge yourself on the pastries, tarts and muffins on show. The melting moments ($2.50) literally dissolve on impact.

main: $6.50-$6.90
dessert: $1.50-$4

AE BC MC V

Open: Mon-Fri 7am-6pm, Sat & Sun 8am-6pm; reservations not accepted; unlicensed

CROWS NEST

Ying's Seafood Restaurant
Chinese

☎ 9966 9182
2/270 Pacific Hwy

Map 17 A1

Private parking

Wheelchair access

Ying's is no ordinary Chinese restaurant. For starters, it's smoke free, smartly minimalist, spacious, airy, and has a very good wine list. And, yes, the food is phenomenal. Ying's culinary artists can be viewed in action in the open plan kitchen at the rear. If you feel like splurging on lobster, this is the place to do it. While some of the fresh flesh is served up as entree – sashimi, on ice, in the shell – the rest is being stir-fried with ginger and shallots, steamed with Chinese wine or deep fried with spicy salt and pepper. A party of at least four is recommended to do justice to the experience and to your wallet. Though seafood is their speciality, chef's chicken hotpot ($14) cooked in a rich anise-infused sauce is also a must-try. Going by the steamed dumplings, the yum cha, served daily from 11am to 3pm should be a real treat too.

starter: $5-$20
main: $8-$55
dessert: $4-$6
Set menu by request

AE BC DC MC V

Open: daily 11am-3pm, 5.30pm-11pm; reservations advisable; licensed & BYO (corkage $3/person)

HORNSBY

Steps
Modern Australian

☎ 9482 7364
188 Pacific Hwy

Map 19 A2

Private parking

Separate smoke-free dining available

Steps surprises with its old-world charm, as it stands rather exposed on the Pacific Highway, near Hornsby junction. Inside, it has that cosy Blue Mountains feel, evoked by a collection of separate rooms, upstairs and down. The menu offers 'beginnings' which includes tapas ($12.50), bruschetta ($8.50) and garlic-fried Tasmanian salmon and black tiger prawns ($13.50). Mains of veal ($23.50), barramundi ($21.50) and rib-eye beef ($20.50) are hearty and appropriately sauced. Desserts are baked on the premises and worth saving room for. Warm apple and walnut cake ($10.50) was given the thumbs up by a cake-baking expert at our table. The Kahlua chocolate terrine ($10.50) with plump strawberries lives up to expectations. A 'healthy alternative' (black pepper spiced pears, $9.50) appears on the dessert menu along with a full calorific and fat breakdown – and it still sounds delicious. The service is friendly and helpful, adding to Step's intimacy.

starter: $8.50-$15.50
main: $17.50-$23.50
dessert: $9.50-$12.50

AE MC V

Open: Tues-Fri noon-2.30pm; Tues-Sat 6pm-10.30pm; reservations advisable; licensed & BYO (corkage $2/person)

KIRRIBILLI

NORTH SHORE

Map 17 C2
Wheelchair access
Smoking after 10pm

Cloudstreet
Modern Australian

☎ 9922 1512
Shop 3, 34 Burton St

Unlike the battered old house central to Tim Winton's popular novel, Cloudstreet is classy. Witness the tasteful terrazzo floor, sculptural blond-wood chairs, soothing jazz and moody lighting. White walls sport a changing display of modern art selected from the owner's family collection; even an exposed air-conditioning duct has style. Personable staff add warmth to the room, while the artistry extends from the walls to the food. Quail breast stuffed with shiitake mushrooms wrapped in Chinese pastry ($16) is a mini-work of 3D modernism. Eating art is generally frowned upon, but the crunchy pastry and subtle contents defy restraint. A roast onion, pumpkin and fetta risotto ($15), though good, can't compete. Sirloin steak ($24) and kangaroo loin ($23) mains are perfectly done, and a hastily ordered side of buttered beans arrives speedily. Rosella and blueberry cheesecake ($11) is another piece of irresistible edible art. The thoroughly agreeable combination of food, ambience and service sees you floating out the door slightly above the ground.

starter: $12-$16
main: $22-$25
dessert: $8-$15
AE BC DC MC V

Open: Tues-Fri 12pm-4pm, Tue-Sat 6pm-midnight; reservations advisable (especially Fri & Sat evenings); licensed & BYO (corkage $4/bottle)

Map 17 C2

Stir Crazy Thai
Thai

☎ 9922 6620
1 Broughton St

From a niche in the wall, a serene gold Buddha overlooks the activity at this small Thai eatery. A huge flower arrangement decorates the kitchen counter, wall colours are tasteful, music subtle and the tables are packed. It's the unexpected stylish touches that take this place beyond the usual budget experience. These touches extend to the food itself, which comes in generous servings and arrives promptly. The delicious chicken and sweet potato stir-fry ($9.90) with its creamy curry sauce is jauntily garnished with a red chilli cut into a flower and contrasting green coriander sprigs. A tangy Thai beef salad ($9.90) provides completely different flavours, combining the freshness of chilli, mint and lemon. Out on the pavement, staff take orders for takeaway and customers wait for tables. It's not the place for a leisurely meal, but otherwise, the food and the karma are right.

starter: $4.90-$5.90
main: $7.50-$18
cash only

Open: Mon-Fri noon-10.30pm, Sat & Sun 5pm-10.30pm; reservations not accepted; BYO (no corkage)

McMAHONS POINT

Thomas Street
Modern Australian

☎ 9955 4703
2 Thomas St

Map 17 C1

- No smoking inside
- Covered courtyard

Dine in the paved courtyard of Thomas Street at McMahons Point in spring and you'll be sheltered by the mauve blossoms of a jacaranda. Deck-style tables and chairs are organised around the tree's base, its branches stretching overhead like bronzed fingers reaching towards the sun. Tucked behind bustling Blues Point Rd, the cafe serves up tempting dishes in a relaxed atmosphere. Start with the meze plate, a tantalising combination of oven-fresh bread and Mediterranean favourites ($11.50). Offal aficionados should tuck into the char-grilled calf's liver served with braised witlof, potato mash and baby beetroot ($18.50). Add a crisp Greek salad ($7), bottles of olive oil and vinegar on each table let you mix your own dressing. But the dish de jour for us was undoubtedly the smoked salmon, Spanish onion and roast tomato pizzettas ($12.50) – garnish lightly with cracked pepper and devour. You'll want to linger here, so bring an extra bottle of vino.

starter: $11.50-$12.50
main: $18-$19.50
dessert: $7

AE DC BC MC V

Open: Tue-Sun 8am-4pm; reservations advisable; BYO (corkage $1.50/person)

NORTH SHORE

Cala Luna (p 196)

MOSMAN – THE SPIT

Map 18 C5
Wheelchair access
No smoking inside
Pavement & courtyard tables

starter: $11-$15
main: $13-$27
dessert: $8
AE BC DC MC V

Cala Luna
Italian

☎ 9968 2426
235 Spit Rd

Bib on, finger bowl at the ready, it's time for an assault on Sydney's biggest and tastiest fish soup ($27.90). A rich tomato broth with more than a hint of chilli overflows with hunks of salmon, tender calamari, meaty crab legs and fat, creamy mussels. You *could* eat other things here. Imported fish roe form the basis of spaghetti alla bottarga* ($14.50), as popular here as in the chef's native Sardinia. Something heavier? How about roast suckling pig ($22.50)? Basic spag bol ($10.80), gnocchi ($10.20), chicken, beef and three types of veal ($18.90-$19.60) pad out the menu for the less adventurous. Desserts? Make sure you have something accompanied by the superb home-made ice cream; just don't believe the waiter when he says it's low fat. Cala Luna is an unexceptional looking eatery, the type of place you'd drive past at speed as you cross Spit Bridge. Might be worth a stop next time.

Open: Tues, Wed, Fri noon-2.30pm, Tues-Sat 6.30pm-9.30pm; reservations essential; BYO (corkage $1/person)

Map 18 C5
Wheelchair access
Nonsmoking tables available

starter: $15-$18
main: $24-$28
dessert: $9-$12
AE BC DC MC V

Fergusons
Modern Australian

☎ 9960 8233
83 Parriwi Rd

There's a smattering of restaurants lining the Spit foreshore but this is many a local's favourite. There's sleek black table settings, timber floors and fixtures, an open kitchen and endless panels of glass – perfect for ogling the 'serious money' moored out front. Yet despite its location and well-heeled clientele, there's not a whiff of pretension in the sea air: the staff are friendly and efficient; the mood relaxed and informal. The food, however, screams out for attention. The roasted rack of veal ($28) arrives atop a blazing beetroot mash, straddled by wisps of asparagus and topped with a king prawn and bernaise sauce. The fiery chilli spatchcock marches out of the kitchen amid dollops of spicy avocado and onion salsa. Fergusons is big on colour and unexpected food combos. Salmon is teamed with pea mash, eggplant caviar and pickled cucumbers, baby cuttlefish is enhanced by a lemon and pickled ginger salad. Desserts pale into insignificance.

Open: Wed-Sun noon-2.30pm, 6pm-10pm (breakfast: Sat & Sun 8am-11am); reservations advisable; BYO (corkage $2.50/person)

MOSMAN – THE SPIT

The Mosquito Bar
Moroccan

☎ 9968 1801
Shop 5, 142 Spit Road

Map 17 C5

Wheelchair access

Smoking throughout

Jewel-bright seat cushions, solid teak tables and chairs, and lively Arabic music at the Mosquito Bar transport you from the well-to-do suburb of Mosman to the heart of colourful Morocco. Add a deliciously spicy menu and your journey's complete. We started with bissara* dip – smothering our pappadams with the broad bean, garlic and cumin mix – then devoured Marrakech express brochettes – lamb fillets marinated in olive oil, coriander, cumin and paprika – and cooled the palate with side dishes of diced banana rolled in shredded coconut, and chilled tomato, cucumber and yoghurt salad. Be sure to stop at the bottle shop on Spit Road, just around the corner, for something refreshing – a light white wine or crispy cold beer. The perennially upbeat staff will put it straight on ice, they're masters of quick and efficient service. Make this your next dinner party location.

starter: $1.90-$9.90
main: $10.90-$13.90

AE BC MC V

Open: Tues-Sat 6pm-11pm; reservations essential (Sat & Sun evenings); BYO (corkage $1/person)

Orso Bayside Restaurant
Seafood/Italian

☎ 9968 3555
79 Parriwi Rd

Map 18 C5

Smoking at the bar only

Jostling for position along Middle Harbour's restaurant strip is Orso Bayside Restaurant. Dining here is a leisurely affair. The floor-to-ceiling windows open out, quite literally, onto the bay, where a flotilla of boats and the odd gull happily bob up and down inches from your table. The sound of clinking masts and the fresh sea air fluttering your crisp white tablecloth will soon turn your attention to seafood. Try the ocean king prawns ($18.50) served on a hearty bed of baby potato salad or a delicate serve of seared scallops in porcini spice ($18.50). Main courses of seared yellow fin tuna steak ($27.50) and grilled lobster ($39.50) impress. The extravagance of the seafood platter ($52.50) we left to the serious seafood lovers. Refresh the palate with the vanilla bean panna cotta and citrus salad, a shot of coffee and enjoy the view.

starter: $13.50-$26
main: $25.50-$52.50
dessert: $11.50-$15.50

AE DC BC MC V

Open: daily noon-3pm, 6pm-10pm; reservations advisable; licensed, no BYO

NEUTRAL BAY

Map 17 A3

Domo
Japanese

☎ 9909 3100
Shop 5, 207 Ben Boyd Rd

The tangerine and salmon decorated Domo might be small, but it can hold its head high with the big boys of Neutral Bay's Japantown when it comes to cooking. There's serious artistic culinary intent here. One of the specials – pickled mackerel and vegetable rolls ($7.50), with slices of fish, shredded carrot and cucumber, and omelette wrapped in paper-thin white radish, with a garnish including three types of seaweed and a sweet miso sauce – had the look of a minature Kandinsky. The sushi is of supermodel status, slinky and beautifully deported; for the best quality go for the $23 special selection including eel. Agedashi ($6.80), deep-fried oval patties of minced chicken sandwiched by zucchini and bathed in a mouthwatering tempura sauce, demonstrates the expertise extending to the hot dishes. Even the miso soup ($2.50) is way above average, graced with liberal amounts of seaweed, green vegetables and silky tofu. Appropriately the restaurant's name translates as 'thank you'.

starter: $5.20-$8
main: $12-$23.50
dessert: $2.50
AE BC DC MC V

Open: Tue-Sun 6pm-10pm; reservations advisable (especially weekends); BYO (corkage $1/person)

Map 17 A3

Smoking after 9.30pm

Just Hooked
Seafood

☎ 9904 0428
236 Military Rd

No wonder this place reels in the crowds. The atmosphere's cheery, the food's excellent, prices are reasonable and the service charming. Painted hessian cloths in green, blue and earthy-red brighten the walls. Throw in high-backed stools, stencilled tables and a token fish tank and you've got the comfortable, happy vibe that is Just Hooked's trademark. The food here looks almost too good to eat. Skewered garlic king prawns with a spicy tomato relish make their entrance nestled in a grand banana flower leaf ($11.50), accompanied by a handful of cassava chips. Other gems include chilli salt squid ($9.50) and lime-cured ocean trout ($10.50). But it was the Atlantic salmon ($19.90) that really did our heads in. Balanced on a sweet potato galette and seared to perfection, the flesh remained tender and moist right through to the centre. Indulge yourself with the banoffen pie ($7.50) – a lavish ensemble of toffee, banana and double cream.

starter: $5.90-$11.50
main: $15.90-$19.90
dessert: $7.50
AE BC DC MC V

Open: Mon-Sat 6pm-10pm; reservations advisable; BYO (corkage $2/person)

NEUTRAL BAY

Kintaro
Japanese

☎ 9904 5188
Shop 1, 24 Young St

Map 17 A3

Try everything – from the hand-sized cupfuls of tasty miso to the sashimi mixed platter – Kintaro at Neutral Bay will quickly become a favourite. You can point to the dual-language menu if you have trouble communicating with the all-Japanese staff. Look beyond the standards to dishes such as maguro tataki, melt-in-your-mouth slices of lightly braised tuna served in a mild vinegar sauce, or koimono nitsuke, steamed bite-sized taro potatoes. There's no glamour at Kintaro – raw timber tables and chairs are set square in the room – but there's no need. Just ask Jana Wendt who left a handwritten testimonial pinned to the green sponge-painted walls. Bring your own wine – try the bottle shop at the Oaks, a humming pub just a block away – or pay $19.50 for the house variety. Alternatively, order a can of Sapporo Kuro, a mild Japanese ale ($5).

starter: $2-$10
main: $9-$38
dessert: $3.50

BC MC V; Eftpos

Open: Tues-Sun 6pm-10pm, Sun noon-2pm; reservations essential (Thurs-Sun evenings); BYO (corkage $2/person)

North China Restaurant
Chinese (Northern)

☎ 9909 2438
238 Military Rd

Map 17 A3

Smoking throughout

The best in northern Chinese dining is to be found in Neutral Bay on the main stretch of Military Road. Chinese locals boast that it's the most authentic example of northern style cooking in Sydney. Their specialities are dumplings, buns and hand-made noodles. Deft chef Jeff Li can be seen casually 'throwing' noodle portions fresh with each order. Northern fried dumplings ($6.80) are literally mouth watering with a pork and chive filling. The heavier fare is balanced with an inventive selection of stir-fries. Cashew nuts with celery ($7) and shredded potato in hot sauce ($7.80) – the thinnest potato slivers singed with chilli oil – are great companions to Xinjiang-style roasted lamb buns ($7). Sister to Chinatown's tiny Chinese Noodle Restaurant, the larger, more comfortable dining room at the North China is popular on weekdays and packed at weekends.

starter: $2-$6.80
main: $6.80-$18.80

BC MC V

Open: Mon-Fri 11am-10pm, Sat-Sun 5pm-10pm; reservations advisable; BYO, no corkage

On Your Plate **Japanese**

Say it's a sign that Sydney has truly taken Japanese food to its heart. In the basement food hall of that rejuvenated grand dame of Martin Place, the GPO building, groovers now gather at Sosumi to pick at designer sushi from a sleek conveyor belt. There's no doubting that this is currently the trendiest spot to begin a love affair with Japanese cuisine.

Not that we'd normally recommend a revolving sushi bar; there are far too many dodgy ones in Sydney for that. But it's certainly cause for celebration when city stalwart Masuya (see review p 46), gets in on the scene with its excellent – and very reasonably priced – Sushi Bar Makoto, a fantastic fast food substitute for the greasy burger/kebab vendors of nearby George St. Fashion aside, Sydney's no slouch on the world Japanese food scene. An army of experienced Japanese chefs; a discerning base of ex-pats and locals to keep them on their toes; readily available traditional ingredients, including the South Sea's best seafood – it's a recipe for top class cooking. Your brain can relax when menus are in English and your wallet can take a breather when dishes, such as shabu-shabu (a kind of beef and vege fondue), expensive in Japan, come in at around $20 a head down under.

In the 'Japantown' district of Neutral Bay, the ever-popular Shimbashi Soba, home of the best comfort food noodles this side of Shikoku, now jostles for pole position with a score of rivals including Domo (see review p 198) with its elegant sushi platters, beautifully prepared.

When money's no object, traditional Japanese dining – the oshibori (hot towel) to cleanse the hands, the beautiful pottery and lacquerware to complement the expertly presented food – doesn't get much better than at Arakawa or Unkai (see reviews pp 26, 51), which still has the city's classiest sushi bar with a penthouse view. For fine Japanese with a twist, try Yoshii or Uchi Lounge and ultra-famous Tetsuya's (see reviews pp 46, 84, 38).

Cheap and simple dishes don't get much better than at Matsuri and Sushi Suma in Surry Hills and Masuya in Pyrmont (see reviews pp 80, 75, 46). And try Sydney Fish Markets, where for just under $20 you can sample the freshest sushi and sashimi set meals this side of Tokyo's Tsukiji Fish Market.

Fish Market Sushi Bar Sydney Fish Market,
Shop 5, Blackwattle Bay, Pyrmont ☎ 9552 2872 Map 8 A6
daily 11am-3pm

Sosumi
GPO, 1 Martin Place, City ☎ 9229 7788 Map 3 B1
Mon-Sat 11.30am-3pm & 5.30pm-8.30pm

Sushi Bar Makoto Basement of the Avillion Hotel,
119 Liverpool St, City ☎ 9283 6767 Map 4 A3
Mon-Fri noon-2.30pm, dinner Mon-Sat 5pm-10pm

Simon Richmond

Sydney-based writer Simon Richmond developed a taste for sushi and soba during over two years spent working in Tokyo. He's written books about Japan, Central Asia and South America, and contributed to newspapers and magazines around the world, including the Sydney Morning Herald and the Australian.

NEUTRAL BAY

Thelma & Louise
Modern Australian

☎ **9953 7754**
Shop 1, 1 Hayes St

Map 17 B2

Balcony tables

Chris and Wendy, proprietors of Thelma & Louise – a breezy cafe nestled on Sydney Harbour at Neutral Bay – chose the name of the feel-good feminist road movie to convey their establishment's carefree ambience. Book a table on the east-facing undercover deck: water lapping on the sandy beach below is the perfect accompaniment to your seafood meal. Try the crab and green pawpaw salad – the delicate flavour of the crab enhanced by the fruit – or Balmain bug tails cooked in a lime and basil butter sauce and served on a bed of seasonal salad. Say yes to dessert: the citrus cake tingles, while the apple and blueberry crumble, served steaming with ice cream or cream, is reminiscent of grandma's best. Now, settle in with their gourmet-blend coffee and stay all afternoon.

starter: $4-$10
main: $14-$17
dessert: $3-$8

AE MC V; Eftpos

Open: Tues-Fri 6am-4pm, Sat & Sun 8am-4pm (breakfast: Tues-Sun until noon); reservations advisable (Sat & Sun); BYO (corkage $1/person)

NORTH SYDNEY

Fare Go Gourmet
*Modern American/
Southern American*

☎ **9922 2965**
69 Union St

Map 17 C1

The greeting at Fare Go Gourmet should be 'passionfruit soufflé'. Their heavenly seasonal fruit soufflés ($11) – could be passionfruit, maybe berry, or pear and amaretto – require around 15 minutes extra preparation time to bake, so be at the ready. Dessert sorted, let's work on back up the list. Blue corn tortillas go just right with vine-ripened tomato soup with coriander ($12.50). Maple glazed quail is cute with a black-eyed pea salad ($14.50). Cornmeal-coated oysters come served with crispy leeks and Creole mustard sauce ($15.50). Chef and owner Forrest Moebes knows his maize and has the accent to prove it. His mains are simarly influenced: barbecued salmon and prawns on a bed of roasted corn succotash ($24.50), rack of lamb with sweet potato polenta and jalapeno preserves ($23.50), grilled swordfish with black bean mango and avocado vinaigrette ($24.50). The secret to Fare Go's success is that the menu tastes just as good as it reads.

starter: $12.30-$15.50
main: $23.50-$25
dessert: $11

AE BC DC MC V

Open: Tues-Sat 6.30pm-late; reservations advisable; BYO corkage $2/person

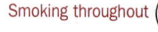

NORTH SYDNEY

Map 17 B2
Smoking throughout
Pavement tables

Isshin
Japanese

☎ 9922 4370
121 Walker St

Isshin has been operating next to Walker Street cinema for 12 years, but don't expect glamour with your sushi. Flowery prints and Japanese hangings are not enough to disguise pale pink walls and an office-style panel ceiling. Adding to the office feel a big whiteboard lists specials. Japan meets IKEA with chunky pine tables and chairs; ashtrays are plastic, table-mats vinyl and chopsticks disposable. The food is homely rather than spectacular. Steamed crab meat dumplings ($6.90) were rather stodgy, but deep-fried eggplant ($6) is squishy and sweet, served in its skin topped with miso sauce and sesame seeds. Salmon nabe for one ($12), a special, is a steaming hotpot of rice and soy sauce soup adorned with grilled salmon and an egg. Thinly sliced beef shogayaki ($13.50) comes with a sweet ginger/soy sauce and a bowl of sticky sushi rice. It's not gourmet fare, but fair prices in this neck of the woods for a solid meal.

starter: $6-$8
main: $10-$16
dessert: $3.50-$5.50

AE BC DC MC V

Open: Mon-Wed noon-2.30, Thu-Fri noon-3pm, Mon-Thu 6.30pm-10pm, Fri-Sat 6.30pm-10.30pm; reservations accepted; BYO (corkage 80c/person)

Map 17 B2
Wheelchair access
Smoking throughout

Malaya Restaurant North Sydney
Malaysian/Chinese

☎ 9955 4306/9957 3775
86 Walker St

If you eat out often, good service instantly impresses. Our waitress suggested dishes, ordered a time-consuming special immediately, filled our bowls and cracked jokes. It's a lively night at the Malaya, where tables are packed, calligraphy hangs on cream walls and trolleys dash over oddly tartan carpet. The name implies Malaysian food but the menu ranges over Indonesian (beef gulai curry $11) and Sichuan (kung pao beancurd $10.50) specialties as well as Chinese standards (chicken chow mein $12). A plastic stand on our table announces two new dishes, a fish curry and seafood noodles (both $15.50) – the waitress recommends snowpeas with beansprouts and mushrooms ($10.50) as accompaniment. All are excellent, but the fish curry stands out, its tender blue-eye cod enhanced by a spicy sauce, fresh tomato, eggplant and okra. Prawn and scallop rolls ($5.50) are the prize starter. Malaya North Sydney has been here for 25 years – now we know why.

starter: $4.50-$11
main: $9.50-$17.50
dessert: $3-$4.50
Banquet $20, $22 or $25
(min 5 people)

AE BC DC MC V

Open: Mon-Fri noon-3pm, Mon-Wed 5pm-10pm, Thu-Fri 5pm-11pm, Sat 6pm-10.30pm; reservations recommended (especially lunchtime); licensed, no BYO

TERREY HILLS

NORTH SHORE

Kaiser Stub'n
Austrian

☎ 9450 0300
Cnr McCarrs Creek and Mona Vale Rds

Map 20 B3

Private parking

No smoking inside

Despite its out-of-the-way location, Kaiser Stub'n's authentic Austrian fare and friendly, homely atmosphere ensures a thriving trade. Plenty of homesick expats flock here for their regular fix of wiener schnitzel or dumplings with sauerkraut. The chalet-style theme doesn't quite come off but it's helped along by lots of cow-bells, Euro knick-knacks, postcard shots of the alps and German-speaking waiters. Make what you will of the giant mounted bore and stag heads. Pork and veal dominate the selection, although fish, venison and chicken make a minor appearance. Servings are huge: the wiener schnitzel ($15.50) literally swamps the plate, while the veal fillet with a mushroom sauce ($22.50) consumes an entire cast-iron frypan. There's nothing flash about the presentation, but it's good hearty fare that's filling and tasty. The ice cream with warmed fresh raspberries and cream is a Mittle European favourite and goes down a treat with a few apple schnapps.

starter: $6.50-$12.80
main: $15.50-$24.80
dessert: $7-$8
Set menu $31.50

AE BC DC MC V

Open: Wed-Thurs, Fri & Sun noon-2.30pm, Tues-Sun 6pm-10pm; reservations essential (Sat & Sun); licensed & BYO (corkage $4/bottle)

Fare Go Gourmet (p 201)

THORNLEIGH

Map 19 B1

Shopping centre car park **P**

Istana Restaurant
Malaysian/Chinese

☎ 9481 8855
Shop 15, 230-238
Pennant Hills Rd

Tremendously popular Istana draws crowds from all over Sydney. It's large and smoke free with tightly packed tables and a cheery ambience. Regulars return again and again for the authentic Malaysian/Chinese fare. It would be a shame not to have roti channai ($2.90) to plunge into the coconut and potato curry of kapitan chicken ($10.80). Spicy king prawns braised in a rich tamarind sauce are almost cruelly tangy and spicy ($16.80). Blachan long beans ($10.80) and blachan kangkong (water convolvulus stir-fried with garlic, shrimp paste and chilli) should be sampled too. It's hard to force yourself away from favourites. Once you do, the choice is even harder. Will it be chilli mud crab, squid with spicy salt, kway teow, lobah or laksa? Freshly made glutinous rice cakes and Malaysian pastries top it all off on Saturdays and Sundays.

starter: $4–$8
main: $10–$20
dessert: $5

Open: daily noon-3pm, Sun-Thurs 5pm-10pm, Sat & Sun 5pm-11pm; reservations advisable; licensed, no BYO

WAHROONGA

Map 19 A3

No smoking inside

Pavement tables

Coonanbarra Cafe
Modern Australian

☎ 9489 0980
64 Coonanbarra Rd

In an area relatively bereft of good coffee drinking opportunities, old-world Coonanbarra Cafe, in the building that once housed the Wahroonga general store, has a coffee selection that rivals any inner-city caff. The lunch menu is ample, from basics like cheese melts ($8.50) to fancier dishes such as pan-fried salmon ($17.50) with green beans, pinenuts and a sage and lime dressing. The dinner menu features Hawkesbury calamari wth parsley, garlic, lemon zest and crushed croutons ($13) and a piquant duck roasted with cardamon and honey on an orange and witlof salad ($25.50). Desserts are worth a special visit. By day it's cakes, scones, tarts and biscuits, by night there's dark and white chocolate mousse with fresh rasberries or rhubarb and vanilla meringues with strawberry consomme ($10.50). The piéce de résistance for the kids and parents, however, is the great playground in leafy Wahronga Park next door.

starter: lunch $8.50-$12.50,
dinner $10.50-$14.50
main: lunch $15.50-$18.50,
dinner $20.50-$24.50
dessert: lunch $3-$12.50,
dinner $9.50-$14.50
AE BC DC MC V

Open: daily 9.30am-4.30pm (breakfast: Sat & Sun 9am-11am), Wed-Sat 6.30pm-9.30pm; reservations advisable for groups of 6 or more; BYO (no corkage)

WESTLEIGH

Scoozi Trattoria
Italian

☎ 9484 5165
Shop 9, Westleigh Shopping Centre, Eucalyptus Drive

Map 19 A1

Shopping centre car park

Verandah tables

Scoozi, in true trattoria style, feels warm and welcoming, with rich brown terracotta tiles and a tremendous wood-fired oven, its cavernous fiery grin to be seen through the terrazzo-decorated wall of the open kitchen. Just a stone's throw from Hornsby and Pennant Hills you'll find casual dining that includes boutique pizza – spinach and pesto with roast sweet potato, grilled eggplant, mushroom, onion and fetta ($12.90) – and pastas like penne with spicy sausage, artichoke, olives and fresh tomato sauce ($8/$12). The à la carte menu is a treat too: seared duck liver tartlet ($10.50) or char-grilled sardines, thick and moist on a bed of parmesan risotto with sun-dried tomato and olive salsa ($16.50). The kid's menu at $6.50 for spag bol or pizzetta with ham, cheese and tomato is a real find. Scoozi really is something to sing about.

starter: $8-$10.50
main: $12-18.50
dessert: $8-$9.50

Open: Tues-Sat 6pm-10pm; reservations essential; BYO (corkage $1/person)

BC MC V

WILLOUGHBY

Grape Garden
Chinese (Northern)

☎ 9967 2001
52 Penshurst St

Map 18 B2

Although looking more stylish since it's move from Marrickville, Grape Garden's food is just as good and as authentically northern. Peking duck is recommended, the ducks hailing from South Windsor. Only an hour's notice is required for this Beijing speciality ($35 serves six people). Delicious cabbage and chive dumplings ($9.60) are boiled and then quickly grilled to give their prison stripe appearance. Pork slices are flung from a spitting hotpot onto a dish of crisp rice crust, to make guo ba ($11.80). Tasty little shreds of pepper lamb ($11.80) and crispy chicken legs keep good company with the vegetable fried rice ($8.80). The steam boat offers two choices: hot & sour Sichuan ($18 per person) and regular meat ($12 per person). It's very satisfying to take leave of the banquet at night's end, survey the scene and see an apocalypse of ravished plates, simmering cookers and empty bottles.

starter: $2.80-$8
main: $7.80-$26.80
dessert: $2.40-$12.80

Open: daily noon-3pm, 5.45pm-10.30pm; reservations accepted; BYO (corkage $2/person)

BC MC V; Eftpos

Back for More

Claudine's
Gallery level, Chatswood Chase, 354 Victoria Ave, Chatswood ☎ 9411 1688 Map 18 A1
Set your doubts aside about the shopping mall location and take the escalator to one of Sydney's most elegant French restaurants. Prices are steep but this is serious food. Try duck roasted in hay and served at the table, and the soufflé and brûlée desserts.

Chon Mage
258 Pacific Hwy, Crows Nest ☎ 9439 1494 Map 17 A1
Chanko-nabe, the chuck-it-all-in sumo wrestler stew, is the speciality here. Starters are a simple flat $5 and mains are $10 – at $20/person the banquet menu is simpler still.

✱ *Write to us: Where do you go to eat time and time again? Is it fabulous food, divine décor, great service, or a place to do business that brings you back? Write or email us (see p 11 for details) and the best suggestions will receive the next edition free.*

NORTHERN BEACHES

Avalon

Clareville

Collaroy

Cottage Point

Dee Why

Harbord

Manly

Narrabeen

North Curl Curl

Palm Beach

Whale Beach

Map 21 - Manly

Narrabeen

- Stella Blu Cafe
- Soleil
- To Food for Thought 2km
- Emilia's Vegetarian Restaurant
- Freshwater Restaurant
- Ash's Table
- Fresh at Manly
- Barking Frog
- Brazil
- Calacoci
- Ceruti's Bistro Italiano
- Out of Africa
- Cafe Tunis
- eden
- The Belgian Waffle Shop
- The Bower Restaurant
- Le Kiosk

Areas: DEE WHY, NORTH CURL CURL, CURL CURL, NORTH MANLY, HARBORD, MANLY

Features: Dee Why Beach, Dee Why Head, Curl Curl Lagoon, Curl Curl Beach, Tasman Sea, Queenscliff Bay, Manly Lagoon, Manly Golf Course, North Steyne Beach, Manly Beach, Cabbage Tree Bay, Manly Wharf, Manly Cove

Streets: Dee Why Pde, The Strand, May Rd, Pittwater Rd, Warringah Rd, Harbord Rd, Griffin Rd, Pitt Rd, Lagoon St, Waterloo St, Albert St, Ocean St, Narrabeen Beach, Adams St, Carrington Pde, Oliver St, Evans St, Lawrence St, Moore Rd, Queenscliff Rd, Kenneth Rd, Balgowlah Rd, Pittwater Rd, North Steyne, Raglan St, Sydney Rd, The Corso, South Steyne, East Esp, Darley Rd, Bower St

0 m 100 / 0 yd 100

0 m 400 800 / 0 yd 400 800

Some minor streets are not depicted

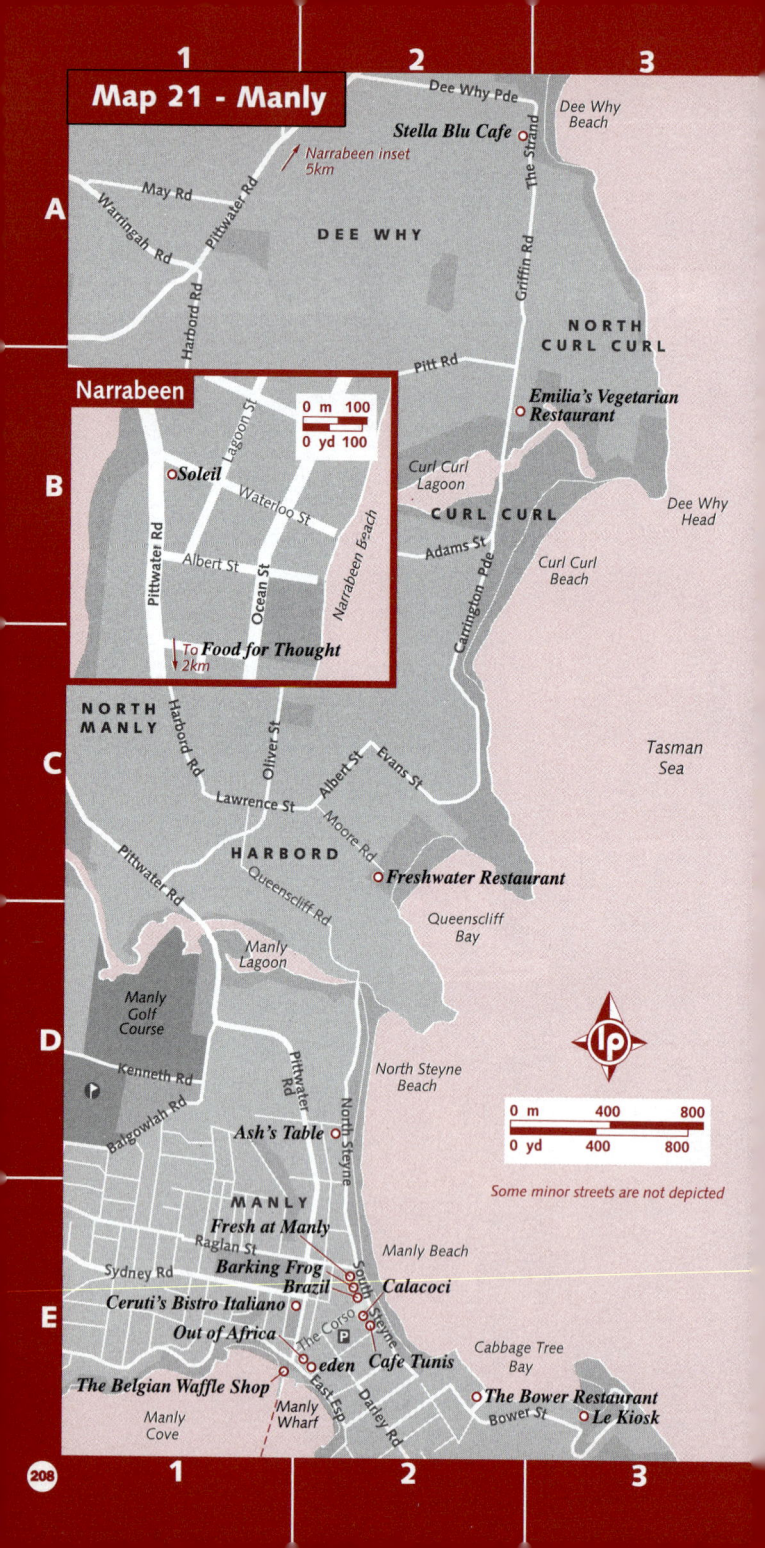

208

Map 22 - Avalon & Palm Beach

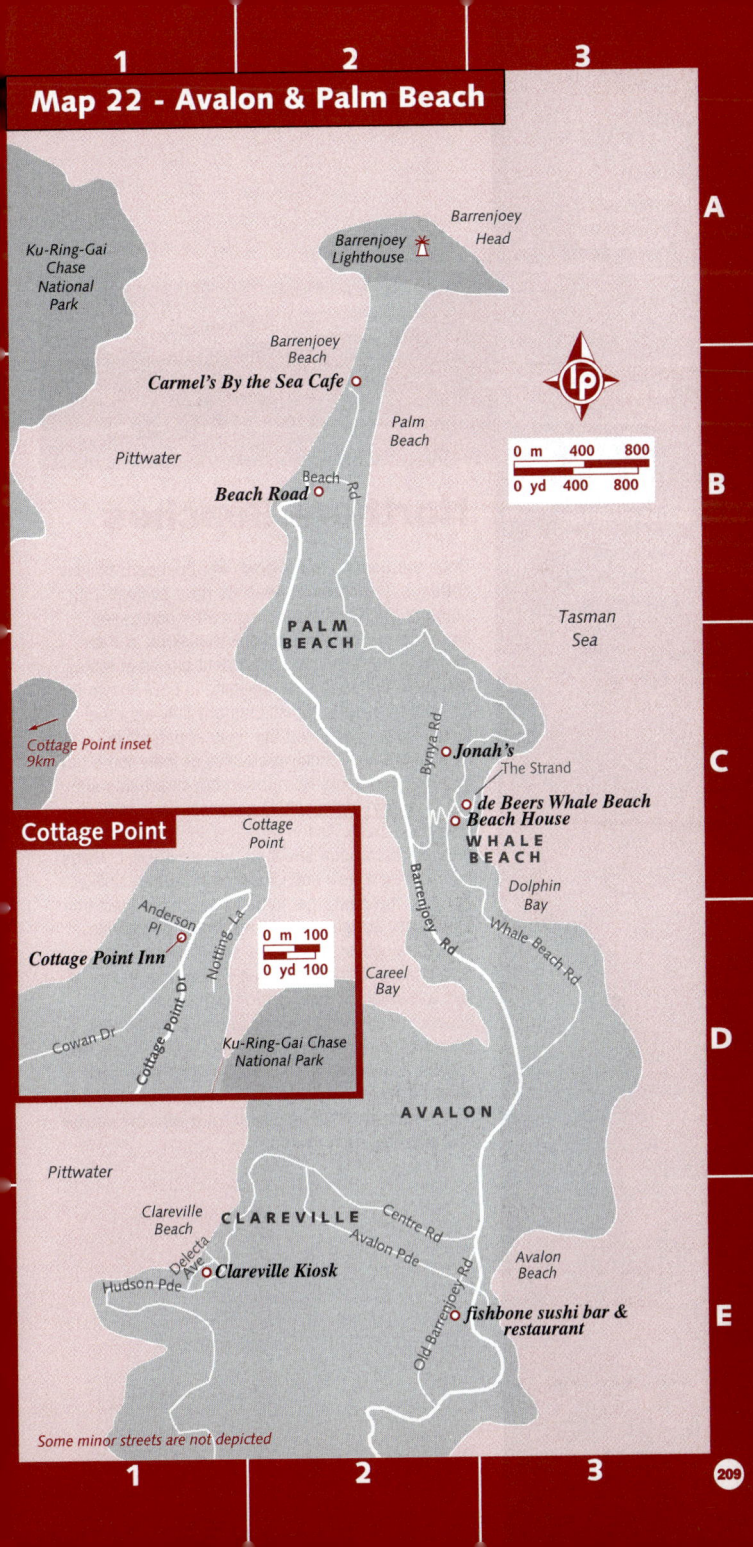

Ku-Ring-Gai Chase National Park

Barrenjoey Lighthouse
Barrenjoey Head
Barrenjoey Beach
Carmel's By the Sea Cafe
Palm Beach
Pittwater
Beach Road
Beach Rd
PALM BEACH
Tasman Sea
Cottage Point inset 9km
Bynya Rd
Jonah's
The Strand
de Beers Whale Beach
Beach House
WHALE BEACH
Dolphin Bay
Barrenjoey Rd
Whale Beach Rd
Careel Bay
AVALON
Pittwater
Clareville Beach
CLAREVILLE
Centre Rd
Delecta Ave
Avalon Pde
Clareville Kiosk
Hudson Pde
Old Barrenjoey Rd
Avalon Beach
fishbone sushi bar & restaurant

Some minor streets are not depicted

Cottage Point

Cottage Point
Anderson Pl
Cottage Point Inn
Notting La
Cottage Point Dr
Cowan Dr
Ku-Ring-Gai Chase National Park

BEST

- **Emilia's Vegetarian Restaurant**
  Relaxed beachy vibe, locals love it

- **Freshwater Restaurant**
  Weatherboard beauty with a view

- **Out of Africa**
  Aromatic African and a lively atmosphere

Northern Beaches

Once the domain of run-down weatherboard holiday cottages, the northern beaches have evolved into some of Sydney's most sought-after addresses. From the celebs' million-dollar mansions at Palm Beach to the flash new apartment blocks in Manly, this beautiful stretch of coastline is best known for its natural assets, rather than any culinary excellence. Aptly nicknamed the 'insular peninsula', locals here are fiercely protective of their home turf. In 1999, residents from the trendy beachside suburb of Avalon successfully quashed plans to film Baywatch there. And in the early 1990s, locals living north of Narrabeen snubbed their southern cousins and formed a new council called Pittwater. Unlike Bondi in the east, the northern beaches (apart from Manly) are not geared up for tourists or nightlife. Suburbs such as Mona Vale and Newport are almost comatose by midnight, and it's near impossible to find a restaurant serving food after 10pm. Accommodation is confined to one caravan park, a couple of backpacker hostels and a few hotels and motels. Traversing the peninsula is no easy task either. Residents love to gripe about the pathetic bus system and the argument for a light rail service has been raging for years.

AVALON

fishbone sushi bar & restaurant
Seafood/modern Australian

☎ 9973 2688
Level 1,
50 Old Barrenjoey Rd

Map 22 E2

Balcony tables

The northern beaches peninsula isn't big on watering holes if you're not into the club scene. Fishbone sushi bar & restaurant provides a comfy trendy bar for young locals who down oyster shooters (a shot glass with an oyster marinated in bourbon) and the combination sushi and sashimi plate with wasabi and pickles ($12). The adjoining restaurant has pricier modern Australian-Japanese fusion creations. Tempura battered beef nori rolls are packed with beef, roasted peppers and coriander making a novel filling starter ($16.50) while the fishbone seafood chowder ($12.50) is a tasty broth, served with herb toast and a rather bland prawn butter. Salmon fillet with steamed miso flavoured ramen noodles and greens ($25.50) and the crustacean and seafood plate ($32) with lime and crisp bread were disappointing. It's pleasant balcony dining, though. Inside, the spaciously Mediterranean décor dons a pot-belly stove suggesting some cosy winter meals.

starter: $12-$20
main: $19.50-$32
dessert: $9
Set lunch $20

AE BC DC MC V

Open: daily 5.30pm till late, Thurs-Sun 11.30am-3pm; reservations advisable; licensed, no BYO

CLAREVILLE

Clareville Kiosk
Modern Australian

☎ 9918 2727
27 Delecta Ave

Map 22 E1

No smoking inside

Covered deck

Tantalisingly close to the sparkling blue waters of Pittwater, the Clareville Kiosk is nestled snugly among the leafy residences of this tranquil beach suburb. The bright and airy weatherboard beach house-cum-restaurant blends exquisite cuisine with intimate simplicity. Entrées like a warm salad of smoked lamb with roasted tomato, spinach, brie and a capsicum coulis ($14.50) and duck and goose-liver pâté with linseed lavoche ($14.50) are teasers for the delights to come. Try the imaginative black band snapper fillet with coriander, yoghurt, kipfler potatoes and harissa sauce ($26.50) or blackfish fillets with zucchini fritters and tomato jam ($25) – all the seafood is caught daily. If your palette's not fully satiated, order the mountainous cheese platter ($16) or a delicate passionfruit curd tart ($12.50) – both are far too good to resist. As is the setting sun painting the aromatic frangipani trees the palest pink.

starter: $14.50-$16.50
main: $25.00-$26.50
dessert: $12.50

AE D BC MC V

Open: Tue-Sat 6.30pm-9pm, Sat-Sun noon-3pm; reservations recommended; BYO (corkage $3/person)

COLLAROY

Map 21 C1

No smoking inside

Pavement tables

Food for Thought
Thai/cafe fare

☎ 9971 2152
1085 Pittwater Rd

Coupling Thai curries with hamburgers may seem a risky combination but Food For Thought manages to pull it off. For seven years, the Thai/English owners have satisfied the hungry droves who frequent this beachside suburb. It's a cosy little place with friendly service and good music. Grab one of the few tables on offer or head across to the beach with some takeaway loot. The Mexican burger ($4.50) is a monster of a creation, dripping with cheese, salsa, avocado and sour cream. But it's the vegetarian house speciality that locals swear by – a tasty patty packed full of vegetables served in a flour damper with salad, salsa or hummus. And of course there's lots of fresh juices and smoothies to wash it all down. In the evenings, the keenly-priced Thai food is popular among those visiting Collaroy's famous Art Deco cinema.

starter: $5.50-$6
main: $7.90-$10.90
(burgers $4-$5)
dessert: $1-$3
cash only

Open: daily 8am-9.30pm (closed Wednesdays); reservations not accepted; BYO (no corkage)

COTTAGE POINT

Map 22 D1

No smoking inside

Verandah tables

Cottage Point Inn
Modern Australian

☎ 9456 1011
2 Anderson Place

Cottage Point Inn enjoys an idyllic waterfront location on the edge of the beautiful Ku-ring-gai Chase National Park. Originally a boatshed and general store, it was converted to a restaurant in the '70s and quickly earned a reputation for excellent food and service. Relax on the timber deck, soak up the fantastic view and watch fellow diners arrive by seaplane or boat. The seafood-dominated menu includes gems like seared sea scallops with green pea purée, warm carrot emulsion and bacon chips ($19.50) or a perfectly-cooked Tasmanian Atlantic salmon fillet ($26.50) enhanced with a port and orange jus. There's some pretty over the top desserts on offer; our favourite being a caramelised banana with banana mousse, white chocolate ice cream and chocolate sauce. Top off a great meal with a choice drop from the predominantly Australian wine list.

starter: $12.50-$20
main: $26-$28
dessert: $12
Set menu (Sunday) $70
AE BC DC MC V

Open: daily noon-3pm, Wed-Sun 6.30pm-9.30pm; reservations essential (Sat & Sun); licensed, no BYO

DEE WHY

Stella Blu Cafe
Italian/modern Australian

☎ **9982 7931**
18 The Strand

Map 21 A2

Wheelchair access

Separate smoke-free dining available

Courtyard tables

Once a rather tatty beachside area, Dee Why Strand has metamorphosed into a trendy restaurant strip popular with the cafe set. Stella Blu's courtyard tables face the beach, giving the cafe a light and airy atmosphere. The food is a mix of traditional Italian and modern Australian. Some combinations are unusual, but you'll find lots of old favourites – the spaghetti marinara ($17.50) is a feast of fresh seafood tossed in a white-wine basil sauce. Meat eaters will enjoy the char-grilled lamb loin fillets with a rosemary glaze ($17.90). Good coffee is served all day long, accompanied by a sumptuous range of Italian delicacies, including tiramisú ($7.50), gelato ($5.50) and shortbread biscuits ($2.50). Work off that post-meal lethargy by taking the nearby cliff-top bushwalk to spectacular Dee Why head.

starter: $11.50-$14.90
main: $12.50-$21.50
dessert: $7.50-$8.50
Banquet $29.50, $32.50 or $37.50

AE BC DC MC V

Open: daily 9am-10pm; reservations essential (Sat & Sun); licensed & BYO (corkage $2/person)

HARBORD

Freshwater Restaurant
Modern Australian

☎ **9938 5575**
Moore Rd

Map 21 C2

No smoking inside

Perched above Freshwater Beach (where Hawaiian athlete Duke Kahanamoku introduced surfing to Australia in 1915) this beautiful weatherboard kiosk was built in 1908, designed as a combination tearoom and guesthouse. It's now a restaurant with lovely ocean views and good food. The vista can best be enjoyed at lunchtime, but evenings are more romantic. White-painted wood, leadlight glass features and raffia floor covering give the interior a light, airy feel, like an elegant beach house. Service is cheery rather than formal, and the menu focuses on fresh seafood such as black mussel soup ($13) and spice crusted blackened fish ($25). Crispy fried green prawns ($16.50), juicy and lightly battered, are highly recommended. Non-marine options include five-spice duckling ($26), a heady dish of succulent skin, soft meat and slippery Asian mushrooms. Your arteries may protest at the chocolate tart ($11) but your taste buds won't, and coffee is served with equally irresistible truffles.

starter: $12.50-$16.50
main: $20-$26
dessert: $11
Set menu $50/person (min 12 people)

AE BC DC JCB MC V

Open: daily noon-2.30pm, 6pm-10pm; reservations advisable (especially Sat dinner & Sun lunch); licensed, no BYO

NORTHERN BEACHES

Manly

Manly was originally envisioned by the British colonialists as an ersatz Brighton in the Antipodes – an escape from the increasingly congested and polluted Sydney Cove settlement. The vision almost got there by the early 1900s, with a silent movie 'pleasure palace' on every corner and Norfolk Island pines casting their tall shadows over the Big Pool (touted as the largest enclosed bathing area in the world). But by the latter decades of the 20th century, Manly fell into a long period that could be called 'the Tacky Times'. The era of Coca Cola Surf Classics, Chicko Rolls and pre-cut pizza tiles sunning themselves under glass displays had arrived by the 1970s – food that would have made the stomachs of those early constitution-conscious colonials turn in their graves. So, perhaps, would the oceanarium shark dives and hotels with aquarium-theme gambling rooms. Today the sleepy beach shacks are being turned into private palaces and Manly is moving upmarket again. You can still buy your fish and greasies to share with the Manly beach seagulls, but you're just as likely to walk into the middle of a food and wine festival, or a 'jazz on the sand' session. A number of new eateries have opened their doors in recent years – with a fair smattering of Mediterranean and African flavours in what has hitherto verged on being an almost pathologically Anglo enclave (this is the suburb that hosts One Nation's head office). The Steyne boulevard has many splashy new cafes with flashy beachfont views – but some are all front and no depth. Choose carefully.

MANLY

Ash's Table
Modern Australian

☎ 9976 3382
93-95 North Steyne

Map 21 D2

Smoking throughout

Pavement tables

If Manly's Corso is heaving with crowds, try wandering north, away from the main drag. Opposite North Steyne's surf lifesaving club is Ash's Table, a favoured local hang-out. Big glass sliding doors opening to ocean views, no bookings taken, nothing over $15, magazines stacked on the counter next to a box of toys – it's surfie casual with wooden floorboards and Afghani artefacts on the walls. Breakfast is served until 2pm, and the lunch/dinner menu covers pasta, pizza, salads and mod Oz mains. Dishes are hit and miss – the yearling scotch fillet on garlic mash ($15) is nicely done, but barramundi fillets ($15) were overwhelmed by a messy sauce. Homemade dips ($8.50) served with a mound of Turkish pide are gobbled up, while moquecca ($14.50), fresh seafood in a coconut sauce, was salty. Toasted banana loaf with banana and caramel sauce ($7) is an ideal post-surf pig-out.

starter: $4.50-$14
main: $10.50-$15
dessert: $7

AE BC MC V; Eftpos

Open: Mon-Thu & Sun 8am-10pm, Fri & Sat 8am-11pm (breakfast: 8am-2pm); reservations not accepted; licensed & BYO (corkage $1.50/person)

THE barKING FROG
Modern Australian

☎ 9977 6307
48 North Steyne

Map 21 E2

No smoking inside

Pavement tables

On a breezy Saturday morning, the front windows at this popular cafe let the sun shine on you while you decide on breakfast: fruit toast with praline butter ($5.50), cranberry and buckwheat pancake ($8.50), muesli with pear and mascarpone ($7.50). Coffee is a serious matter with specials like coffee bowl ($3.50), a double caffeine shot in a bowl. Outside, two muscle-bound Kojaks check their mobiles before tucking into eggs, bacon, tomato and doorstop toast ($8.50) and a lone bookworm munches away. Good coffee, smiley service, classic Stevie Wonder music; life feels fine. Evenings, the tone changes to more serious dining with clothed tables, soft lighting and a mod Oz menu which includes an assorted daily tapas selection ($15.50) and exciting roasted baby beetroot and pumpkin salad with sheeps milk dressing ($12.00). Mains, like the cardamon spiced duck with sweet rhubarb jus ($23.00), come with wine suggestions.

starter: $12-$16.50
main: $17-$23
dessert: $8.50
Set menu from $32/person (min 10 people)

AE BC MC V

Open: Mon-Thu & Sun 8am-10pm, Fri & Sat 8am-11pm (breakfast: 8am-noon); reservations advisable (especially weekends); licensed & BYO (corkage $2/person)

MANLY

Map 21 E2

Nonsmoking tables available

Pavement tables

Brazil
Modern Australian

☎ 9977 3825
46 North Steyne

Brazil is one of the stayers on the Manly restaurant scene, thanks to its innovative cuisine, swanky décor and prominent beachfront location. It's a busy little operation, kicking off with brekky at 8am and churning out dinners until 10.30pm. Groovy white chairs and black plastic tables hustle for space within the narrow confines, and there's some pretty interesting photos lining the walls – we're still trying to work out if the pics are of body parts. Brazil food is packed with flavour, although the liberal use of sauces and spices can be overwhelming – a fate suffered by the char-grilled octopus with a Sichuan-crusted tofu salad and coriander pesto ($13.50). The pan-fried cod fillet (22.50) fared a little better, with a red wine sauce. You'll need a jog along Manly Beach after wolfing down the lethal concoction of chocolate meringue, mixed berry parfait and chocolate sauce ($8.50).

starter: $12.50-$15.50
main: $19.50-$23.50
dessert: $8.50

AE BC DC MC V

Open: daily 8am-midnight (breakfast: 8am-noon); reservations advisable; licensed & BYO (corkage $2/person)

Map 21 E2

Smoking throughout

Pavement tables

Cafe Tunis
North African/Mediterranean

☎ 9976 2805
30-31 South Steyne

There are worse places to be on a sunny afternoon than sitting at a pavement table facing Manly Beach, tucking into spicy grilled merguez sausage on couscous with char-grilled vegetables and minted yoghurt ($11.50). Or investigating the different flavours and textures of a mixed platter piled with dips, olives, octopus, artichokes and sausage ($12.50). The North African-style food is supported by a bright interior of yellow walls, terracotta floor tiles, and a long Arabic-style feature painting. Suitable music sets the mood. At night, unless it's moonlit, the sea is no longer visible, but who minds when the food is this good. Blue-eye cod over sweet potato puree, crunchy broccoli, charmoula and spicy Tunisian tomato glaze ($17) work well together. The chocolate tart ($6) is rather gelatinous and service somewhat erratic, but it's a nice change from fish and chips (though grilled fish and chips, $16.50, is on the lunch menu, with kaftaji*).

starter: $7-$12.50
main: $17-$18
dessert: $6
Set menu $25/person
AE BC DC MC V

Open: daily 7am-10pm; reservations advisable (especially Sat & Sun); licensed & BYO (corkage $2/person)

MANLY

Ceruti's Bistro Italiano
Italian

☎ 9977 7600
15 Sydney Rd

Map 21 E2

Entertainment: flamenco guitarist Fri & Sat 7.30pm-11pm

🚭 Nonsmoking tables available

Pavement tables

With so many restaurants vying for attention in Manly, it's not easy to stand out in the crowd. But Ceruti's has more to offer than most. Smart timber and iron table settings provide an excellent vantage point for people-watching while the endlessly long bar whips up a pretty mean cocktail. On the food front, you'll find pasta dishes galore, as well as duck, fish, veal and beef. Try the mediterranean salad ($11.90/ $13.90) – an interesting mix of roasted peppers, marinated eggplant, char-grilled field mushrooms, fetta, olives and basil – buonissimo! There's lots of favourites on the dessert menu – go for the creamy Tuscan chocolate torte ($8.50) or some home-made ice cream. After you've twirled your way through pasta and sampled a dessert or two, head upstairs to the wine bar and cigar lounge, where you can groove to live Latin and funk bands.

starter: $10.90-$13.90
main: $15.90-$26.90
dessert: $8.50-$10.50
Banquet $35, $55
or $85/person
(min 6 people)
AE BC DC MC V

Open: Tues-Sun noon-11pm; reservations essential (Thurs-Sat); licensed & BYO (corkage $3/person)

NORTHERN BEACHES

Ash's Table (p 215)

MANLY

Fresh at Manly
Cafe fare

☎ 9977 7705
1/49 North Steyne

Map 21 E2
No smoking inside
Courtyard tables

The staff at Fresh look almost as wholesome and pure as the vitamin-packed goodies they dish up. With cheerful enthusiasm they cram turkish bread, foccacia, rolls or sandwiches with as many fillings as you like – and the price doesn't change no matter how greedy you get! There's every type of salad combination imaginable, including novel additions like carrot purée, zucchini fritters, or lentil burgers with satay sauce. Servings are monstrous here – there's barely room for a cookie or muffin afterwards. Early birds can enjoy scrambled eggs, home-made muesli or porridge, while banana bread and freshly-squeezed juices are on tap all day. Species like Fresh are almost extinct in Manly. So make the most of a seat by the beach and a good feed for under $10 while you can.

main: $4-$6.50
dessert: $2-$2.50
cash only

Open: daily 8am-4pm; reservations not accepted; BYO (no corkage)

Out of Africa
North African

☎ 9977 0055
43-45 East Esplanade

Map 21 E2
Entertainment: African band Thurs & Sun 5pm-10pm
Nonsmoking tables available
Courtyard tables

Out of Africa is for those looking for something off the beaten track – but don't go on a Thursday or Sunday night if you want some quiet conversation, as the African band's volume control is set at full bore. It's not too quiet on other nights either: the restaurant is often jam-packed, making for a lively, even boisterous, evening. The food is definitely original. The mixed dips starter ($8.90) is likely to include sun-dried tomato, pumpkin and leek, or artichoke and pea. The reef and beef ($21.90) takes on a new twist with an exotic sauce of lemon, sun-dried tomato, saffron and coconut. Or lash out and try the couscous royale ($32.90 for two) – a grand combination of lamb, chicken and sausages served on a sizzling hot plate. Moroccan coffee ($2.50) or green mint tea ($3.50) are aromatic afters.

starter: $7-$10
main: $14.90-$22
dessert: $7.50-$9.20
Banquet $30
AE BC DC MC V

Open: Mon-Wed 6pm-10.30pm, Thurs-Sun noon-10.30pm; reservations essential (Fri-Sun); BYO (corkage $2/person)

Cafe Crawl – North

Whatever side of the harbour you find yourself on there's great coffee to be had. So bridge out and try one of these delights.

Barcelos Cafe
292 Willoughby Rd, Naremburn ☎ 9439 8990 Map 18 C2
Consistently good food and great breakfasts in an area where cafes are about as common as a cup of Nescafe in Darlinghurst. Try the 'Barcelos special' (eggs benedict) for breakfast and the open ravioli for lunch.

The Belgian Waffle Shop
Kiosk 1, Manly Wharf, Manly ☎ 9949 8180 Map 21 E1
It's a life-saving, heart-starting spot for manic Manly-ites running to board the Jet Cat to the other side of the harbour. During the day, the too young and too beautiful make out that the polished dark wood stools and benches is their mobile office (not that anyone has actually seen any work going on).

Calacoci
112 The Corso, Manly ☎ 9977 1458 Map 21 E2
One of the last old-time Manly milkbars still left standing – complete with a period bubble-gum machine. Self-styled mayors of Manly meet around the plastic tables, sipping Vittoria coffee in front of a backdrop of hundreds of postcards from those who've passed this way and sipped before them.

eden
41-42 East Esplanade, Manly ☎ 9977 1474 Map 21 E1
A chic lounge room for surf-loving backpackers, young mums and the more elegant end of the herbal hippie spectrum. Numbers are swelled by enthusiasts of the tai chi, Feldenkrais and life drawing classes in the adjoining 'spaces'.

Old Fish Shop
94-96 Alfred St, Milsons Point ☎ 9460 2698 Map 17 C2
The laid-back atmosphere is the key. Magazine editors and computer industry buffs join locals who bring their mugs for takeaway coffee. The formula of chillies, miniature onions, broad beans, garlic, and bunches of dried roses hanging from the ceiling (along with the trademark malnourished polystyrene shark) was a success in Newtown, but this is the last one in the group owned by the original management.

Otello
181 Military Rd, Neutral Bay ☎ 9953 2344 Map 17 B3
Not strictly a cafe (it's also a gift shop that sells candles and Fortnam & Mason teas) but the Segafredo coffee, handmade chocolates and truffles, the Queen of Sheba Japonaise (a chocolate mousse cake) and walnut shortbread keep the limited seating (for 12) in good use.

NARRABEEN

Map 21 B1
Smoking after 10pm only

Soleil
International

☎ 9970 7349
1336 Pittwater Rd

Don't be put off by Soleil's busy main road location. Inside this elegant establishment lies a tranquil atmosphere, fine dining and tables spaced so far apart you almost feel lonely. It's simple but elegant, with attractive furnishings and unobtrusive staff who blend in with the surrounds. There's plenty of action on the menu though, with dishes like lambs brains ($12.50) or a duo of white rabbit and hare ($27.50). Simple food devotees will cringe at the wordy menu and complex food combos but others will feel right at home. The open seafood crêpe glazed with a pesto cream sauce fires up the taste buds while the tender beef fillet with a châteaubriand sauce and brandy cream ($25.50) is heaven. Savour the 'celebration of desserts'($14.50) – was the dark chocolate tart or the citrus fruit ravioli our favourite?

starter: $8.50-$18.50
main: $19.50-$28.50
dessert: $7.50-$14
AE BC DC MC V

Open: Tues-Sat 6.30pm-9.30pm, Thurs & Fri noon-2pm; reservations essential (weekends); BYO (corkage $2/person)

NORTH CURL CURL

Map 21 B2
Pavement tables

Emilia's Vegetarian Restaurant
Vegetarian

☎ 9939 1317
41 Griffin Rd

It's not just the food that disappears fast at Emilia's. Some bad-mannered vegans have taken to swiping the cutesy marine decorations from the colourful outdoor dunnies. Hence the 'Please don't steal our fish' sign on the back of the toilet door. Not to worry – it doesn't affect the cosy, feel-good atmosphere going on inside this former beach cottage. A statue of buddha and the smiling face of Indian yoga master Swamiji watch approvingly as the wholesome dishes emerge from the little kitchen. Emilia's menu has remained unchanged for years – locals kick up a fuss whenever a variation is mooted. The chickpea and vegetable curry ($11) is fragrant and tasty while the spinach and cheese enchilada puts most Mexican restaurants to shame. And it's hard to believe something tasting as fine as the chocolate and zucchini cake ($3.50) could actually be good for you. The musically inclined are welcome to strum one of the many hand-made guitars adorning the walls.

starter: $8
dessert: $3.50
cash only

Open: Tues-Sun 5.30pm-10pm, Sat & Sun 10.30am-2.30pm; reservations essential; BYO (corkage $1/bottle)

PALM BEACH

Beach Road
Modern Australian

☎ **9974 1159**
1 Beach Rd

Beach Road's sisal matting, louvred windows and outdoor loo evokes an oh-so-tasteful holiday home. The relaxed but attentive staff seem as delighted to be here as our fellow diners – a collection of tourists, film-industry locals and forty-something surfers. Nestled in a kink of road between Palmies' spectacular sweep of ocean and the calmer Pittwater, Beach Road's considered emphasis on natural fibres, light and air, offset the lack of water views. The designer-touch extends to the presentation of the food. Tiny Northern Thai-style scallop and prawn sausages ($21.50) are exquisitely placed among a green mango salad – a combination that leaves us wishing for more. Fish lovers will appreciate the seafood-dominated menu, although the alternatives are also attractive. Slow-grilled corn fed duck ($28.50) is salivatingly tender, and spiced up nicely with pear and green peppercorns. Loosen your belt a few notches for the white chocolate and honeycomb ice cream sandwich ($14) – our pick of the dessert menu.

Open: summer daily noon-3pm, 7pm-10pm, winter Fri-Sun noon-3pm, Wed-Sat 7pm-10pm; reservations essential; licensed, no BYO

Map 22 B2

Ⓟ Private parking

Entertainment: live jazz Fri 8pm-11pm

Smoking at the bar only

Terrace tables

starter: $14-$26
main: $27-$30
dessert: $14-$16

AE BC DC MC V; Eftpos

NORTHERN BEACHES

Map 22 B2
No smoking inside
Deck tables

Carmel's by the Sea Cafe
Cafe fare

☎ 9974 4374
Barrenjoey Boathouse, Governor Philip Park

Carmel's could not be any closer to the water. The calm tides of Pittwater lap the boards underneath, sea planes take off for your sheer entertainment while divers pop up now and then to check that you're having a good time. Carmel's vegetarian bake and chicken satay burgers are tops. Their pots of good tea and plunger coffee go well with oven fresh scones ($5.50). Who needs espresso at a location like this? Early breakfast is simple and peaceful, with freshly chopped fruit salad ($4.50) and a satisfying bacon and egg roll ($4.50). It's a no-nonsense place, so you order at the counter and collect your tray when called. If you try the strenuous but manageable climb to near-by Barrenjoey Lighthouse, then the home-style delights of Carmel's are a welcome reward.

main: $5-$8.50
dessert: $5.50
cash only

Open: daily 9am-5pm (breakfast: Sat & Sun 8am-noon); reservations not accepted; BYO (no corkage)

PALM BEACH

Jonah's
Modern Australian

☎ 9974 5599
69 Bynya Road

Map 22 C2

Private parking

Entertainment: live jazz Fri 8pm-11pm

Smoking at the bar only

Terrace tables

A favourite with young lovers popping the question and older couples celebrating the anniversary of the answer, Jonah's is the place to go when you're out to impress. The restaurant is perched precariously on a secluded cliff top, offering 180-degree views over spectacular Whale Beach. Romantic evenings start with a drink at one of the two open fireplaces, before moving on to the Mediterranean terrace. Jonah's offers one of Sydney's most succulent steaks: Angus beef tenderloin with baby bok choy, spinach, parsnip and a soy butter sauce ($38.50). The place also has a name for its house-smoked ocean trout and salmon. The trout ($27.50) is served rare with a cauliflower purée and dreamy ginger and coconut cream sauce. Worth noting is Jonah's absolutely mind-boggling wine list, with some drops priced at close to $1000 a bottle. Cigars (up to $88) are available to round off the meal.

starter: $14-$26
main: $27-$30
dessert: $14-$16

Open: daily noon-3pm, Mon-Fri 6.30pm-10pm, Sat 7pm-10pm; reservations essential; licensed, no BYO

AE BC DC MC V; Eftpos

WHALE BEACH

Beach House
Seafood/modern Australian

☎ 9974 2727
227 Whale Beach Rd

Map 22 C2

The view at Beach House will sweep you off your feet. Brilliantly blue in the sunshine stretching right out to the Pacific horizon. Dusty grey under cloud. Such a stunning location is the perfect place for a lazy Sunday breakfast. The buffet includes fresh fruits, stewed peaches, juices, cereals, creamy yogurt and a great array of just baked pastries. Follow with generous servings of scrambled, fried or eggs benedict, accompanied by bacon, sausages and grilled tomato. In the evening relax in the comfortable décor and choose from a menu including sugar cured salmon with vodka and dill créme fraîche ($16) to start, roast pork fillet with prune and chipotle chilli stuffing ($25) or, maybe, whole barramundi with green curry sauce ($25) for main and finish with fig parfait with quince and spiced plums. At the day's end it's not just the view that's good.

starter: $14-$16
main: $19.50-$25
dessert: $11
Set menu breakfast on Sunday $20/adult, $10/child

Open: Tues-Sat 6pm-last booking, Thurs-Sat noon-3pm, Sun 9am-11am, 12.30pm-3pm; reservations advisable; licensed only

AE BC DC MC V

Frying Kangaroo

Protests in Britain, where animal rights groups are well organised, have seen kangaroo removed from supermarket shelves and restaurant menus. Should we be eating kangaroo?

Kangaroo meat has its own industry, like beef and chicken. However, instead of being intensively farmed, kangaroos are sourced from the bush. Every year the Australian Government uses research regarding kangaroo populations to set quotas outlining how many kangaroos may be killed commercially. A small number of trained, licensed shooters kill kangaroos from areas of New South Wales, Queensland, South Australia and Western Australia. Hunting kangaroos in Australia's 68 million hectares of conservation reserves, national parks and state forests is prohibited. The trade in kangaroo meat is managed with care to protect both kangaroo populations and rural production.

A Code of Practice for the Humane Killing of Kangaroos requires hunters to shoot the animals in the head with a high-powered rifle, therefore causing instant death. The RSPCA claims this method to be a humane form of animal slaughter but other welfare organisations argue that the hunt itself is extremely stressful for the animals. It is illegal to use devices such as steel-jawed traps and archery equipment that may cause prolonged suffering prior to death. After killing, the animals are taken to abattoirs and inspected by officials from the Australian Quarantine and Inspection Service (AQIS) before the meat is processed. AQIS ensures that the kangaroos have been shot in the head. The latest study completed by the RSPCA found that 95% of kangaroos killed commercially in New South Wales and 84% in South Australia were shot in the head.

While farming has been an alternative to hunting for Australian animals like crocodiles and emus, attempts to intensively farm kangaroos have so far been unsuccessful. Killing by licensed shooters is currently the only legal means of obtaining kangaroo meat.

Until recently, farmers saw the kangaroo as a pest. However, landowners are now encouraged to look at the kangaroo as a resource and to manage their properties to allow room for the kangaroos. As for us, we may see a lot more 'braised kangaroo tail' turning up on menus, in Australia if not in Britain.

Courtney Centner

WHALE BEACH

de beers Whale Beach
Modern Australian

☎ **9974 4009**
24b The Strand

Map 22 C2
Wheelchair access
No smoking inside
Courtyard seating

Steeped in history (first opening as the Pacific in 1913), de beers has been transformed into an elegant modern dining room. Subtly featuring the work of local artists, de beers' food and ambience is a perfect match. Each dish resembles a work of modern art. Roger Haldane's Victorian buffalo-milk yogurt is served as a neatly cubed terrine, a fresh fig with its top chopped, winking tiny pink seeds from the centre ($17.50). The duck ($29), appears as an oblong brick of crispy aromatic duck skin, encasing a confit of duck meat infused with olive oil and spices. Served with a delightfully moist spinach dumpling, slivers of shiitake mushroom spill into the sesame-scented juices. Dessert-wise, strawberry and raspberry fusion ($14) combines strawberry ice cream with praline and soft Italian-style raspberry meringue, all caramelised on top. This beachside reverie serves skilfully executed food fit for its stunning location.

Open: Wed-Sat 6.30pm-9.30pm, Fri-Sat 12.30-3.30pm, Sun noon-4pm (garden char-grill open weather permitting: Wed-Sun from noon; breakfast Sat & Sun 8.30-11.30am); reservations advisable; licensed & BYO (corkage $5/bottle)

starter: $17.50-$21
main: $23-$31
dessert: $13.90-$14
AE BC DC JCB MC V; Eftpos

NORTHERN BEACHES

Jonah's (p 223)

Back for More

The Bower Restaurant
Cnr Bower Lane & Marine Pde, Manly ☎ 9977 5451 Map 21 E2
An unpretentious spot for any meal of the day, the Bower is halfway between a relaxed cafe and a proper restaurant at the halfway stop between the scenic walks connecting Manly and Shelly Beaches. There's a constant wave of passing surfers, scuba divers and bathers at the Fairy Bower rock pool.

Le Kiosk
1 Marine Pde, Shelly Beach, Manly ☎ 9977 4122 Map 21 E3
Right on Shelly Beach, Le Kiosk is so Sydney it's practically got sunscreen and Speedos on. Fresh fish that's grilled, baked or fried with modern Australian salads and a relaxed outdoor dining area. At night, an open fire makes for a romantic setting, especially if you've taken the beachside path to arrive.

✱ *Write to us: We think we've got Sydney well-covered – even so, there are always new places to try. Our tastebuds will travel, so let us know about suburbs where there's more to discover. Write to us or email us (see p 11 for details) and the best suggestions will receive the next edition free.*

OUTER WEST

Auburn

Bankstown

Beverly Hills

Cabramatta

Campsie

Lakemba

North Strathfield

Parramatta

St Marys

Map 23 - Outer West

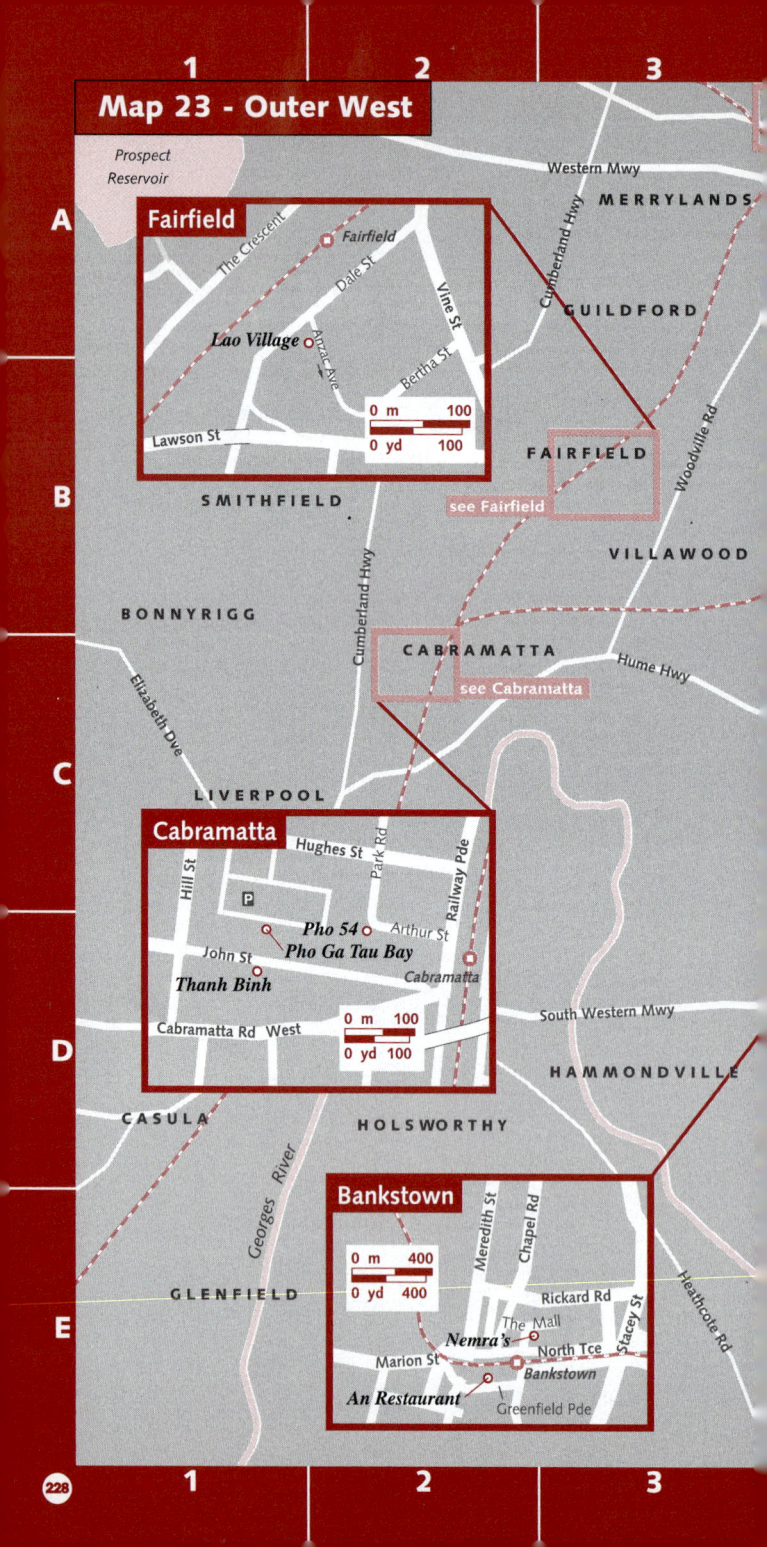

Prospect Reservoir

Fairfield

- The Crescent
- Fairfield
- Dale St
- Vine St
- Anzac Ave
- Bertha St
- *Lao Village*
- Lawson St

0 m 100
0 yd 100

SMITHFIELD
MERRYLANDS
Western Mwy
Cumberland Hwy
GUILDFORD
Woodville Rd
FAIRFIELD
see Fairfield
VILLAWOOD
BONNYRIGG
Elizabeth Dve
Cumberland Hwy
CABRAMATTA
see Cabramatta
Hume Hwy
LIVERPOOL

Cabramatta

- Hill St
- Hughes St
- Park Rd
- Railway Pde
- *Pho 54*
- Arthur St
- John St
- *Pho Ga Tau Bay*
- *Thanh Binh*
- Cabramatta
- Cabramatta Rd West

0 m 100
0 yd 100

South Western Mwy
HAMMONDVILLE
CASULA
Georges River
HOLSWORTHY

Bankstown

0 m 400
0 yd 400

- Meredith St
- Chapel Rd
- Rickard Rd
- Stacey St
- Heathcote Rd
- The Mall
- *Nemra's*
- North Tce
- Marion St
- Bankstown
- *An Restaurant*
- Greenfield Pde

GLENFIELD

228

Auburn

Ben Da Vietnamese Restaurant

North Strathfield

Abhi's

Minor streets are not depicted

Lakemba

La Roche

To **Masthai Seafood Restaurant** 2.4km

Some minor streets are not depicted

Campsie

Yuan's BBQ
Se Joung Restaurant

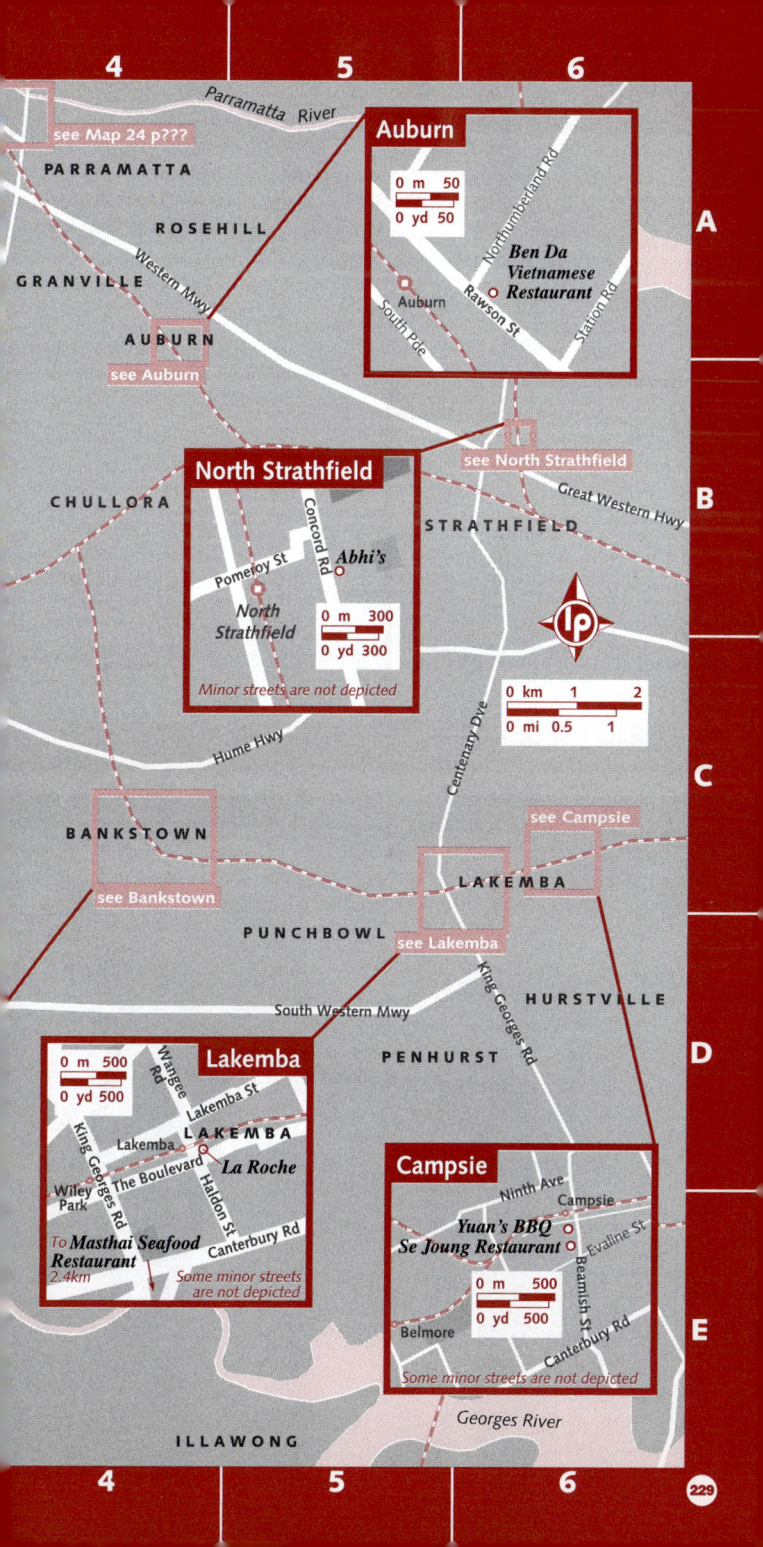

Some minor streets are not depicted

Map 24 - Parramatta

1 2 3

A
PARRAMATTA
St Marys inset 20km

O'Connell St
Marsden St
Church St
Phillip St
Horwood Pl
Smith St
Wilde Ave
Parramatta River

○ Costa Esmeralda
○ La Porchetta
○ La Bella Vista
○ Fiderio
George St
○ Carne Station

St Marys

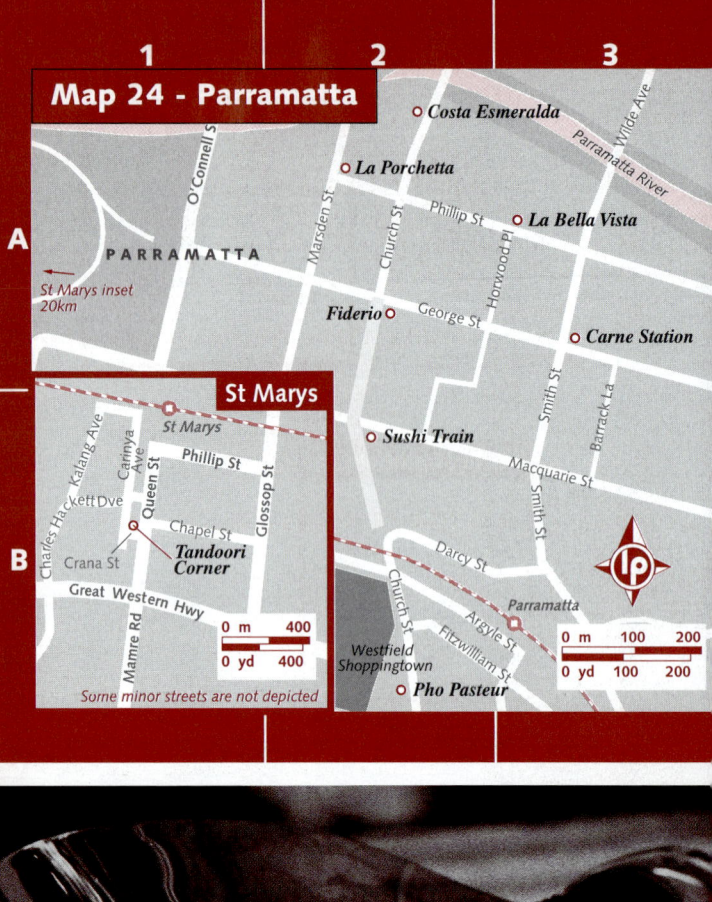

Charles Hackett Dve
Kalang Ave
Carinya Ave
Queen St
Phillip St
Glossop St
St Marys
Chapel St
Crana St
Tandoori Corner
Great Western Hwy
Mamre Rd

0 m 400
0 yd 400

Some minor streets are not depicted

B
○ Sushi Train
Smith St
Macquarie St
Barrack La
Darcy St
Church St
Argyle St
Fitzwilliam St
Parramatta
Westfield Shoppingtown
○ Pho Pasteur

0 m 100 200
0 yd 100 200

BEST

- **Ben Da Vietnamese Restaurant**
  One visit just isn't enough

- **Se Joung Restaurant**
  Kimchi on cushions in Campsie

Outer West

Since the end of WWII, Sydney's west and south-west have provided the setting for a relentless suburban advancement. In the prosperous '50s, rural areas were replaced by quarter-acre blocks and simple fibro kit homes. Streets of blond brick were soon on the landscape, as newlywed baby-boomers moved into adjoining suburbs, and migrant communities ebbed away from the city to secure their own place in the sun. Known in recent decades as the home of Sydney's working class (and subsequent first-generation middle class) the west and south-west take in dozens of regions. These range from expansive areas of young populations, walled-in private housing estates with security patrols and utopian names like 'Cherry Haven Gardens', to big, outlying suburbs with strong ethnic identities. The west sprawls around major business centres such as Parramatta (an early settlement now subsumed by Sydney suburbs) and Liverpool and, as elsewhere in Sydney, multi-layered malls have claimed much trade. But it's not all burger chains and food courts. The sheer size of the place and the diversity of the populace account for an open-ended range of restaurants. Older shopping strips are becoming popular for their acute local flavours, such as Cabramatta, a marketplace of Vietnamese eateries, and St Mary's, home to Fijian-Indian cuisine.

AUBURN

Map 23 A6
Smoking throughout

starter: $5.50-$7
main: $5.50-$26.80
dessert: $1.50
Set menu available
BC MC V

Ben Da Vietnamese Restaurant
Vietnamese

☎ 9649 5657
71 Rawson St

Ben Da boasts an eclectic menu in the best Vietnamese tradition, in an intensely diverse part of western Sydney. Opposite Auburn Station, it shares the block with a Turkish pastry shop and Asian grocers. Light ricepaper rolls on vermicelli ($6), daubed with peanut sauce, are a great start, as are mini spring rolls ($5.50) served with lettuce and mint for wrapping. One of the fifteen varieties of noodle soup, such as shredded-chicken and pea vermicelli soup ($5.50) might also do the trick. Minced barbecue prawns on sugar-cane ($5.80 per piece), are heavenly hot from the pan. Beef cubes fried with butter ($16.80) is succulent and the favourite at our table. Baby bok choy fried with garlic is crisp and tasty, as are the stir-fried snow pea leaves (both $9.80). Bowls of sago in coconut milk with finely chopped melon ($1.50) sweetened us up to finish. We will return to comfortable, friendly Ben Da.

Open: Mon-Fri 11am-3pm, 5pm-10pm, Sat & Sun 11am-10pm; reservations advisable (dinner Fri & Sat); BYO (corkage $3/bottle)

BANKSTOWN

Map 23 E2
Nonsmoking tables available

main: $6.50-$8
cash only

An Restaurant
Vietnamese

☎ 9796 7826
29-31 Greenfield Pde

Specialising in north Vietnamese pho, An Restaurant is one of many eateries along Greenfield Pde. Although to see its popularity among the local Vietnamese community you'd think it was the only place in town. Essentially a dining hall with roving waiters and an economical eight dishes, An's big board menus are in Vietnamese only, so ask at the counter for an English version. The soups on offer are variations of beef and chicken-based pho. Of the beef stylings that top An's 'hot secret recipe soup', the rare beef seems most popular; cut very thin, it is seriously rare and has a lively cinnamon flavour. The pho topped with chicken combination is a swampy pick-me-up that really makes the most of the chook, afloat with breast meat, heart, liver, giblet, blood jelly and egg.

Open: daily 7am-9pm; reservations accepted; unlicensed

OUTER WEST

BANKSTOWN

Nemra's
Lebanese

☎ **9793 7247**
Shop 2a, 57 The Mall

Map 23 E2

Nonsmoking tables available

Locating a cheap Lebanese restaurant in Sydney is as easy as finding potholes along Parramatta Rd. But not too many plate up wonderfully soft lamb, perfectly formed felafels and crisp baklava. Nemra's is such a place, and even better, it's a tad more comfortable than your typical kebab shop. Our tip is to order the mixed plates. An entrée platter ($10.90) comes with creamy hummus and tahini piled next to a heap of lemony tabouli. Add in just-made felafels, thin slices of lamb and a whole lotta pita (two types, crispy and fresh) and you're on your way. Undo your zipper because next is the mixed grill ($9.90). Tender, smoky-flavoured, barbecued lamb, chicken, beef and sausages come with the garlickiest garlic dip we've ever tasted. We dare you to finish with the crunchy, nutty baklava ($1.60).

starter: $4.50-$7.50
main: $10.50-$14.90
dessert: $1.60-$7.50
Banquet lunch $12.50, banquet dinner $16.90/$19.90

AE BC MC V

Open: Sun-Thurs 10.30am-10pm, Fri & Sat 10.30am-midnight; reservations accepted; BYO (no corkage)

BEVERLY HILLS

Map 23 E4
Smoking throughout

Masthai Seafood Restaurant
Cantonese (Hong Kong)

☎ 9580 5609
495 King Georges Rd

Masthai doesn't need an English menu. Chinese diners descend on the place from miles around to eat the ru ge – suckling pigeon ($14.80 per bird). It's duck-like flesh is roasted whole, quartered for easy eating and served with side dishes of sea salt and soy sauce. And if the little beak is pointing your way – then the head is yours. Other draw cards include hao, giant NZ oysters, steamed with slivers of shallot ($9.80). Thinly sliced abalone, bao yu, can be enjoyed in seafood hotpot. Salt and pepper deep-fried crab is gnawish too (both market price). Small bowls of warm red-bean soup are provided gratis as a sweetener at the end of your meal along with the obligatory sliced fresh fruit. If you are new to Chinese dining, ask one of the charming waiters to navigate the lengthy menu with you. Or look for the most enthusiastic faces around you and say you'll have what their having.

starter: $6-$14
main: $12-$18
BC MC V

Open: daily 5.30pm-2am; reservations advisable; licensed & BYO (corkage $1.50/person)

OUTER WEST

CABRAMATTA

Map 23 D1

Pho Ga Tau Bay
Vietnamese

☎ 9724 7162
Shop 15, 107 John Street

Venture into a sideshow alley of trinket shops and frenzied fishmongers and you'll find the Pho Ga Tau Bay in one of Cabramatta's many bazaar-like arcades. The street numbering isn't exactly sequential, so you may have to look twice to find this very simple restaurant where the focus on pho soup is evident in the menu of only eleven dishes at $6 apiece. Such specialisation pays dividends for the diner: the crab meat and pig trotter rice noodle soup has a creamy but punchy balance, and the chicken pho is boiled just enough to really get the most out of the meat and skin. There is an almost subterranean and very immediate feel about the place – the cooks sit at tables chopping vegetables bought at a grocery three metres from the door. While in town, you might want to stock up on ingredients and try your own pho – but don't expect to replicate what they have on offer here.

main: $6
cash only

Open: daily 8am-7pm; reservations accepted; unlicensed

Manic Organic

With the uncertainties surrounding GM (genetically modified) food, Australians are undoubtedly becoming more concerned about what they're eating. Many are looking to organic products for assurance that what they are consuming is a closer form of 'pure' than what is created in a lab or on a factory farm.

It's been impossible not to notice the speed with which organic food has taken off in the UK. The media is rife with everything organic – from beef to ice cream – and agribusiness will never be the same. At UK supermarket giant Sainsbury's you can even buy chemical-free fare for your organic-minded pooch.

Organic farming is not a new concept in Australia, but suddenly it has hit us head on. Everyone wants to be a part of it. You can get pesticide-free produce delivered to your door through the Green Line or find it on the web at goorganic.com.au. Restaurant menus are speckled with the word 'organic' reflecting the trend. But, is it *really* organic? Organic farming rejects such practices as use of growth hormones, pesticides, artificial fertilisers and chemicals. Genuine organic products carry an authenticating label by one of the various certification bodies such as the Biological Farmers of Australia (BFA) or the National Association for Sustainable Agriculture Australia (NASAA). However, it is an 'on-going battle' to make certain that you get what you pay for when a product is labelled organic – retailers and restauranteurs must continuously follow up with suppliers, double checking the source of the produce and the methods of its production.

But organics are hip and it looks as if the demand for organics will increase as people become aware of their environment and more concerned about the effects of the chemicals they're ingesting.

For organic and macrobiotic delights try Macro Wholefoods in Bondi Junction (see review p 143) and Iku Wholefoods (see cafe crawl p 119) with branches in Glebe, Darlinghurst and Neutral Bay.

Courtney Center

CABRAMATTA

Map 23 D1

Smoking throughout

Thanh Binh
Vietnamese

☎ 9727 9729
52a John St

A widely celebrated Vietnamese favourite, the Thanh Binh makes for a good lunch stop during a day out and about in the thronging hub of downtown Cabra'. A standard formica-table-and-mirrored-wall affair that gridlocks at peak hours, Thanh Binh's good name seems to come from a precise, superior balance of flavours and a sheer freshness of ingredients. A formidable menu offers 251 dishes; it's a bit like reading a form guide where no odds or tips are given but all the horses have exciting names. The sugar-cane prawns seem to be a big hit with the regulars. The lemongrass chicken is clean and sharp and well-complemented by bright shavings of chilli, while the duck with mushrooms is nice and smoky. Its elbow to elbow most of the time, and you'll be sharing sauce bottles with local folk and the odd outlander in town for the spectacle, the bargains and the far-famed food.

starter: $3-$6
main: $5.50-$25
dessert: $2.50-$4

AE BC MC V; Eftpos

Open: daily 9am-9pm; reservations accepted; BYO (corkage $2/person)

CAMPSIE

Map 23 E6

Smoking throughout

Se Joung Restaurant
Korean

☎ 9718 4039
68-72 Evaline St

Settling on red and blue satin cushions in a wood-panelled room while a waitress brings you bowl after bowl of kimchi*, it's hard to believe that Koreans have only been in Australia in large numbers since the mid-1980s. You can pick the cafe-style room with pine tables, or the table-top barbecues with cushioned floor seating. A picture-assisted menu covers everything from Japanese-style sashimi ($15), and cold buckwheat noodles in blood red chilli sauces to dinner-plate sized spring onion pancakes (wonderfully doughy $8). Giant belts of marinated beef ribs arrive raw, and a scissors- and tong-wielding waitress cooks and cuts it for you to wrap in lettuce with kimchi. After the complimentary watermelon dessert, you won't leave anything but a devastating scene of bowls, empty cola cans (and perhaps a well-drained Soju bottle – a vodka/rice wine hybrid).

starter: $8-$17
main: $11-$28

AE BC MC V; Eftpos

Open: daily 11am-11pm; reservations advisable; licensed & BYO (corkage $3/bottle)

CAMPSIE

Yuan's BBQ
Chinese (Shanghai)

☎ 9787 9896
Shop 13, 199 Beamish St

Map 23 E6

Smoking throughout

This bright Shanghainese place directly opposite Campsie Station has a bain-marie exhibiting delicacies fit to cure homesickness in many a regular: salted pork stomach or salted duck gizzard ($6.80), chicken feet ($4.80) and chewy, sinuous sliced pigs' ears. These are eaten cold as starters. Á la carte options include a variety of dumplings, steamed or fried, pork buns and noodle soups such as the popular noodle with pork chop in soup ($6). The attraction is authenticity: pan-fried finless eel ($10.80) and braised sea cucumber with barbecue sauce ($15.80) are considered common fare. Vegetarian choices are many, such as gluten-based vegetarian chicken in brown sauce ($5.80), soy sauce bean curd, Suzhou flavour ($4.80) and straw mushrooms with vegetables and oyster sauce ($9.80). Simple décor, friendly service and its convenient location add to the pleasures of a quick meal on the way home or indeed, an adventurous trek to this booming stretch of Beamish St.

starter: $3.50-$7.80
main: $5.50-$16.80
dessert: $3.00-4.60

cash only

Open: daily 10am-10pm; reservations accepted; BYO (no corkage)

LAKEMBA

La Roche
Lebanese

☎ 9759 9257
5/61 Haldon St

Map 23 D4

Smoking throughout

Well-regarded by the Lebanese community across Sydney as a reliable takeaway outlet, La Roche also provides tables and service if you want to kick back and feed at the source. The kitchen is a hissing, roisterous engine room that even on a quiet night is packed with half a dozen brawny cooks; perhaps this ethos of heavy industry is what keeps the punters coming in. Best bet is the mixed plate (a bargain at $8) that guarantees you a bountiful range of shish kebab, tabouli, hummus and baba ghanoush. On top of these staples, it also comes with fresh, sweet felafels and the shish tawouk – which sounds like a George Lucas character if there ever was one – the house special of chicken with vinegar and garlic and a warming, fruity sting to it.

starter: $3.50-$5.50
main: $4-$8

cash only

Open: daily 8am-9pm; reservations accepted; unlicensed

NORTH STRATHFIELD

Map 23 B5

Abhi's
Indian

☎ 9743 3061
163 Concord Rd

starter: $8.80-$12.80
main: $12.80-$15.80
dessert: $7.80
Banquet $25.50 or $30/person (min four people)

AE BC DC MC V

If it wasn't for the gods Ganesh (perched above the entrance) and Shiva (sitting serenely above the polished wood bar), you could be excused for thinking you'd stumbled upon another chic Italian pizzeria. And while all over Sydney sub-continental cuisine seems to be suffering from the locals' love affair with Thai, the queues here regularly spill out onto the street. Delicately sautéed crab meat with a mild chilli flavour served on snow peas ($12.80) is one of the most popular options. So is a crisp and perfectly round pancake cylinder of masala dosa, served with a tangy coriander and coconut paste that's the colour and texture of Japanese wasabi ($8.80/$12.80). The dhal tarka ($6.80) is highly recommended, but be warned that some of the vegetarian options can be surprisingly hot. But there's nothing subcontinental about desserts like thin, towering cones of sorbet in moats of berry coulis ($7.80).

Open: Mon-Fri noon-3pm, daily from 6pm; reservations advisable (especially weekends); licensed & BYO (no corkage)

PARRAMATTA

Map 24 A3
Wheelchair access
Smoking throughout

Carne Station
Korean

☎ 9633 5788
100 George St

Set menu $13 (daily lunch), $17 (Sun-Thurs dinner), $19 (Fri & Sat dinner), children 4-7 years $6, 8-11 years $11

AE BC MC V; Eftpos

Carne Station is a revelation in just how much Korean culture and the Aussie-backyard culture have in common: the buffet, the beer and the BBQ. It's an all-you-can-eat deal in a large, brightly-lit room resembling a roadhouse diner, where the tabletop cookers will have you fighting to play dad with the tongs. Front up to the buffet to fill your plates with kimchi, raw vegetables, piles of raw onion and garlic and a dozen different marinated meats – the cover charge even includes mussels and octopus. When your cooking's done, dunk the results in your personal bowl of dipping sauce – it has a delightful sweet, gingery miso flavour. For those who are still a bit fearful when it comes to the unfamiliar, there's even a tray full of snags, cold pasta salad and caramel sponge and a dozen photographs of the Harbour Bridge and Sydney to make you feel at home.

Open: daily noon-3pm, 5pm-10pm; reservations advisable (Fri-Sun); licensed & BYO (no corkage)

Church St, Parramatta

When the First Fleeters arrived on the rocky sandstone shores of Port Jackson and tried (with very little success) to grow their English seeds, it was only the discovery of Parramatta's alluvial plains that saved the crops. But ever since then, the suburbs in the east have been turning up their noses at the culinary aromas of the west. Now Church St's thriving new dining scene is putting Parramatta back on the foodie map.

The eating precinct's northern end is bounded by the Parramatta River, Prince Alfred Park and St Patrick's Cathedral (left with an iron skeleton roof after a suspected arson attack). Walking south, there's a piece of Rome down a little laneway at the Costa Esmeralda, with its heavy brass doors and clubby atmosphere (Frank Sinatra's career would have started in a place like this). Franchises such as City Extra and Victoria's budget pizza purveyor La Porchetta (housed in the shell of another old church) are here too. At night, the Parramatta public procure bowls of pasta in a frenetic alfresco scene that's mainly Mediterranean. Keep heading south towards the southern shopping district end and Church Street becomes a tree-lined mall that hosts old fashioned Italian coffee shops and something that's more 'nouveau Italo': Fiderio (see review p. 240). There's the kitsch Sushi Train and the bordering-on-kitsch pink Town Hall as well. Opposite is St John's Cathedral (still intact) – reputedly the only church in the colony when it opened in 1803. The mall ends with the Westfield Shopping Centre and the best value cafes are at this end, in Parramatta's South-East Asian quarter. Alongside the golden arches is an outlet of another much smaller chain, Pho Pasteur – their beef and chicken noodle soups, praised all over Sydney Town.

Costa Esmeralda 333 Church Street, Parramatta ☎ 9689 2989 Map 24 A2
La Porchetta 2 Phillip Street, Parramatta ☎ 9687 0470 Map 24 A2
Pho Pasteur 137 Church Street, Parramatta ☎ 9635 0782 Map 24 B2
Sushi Train Shop 3, 188 Church Street, Parramatta ☎ 9891 1399 Map 24 B2

Map 24 A2

No smoking inside

Pavement tables on Church St Mall

Fiderio
Italian

☎ **9687 3077**
262 Church St
(cnr Church and George Sts)

Fiderio started off more mod Oz than traditional Italian. Its emphasis now though is definitely Italian serving antipasto and veal cutlets with bocconcini and roma tomatoes ($23). And even with the gelato bar facing out to the Church St mall, Fiderio is still Parramatta's smartest new restaurant. It's the linen service, high-backed archbishop chairs and banquettes. Not to mention the helpful suggestions of wine by the glass for each main course. The dish of three large seafood-filled ravioli ($27) gets maximum points for presentation: orange and black fettucine are placed in a gingham pattern over each ravioli. The accompanying white cream sauce and decorative lobster are lovely, but the pasta's chewy pancake texture lets the whole thing down. Much better is the beef ($23) wonderfully raw and served with a smoky mushroom mix (including morrel) and asparagus.

starter: $14-$16
main: $23-$27.50
dessert: $10-$11
AE BC DC MC V

Open: daily 8am-9.30pm (breakfast: 8.30am-11.30am); reservations advisable; licensed, no BYO

PARRAMATTA

La Bella Vista
Italian

☎ 9633 3718
40 Phillip St

Map 24 A3
Entertainment: jazz band on Fri and Sat nights

Smoking downstairs only

Courtyard tables

The walls at La Bella Vista are painted blue, red and purple and covered in a salon of photos – from family snaps to postcard pics of Rome's Trevi Fountain. So why the sad country and western music? After the waitress wins the battle to keep the volume below stadium level, she takes our order and five prawns promptly arrive on a sizzling platter in a very garlicky tomato sauce that leaves a pleasingly tangy lemon aftertaste ($13.50). A bocconcini salad ($8.50) is doused in lovely vinegar and olive oil. The gnocchi ($12.50) are a bit too heavy and chewy, but they're served with a tasty tomato-based pesto sauce. The risotto will please those who like a light meal – its fresh mushrooms, spring onions and capsicum are delightful, even if the texture is akin to boiled rice in thick stock ($13.50). Good garlic and olive oil and the trattoria atmosphere keep us happy.

starter: $8-$18
main: $16.50-$25
dessert: $5.50-$6.50
Set menu $27.90 or $35
AE BC DC MC V

Open: daily noon-3pm, 5.30pm-10.30pm; reservations advisable; licensed & BYO (corkage $2.50/person)

ST MARYS

Tandoori Corner
Indian

☎ 9833 2590
5 Crana Street

Map 24 B1

Smoking throughout

Set among plains stretching from the Blue Mountains out to the Hawkesbury River, the shopping centre attests to a varied population and the local restaurants are no exception. Tandoori Corner, next to an Indian spice and video shop, offers a much longer menu than your average curry house, taking in regional specialities from all over India. The entrées – such as marinated chicken pakora ($7.50) and samosas ($3.80) – are served with home-made mint chutney and for the consummate Indian feed there's a selection of side dishes; cucumber raita (with yoghurt and spices), mixed pickles, date and tamarind chutney ($1.60 each). The savoury bombay potatoes ($8.20) will appeal to both vegetarian and wolfish meat-lover, and the lamb dishes – dal ghosht ($8.90) and lamb nentara – are brimming with that complex Indian tang. For dessert try the fried dumplings in rosewater syrup or the mango ice cream.

starter: $3.80-$8.50
main: $6.50-$11.50
dessert: $2.50-$3.50
Set menu $22.90/person (min 4 people)
AE BC DC MC V; Eftpos

Open: Tues-Sun 5.30pm-10.30pm; reservations accepted; BYO (no corkage)

OUTER WEST

Back for More

Pho 54
54 Park Rd, Cabramatta ☎ 9726 1992 Map 23 D2
They are experts in the French-Vietnamese tradition of making soup stock over eight hours. The beef pho is a speciality, as is the bún bó xai – if you don't exhibit early proficiency with your chopsticks, you may find one of the well-meaning staff tossing this warm salad for you.

Lao Village
1-3 Anzac Ave, Fairfield ☎ 9728 7136 Map 23 A2
Dishes are amazingly cheap here, with nearly everything costing less than $10. Although the Lao family who run this place say they don't make their chilli prawn soup as hot as the Thai do, it's still tear-jerkingly delectable. Most nights of the week it's filled with cigarette smoke and plenty of locals.

✱ **Write to us:** *Where do you go to eat time and time again? Is it fabulous food, an authentic atmosphere, great service, or a welcome for the kids that brings you back? Write or email us (see p 11 for details) and the best suggestions will receive the next edition free.*

BLUE MOUNTAINS

Blackheath

Katoomba

Leura

Map 25 - Blue Mountains

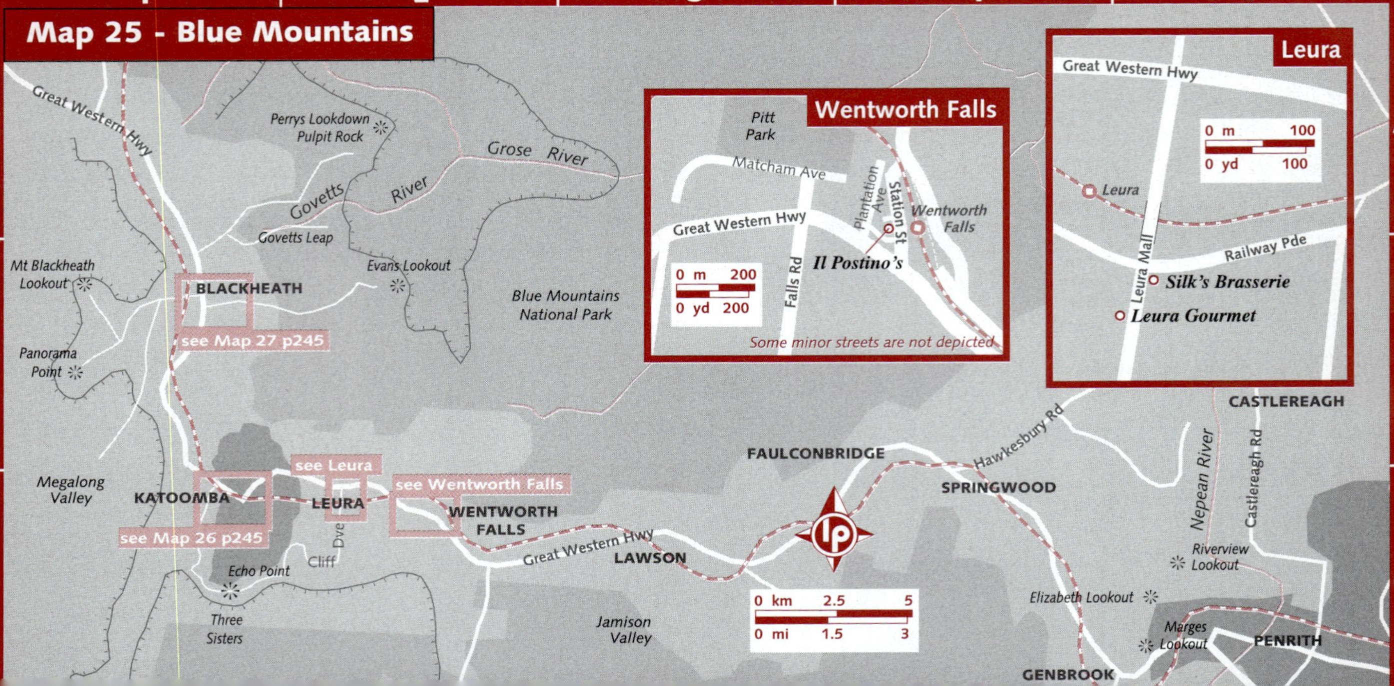

Map 26 - Katoomba

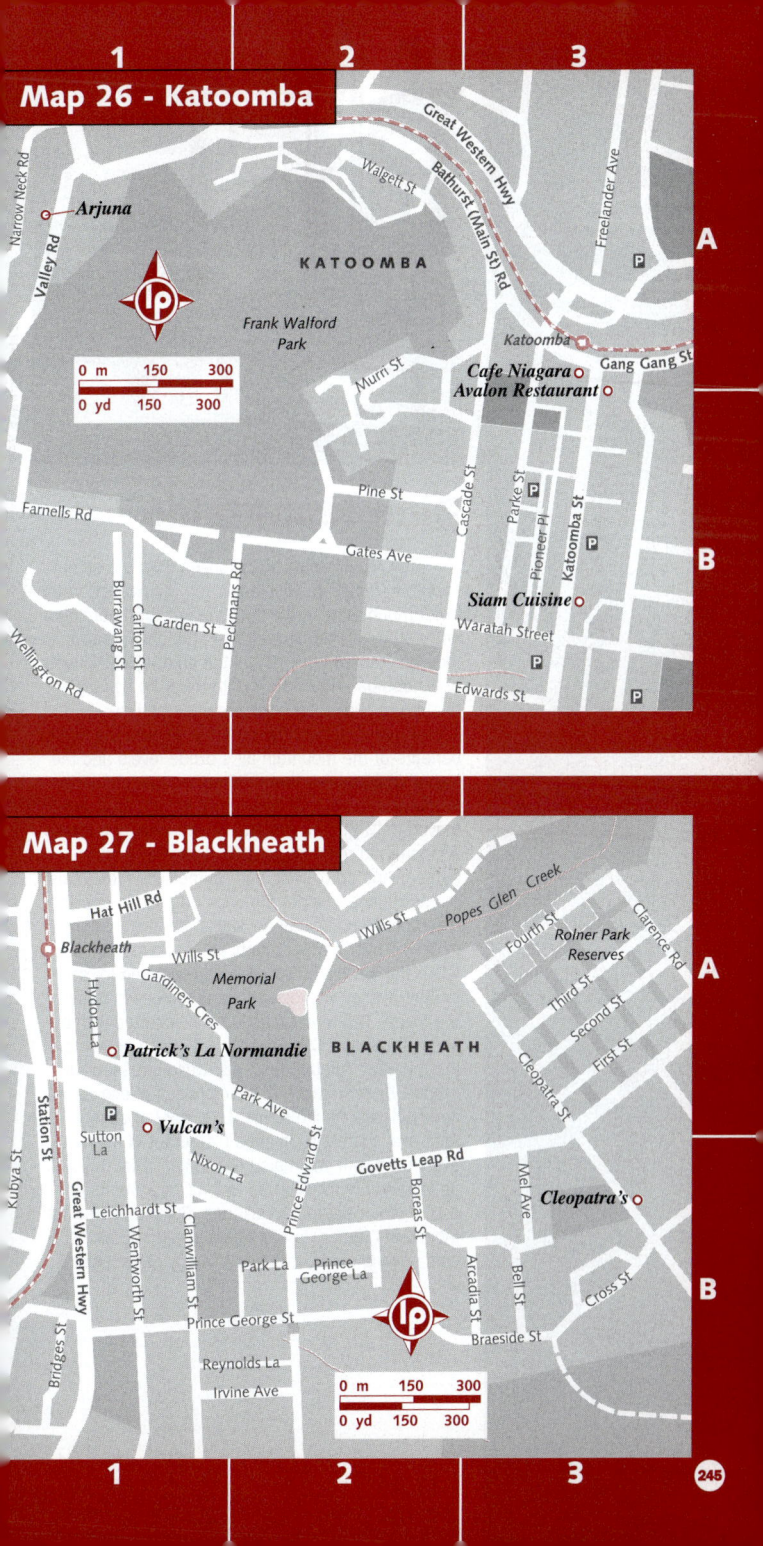

Map 27 - Blackheath

BEST

- **Patrick's La Normandie**
  Superb food served with gracious ease

- **Silk's Brasserie**
  Art Deco dining doesn't get any better

Cafe Niagara (p 249)

Blue Mountains

The Blue Mountains district ranges from the semi-suburban Blaxland, Glenbrook and Springwood in the lower mountains, to the haute resort towns of Leura and Katoomba sitting prettily on the chilly, misty mountaintops. In the 1920s the grand guesthouses of Katoomba and Medlow Bath were the holiday destination of choice for honeymooners and royalty. Tourist pamphlets of the period promoted the health benefits of the mountain air's ozone levels and the 'sybaritical luxuries that awaited the peregrinating tourist traffic'. In later years, the art and craft set moved in, with their potters' wheels, weaving looms and jam and relish recipes. By the 1980s, exponents of the art-of-living had claimed the Mountains as their home (they're the ones dressed in designer dreadlocks and crystal necklaces reading numerology books over bowls of lentil and kumera soup). While the area is now increasingly a home for commuting Sydney workers, rest and recreation is still the focus. The winter solstice is celebrated with a second round of Christmas pudding and presents at the mid-year Yuletide festivals, while stressed-out executives are drawn by the promises of eco-resorts and secluded health farms. Like most of country Australia, there's a Chinese restaurant in nearly every town, but you'll also find Indian, Thai, Swiss, Italian and French food as well as vegan eateries and organic vegetarian bakeries. But the archetypal Mountains' eatery is the carefully restored art deco cafe serving mod Oz as good as any city cousin.

BLACKHEATH

Patrick's La Normandie
French

☎ **4787 6144**
124 Wentworth St

Map 27 A1

Private parking

Verandah tables

It's Sara who these days holds the reins at Patrick's La Normandie, and she holds them with confidence. The nonchalant ease with which she manages this backstreets cottage restaurant is enviable. Here's a place with a chameleon atmosphere (being cosy, businesslike, light-hearted or romantic), a warm, poised and gracious service and consistently excellent food. The scallops with chef's tartare ($12) are succulent, while the goat's cheese in puff pastry with a herbed-tomato coulis ($12) represents Mediterranean French cuisine at its sunniest. Mains are more northern-focused, with dishes like baked duck with caramelised pears ($21) and char-grilled rib eye in a red wine and tarragon sauce ($21) demonstrating a richness permissible only in a cold climate. The homemade raspberry ice cream in a meringue basket ($9) makes a sweet finale. It's a dining experience that could be called impeccable, if that wasn't too studied a word for something that comes so naturally.

Open: Mon-Sat 6.30pm-late; reservations advisable; BYO (no corkage)

starter: $9-$12
main: $21
dessert: $9

AE BC MC V; Eftpos

Vulcan's
Modern Australian

☎ **4787 6899**
33 Govetts Leap Rd

Map 27 A1

No smoking inside

Courtyard tables

Located on the site of the old Blackheath bakery, Vulcan's prides itself on its venerable wood-fired oven – but the food that emerges from it is up-to-date Mod Oz, with strong Asian influences. A starter of firebox squid is flavoured with Sichuan pepper and sits on ribbons of cucumber dressed with mirin and soy. The emphasis is on slow-roasted meats, but again Asian flavours add an extra dimension. Aromatic pot-roasted veal with lemongrass and yellow beans lives up to its name, and the meat melts in the mouth. Make sure you order a copper baking dish of roast potatoes and vegetables ($5), and have a hunk of sourdough bread (50c) on hand to mop up the juices. Even after such robust fare, you'd be mad to resist Philip Searle's famous chequerboard ice cream ($12), with its alternate squares of pineapple and anise ice cream outlined with a black smudge of liquorice.

Open: Fri-Sun noon-3pm, 6pm-11pm; reservations essential; BYO (corkage $2/person)

starter: $13
main: $19
dessert: $9-$12

AE BC DC MC V

KATOOMBA

Map 26 A1
Wheelchair access
Separate smoke-free dining available
Balcony tables

Arjuna
Indian

☎ 4782 4662
16 Valley Rd

Don't judge a book by its cover. Arjuna's purpose-built exterior and outdated interior with ski-chalet style wood panelling belie continuing excellence in the kitchen. The food would rival Sydney's best Indian eateries. Our lamb saag with spinach ($12.90) was tender and tasty and avoided falling into the common trap of being too oily. The creamy sauce on the Goan-style chicken xacuti ($12.50) is a delicate melange of spices, lime rind and coconut with a bit of heat that may catch you by surprise. The naan was perhaps a little doughy, but what it lacked in quality it made up for in quantity – one serve between two was heaps. The super-speedy service makes you want to rush your meal, but it's worth lingering on the outdoor balcony to enjoy the sunset across the Megalong Valley. An added attraction: Arjuna is one of the few places in Katoomba open on a Monday evening.

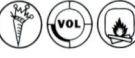

starter: $5-$6.50
main: $6-$15.50
dessert: $3.50-$5
AE BC MC V; Eftpos

Open: Thurs-Mon 6pm-9.30pm; reservations essential; BYO (corkage $1/person)

Map 26 A3
Smoking at the bar only

Avalon Restaurant
Modern Australian

☎ 4782 5532
18 Katoomba St

When the elegantly ramshackle Avalon Cafe burnt down in late 1999, a great loss was suffered by the residents of Katoomba and beyond. Nothing, it was felt, could ever replace the Avalon. But they were wrong. In double-quick time, owners Gayle Pollard and Glenn Puster relocated to Katoomba's old Savoy cinema, en route renaming their venture the Avalon Restaurant. Visually, it's a feast. Below the kitchen, located in the old projectionists' room, cascade four balustraded platforms scattered with Art Deco tables and chairs, standard lamps, mirrors, silver candlesticks, and paintings. The food is a match for the furnishings. The smoked salmon and avocado platter ($13.50) is light and elegant, while the chicken cooked in a macadamia, coconut and lime curry sauce ($17.80) offers a wonderful ensemble of flavours. The baked lime cheesecake ($7.80) is as sweetly tart as you could wish it – a lovely finish to a sensuous dining experience.

starter: $7.50-$13.50
main: $13.90-$18.50
dessert: $5.80-$7.80
AE BC MC V

Open: daily noon-2pm, 6.30pm-9.30pm; reservations essential (Fri-Sun); BYO (corkage $1/person)

KATOOMBA

Cafe Niagara
Modern Australian

☎ **4782 4001**
92 Main St

Well positioned opposite Katoomba railway station, Cafe Niagara is as popular for all-day breakfasts as it is for whiling away a rainy winter's afternoon. It is an Art Deco experience, with its elegant street frontage, slightly subdued interior and pressed metal ceiling. Modern recessed lighting and large, roomy booths don't detract from the old-fashioned ambience. A typical mod Oz cafe menu includes wok-seared Asian vegetables and noodles – predictable but tasty. The addition of pesto, chilli relish and mozzarella to the Niagara burger ($10.90) gave a lift to a standard dish. After a hard morning's bushwalk tuck into comfort desserts/cakes ($5.50) such as slow baked lemon and lime tart or rich fig and brandy cheesecake. Friendly and efficent service makes it a good place for either a quick bite or a more leisurely sitting – especially on Friday nights when the place hosts the best drag show in the Blue Mountains.

Open: Mon-Fri 10am-10pm, Sat & Sun 8am-11pm (breakfast: all day); reservations accepted; BYO (corkage $1.50/person)

Map 26 A3

Entertainment: cabaret and drag show Fri from 7pm

Pavement tables

starter: $5.50-$10.90
main: $11.90-$16.90
dessert: $3.60-$5.50

BC MC V

Siam Cuisine
Thai

☎ **4782 5671**
172 Katoomba St

The Katoomba drizzle has duly arrived on another cold mountain night, and we're half expecting the terracotta pot of rice to arrive with a tea cosy. Without a doubt, the hottest thing in Katoomba is a plate of Siam Cuisine's chicken larb salad ($8). The rough mince comes with coriander and onion and more than a handful of dried chilli. Somewhat milder is the creamy red curry with prawns ($12.50) and the tom kar gai soup that's simultaneously sweet and sour and creamy ($5.50). The dishes go on and on (numbers 1-90) with barbecued and marinated arrangements and a curious-sounding 'boneless duck with cucumber and special sauce' ($9.50). The wood veneer-lined room and plastic floral tablecloths are almost romantic at night – which just goes to show what you can do with tasteful Thai wooden statues and a front window with more fairy light strings than a Mardi Gras float.

Open: Tues-Sun 11.30am-2.30pm, 5.30pm-10pm; reservations advisable (especially weekends); BYO (no corkage)

Map 26 B3

No smoking inside

starter: $4.80-$6.90
main: $8-$15
dessert: $4-$5
Banquet menu $19.20 and $23/person (min 4 people)

BC MC V; Eftpos

BLUE MOUNTAINS

LEURA

Map 25 B5

Silk's Brasserie
Modern Australian

☎ 4784 2534
128 The Mall

Their home-made bread is possibly *the* best we've ever tasted: a sensational nutty flavour with (we're told) a touch of pepper. The rest of the food isn't bad either: a rack of lamb ($25.50), tender and hearty enough to satisfy a hungry post-bushwalk appetite, and roast Peking duck ($27.50) matched well with Asian greens and a spicy marinade. Our eyes strayed to the next table where a voluminous Yorkshire pudding threatened to suffocate a tasty looking fillet of beef ($27.50). The plate of five excellent and perfectly ripe cheeses is a good way to finish off your red wine, although the sweet toothed can seek solace in desserts you can get away with only in the mountains, including sticky date ($10.50) or lemon and lime pudding ($12.50). Despite the often cold mountain air, the wall of glass bricks and the high Art Deco ceiling, the atmosphere is warm and cosy.

starter: $16-$16.50
main: $24-$27.50
dessert: $9-$12.50

AE BC DC MC V

Open: daily noon-3pm, 6pm-9.30pm; reservations essential (Fri-Sun); licensed, no BYO

Back for More

Cleopatra's
118 Cleopatra St, Blackheath ☎ 4787 8456 Map 27 B3
This Blue Mountains guesthouse and regional centre of French cooking flair has changed hands, with Sydney's Damien Pignolet (Bistro Moncur chef) now serving up the set-price, three-course feasts ($80 Fri & Sat, $60 weekdays).

Leura Gourmet
159 The Mall, Leura ☎ 4784 1438 Map 25 B5
The place to pick up chocolates imported from Europe, curry pastes from some of Sydney's best restaurants, locally made quince jams, and passionfruit and lemon butter. If you can get past all this (displayed in the front of the shop), the breakfast views from the dining room look out onto a pretty valley scene.

Il Postino's
13 Station St, Wentworth ☎ 4757 1615 Map 25 A4
Another old post office that's been transformed into a toast office: bacon and eggs and hollandaise accompany the toast, or order one of the fancy melts, affordable pastas and fast focaccias. Nothing's over $11.90, and the original black metal post boxes are filled with info on things to do in the local area.

On the Grapevine

The Australian wine industry is riding the crest of a wave. Export markets can't get enough of our fresh, fruit-driven styles and the noble drop is enjoying unprecedented popularity at home. Australia now boasts more than 1200 wineries, with another one opening up every 94 hours.

Wine drinkers are a fickle lot. During the eighties, chardonnay was so ubiquitous that it spawned its own social phenomenon. But these days the 'chardonnay set' has probably moved onto shiraz, because the white wine boom that began in the mid-seventies fizzled out twenty years later. Since the mid-nineties, wineries have been falling over themselves in the rush to plant shiraz. In 1999, a massive 192,000 tonnes of the grape were crushed and that figure is expected to increase dramatically over the next few years.

Gourmets that we increasingly are, Australians are showing quite an interest in the matching of food and wine. But our current preference for the light, lean flavours of Mediterranean and Asian food doesn't easily gel with our love affair with big red wines like shiraz. Perhaps this explains why a small, but growing band of winemakers are looking beyond the classic French varieties like cabernet sauvignon, shiraz and pinot noir.

Italians have long understood that wine is meant to be drunk with food and must complement rather than overpower or clash with it. In recent years Australian winemakers have begun to produce excellent wines with Italian varieties like sangiovese, nebbiolo and barbera. These grapes make dry, lean, less fruity red wines than those we're used to; wines that pair beautifully with tomato-based pastas and olive oil-based chicken, veal, pork and fish dishes.

Chardonnay faces increased competition from varieties like riesling and semillon, though it still continues as the undisputed prince of white wines. Riesling is proving to be a perfect partner for spicy Thai and fresh, fragrant Vietnamese dishes, as is the aromatic German variety, gewürztraminer.

Another grape variety that's on the way up in Australia is pinot gris. This French variety is being made into a crisp, complex unwooded white wine.

Australian winemakers are increasingly willing to experiment with varieties other than the French classics. All that remains to be done is to convince more wine drinkers that there's a world beyond chardonnay and shiraz.

Carolyn Holbrook

Best Australian Wine

Even at modest price levels Australian wines are world class. In selecting your wine there are two reliable pointers to both quality and style. These are (1) grape variety and (2) the region where the grapes are grown. This table brings the two together but is not exhaustive and generalisations have been made. If a wine list doesn't indicate the region ask the sommelier or read the label before making your decision. Use the table as a guide only and feel free to experiment with other regional/varietal combinations. Cheers!

Grant Van Ev[...]

REGION / VARIETY	Sparkling	Riesling	Sauvignon Blanc	Semillon	Chardonnay	Pinot Noir	Shiraz	Cabernet Sauvignon
New South Wales								
Hunter Valley	*	*	*	***	***	*	***	*
Orange	**	**	**	**	***	**	**	**
Riverina	*	*	*	**	**	*	***	*
Mudgee	*	*	*	**	***	*	***	*
Cowra					*		**	**
Victoria								
Yarra Valley	***	**	**	**	***	***	**	***
Mornington	***	*	**	*	***	***	**	*
Geelong	**	*	**	*	***	***	***	*
Macedon	***	*	**	*	***	***	***	*
Pyrenees	***	*	**	**	**	*	***	***
Rutherglen	*	**	*	*	*	*	***	**
Gippsland	**	*	*	*	***	***	**	**
Grampians	**	***	**	*	**	*	***	***
Bendigo	**	**	**	*	**	*	***	**
Ballarat	**	**	**	*	**	*	***	**
Goulburn Valley	**	**	*	***	**	*	***	**
High Country	***	***	***	*	**	***	**	*
South Australia								
Barossa	*	***	*	**	**	*	***	*
McLaren Vale	**	*	*	*	***	*	***	**
Clare Valley	*	***	**	**	**	*	***	**
Adelaide Hills	***	*	***	**	***	***	**	**
Coonawarra	**	**	**	*	**	*	***	***
Riverland	*	*	*	*	**	*	**	**
Padthaway	**	*	**	*	***	*	**	**
Langhorne Creek	*	**	*	*	**	*	**	**
Western Australia								
Margaret River	**	**	**	**	***	**	**	***
Pemberton	**	***	**	**	***	***	***	**
Great Southern	**	***	**	**	***	***	***	**
Tasmania	***	**	**	*	***	***	*	*

Other Varieties	
Dessert wine (semillon)	
Pinot grigio	
Fortified wine	
Marsanne	
Dessert & fortified wine	
Dessert & fortified wine	
Dessert wine (riesling)	
Dessert wine (riesling)	
Sem./sav.bl blend & dessert wine (semillon)	

Beppi's (p 65)

***	The variety is a speciality of the region. Many of the finest examples of the variety come from the region.
**	While not a classic, this regional/varietal combination has the ability to produce high-quality wines.
*	Usually better to select another combination, but individual producers may provide surprising exceptions to the rule.

BEST AUSTRALIAN WINE 253

Glossary

A

achars: *Indian/Nepalese;* pickled and salted relishes. These can be sweet or sour depending on seasoning. A version of these can also be found in South-East Asian cuisine.

B

barfi: *Indian;* fudge-like Indian sweet made from nuts and condensed milk.

bavette: *Italian;* long pasta strips, like a flattened spaghetti.

bissara: *North African;* a thick soup or dip of fava beans, spiced with harissa, originating in Egypt.

bisteeya: *North African;* an immense pie of thin, flaky pastry filled with spiced pigeon, chicken or fish, lemony eggs, tangy onion sauce and toasted sweetened almonds, baked and then dusted with cinnamon and sugar. Also called bastela or bastilla.

bottarga: *Italian;* salted, pressed and dried roe of tuna or grey mullet.

bresaola: *Italian;* air-dried salted beef originally from Lombardy. Usually served thinly sliced and drizzled with oil.

C

cotechino: *Italian;* a large pork sausage made with both lean and fat meat and lightly spiced with nutmeg and cloves. Originates from the Emilia-Romagna region.

I

involtini: *Italian;* rolled meat usually stuffed with meat and/or vegetables.

izakaya: *Japanese;* Japanese 'pub', serving alcohol such as beer and saki and an extensive list of snacks and small dishes. The atmosphere is usually boisterous and in Japan izakayas are identified by their rustic facades and an outside red lantern.

K

kaftaji: *North African;* a spicy mash, often consisting of pumpkin, fresh coriander, capsicum, chilli and Tunisian spices with an egg.

kimchi: *Korean;* a common Korean accompaniment of spicy, pickled Chinese cabbage which has been fermented in an earthenware pot with chilli, garlic and ginger.

L

larb: *Thai;* salad made with spicy minced meat (pork, poultry or freshwater fish) tossed with lime juice, fish sauce, chillies, fresh mint leaves, spring onion and dry-roasted pulverised rice, originating from the North-East.

M

mole poblano: *Mexican;* a rich, dark sauce traditional to Mexican cuisine. Usually a blend of onion, coriander, garlic, and deseeded poblano chillies and a small amount of bitter chocolate.

momos: *Nepalese;* a dumpling much like dim sum. They are traditionally filled with minced meat but can also be filled with chicken or vegetables and can be either steamed or fried.

mozzarella di bufala: *Italian;* mozzarella (a spun-curd cheese) made from the milk of a water buffalo. Originally all mozzarella was made from buffalo milk but it is now considered a delicacy.

O

okonomiyaki: *Japanese;* known as Japanese pizza or pancake: an egg batter with shredded cabbage, other vegetables, meat and seafood. Coated in a sweet brown sauce and/or mayonnaise and sprinkled with dried seaweed and bonito flakes.

P

ponzu: *Japanese;* a light tangy sauce made with mirin (sweet cooking sake), lemon juice and soy sauce. Used as a dipping sauce with sashimi.

Y

yemista: *Greek;* to stuff, usually with a filling of rice and herbs.

Z

zuppa di fagioli: *Italian;* a thick autumnal soup made with borlotti beans and pasta.

Chinese Cuisine

Cantonese (far south): seafood, stir-fries and sweeter tastes dominate.

Hong Kong (far south): similar to Cantonese in style. Western ingredients such as stewed ox tongue make appearances. Also influenced by Chaozhou cooking, another southern coastal style famous for its seafood.

Beijing (north): wheat is a staple with noodles and steamed dumplings being common. Known for dishes such as Mongolian hotpot (lamb) and Peking Duck served with pancakes.

Sichuan & Hunan (south west): spicy, hot and sour flavours.

Xinjiang (north west): staples include lamb, steamed buns, handmade noodles.

Shandong (north east): fried meat-stuffed dumplings, preserved cabbage, generous use of salt.

Shanghai (south east): lighter than northern fare, but often considered rich and heavy due to a generous use of oil. Favourites include 'xiao long bao' (steamed dumpling) and pork chops with noodles.

Taiwan (island off southern China): simply cooked vegetarian and seafood predominate with diffuse Japanese influence and heavy use of sugar and spice.

Special Order
A Glossary for All Tastes

Devouring a plate of eggs and bacon may not seem to many to require much deliberation but it's a choice shaped by a mosaic of social and cultural considerations. Conscious or unconscious, we are all influenced by religious, health and moral codes when deciding what to eat. Here is a small guide to the most common dietary philosophies or health regimes:

vegetarian: one who does not eat the flesh of animals, including fish and seafood.

lacto-ovo vegetarian: a vegetarian who eats eggs and dairy products.

vegan: a vegetarian who doesn't eat dairy products or eggs and does not buy or use any other animal products, including leather, wool, silk and, often, honey.

macrobiotic: an eating practice which uses wholefoods, locally grown vegetables, pulses, sea vegetables and complex carbohydrates to achieve health and a yin-yang balance. A macrobiotic lifestyle excludes red meat, poultry and dairy products, but allows a small amount of white-meat fish and shellfish.

Pritikin: guidelines for a healthy lifestyle which exclude the intake of most meat, poultry, fish, eggs, processed grains and fat. Created by Nathan Pritikin more than 20 years ago to cure his own heart disease, the diet is used to reduce the effects of health problems such as angina, arthritis, cancers, diabetes and hypertension.

kosher: prepared in accordance with Jewish dietary laws. Animals must be slaughtered by a trained kosher slaughterer, and their flesh must undergo the prescribed koshering processes. Mammals may become kosher if they are cloven hoofed and chew their cud. Kosher poultry is usually limited to chicken, duck, geese and turkey. Shellfish are not kosher, but fish which have fins and scales may be. The combination of dairy products and meat on utensils, in sinks and in the same meal is forbidden. Dairy products are kosher if they come from a kosher animal.

halal: prepared in accordance with Muslim dietary laws. Animals must be slaughtered by a Muslim who cuts the animal's jugular vein, oesophagus and respiratory tract with a stainless-steel knife (which is rinsed after each slaughter). The animal must be dead prior to skinning. Dogs, donkeys, pigs, amphibians, animals with protruding canine teeth, birds of prey and carnivores are not halal. Alcohol and blood are also prohibited.

celiac: a person who suffers from celiac disease, where glutens destroy the villi in the small intestine, which results in the malabsorption of nutrients. Celiacs must maintain a gluten-free diet, abstaining from barley, oats, rye, wheat and products made from these grains. Prohibited products include durum, semolina, spelt, kamut, and grain alcohols such as beer, bourbon, gin and whisky.

lactose intolerance: an inability to digest the lactose (milk sugar) in dairy products, due to insufficient production of lactase, the enzyme which digests lactose. People with lactose intolerance can often tolerate dairy products low in lactose, like butter, margarine, aged cheeses and yoghurt but must reduce their consumption of foods containing high amounts of lactose.

Lonely Planet Offices

Australia
PO Box 617, Hawthorn VIC 3122
☎ 03 9819 1877
fax 03 9819 6459
email: out2eat@lonelyplanet.com.au
talk2us@lonelyplanet.com.au

from Jan 2001:
90 Maribyrnong St, Footscray
Locked Bag 1, Footscray VIC 3011
☎ 03 9689 4666
fax 03 9689 6833

USA
150 Linden St, Oakland,
CA 94607
☎ 510 893 8555
TOLL FREE: 800 275 8555
fax 510 893 8572
email: info@lonelyplanet.com

UK
10a Spring Place,
London NW5 3BH
☎ 020 7428 4800
fax 020 7428 4828
email: go@lonelyplanet.co.uk

France
1 rue du Dahomey,
75011 Paris
☎ 01 55 25 33 00
fax 01 55 25 33 01
email: bip@lonelyplanet.fr

Web
www.lonelyplanet.com
or AOL keyword: lp

Lonely Planet Images
lpi@lonelyplanet.com.au

Thanks

Thanks to all the restaurants who kindly allowed us to take photographs for this edition:

Ash's Table, Asian Kitchen, Beach Road, Beppi's, Bodhi, Café Niagara, Cala Luna, Carmel's by the Sea Cafe, Cine, Enigma 88, Fare Go Gourmet, Jonah's, La Bella Vista, Le Sands Restaurant, Lebanon & Beyond, passionflower, Sejuiced at Bronte Beach, Spanish Tapas, Tanjore, Tum Tum's, Yak & Yeti.

City Products

City Guides offer an in-depth view to over 50 cities around the globe. Featuring the top restaurants, bars and clubs as well as information on accommodation and transport, these guides are suited to long-term and business travellers and anyone who wants to get the most out of a city. They come with reliable, easy-to-use maps, cultural and historical facts and a run-down on attractions, old and new.

For the discerning short-term visitor, **Condensed** guides highlight the best a destination offers in a full-colour pocket-sized format designed for quick access. From top sights and walking tours to opinionated reviews of where to eat, stay, shop and have fun.

CitySync lets travellers use their Palm™ or Visor™ hand-held computers to discover a city's highlights with tips on transport, history, cultural life, major sights and shopping and entertainment options. It can also quickly search and sort hundreds of reviews of hotels, restaurants and attractions and pinpoint the place on scrollable street maps. Go to www.citysync.com for downloads.

Food Guides

For people who live to eat, drink and travel, the **World Food** series explores the culinary culture of various countries. Entertaining and adventurous, each guide is packed with detail on staples and specialities, regional cuisine and local markets, as well as sumptuous recipes, comprehensive culinary dictionaries and lavish photos good enough to eat.

Lonely Planet Online

Lonely Planet's award-winning web site, has insider information on hundreds of destinations complete with interactive maps and relevant links. There's also the latest travel news, 'on the road' reports, guidebook upgrades, travel links, online book sales and a lively traveller's chat area. Go to www.lonelyplanet.com or AOL keyword: lp.

INDEX

RESTAURANT NAME	PAGE NUMBER	Wheelchair access	Business	Outdoor	Breakfast	Easy on the pocket	Children friendly
The Abbey, Glebe ☎ 9660 4792	106		●				●
Abhi's, North Strathfield ☎ 9743 3061	238					●	●
Alio, Redfern ☎ 8394 9368	74	●	●				●
All India Restaurant, Balmain ☎ 9555 8844	97			●		●	
Angkor Wat, Darlinghurst ☎ 9360 5500	58						●
Angler's Rest Hotel, Brooklyn ☎ 9985 7860	185	●	●	●			●
An Restaurant, Bankstown ☎ 9796 7826	232				●	●	
Aqua Luna, Circular Quay East ☎ 9251 0311	24	●	●				●
Arakawa, City ☎ 9229 0191	26	●	●				●
Arena Bar and Bistro, Moore Park ☎ 9361 3930	146	●	●	●			●
Aria, Circular Quay East ☎ 9252 2555	24		●	●			
Arjuna, Katoomba ☎ 4782 4662	248	●		●		●	
Asakusa, Newtown ☎ 9519 8530	116						●
Ash's Table, Manly ☎ 9976 3382	215			●	●	●	●
Asian Kitchen, Moore Park ☎ 9358 4488	147	●		●			
Avalon Restaurant, Katoomba ☎ 4782 5532	248		●				
Ayam Goreng, Kingsford ☎ 9697 0030	171					●	
Azteca's Mexican Restaurant, Randwick ☎ 9398 1020	173						●
Azuma, Crows Nest ☎ 9436 4066	190		●				
Bacchus, Cronulla ☎ 9544 3883	167	●			●		●
Balkan Seafood Restaurant, Darlinghurst ☎ 9331 7670	58						●
Balmain Stars at Gigis, Balmain ☎ 9818 2170	97			●			
Bambini Cafe Bar, City ☎ 9264 9550	26		●		●		
Bambini Trust Cafe, City ☎ 9283 7098	27		●		●		
Banc, City ☎ 9233 5300	27		●				●
THE barKING FROG, Manly ☎ 9977 6307	215		●	●	●		
Barzura, Coogee ☎ 9665 5546	167			●	●		●

INDEX

RESTAURANT NAME	PAGE NUMBER	Wheelchair access	Business	Outdoor	Breakfast	Easy on the pocket	Children friendly
The Bathers' Pavilion Café, Balmoral ☎ 9969 5050	182	●	●		●		●
Bayswater Brasserie, Kings Cross ☎ 9357 2177	69		●	●			●
Bay Tinh, Marrickville ☎ 9560 8673	115					●	●
BBQ King, City ☎ 9267 2586	29						●
Beach House, Whale Beach ☎ 9974 2727	223		●		●		●
Beach Road, Palm Beach ☎ 9974 1159	221		●	●			●
bel mondo, The Rocks ☎ 9241 3700	47		●	●			
Ben Da Vietnamese Restaurant, Auburn ☎ 9649 5657	232		●			●	●
Bennelong, Circular Quay ☎ 9250 7548	23		●				●
Beppi's, East Sydney ☎ 9360 4558	65		●				
Berowra Waters Tea House, Berowra Waters ☎ 9456 1454	184	●	●	●	●		
Big Mama, Woollahra ☎ 9328 7629	156			●			●
bills, Darlinghurst ☎ 9360 9631	59				●	●	●
Billy Kwong, Surry Hills ☎ 9332 3300	76		●				
Bistro Moncur, Woollahra ☎ 9363 2519	157		●	●			●
blackbird, Cockle Bay ☎ 9283 7385	39	●	●	●	●	●	●
The Boathouse on Blackwattle Bay, Glebe ☎ 9518 9011	106	●	●				●
Bocca, Bondi Beach ☎ 9130 8611	133		●	●			●
Bodhi, Haymarket ☎ 9212 2828	41					●	●
bonne femme, East Sydney ☎ 9331 4455	66		●				
Boulders at The Rocks, The Rocks ☎ 9241 1447	48		●		●		
Brazil, Manly ☎ 9977 3825	216		●	●	●		
Buon Ricordo, Paddington ☎ 9360 6729	150		●				●
Café Barzu, Leichhardt ☎ 9550 0144	110			●			●
Cafe Niagara, Katoomba ☎ 4782 4001	249			●	●	●	
Café Pacifico, East Sydney ☎ 9360 3811	66						●
Cafe Sydney, Circular Quay ☎ 9251 8683	23	●	●	●			●

INDEX

RESTAURANT NAME	PAGE NUMBER	Wheelchair access	Business	Outdoor	Breakfast	Easy on the pocket	Children friendly
Cafe Tunis, Manly ☎ 9976 2805	216		●	●	●		●
Caffeine, Erskineville ☎ 9516 4207	105			●	●	●	●
Cala Luna, Mosman ☎ 9968 2426	196	●		●			●
Camperdown Canteen, Camperdown ☎ 9557 4106	100			●	●	●	●
Carmel's by the Sea Cafe, Palm Beach ☎ 9974 4374	222			●	●	●	
Carne Station, Parramatta ☎ 9633 5788	238	●				●	●
Catalina Rose Bay, Rose Bay ☎ 9371 0555	155		●	●			
Ceruti's Bistro Italiano, Manly ☎ 9977 7600	217		●	●			●
Chatswood BBQ Kitchen, Chatswood ☎ 9419 6532	186					●	●
Chicane, Darlinghurst ☎ 9380 2121	59	●	●	●			●
Chilli Lime Too, Cremorne ☎ 9909 0882	187					●	
Chinese Noodle Restaurant, Haymarket ☎ 9281 9051	41					●	●
Chinta Ria...The Temple of Love, Cockle Bay ☎ 9264 3211	40	●	●	●			
Cicada, Potts Point ☎ 9358 1255	73		●				
Cine, Moore Park ☎ 9332 1409	150	●		●			●
Cinque, Newtown ☎ 9519 3077	117	●			●	●	
Clareville Kiosk, Clareville ☎ 9918 2727	211			●			●
Clock Hotel, Surry Hills ☎ 9331 5333	76			●			●
Clonny's on the Beach, Clontarf ☎ 9948 2373	187		●				●
Cloudstreet, Kirribilli ☎ 9922 1512	194	●					●
the clove, Darlinghurst ☎ 9361 0980	60					●	●
Coonanbarra Cafe, Wahroonga ☎ 9489 0980	204		●	●	●		●
Corinthian Rotisserie Restaurant, Marrickville ☎ 9569 7084	115					●	●
Cortë, Brighton-Le-Sands ☎ 9597 3300	164	●		●			●
Cossie's Cafe-Restaurant, Surry Hills ☎ 9699 8482	77			●	●		●
Cottage Point Inn, Cottage Point ☎ 9456 1011	212			●			●
Crave, Bellevue Hill ☎ 9327 1670	133			●	●	●	

INDEX

RESTAURANT NAME	PAGE NUMBER	Wheelchair access	Business	Outdoor	Breakfast	Easy on the pocket	Children friendly
Danish Deli, Marrickville ☎ 9572 7988	116				●	●	●
Dante, Leichhardt ☎ 9550 0062	111	●	●	●			●
de beers Whale Beach, Whale Beach ☎ 9974 4009	225	●	●	●	●		●
DIG, Bondi Beach ☎ 9365 6044	134		●	●	●		●
Domo, Neutral Bay ☎ 9909 3100	198						
Ecco, Drummoyne ☎ 9719 9394	101		●				●
Edna's Table, City ☎ 9267 3933	29		●				●
Eleni's, East Sydney ☎ 9331 5306	67		●				
Elio, Leichhardt ☎ 9560 9129	111		●	●			
Emilia's Vegetarian Restaurant, North Curl Curl ☎ 9939 1317	220			●		●	●
Enigma 88, Brighton Le Sands ☎ 9556 3611	164		●				
Erciyes Restaurant, Redfern ☎ 9319 1309	75					●	●
Fare Go Gourmet, North Sydney ☎ 9922 2965	201		●				
Fat Duck, Paddington ☎ 9380 9838	151		●	●	●	●	
Fergusons, Mosman ☎ 9960 8233	196	●	●		●		●
Fiderio, Parramatta ☎ 9687 3077	240		●	●	●		●
Fifi's Cafe, Enmore ☎ 9550 4665	102					●	●
fishbone sushi bar & restaurant, Avalon Beach ☎ 9973 2688	211		●	●		●	●
Food for Thought, Collaroy ☎ 9971 2152	212			●	●		●
Forty One, City ☎ 9221 2500	30	●	●				●
Fresh at Manly, Manly ☎ 9977 7705	218			●	●	●	●
Freshwater Restaurant, Harbord ☎ 9938 5575	213		●				●
fuel, Surry Hills ☎ 9383 9388	77		●	●	●		
fu-manchu, Bondi ☎ 9300 0416	134			●		●	
Furusato, Pyrmont ☎ 9660 0477	45		●	●			●
Gelbison, Bondi ☎ 9130 4042	136			●		●	●
Golden Kingdom Beijing House Restaurant, Kensington ☎ 9662 1616/9662 1122	170		●				●

INDEX

RESTAURANT NAME	PAGE NUMBER	Wheelchair access	Business	Outdoor	Breakfast	Easy on the pocket	Children friendly
Grand National, Paddington ☎ 9363 4557	151	●	●				●
grand pacific blue room, Paddington ☎ 9331 7108	152						
Grand Taverna, City ☎ 9267 3608	30			●			
Grape Garden, Willoughby ☎ 9967 2001	205		●			●	●
Grappa, Leichhardt ☎ 9560 6090	113	●	●	●			●
Great Wall, Ashfield ☎ 9798 6930	95					●	
Hannibal, Bondi ☎ 9130 4605	136					●	
hickson one, Walsh Bay ☎ 8298 9912	51	●	●	●			
Himal, Crows Nest ☎ 9460 9058	190		●			●	
Hot Gossip Cafe, Paddington ☎ 9332 4358	152		●	●	●	●	
Hyde Park Barracks Cafe, City ☎ 9223 1155	31	●	●	●	●		●
Il Piavé, Rozelle ☎ 9810 6204	124	●	●				●
Indochine, Bondi ☎ 9387 4081	137			●		●	
Inside, City ☎ 9241 1978	31		●		●		
International Restaurant & Bar, Kings Cross ☎ 9360 9080	69		●				
intra Thai, Bondi Beach ☎ 9130 3324	137					●	●
Isaribi, Elizabeth Bay ☎ 9358 2125	68						●
Isshin, North Sydney ☎ 9922 4370	202		●	●		●	
Istana Restaurant, Thornleigh ☎ 9481 8855	204		●			●	●
Jonah's, Palm Beach ☎ 9974 5599	223		●	●			●
J.P. Bastiani, City ☎ 9238 7088	32	●	●		●		
Ju Ju, Kings Cross ☎ 9357 7100	72					●	
Just Hooked, Neutral Bay ☎ 9904 0428	198						●
Kaiser Stub'n, Terrey Hills ☎ 9450 0300	203						
Kamari Greek Taverna Café, Brighton Le Sands ☎ 9556 2533	166						●
Kam Fook Shark's Fin Restaurant, Haymarket ☎ 9211 8388	42		●		●		●
Kazbah on Darling, Balmain ☎ 9555 7067	99		●	●			

INDEX

RESTAURANT NAME	PAGE NUMBER	Wheelchair access	Business	Outdoor	Breakfast	Easy on the pocket	Children friendly
Kilimanjaro, Newtown ☎ 9557 4565	117					●	
Kintaro, Neutral Bay ☎ 9904 5188	199		●				●
kök, Enmore ☎ 9519 0555	104	●	●				●
Kokum, Pyrmont ☎ 9566 1311	45		●	●			●
La Bella Vista, Parramatta ☎ 9633 3718	241		●	●			●
La Disfida, Haberfield ☎ 9798 8299	110					●	
Lam's Seafood Restaurant, City ☎ 9281 2881	33		●				●
La Persia, Surry Hills ☎ 9698 4355	79			●		●	
La Roche, Lakemba ☎ 9759 9257	237				●	●	●
Laundro.Net.Cafe, Bondi Beach ☎ 9365 1211	138				●	●	
Lebanon and Beyond, Randwick ☎ 9326 5347	173			●		●	●
Lillipilli on King, Newtown ☎ 9516 2499	120	●	●				●
Longrain, Surry Hills ☎ 9280 2888	79	●	●				●
Lord Nelson Brewery Hotel (Bistro), The Rocks ☎ 9251 4044	48	●				●	
Lucio's, Paddington ☎ 9380 5996	153		●				
Lou Jack's, Newtown ☎ 9557 7147	120			●	●	●	●
Lunch, Castlecrag ☎ 9958 8441	186		●	●	●		
Macro Wholefoods Cafe, Bondi Junction ☎ 9389 7611	143			●	●	●	
Malabar, Crows Nest ☎ 9906 7343	191		●			●	●
Malaya Restaurant North Sydney, North Sydney ☎ 9955 4306/9957 3775	202	●	●			●	●
Marque, Surry Hills ☎ 9332 2225	80		●				●
Martini, Leichhardt ☎ 9568 3344	113	●	●	●			
Masthai Seafood Restaurant, Beverly Hills ☎ 9580 5609	234						●
Masuya, Pyrmont ☎ 9566 2866	46			●		●	
Matsuri, Surry Hills ☎ 9690 1336	80						
Maya Sweets Centre, Surry Hills ☎ 9699 8663	81					●	●

INDEX

RESTAURANT NAME	PAGE NUMBER	Wheelchair access	Business	Outdoor	Breakfast	Easy on the pocket	Children friendly
MCA Cafe, The Rocks ☎ 9241 4253	49	●	●	●	●		●
Mezzaluna, Potts Point ☎ 9357 1988	73		●	●			●
MG Garage, Surry Hills ☎ 9383 9383	81	●	●				
Minh, Dulwich Hill ☎ 9560 0465	102					●	●
Mio, Newtown ☎/fax 9519 5328	121		●				●
MoS Cafe, City ☎ 9241 3636	33		●	●	●		●
The Mosquito Bar, Mosman ☎ 9968 1801	197	●	●			●	
Mother Chu's Vegetarian Kitchen, City ☎ 9283 2828	34					●	
Mykonos on Crown, Darlinghurst ☎ 9368 7900	61			●	●		●
Nemra's, Bankstown ☎ 9793 7247	233						●
The Nepalese Kitchen, Surry Hills ☎ 9319 4264	83			●		●	●
New Orient Take Away, Randwick ☎ 9398 6929	174					●	
Newsbar, City ☎ 9238 9460	34	●	●		●		●
Nielsen Park Kiosk, Vaucluse ☎ 9337 1574	156		●	●	●		●
North China Restaurant, Neutral Bay ☎ 9909 2438	199		●			●	
The One That Got Away, Bondi ☎ 9389 4227	139					●	●
Original Ploy Thai, Bondi Beach ☎ 9369 3949	139					●	●
Orso Bayside Restaurant, Mosman ☎ 9968 3555	197		●				●
Otto Ristorante Italiano, Woolloomooloo ☎ 9368 7488	85	●	●	●			
Out of Africa, Manly ☎ 9977 0055	218		●	●			●
Paramount, Potts Point ☎ 9358 1652	74		●				
passionflower, Haymarket ☎ 9281 8322	42	●					●
Patrick's La Normandie, Blackheath ☎ 4787 6144	247		●	●			●
Pavilion on the Park, City ☎ 9232 1322	36	●	●	●			●
Phatboys, Darlinghurst ☎ 9332 3284	61			●			
Pho Ga Tau Bay, Cabramatta ☎ 9724 7162	234				●	●	
Pier Restaurant, Rose Bay ☎ 9327 6561	155		●	●			

INDEX

RESTAURANT NAME	PAGE NUMBER	Wheelchair access	Business	Outdoor	Breakfast	Easy on the pocket	Children friendly
The Pig & The Olive, Cremorne ☎ 9953 7512	189						●
Pino's Pizzeria, Crows Nest ☎ 9439 2081	191		●	●			●
Point of View, Bondi Beach ☎ 9365 5166	140		●	●			
Pompei's, Bondi Beach ☎ 9365 1233	140			●		●	●
The Pool Caffé, Maroubra ☎ 9314 0364	172			●	●		●
Portofino, Leichhardt ☎ 9550 0782	114		●	●			●
Post, City ☎ 9229 7744	36	●	●				●
Prasit's Northside on Crown, Surry Hills ☎ 9319 0748	83		●				
Pruniers, Woollahra ☎ 9363 1974	157		●	●			●
Raw Bar, Bondi ☎ 9365 7200	142		●	●			●
Red Chilli, Double Bay ☎ 9328 2558	146					●	●
Restaurant CBD, City ☎ 9299 8911	37		●				
Restaurant Dish, Crows Nest ☎ 9906 2275	192		●	●			
The Restaurant on Berowra Waters, Berowra Waters ☎ 9456 1027	184		●		●		●
Restaurant Portugal, Petersham ☎ 9564 1163	124						●
Riverside Brooklyn Restaurant, Brooklyn ☎ 9985 7248	185		●	●		●	●
Riverview Hotel Dining Room, Balmain ☎ 9555 9899	99		●				
Rockpool, The Rocks ☎ 9252 1888	49		●				●
The Rose Hotel, Chippendale ☎ 9318 1133	101			●			
Rozelle Fish Bowl, Rozelle ☎ 9555 7302	125			●			●
Safari, Newtown ☎ 9557 4458	121					●	●
Sailors Thai, The Rocks ☎ 9251 2466	50		●	●			
Sailors Thai Canteen, The Rocks ☎ 9251 2466	50			●			●
Salt, Darlinghurst ☎ 9332 2566	64	●	●				
Savion, Bondi ☎ 9130 6357	142			●		●	●
Scoozi Trattoria, Westleigh ☎ 9484 5165	205		●	●		●	●
Sean's Panorama, Bondi ☎ 9365 4924	143			●			

INDEX

RESTAURANT NAME	PAGE NUMBER	Wheelchair access	Business	Outdoor	Breakfast	Easy on the pocket	Children friendly
Se Joung Restaurant, Campsie ☎ 9718 4039	236						●
Sejuiced at Bronte Beach, Bronte ☎ 9389 9538	144			●	●	●	
Shimbashi Soba on the Sea, Woolloomooloo ☎ 9357 7763	85		●	●			
Siam Cuisine, Katoomba ☎ 4782 5671	249					●	●
Silk's Brasserie, Leura ☎ 4784 2534	250		●				●
Silver Spring, Haymarket ☎ 9211 2232	44	●	●			●	●
Slip Inn, City ☎ 9299 1700	37	●		●			
Soleil, Narrabeen ☎ 9970 7349	220						
Spanish Tapas, Glebe ☎ 9571 9005	107						●
Stella Blu Cafe, Dee Why ☎ 9982 7931	213		●	●	●	●	
Steps, Hornsby ☎ 9482 7364	193		●				●
Stir Crazy Thai, Kirribilli ☎ 9922 6620	194					●	
The Summit, City ☎ 9247 9777	38	●	●				●
Surjit's Indian Restaurant, Annandale ☎ 9569 8884, 9564 6600	95					●	●
Sushi Suma, Redfern ☎ 9698 8873	75					●	●
Swiss Hut, Maroubra ☎ 9344 7755	172	●					
Tabou, Surry Hills ☎ 9319 5682	84		●				●
Tandoori Corner, St Marys ☎ 9833 2590	241					●	●
Tandoori Hut, Enmore ☎ 9519 8140	104					●	●
Tanjore, Glebe ☎ 9660 6332	107						●
Taqsim, Paddington ☎ 9361 6001	154			●			
Tarifa, Bronte ☎ 9386 9456	145			●	●	●	●
Tea Inn, Kingsford ☎ 9697 2789	171					●	
Teascapes, Randwick ☎ 9398 7994	175						
Tetsuya's, City ☎ 9267 2900	38		●				
Thai FireFry, Randwick ☎ 9326 4203	175			●		●	●
Thai I-San Classic, Eastlakes ☎ 9693 5046	169					●	●

INDEX

RESTAURANT NAME	PAGE NUMBER	Wheelchair access	Business	Outdoor	Breakfast	Easy on the pocket	Children friendly
Thai On Wok, Glebe ☎ 9660 9011	108					●	
Thai Pothong, Newtown ☎ 9550 6277	122		●				●
Thanh Binh, Cabramatta ☎ 9727 9729	236				●	●	●
Thelma & Louise, Neutral Bay ☎ 9953 7754	201		●	●	●		●
Thomas Street, McMahons Point ☎ 9955 4703	195		●	●	●		●
Trovata, East Sydney ☎ 9361 4437	67		●	●	●		
Tuk Tuk Real Thai, Balmain ☎ 9555 5899	100			●			
Tum Tum's, Darlinghurst ☎ 9331 5390	64					●	
Uchi Lounge, Surry Hills ☎ 9261 3524	84		●			●	
Unkai, The Rocks ☎ 9250 6123	51	●	●		●		●
Uno 53, Leichhardt ☎ 9572 8992	114	●		●			●
Vera Cruz Restaurant & Bar, Cremorne ☎ 9904 5818	189						
Vinyl Lounge, Elizabeth Bay ☎ 9326 9224	68			●	●	●	●
Vulcan's, Blackheath ☎ 4787 6899	247			●			
Watermark, Balmoral Beach ☎ 9968 3433	182	●	●	●	●		●
Wedgetail, Newtown ☎ 9516 1568	123			●			●
Welcome Hotel, Rozelle ☎ 9810 1323	125		●	●			
Well Connected Café, Glebe ☎ 9566 2655	109			●	●	●	
Wet Paint Cafe, Bronte ☎ 9369 4634	145						
Wine Banc, City ☎ 9233 5399	39		●				
Wrapido, Crows Nest ☎ 9438 4946	192			●	●	●	
Xic Lo, Haymarket ☎ 9280 1678	44					●	●
Yak & Yeti, Glebe ☎ 9552 1220	109						
Ying's Seafood Restaurant, Crows Nest ☎ 9966 9182	193		●			●	
Yoshii, Pyrmont ☎ 9211 6866	46		●				
Yuan's BBQ, Campsie ☎ 9787 9896	237					●	●
Yuan's Family Restaurant, Ashfield ☎ 9789 9411	96				●	●	●

INDEX

RESTAURANT NAME	PAGE NUMBER	Wheelchair access	Business	Outdoor	Breakfast	Easy on the pocket	Children friendly
Zaaffran, Darling Harbour ☎ 9211 8900	40		●	●			●
Zagloba, Ashfield ☎ 9716 9119	96					●	●
Zimi, Newtown ☎ 9519 4044	123	●					●

INDEX

By Cuisine

African

Kilimanjaro Newtown	117

Asian

Chilli Lime Too Cremorne	187

Austrian

Kaiser Stub'n Terrey Hills	203

Cafe fare

Carmel's by the Sea Cafe Palm Beach	222
Food for Thought Collaroy	212
Fresh at Manly Manly	218
Teascapes Randwick	175
Well Connected Café Glebe	109
Wrapido Crows Nest	192

Cambodian

Angkor Wat Darlinghurst	58

Cantonese

Kam Fook Shark's Fin Restaurant Haymarket	42
Masthai Seafood Restaurant Beverly Hills	234
Silver Spring Haymarket	44

Chinese

Asian Kitchen Moore Park	147
BBQ King City	29
Billy Kwong Surry Hills	76
Chatswood BBQ Kitchen Chatswood	186
Chinese Noodle Restaurant Haymarket	41
fu-manchu Bondi	134
Golden Kingdom Beijing House Restaurant Kensington	170
Grape Garden Willoughby	205
Great Wall Ashfield	95
Istana Restaurant Thornleigh	204
Lam's Seafood Restaurant City	33
Malaya Restaurant North Sydney North Sydney	202
North China Restaurant Neutral Bay	199
Ying's Seafood Restaurant Crows Nest	193
Yuan's BBQ Campsie	237
Yuan's Family Restaurant (Yuan Zhong Yuan) Ashfield	96

Chinese vegan

Bodhi Haymarket	41
Mother Chu's Vegetarian Kitchen City	34

Danish

Danish Deli Marrickville	116

Egyptian

Taqsim Paddington	154

European/Modern European

Chicane Darlinghurst	59
Pruniers Woollahra	157
Riverview Hotel Dining Room Balmain	99

French/Modern French

Banc City	27
Bistro Moncur Woollahra	157
bonne femme East Sydney	66
Marque Surry Hills	80
Patrick's La Normandie Blackheath	247
Restaurant Dish Crows Nest	192
Swiss Hut Maroubra	172
Tabou Surry Hills	84
Tetsuya's City	38
Vinyl Lounge Elizabeth Bay	68
Wine Banc City	39

Greek/Modern Greek

Corinthian Rotisserie Restaurant Marrickville	115
Eleni's East Sydney	67
Enigma 88 Brighton Le Sands	164
Kamari Greek Taverna Café Brighton Le Sands	166
Lou Jack's Newtown	120
Mykonos on Crown Darlinghurst	61

Indian

Abhi's North Strathfield	238
All India Restaurant Balmain	97
Arjuna Katoomba	248
the clove Darlinghurst	60
Kokum Pyrmont	45
Malabar Crows Nest	191
Maya Sweets Centre Surry Hills	81
Surjit's Indian Restaurant Annandale	95
Tandoori Corner St Marys	241
Tandoori Hut Enmore	104
Tanjore Glebe	107
Zaaffran Darling Harbour	40

INDEX

By Cuisine

Indonesian

Ayam Goreng Kingsford	171
New Orient Take Away Randwick	174
Safari Newtown	121

International

Berowra Waters Tea House Berowra Waters	184
Cafe Sydney Circular Quay	23
Laundro.Net.Cafe Bondi Beach	138
Soleil Narrabeen	220

Iranian

La Persia Surry Hills	79

Italian/Modern Italian

The Abbey Glebe	106
Alio Redfern	74
Aqua Luna Circular Quay East	24
Bacchus Cronulla	167
Balmain Stars at Gigis Balmain	97
Bambini Cafe Bar City	26
Bambini Trust Cafe City	27
The Bathers' Pavilion Café Balmoral	182
bel mondo The Rocks	47
Beppi's East Sydney	65
Big Mama Woollahra	156
Buon Ricordo Paddington	150
Café Barzu Leichhardt	110
Cala Luna Mosman	196
Ceruti's Bistro Italiano Manly	217
Cine Moore Park	150
Dante Leichhardt	111
Ecco Drummoyne	101
Elio Leichhardt	111
Fiderio Parramatta	240
Gelbison Bondi	136
Grappa Leichhardt	113
Il Piavé Rozelle	124
La Bella Vista Parramatta	241
La Disfida Haberfield	110
Lucio's Paddington	153
Martini Leichhardt	113
Mezzaluna Potts Point	73
Newsbar City	34
Nielsen Park Kiosk Vaucluse	156
Orso Bayside Restaurant Mosman	197
Otto Ristorante Italiano Woolloomooloo	85
The Pig & The Olive Cremorne	189
Pino's Pizzeria Crows Nest	191
Pompei's Bondi Beach	140
Portofino Leichhardt	114
Scoozi Trattoria Westleigh	205
Slip Inn City	37
Stella Blu Cafe Dee Why	213
Trovata East Sydney	67
Wedgetail Newtown	123
Zimi Newtown	123

Japanese/Modern Japanese

Arakawa City	26
Asakusa Newtown	116
Azuma Crows Nest	190
Domo Neutral Bay	198
Furusato Pyrmont	45
Isaribi Elizabeth Bay	68
Isshin North Sydney	202
Ju Ju Kings Cross	72
Kintaro Neutral Bay	199
Masuya Pyrmont	46
Matsuri Surry Hills	80
Raw Bar Bondi	142
Shimbashi Soba on the Sea Woolloomooloo	85
Sushi Suma Redfern	75
Tetsuya's City	38
Uchi Lounge Surry Hills	84
Unkai The Rocks	51
Yoshii Pyrmont	46

Korean

Carne Station Parramatta	238
Se Joung Restaurant Campsie	236

Kosher

Savion Bondi	142

Lebanese

Fifi's Cafe Enmore	102
Hannibal Bondi	136
La Roche Lakemba	237
Lebanon and Beyond Randwick	173

Nemra's Bankstown	233	

Malaysian

Chinta Ria... The Temple of Love Cockle Bay	40
Istana Restaurant Thornleigh	204
Malaya Restaurant North Sydney North Sydney	202

Mediterranean

Barzura Coogee	167
Cafe Tunis Manly	216
Caffeine Erskineville	105
J.P. Bastiani City	32
MG Garage Surry Hills	81
Mio Newtown	121
The Pool Caffé Maroubra	172
Trovata East Sydney	67
Uno 53 Leichhardt	114

Mexican

Azteca's Mexican Restaurant Randwick	173
Café Pacifico East Sydney	66
Vera Cruz Restaurant & Bar Cremorne	189

Middle Eastern

Erciyes Restaurant Redfern	75
Fifi's Cafe Enmore	102
Hannibal Bondi	136
Kazbah on Darling Balmain	99
La Persia Surry Hills	79
La Roche Lakemba	237
Lebanon and Beyond Randwick	173

Nemra's Bankstown	233
Taqsim Paddington	154

Modern American/ Southern American

Fare Go Gourmet North Sydney	201

Modern Australian

Arena Bar and Bistro Moore Park	146
Aria Circular Quay East	24
Ash's Table Manly	215
Avalon Restaurant Katoomba	248
Bambini Cafe Bar City	26
THE barKING FROG Manly	215
Barzura Coogee	167
The Bathers' Pavilion Café Balmoral	182
Bayswater Brasserie Kings Cross	69
Beach House Whale Beach	223
Beach Road Palm Beach	221
Bennelong Circular Quay	23
bills Darlinghurst	59
blackbird Cockle Bay	39
The Boathouse on Blackwattle Bay Glebe	106
Bocca Bondi Beach	133
Boulders at The Rocks The Rocks	48
Brazil Manly	216
Café Barzu Leichhardt	110
Cafe Niagara Katoomba	249
Camperdown Canteen Camperdown	100
Catalina Rose Bay Rose Bay	155
Cicada Potts Point	73

Cinque Newtown	117
Clareville Kiosk Clareville	211
Clock Hotel Surry Hills	76
Clonny's on the Beach Clontarf	187
Cloudstreet Kirribilli	194
Coonanbarra Cafe Wahroonga	204
Cortë Brighton-Le-Sands	164
Cossie's Cafe-Restaurant Surry Hills	77
Cottage Point Inn Cottage Point	212
Crave Bellevue Hill	133
de beers Whale Beach Whale Beach	225
DIG Bondi Beach	134
Edna's Table City	29
Fat Duck Paddington	151
Fergusons Mosman	196
fishbone sushi bar & restaurant Avalon Beach	211
Forty One City	30
Freshwater Restaurant Harbord	213
fuel Surry Hills	77
Grand National Paddington	151
grand pacific blue room Paddington	152
hickson one Walsh Bay	51
Hot Gossip Cafe Paddington	152
Hyde Park Barracks Cafe City	31
Inside City	31
International Restaurant & Bar Kings Cross	69

INDEX BY CUISINE (271)

INDEX

By Cuisine

Modern Australian cont

Jonah's Palm Beach	223
Kazbah on Darling Balmain	99
kök Enmore	104
Lord Nelson Brewery Hotel (Bistro) The Rocks	48
Lunch Castlecrag	186
Macro Wholefoods Cafe Bondi Junction	143
MCA Cafe The Rocks	49
MG Garage Surry Hills	81
MoS Cafe City	33
Paramount Potts Point	74
Pavilion on the Park City	36
Pier Restaurant Rose Bay	155
The Pig & The Olive Cremorne	189
Point of View Bondi Beach	140
The Pool Caffé Maroubra	172
Post City	36
Restaurant CBD City	37
Restaurant Dish Crows Nest	192
The Restaurant on Berowra Waters Berowra Waters	184
Riverside Brooklyn Restaurant Brooklyn	185
Rockpool The Rocks	49
The Rose Hotel Chippendale	101
Rozelle Fish Bowl Rozelle	125
Salt Darlinghurst	64
Sean's Panaroma Bondi	143
Sejuiced at Bronte Beach Bronte	144
Silk's Brasserie Leura	250
Stella Blu Cafe Dee Why	213
Steps Hornsby	193
The Summit City	38
Tarifa Bronte	145
Thelma & Louise Neutral Bay	201
Thomas Street McMahons Point	195
Vinyl Lounge Elizabeth Bay	68
Vulcan's Blackheath	247
Watermark Balmoral Beach	182
Welcome Hotel Rozelle	125
Wet Paint Cafe Bronte	145
Zimi Newtown	123

Modern Australian desserts

passionflower Haymarket	42

Moroccan

The Mosquito Bar Mosman	197

Native Australian

Lillipilli on King Newtown	120

Nepalese

Himal Crows Nest	190
The Nepalese Kitchen Surry Hills	83
Yak & Yeti Glebe	109

New York Deli

Crave Bellevue Hill	133

North African

Cafe Tunis Manly	216
The Mosquito Bar Mosman	197
Out of Africa Manly	218

Pakistani

Tandoori Hut Enmore	104

Polish

Zagloba Ashfield	96

Portuguese

Restaurant Portugal Petersham	124

Seafood

Angler's Rest Hotel Brooklyn	185
Balkan Seafood Restaurant Darlinghurst	58
Beach House Whale Beach	223
The Boathouse on Blackwattle Bay Glebe	106
Clonny's on the Beach Clontarf	187
fishbone sushi bar & restaurant Avalon Beach	211
Just Hooked Neutral Bay	198
MCA Cafe The Rocks	49
The One That Got Away Bondi	139
Orso Bayside Restaurant Mosman	197
Pier Restaurant Rose Bay	155
Rozelle Fish Bowl Rozelle	125

Spanish

Grand Taverna City	30
Spanish Tapas Glebe	107

Swiss

Swiss Hut Maroubra	172

Taiwanese

Tea Inn Kingsford	171

Thai

Food for Thought Collaroy	212
intra Thai Bondi Beach	137
Longrain Surry Hills	79
Original Ploy Thai Bondi Beach	139
Phatboys Darlinghurst	61
Prasit's Northside on Crown Surry Hills	83
Red Chilli Double Bay	146
Sailors Thai The Rocks	50
Sailors Thai Canteen The Rocks	50
Siam Cuisine Katoomba	249
Stir Crazy Thai Kirribilli	194
Thai FireFry Randwick	175
Thai I-San Classic Eastlakes	169
Thai On Wok Glebe	108
Thai Pothong Newtown	122
Tuk Tuk Real Thai Balmain	100
Tum Tum's Darlinghurst	64

Turkish

Erciyes Restaurant Redfern	75

Vegetarian

Bodhi Haymarket	41
Emilia's Vegetarian Restaurant North Curl Curl	220
Macro Wholefoods Cafe Bondi Junction	143
Mother Chu's Vegetarian Kitchen City	34

Vietnamese

An Restaurant Bankstown	232
Bay Tinh Marrickville	115
Ben Da Vietnamese Restaurant Auburn	232
Indochine Bondi	137
Minh Dulwich Hill	102
Pho Ga Tau Bay Cabramatta	234
Thanh Binh Cabramatta	236
Xic Lo Haymarket	44

INDEX

By Neighbourhood

Annandale

side-on café 149
Reel to Reel

Surjit's Indian
Restaurant 95
Indian

Ashfield

Great Wall 95
Chinese (Northern)

Yuan's Family Restaurant
(Yuan Zhong Yuan) 96
Chinese (Shanghai)

Zagloba 96
Polish

Auburn

Ben Da Vietnamese
Restaurant 232
Vietnamese

Avalon Beach

fishbone sushi bar &
restaurant 211
Seafood/modern Australian

Balmain

All India Restaurant 97
Indian

Balmain Stars at
Gigis 97
Italian

Cafe Viva 118
Cafe Crawl

Canteen 118
Cafe Crawl

Kazbah on
Darling 28, 99
Middle Eastern/
modern Australian

Pelican's Fine Food 119
Cafe Crawl

Riverview Hotel
Dining Room 99
European

Tuk Tuk Real Thai 100
Thai

Balmoral

The Bathers'
Pavilion Café 182, 183
Modern Australian/
Italian

Watermark 182
Modern Australian

Bankstown

An Restaurant 232
Vietnamese

Nemra's 233
Lebanese

Bellevue Hill

Crave 133
Modern Australian/
New York Deli

Berowra Waters

Berowra Waters
Tea House 184
International

The Restaurant on
Berowra Waters 184
Modern Australian

Beverly Hills

Masthai Seafood
Restaurant 234
Cantonese (Hong Kong)

Blackheath

Cleopatra's 250
Back for More

Patrick's La
Normandie 247
French

Vulcan's 247
Modern Australian

Bondi

Bocca 133
Modern Australian

Bondi Tratt Cafe-
Restaurant 158
Back for More

Brown Sugar 168
Cafe Crawl

DIG 134
Modern Australian

fu-manchu 134
Chinese (Northern)

Gelbison 136
Italian

Gusto 168
Cafe Crawl

Hannibal 136
Lebanese

Hugo's 82
Joy of Food

Indochine 137
Vietnamese

intra Thai 137
Thai

Izmir Turkish Pizza
and Kebab 98
Pizza and Pide

jones the grocer 82
Joy of Food

Laundro.Net.Cafe 71, 138
International

The One That Got
Away 139
Seafood

Original Ploy Thai 139
Thai

Point of View 140
Modern Australian (tapas)

Pompei's 140, 141
Italian

Raw Bar 142
Japanese

The Red Kite Cafe 168
Cafe Crawl

Savion 142
Kosher

Sean's Panaroma 143
Modern Australian

Sports Bard 158
Back for More

Bondi Junction

Macro Wholefoods
Cafe 143
Modern Australian/
vegetarian

Brighton Le Sands

Cortë 164
Modern Australian

Enigma 88 164
Greek

Kamari Greek
Taverna Café 166
Greek

Le Sands
Restaurant 176
Back for More

Bronte

The Bogey-Hole
Café 168
Cafe Crawl

Sejuiced at
Bronte Beach 144, 148
Modern Australian

Tarifa 145
Modern Australian

Wet Paint Cafe 145
Modern Australian

Brooklyn

Angler's Rest Hotel 185
Seafood

Riverside Brooklyn Restaurant 185 Modern Australian	**Bambini Cafe Bar** 26 Italian/Modern Australian	**Slip Inn** 37 Modern Italian
	Bambini Trust Cafe 27, 28 Italian	**Sosumi** 200 OYP Japanese
Cabramatta	**Banc** 27 Modern French	**The Summit** 38 Modern Australian
Pho 54 242 Back for More	**Bar Cupola** 35 Cafe Crawl	**Sushi Bar Makoto** 28, 200 I Want To Be Alone/
Pho Ga Tau Bay 234 Vietnamese	**Bar Quattro** 183 Lowdown on Loos	OYP Japanese
Thanh Binh 236 Vietnamese	**BBQ King** 29 Chinese	**Wine Banc** 39 French
Camperdown	**Bittersweet Coffee** 35 Cafe Crawl	**Clareville**
Camperdown Canteen 100 Modern Australian	**Deli on Market (DoM)** 35 Cafe Crawl	**Clareville Kiosk** 211 Modern Australian
Campsie	**Edna's Table** 29 Modern Australian	**Clontarf**
Se Joung Restaurant 236 Korean	**Forty One** 30, 183 Modern Australia	**Clonny's on the Beach** 187 Modern Australian/seafood
Yuan's BBQ 237 Chinese (Shanghai)	**GPO Food Court** 28 I Want To Be Alone	**Clovelly**
Castlecrag	**Grand Taverna** 30 Spanish	**Direction of Cure** 168 Cafe Crawl
Lunch 186 Modern Australian	**Hyde Park Barracks Cafe** 31 Modern Australian	**Cockle Bay**
Chatswood	**Inside** 31 Modern Australian	**blackbird** 39, 183 Modern Australian
Chatswood BBQ Kitchen 28, 186 Chinese	**J.P. Bastiani** 32 Mediterranean	**Chinta Ria... The Temple of Love** 40 Malaysian
Claudine's 206 Back for More	**Lam's Seafood Restaurant** 33 Chinese	**Collaroy**
Chippendale	**Macchiato** 35 Cafe Crawl	**Food for Thought** 212 Thai/cafe fare
The Rose Hotel 101 Modern Australian	**MoS Cafe** 33 Modern Australian	**Coogee**
Circular Quay	**Mother Chu's Vegetarian Kitchen** 28, 34 Chinese vegan	**Barzura** 167 Mediterranean/ modern australian
Bennelong 23 Modern Australian	**Newsbar** 28, 34 Italian	**Coogee Bite Cafe** 168 Cafe Crawl
Cafe Sydney 23, 183 International	**Orbit Bar at the Summit** 71 Bar Brawl	**Cottage Point**
The Sydney Cove Oyster Bar 183 Lowdown on Loos	**passionflower** 42, 141 Modern Australia desserts	**Cottage Point Inn** 212 Modern Australian
Circular Quay East	**Pavilion on the Park** 36 Modern Australian	**Cremorne**
Aqua Luna 24 Italian	**Pavilion on the Park Café** 35 Cafe Crawl	**Chilli Lime Too** 187 Asian
Aqua Luna Bar 70 Bar Brawl	**Post** 36 Modern Australian	**The Pig & The Olive** 189 Italian/modern australian
Aria 24 Modern Australian	**Restaurant CBD** 37 Modern Australian	**Vera Cruz Restaurant & Bar** 189 Mexican
City	**Sea Bay Restaurant** 52 Back for More	
Arakawa 26 Japanese		

INDEX BY NEIGHBOURHOOD

INDEX

By Neighbourhood

Cronulla

Bacchus 167
Italian

Crows Nest

Azuma 190
Japanese
Bravo Trattoria
Gelato & Coffee Bar 141
Lick It Up
Chon Mage 206
Back for More
Himal 190
Nepalese (Newari)
Malabar 191
South Indian
Pino's Pizzeria 191
Italian
Restaurant Dish 192
Modern Australian/French
Wrapido 192
Cafe fare
Ying's Seafood
Restaurant 193
Chinese

Darling Harbour

Zaaffran 40
Indian

Darlinghurst

Angkor Wat 58, 141
Cambodian
ARQ 70
Bar Brawl
Balkan Seafood
Restaurant 58
Seafood
Bar Coluzzi 148
Reel to Reel
Betty's Soup Kitchen 86
Back for More
bills 59
Modern Australian
Cafe 191 62
Cafe Crawl
Chicane 59
Modern European
the clove 60
Indian
DOV 62
Cafe Crawl
Dug Out Bar 70
Bar Brawl
Eca Bar 62
Cafe Crawl

Fez 86
Back for More
Fix 70
Bar Brawl
Govinda's and the
Movie Room 149
Reel to Reel
Latteria 62
Cafe Crawl
Le Petit Crème 62
Cafe Crawl
Mali Cafe 63
Cafe Crawl
Mykonos on Crown 61
Greek
Phatboys 61
Thai
Salt 64
Modern Australian
Sel et Poivre 63
Cafe Crawl
Tropicana 148
Reel to Reel
Tum Tum's 64
Thai

Dee Why

Stella Blu Cafe 213
Italian/Modern Australian

Double Bay

Red Chilli 146
Thai

Drummoyne

Ecco 101
Italian

Dulwich Hill

Minh 102
Vietnamese

Eastlakes

Thai I-San Classic 169
Thai

East Sydney

Beppi's 65
Italian
Bill & Toni's 98
Pizza and Pide
bonne femme 66
French
Café Pacifico 66
Mexican
Eleni's 67
Modern Greek
Trovata 67
Italian/Mediterranean

Elizabeth Bay

Isaribi 68
Japanese
Vinyl Lounge 68
French/Modern
Australian
The Wedge 63
Cafe Crawl

Enmore

Bank's Thai
Restaurant 126
Back for More
E.M.U Tek Cafe 119
Cafe Crawl
Fifi's Cafe 102
Lebanese
kök 104
Modern Australian
Sarays 98
Pizza and Pide
Tandoori Hut 104
Indian/Pakistani

Erskineville

Aroy Thai 149
Reel to Reel
Cafe Brontosaurus 149
Reel to Reel
Caffeine 105
Mediterranean
She Bistro at the Rose
of Australia Hotel 149
Reel to Reel

Fairfield

Lao Village 242
Back for More

Glebe

The Abbey 106
Italian
Badde Manors 118
Cafe Crawl
The Boathouse on
Blackwattle Bay 106
Modern Australian/
seafood
Different Drummer 70
Bar Brawl
digi.kaf 118
Cafe Crawl
Iku 28, 119
I Want To Be Alone/
Cafe Crawl
Spanish Tapas 107
Spanish
Tanjore 107
Indian

Thai On Wok 108
Thai

Well Connected Café 109
Cafe fare

Yak & Yeti 109
Nepalese

Haberfield

A & P Sulfaro 141
Lick It Up

La Disfida 98, 110
Italian

Harbord

Freshwater Restaurant 213
Modern Australian

Haymarket

Bodhi 41
Chinese vegan

bohem 70
Bar Brawl

Chinese Noodle Restaurant 41
Chinese (North-western)

Golden Century 52
Back for More

Kam Fook Shark's Fin Restaurant 42
Cantonese

passionflower 42
Modern Australian desserts

Silver Spring 44
Cantonese

Xic Lo 44
Vietnamese

Hornsby

Steps 193
Modern Australian

Katoomba

Arjuna 248
Indian

Avalon Restaurant 248
Modern Australian

Cafe Niagara 249
Modern Australian

Siam Cuisine 249
Thai

Kensington

Golden Kingdom Beijing House Restaurant 170
Chinese (Northern)

Kings Cross

Bayswater Brasserie 69
Modern Australian

The Fire Place 183
Lowdown on Loos

Haste 71
Bar Brawl

International Restaurant & Bar 69, 71
Modern Australian

Ju Ju 72
Japanese

Piccolo 63
Cafe Crawl

Kingsford

Ayam Goreng 171
Indonesian

Nasi Uduk Jakarta 176
Back for More

Tea Inn 171
Taiwanese

Kirribilli

Cloudstreet 194
Modern Australian

Stir Crazy Thai 194
Thai

Lakemba

La Roche 237
Lebanese

Leichhardt

Bar Italia 98, 141
Lick It Up/ Pizza and Pide

Café Barzu 110
Italian/Modern Australian

Caffe Sport 118
Cafe Crawl

Dante 111
Italian

Elio 111
Modern Italian

Frattini 126
Back for More

Grappa 113
Italian

La Crimerai 141
Lick It Up

Martini 113
Italian

Martini Bar 71
Bar Brawl

Portofino 114
Italian

Uno 53 114
Mediterranean

Leura

Leura Gourmet 250
Back for More

Silk's Brasserie 250
Modern Australian

Manly

Ash's Table 215
Modern Australian

THE barKING FROG 215
Modern Australian

The Belgian Waffle Shop 219
Cafe Crawl

The Bower Restaurant 226
Back for More

Brazil 216
Modern Australian

Cafe Tunis 216
North African/ Mediterranean

Calacoci 219
Cafe Crawl

Ceruti's Bistro Italiano 217
Italian

eden 219
Cafe Crawl

Fresh at Manly 218
Cafe fare

Le Kiosk 226
Back for More

Out of Africa 218
North African

Maroubra

The Pool Caffé 172
Mediterranean/ Modern Australian

Swiss Hut 172
Swiss/French

Marrickville

Bay Tinh 115
Vietnamese

Corinthian Rotisserie Restaurant 115
Greek

Danish Deli 116
Danish

Post Cafe 119
Cafe Crawl

Mascot

Caffe Wine Bar 168
Cafe Crawl

INDEX BY NEIGHBOURHOOD 277

INDEX

By Neighbourhood

McMahons Point

Thomas Street 195
Modern Australian

Milsons Point

Old Fish Shop 219
Cafe Crawl

Moore Park

Arena Bar and Bistro 146
Modern Australian
Asian Kitchen 147
Chinese
Cine 150, 183
Italian
La Premiere Fox Studios 148
Reel to Reel

Mosman

Cala Luna 196
Italian
Fergusons 196
Modern Australian
The Mosquito Bar 197
Moroccan
Orso Bayside Restaurant 197
Seafood/Italian

Naremburn

Barcelos Cafe 219
Cafe Crawl

Narrabeen

Soleil 220
International

Neutral Bay

Domo 198
Japanese
Just Hooked 198
Seafood
Kintaro 199
Japanese
North China Restaurant 199
Chinese (Northern)
Otello 219
Cafe Crawl
Thelma & Louise 201
Modern Australian

Newtown

Asakusa 116
Japanese
Bacigalupo 118
Cafe Crawl
Cinque 28, 117
Modern Australian
Efes Turkish Pizza 98
Pizza and Pide
Kilimanjaro 117
African
Kuletos 71
Bar Brawl
Lillipilli on King 120
Native Australian
Lou Jack's 120
Greek
Martini Cafe 119
Cafe Crawl
Mio 121
Modern Mediterranean
Safari 121
Indonesian
Satelite Expresso 119
Cafe Crawl
Simply Thai 126
Back for More
Sumalee Thai 126
Back for More
Thai Jaroen 82
Joy of Food
Thai Pothong 122
Thai
Wedgetail 123
Italian (pizza)
Zimi 123
Italian/modern Australian

North Curl Curl

Emilia's Vegetarian Restaurant 220
Vegetarian

North Strathfield

Abhi's 238
Indian

North Sydney

Fare Go Gourmet 201
Modern American/Southern American
Isshin 202
Japanese
Malaya Restaurant North Sydney 202
Chinese/Malaysian

Paddington

The Albury Hotel 70
Bar Brawl
Arthur's Pizza 98
Pizza and Pide
Buon Ricordo 150
Italian
Café Orphée 168
Cafe Crawl
Fat Duck 151
Modern Australian
Grand National 151
Modern Australian
grand pacific blue room 152
Modern Australian
Hot Gossip Cafe 152
Modern Australian
Lucio's 153
Italian
Taqsim 154
Egyptian

Palm Beach

Beach Road 221
Modern Australian
Carmel's by the Sea Cafe 222
Cafe fare
Jonah's 223
Modern Australian

Parramatta

Carne Station 238
Korean
Costa Esmeralda 239
Church St, Parramatta
Fiderio 240
Modern Australian/Italian
La Bella Vista 241
Italian
La Porchetta 239
Church St, Parramatta
Pho Pasteur 239
Church St, Parramatta
Sushi Train 239
Church St, Parramatta

Petersham

Camo's on the Park 118
Cafe Crawl
Perama 126
Back for More
Restaurant Portugal 124
Portuguese

Potts Point

Cafe Hernandez Cafe Crawl	62
Cicada Modern Australian	73
Mezzaluna Modern Italian	73
Paramount Modern Australian	74, 141
Roys Famous Cafe Crawl	63
Spring Espresso Bar Cafe Crawl	63

Pyrmont

Concrete Cafe Crawl	35
Fish Market Sushi Bar OYP Japanese	200
Furusato Japanese	45
Kokum Indian	45
Masuya Japanese	46
Yoshii Japanese	46

Randwick

Azteca's Mexican Restaurant Mexican	173
Lebanon and Beyond Lebanese	173
New Orient Take Away Indonesian	174
Teascapes Cafe fare	175
Thai FireFry Thai	175

Redfern

Alio Modern Italian	74
Erciyes Restaurant Turkish	75
Sushi Suma Japanese	75

Rose Bay

Catalina Rose Bay Modern Australian	155
Pier Restaurant Modern Australian/seafood	155

Rozelle

Il Piavé Italian	124
Ipek Pizza and Pide	98
Rozelle Fish Bowl Seafood/modern Australian	125
Tetsuya's Japanese/French	38
Welcome Hotel Modern Australian	125

St Marys

Tandoori Corner Indian	241

Summer Hill

The Twain Shall Meet Cafe-Gallery Cafe Crawl	119

Surry Hills

Billy Kwong Chinese	76
Clock Hotel Modern Australian	76
Cossie's Cafe-Restaurant Modern Australian	77
fuel Modern Australian	77
Hopetoun Bar Brawl	71
La Passion de Fruit Cafe Crawl	62
La Persia Iranian	79, 141
Longrain Thai	28, 79
Marque Modern French	80
Matsuri Japanese	80
Maya Sweets Centre Indian	81
MG Garage Modern Australian/Mediterranean	81, 183
The Nepalese Kitchen Nepalese	83
Piment Rouge Cafe Crawl	63
Prasit's Northside on Crown Thai	83
Tabou French	84

Uchi Lounge Japanese	84

Terrey Hills

Kaiser Stub'n Austrian	203

The Rocks

Anti Bar at bel mondo Bar Brawl	70
The Australian Hotel Pizza and Pide	98
bel mondo Italian	47
Boulders at The Rocks Modern Australian	48
Glenmore Hotel Bar Brawl	71
Gumnut Tea Garden Cafe Crawl	35
Horizons Bar Bar Brawl	71
Lord Nelson Brewery Hotel (Bistro) Modern Australian	48
MCA Cafe Modern Australian/seafood	49
Rockpool Modern Australian	49
Sailors Thai Thai	50
Sailors Thai Canteen Thai	50
Unkai Japanese	51

Thornleigh

Istana Restaurant Malaysian/Chinese	204

Vaucluse

Nielsen Park Kiosk Italian	156

Wahroonga

Coonanbarra Cafe Modern Australian	204

Walsh Bay

hickson one Modern Australian	51

Wentworth

Il Postino's Back for More	250

INDEX BY NEIGHBOURHOOD

INDEX

By Cuisine

Westleigh

Scoozi Trattoria 205
Italian

Whale Beach

Beach House 223
Seafood/modern Australian

de beers Whale Beach 225
Modern Australia

Willoughby

Grape Garden 205
Chinese (Northern)

La Botte da Ercole 98
Pizza and Pide

Woollahra

Big Mama 156
Italian

Bistro Moncur 157
Modern French

Pruniers 157
European

Woolloomooloo

Harry's Cafe de Wheels 57
Inner East Introduction

Otto Ristorante Italiano 85
Italian

Shimbashi Soba on the Sea 85
Japanese

Map 28 - Regional Sydney

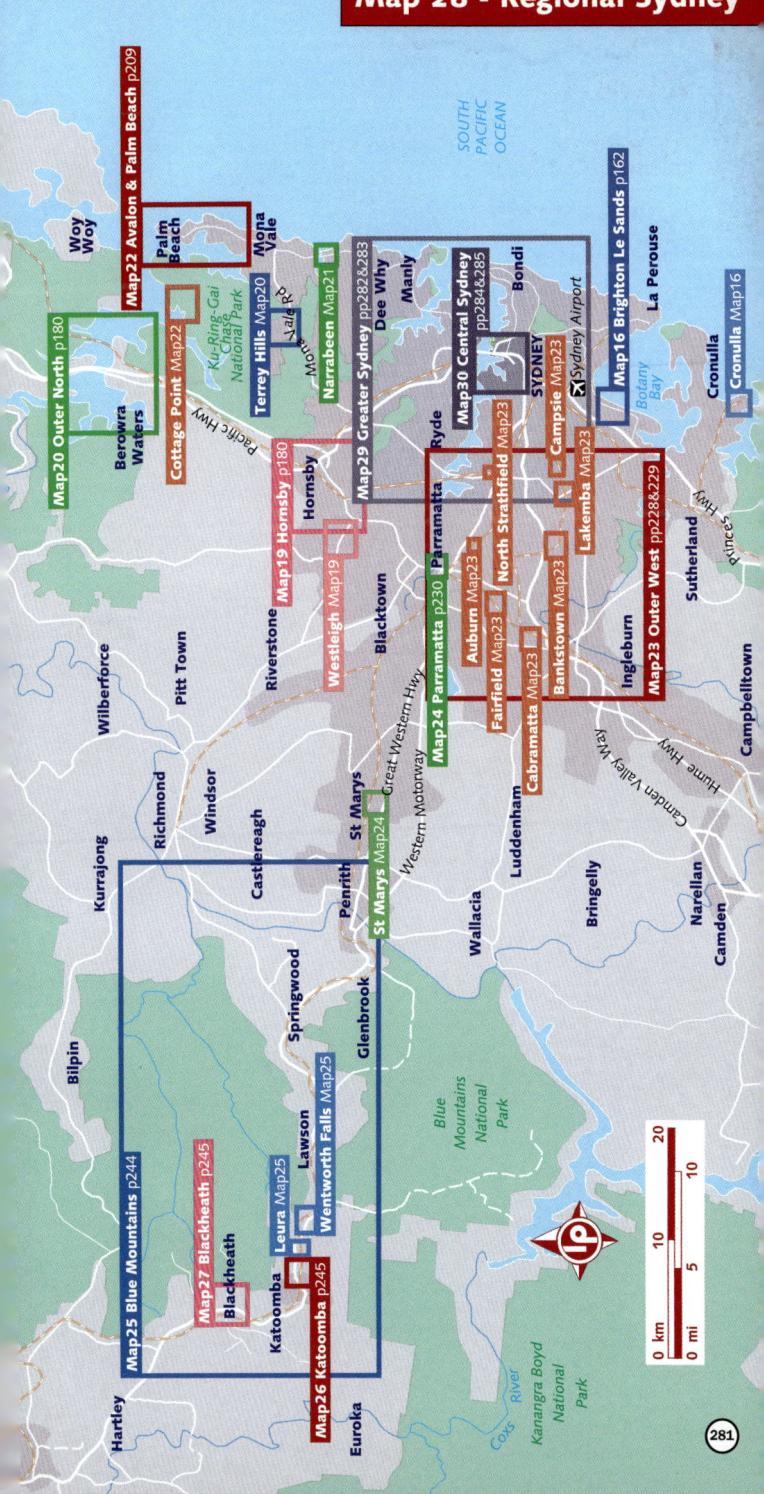

Map 29 - Greater Sydney

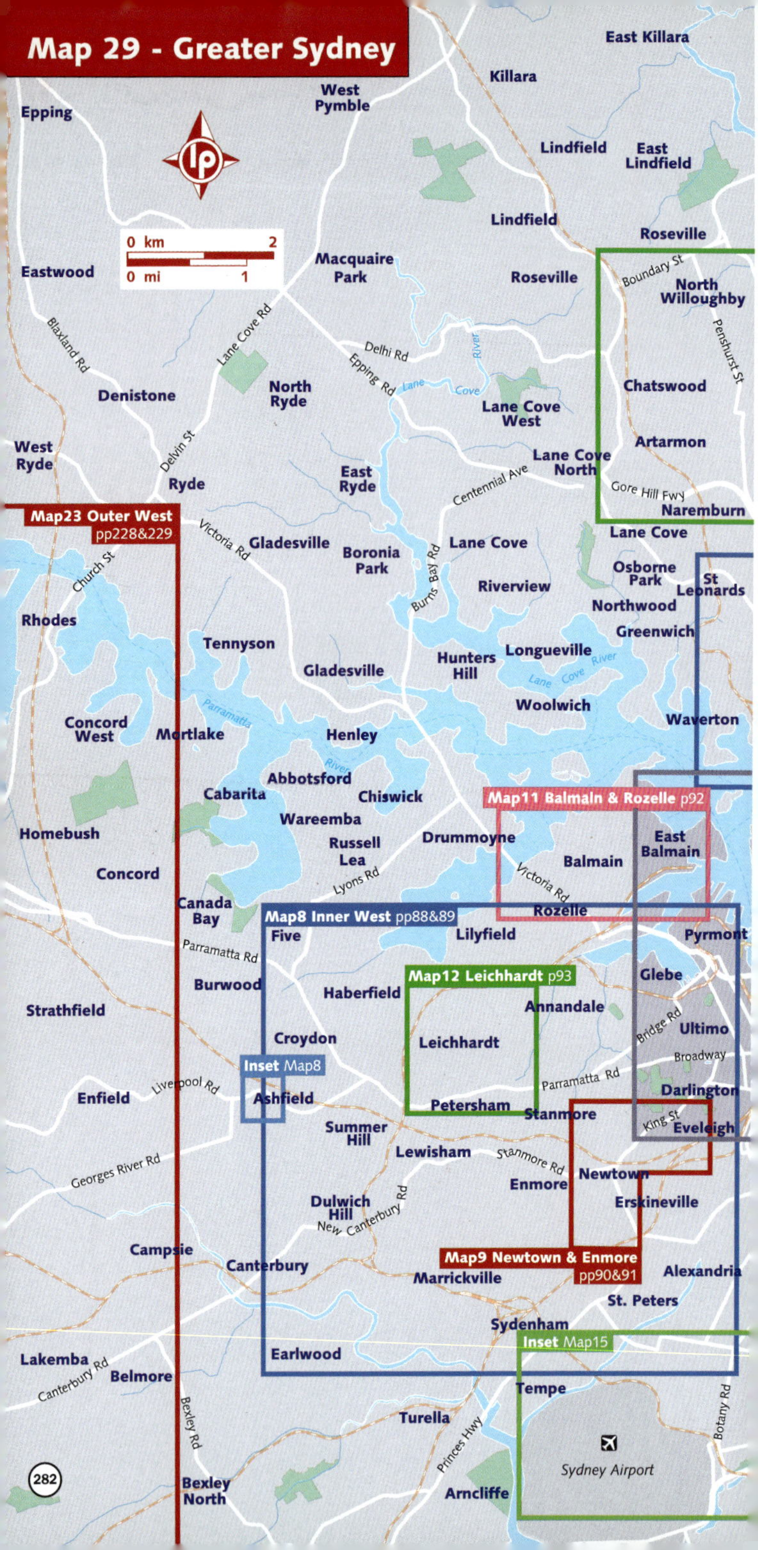

Sydney Area Map Index

Map18 Middle Harbour p179
Map21 Manly p208
Inset Map17
Map17 North Sydney p178
Vaucluse Map13
Map30 Central Sydney pp284&285
Map14 Bondi pp130&131
Map15 South-East pp160&161
Map13 Paddington & Woollahra pp128&129

Locations

Forestville, Warringah Rd, Wakehurst Pkwy, Allambie Heights, Dee Why, North Curl Curl, Brookvale, Wingala, Killarney Heights, Curl Curl, Harboard, Roseville Chase, North Manly, Queenscliff, Condamine St, Pittwater Rd, Castle Cove, Manly Vale, Middle Cove, North Balgowlah, Eastern Valley Way, Seaforth, Sydney Rd, Manly, Castlecrag, Frenchs Forest Rd, Manly Rd, Balgowlah, Fairlight, Willoughby, Clontarf, Balgowlah Heights, Middle Harbour, Beauty Point, Northbridge, Hunters Bay, Crows Nest, Cammeray, Balmoral, North Head, Pacific Hwy, Military Rd, Mosman, South Head, Cremorne, Georges Heights, North Sydney, Neutral Bay, Warringah Fwy, Watsons Bay, Kirribilli, Vaucluse, Hopetoun Ave, The Rocks, Potts Point, Port Jackson (Sydney Harbour), Point Piper, Diamond Bay, Sydney, Darling Point, New South Head Rd, Darling Harbour, Kings Cross, Double Bay, Rose Bay, Old South Head Rd, Dover Heights, Haymarket, Darlinghurst, Bellevue Hill, North Bondi, SOUTH PACIFIC OCEAN, Surry Hills, Paddington, Woollahra, Oxford St, Anzac Pde, Syd Einfeld Dve, Bondi, Campbell Pde, Bondi Beach, Redfern, Bondi Junction, Bondi Rd, Carrington Rd, Tamarama, Waterloo, Waverley, Centennial Park, Bronte, Zetland, Randwick, Clovelly, Rosebery, Coogee, South Dowling St, Kensington, Gardeners Rd, Avoca St, Mascot, Kingsford, South Coogee, Botany, Eastlakes

283

Map 30 - Central Sydney

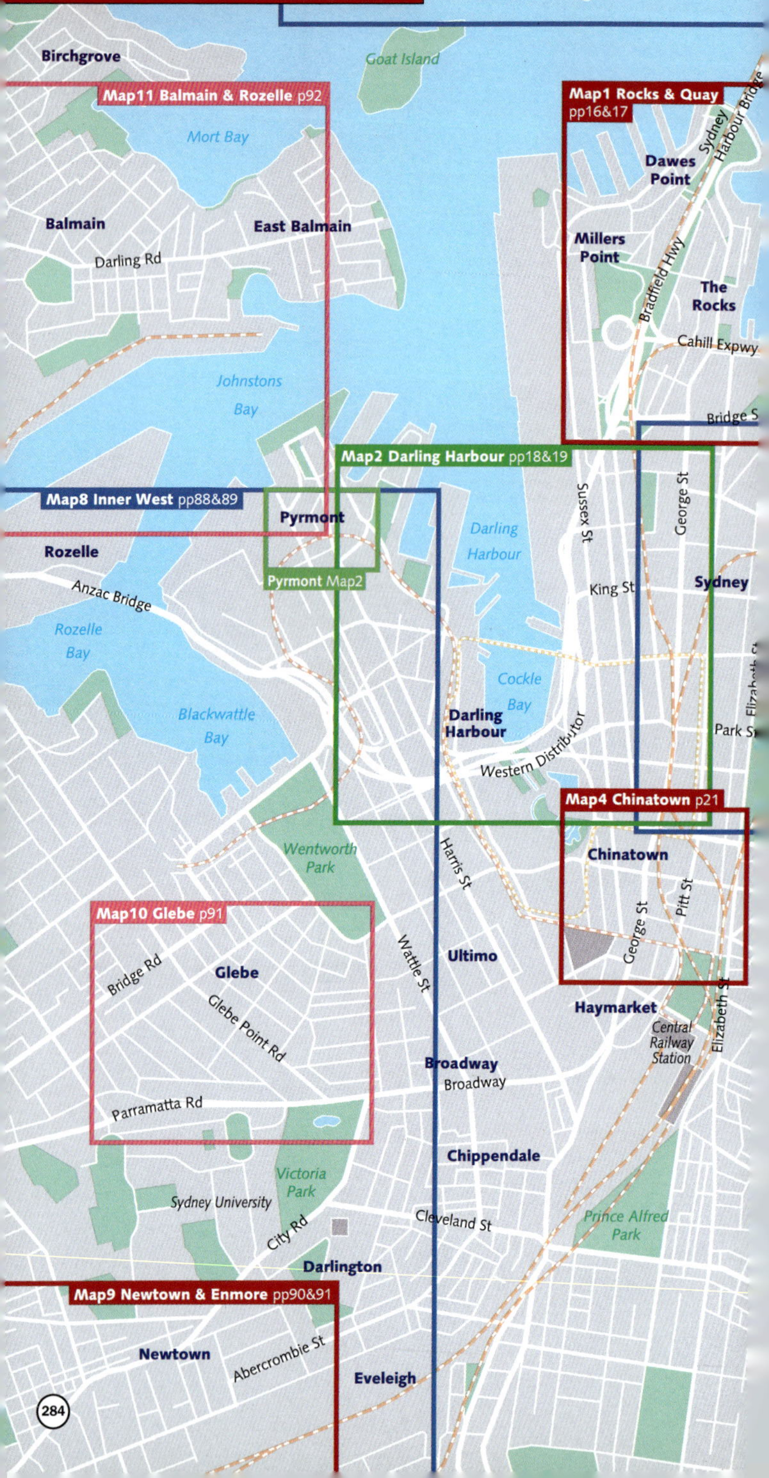

Kirribilli

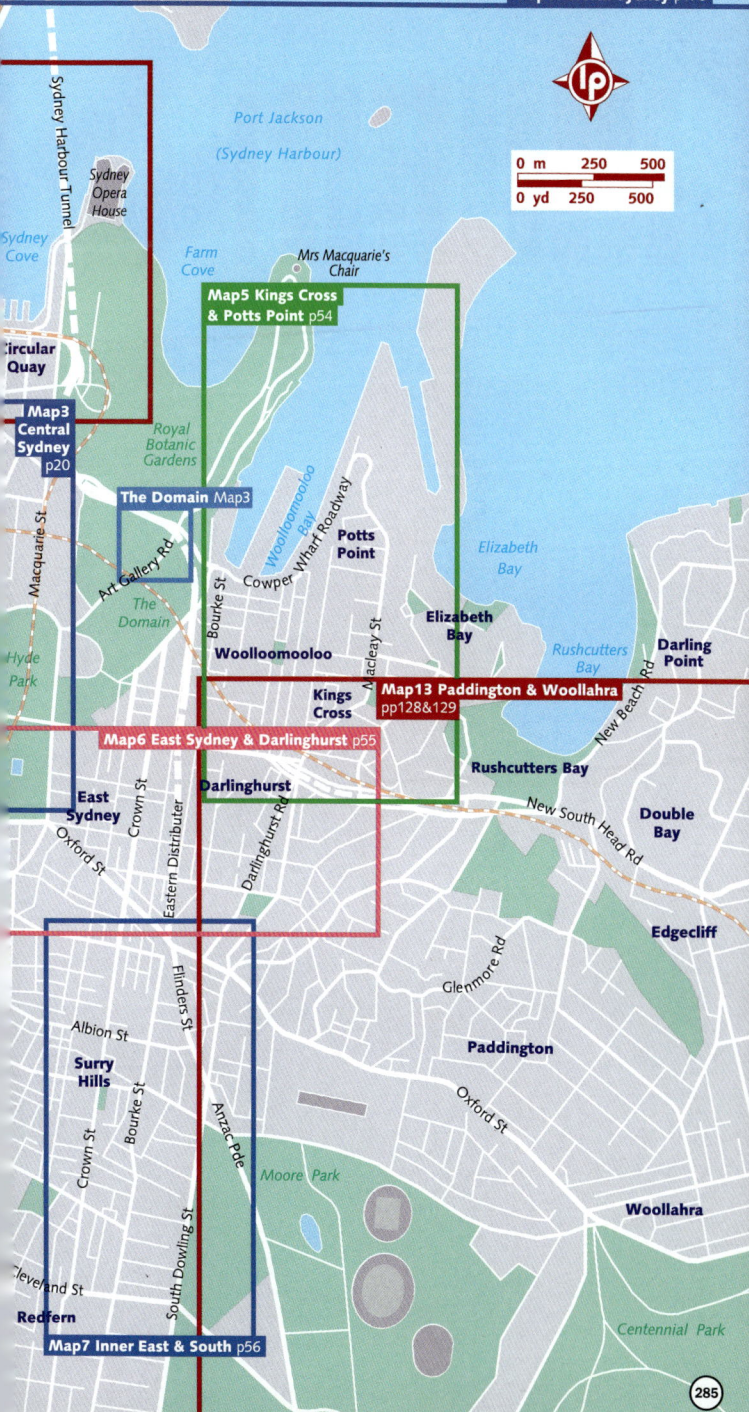

Map17 North Sydney p178

Port Jackson
(Sydney Harbour)

0 m   250   500
0 yd 250   500

Sydney Harbour Tunnel

Sydney Cove

Sydney Opera House

Circular Quay

Farm Cove

Mrs Macquarie's Chair

Map5 Kings Cross & Potts Point p54

Map3 Central Sydney p20

Royal Botanic Gardens

The Domain Map3

Art Gallery Rd

The Domain

Macquarie St

Hyde Park

Bourke St

Cowper Wharf Roadway

Woolloomooloo Bay

Potts Point

Elizabeth Bay

Macleay St

Elizabeth Bay

Rushcutters Bay

Darling Point

Woolloomooloo

Kings Cross

Map13 Paddington & Woollahra pp128&129

East Sydney

Crown St

Oxford St

Eastern Distributor

Darlinghurst Rd

Map6 East Sydney & Darlinghurst p55

Darlinghurst

Rushcutters Bay

New Beach Rd

New South Head Rd

Double Bay

Edgecliff

Albion St

Bourke St

Flinders St

Crown St

Surry Hills

Anzac Pde

Moore Park

Glenmore Rd

Paddington

Oxford St

Woollahra

Cleveland St

Redfern

South Dowling St

Map7 Inner East & South p56

Centennial Park

(285)

Map 31 - Trains

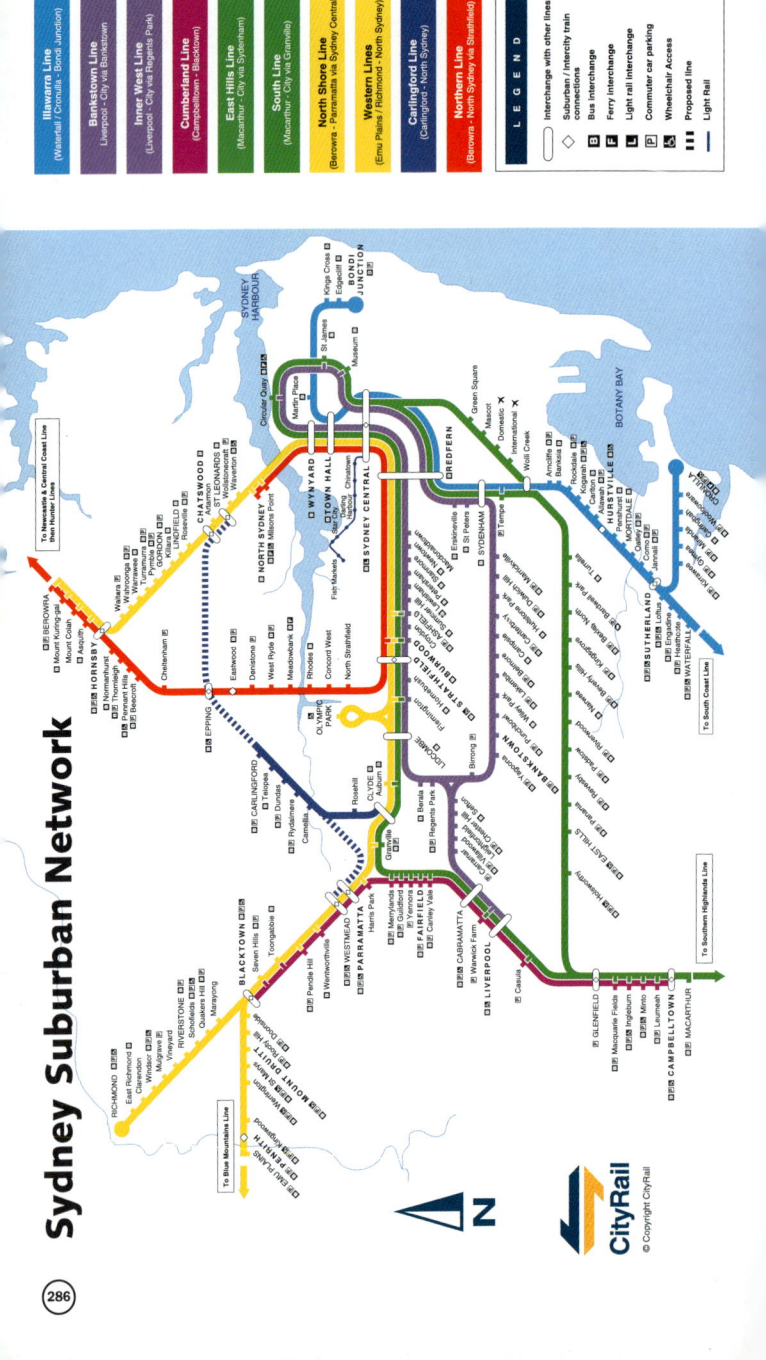

Map 32 - Ferries

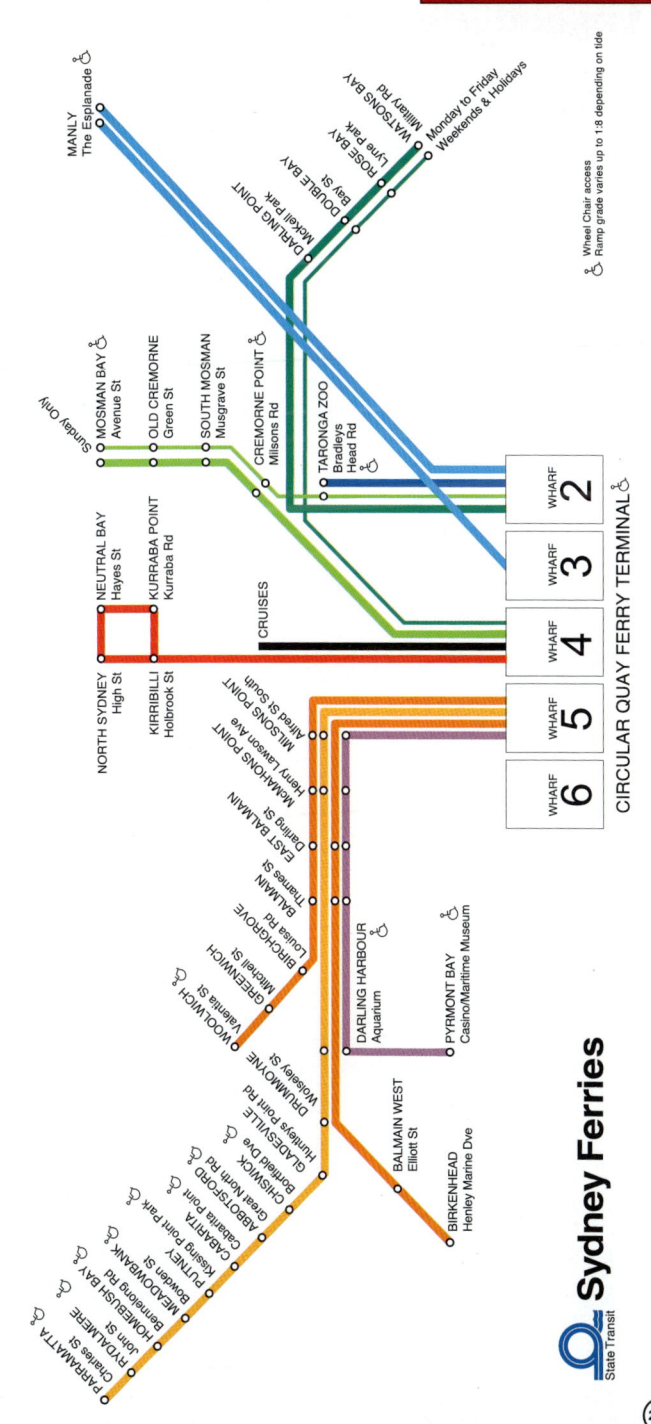

Sydney Ferries — State Transit

Circular Quay Ferry Terminal

- Wharf 2
- Wharf 3
- Wharf 4
- Wharf 5
- Wharf 6

Wheel Chair access
Ramp grade varies up to 1:8 depending on tide

Manly route
- MANLY, The Esplanade

Taronga Zoo / Eastern Suburbs route
- DARLING POINT, McKell Park
- DOUBLE BAY, Bay St
- ROSE BAY, Lyne Park
- WATSONS BAY, Military Rd (Monday to Friday / Weekends & Holidays)
- TARONGA ZOO, Bradleys Head Rd

Mosman route
- MOSMAN BAY, Avenue St
- OLD CREMORNE, Green St
- SOUTH MOSMAN, Musgrave St
- CREMORNE POINT, Milsons Rd

Neutral Bay route (Sunday Only to Kurraba Point)
- NEUTRAL BAY, Hayes St
- KURRABA POINT, Kurraba Rd

North Sydney route
- NORTH SYDNEY, High St
- KIRRIBILLI, Holbrook St

CRUISES

Darling Harbour route
- McMAHONS POINT, Henry Lawson Ave
- MILSONS POINT, Alfred St South
- DARLING HARBOUR, Aquarium
- PYRMONT BAY, Casino/Maritime Museum

Parramatta River route
- EAST BALMAIN, Darling St
- BALMAIN, Thames St
- BIRCHGROVE, Louisa Rd
- GREENWICH, Mitchell St
- WOOLWICH, Valentia St
- DRUMMOYNE, Wolseley St
- BALMAIN WEST, Elliott St
- BIRKENHEAD, Henley Marine Dve
- GLADESVILLE, Humbleys Point Rd
- CHISWICK, Bortfield Dve
- ABBOTSFORD, Great North Rd
- CABARITA, Cabana Point
- PUTNEY, Kissing Point Park
- MEADOWBANK, Bowden St
- HOMEBUSH BAY, Bennelong Rd
- RYDALMERE, John St
- PARRAMATTA, Charles St

Legend (Maps 1-27)

- ○ Restaurant
- ✈ Airport
- 🚌 Bus Station
- ✝ Church
- 🎬 Cinema
- ⛳ Golf Course
- ✚ Hospital
- ℹ Information
- 🗼 Lighthouse
- ☪ Mosque
- 🏛 Museum
- P Parking Area
- ● Point of Interest
- 🏊 Pool
- ✉ Post Office
- ✡ Synagogue
- 🎭 Theatre
- 🐾 Zoo

─○─ Lewisham	**Train** with station
─○─ Convention SLR	**Sydney Light Rail** with station
─○─ Park Plaza	**Monorail** with station
─ ─ ─	**Train** underground
George St	**Major Road**, Freeway
Harwood Rd	**Road**
Gipps St	**Street**
Barnett La	**Minor Street**
←──	**One Way Street**
┄┄┄	**Footpath**
GLEBE	**Suburb**
	Parks, Gardens
	Buildings
	Mall, Market
	Water
see Inset	Extents of **Inset Map**, Overlap or Enlargement